VISIONS & DREAMS OF BALTAZARA

BALTAZARA S. TCHERMNYKH

Table of contents

Prologue

This collection of compelling true life stories of significant events and turmoil had started from my childhood years, these are of meaningful experiences with surprising consequences. The book explores accounts of episodes of mysterious spiritual connections with a loving and profound intangible force such as the Holy Spirit's appearance that had changed my childhood's life, the near-death and out-of-body experience, at the time I remember seeing a heavenly peaceful place, full of white light, and hearing sacred chants. I felt wonderfully loved. In this encounter with "the after life" I met my late grandmother who helped me see that "life after death" really exists. And for me, I feel that we need not fear death, as it is the beginning of real life, "the eternal life." All these unforgettable supernatural events had modified my life's existence.

Are the appearance of visions and vivid dreams warnings or messages from God? Are the series of different struggles are an answer to God's call or are parts of God's plans? Even though these strange phenomena were challenging to understand and interpret at the time, they increased my desire to write them down to share with others. This include my experiences of premonitions, precognitions, and messages from "the other side". The interpretation of my dreams continues to baffle me. A large number of my dreams ended up coming true, and left me amazed.

I was however once guided by Sister Cecile, a nun, who said: "Sarah, there is no reason to fear your visions and dreams, these are signs of God's love for you."

At times, I see strange visions even when I am fully awake, which last a few seconds. Coincidences, hunches and premonitions are all lodged in my memory in a way that make it feel like those events happened only yesterday. However, sometimes I do not recall suspicions revealed in my dreams until later, after the foreseen real events unfold in real life.

My intuitive thoughts made me feel quite distant from other children or adults. I felt ashamed. This made me develop anger against myself, and same time, I was intrigued to know what might be different or unique about my personality.

I am grateful when I have sensed some excellent news such as: upcoming trips, new marriages, births (and whether the child is a boy or girl) and other things. Once I helped a family member find a house, and a friend to find his new job. However, I've often been misunderstood. The information is not seen ahead in any planned fashion, but rather it comes by surprise in a flash, often hard to translate or can be difficult for it to flow.

I chose to participate more in religious and intellectual discussions with adults, rather than to interact with children of my own age. I learned from them different types of stories of successes and shortcomings, giving me new perspectives on life. For me, living in our complex world without spiritual guidance would only enhance trouble and misunderstandings.

Good religious people through my life helped me feel at ease. Many were callous and presumptuous. Some people pretended to be my friends, seeming to be very devoted to their religious activities, and yet, simultaneously, using good works as a mask for their guilt.

I humbly admit I didn't always do the right thing. God knows how many times I have offended Him, and I am asking Him to grant me His pardon. I know He is right and that I should live by His word. I am a sinner, and many times I lost my way. I always need His guidance not to be tempted to live in immorality and hatred or remorse.

Have you ever sensed things that are yet to happen, such as the upcoming death of someone, even though looking at that person, nobody could guess that death was approaching? It is impossible task to tell someone about their coming death because in most cases I never knew exactly when, where or how. This drove me mad. When I have a friend or colleague and foresee that he or she is passing away, I need to take distance. I fear telling him, scared of his reaction. This puts me in a dilemma, whether to inform the family of the forthcoming undesirable event or not. But sharing my incomplete news might cause them to disbelieve more or worse: persecution. To avoid such confusion, I often prevented myself from joining in with groups of people, or avoided looking deep into people's eyes when I had premonitions.

The more I fought sensing the future for people, the more influential the encounter became. Anxieties invaded me every time a precognition occurred without knowing why; it was very upsetting. Any meeting would be even more challenging if the vision concerned a close family member, leading to misunderstandings and unspoken words.

A short ceremony was held during the wake for my father, and many people attended. But I did not expect to be asked to say some words. I was unprepared, and it was difficult to utter even a few words in front of people while fighting back sobs. I was wordless. I was afraid that nobody had understood what I said. However, a man came up to me after the ceremony. He smiled and said, "I agree with you," staring at me. Has he understood me without words? But at the same time, I was bewildered because I had seen a vision of him dead. I became even more upset; I did not understand anymore what he was saying.

The following morning, the man attended my father's burial with his family. He was the father of my nephew's wife. I sensed that to inform them of what would happen to her father would only cause them more grief. I regret being a coward by failing to help them prepare for the coming sad event. But I didn't want them to anticipate their pain of losing him.

Only a handful of close family and friends know that I have this capacity, and that I always feel guilty. Today, although it is difficult to handle, I often keep things to myself to avoid confrontation, and try to make peace with that.

Anyhow, despite some feelings of uncertainty, I felt honoured and flattered when harmless good spirits came to visit me, talk to me mentally; for me, it is a great privilege that they still cared for me from before, and even after they had joined the "other side." It is gratifying to hear when a spirit has had a happy crossover, like my beloved father, Tatay Eco.

Tatay remains forever alive as I keep his legacy of wisdom in me. I am quite reassured, thinking that he is there watching me like a guardian angel, and he is waiting for me when my turn comes.

Sometimes my intuition was so strong that I can't avoid revealing it, even though it was against my will. This can be so embarrassing. However, sometimes impulses needed to be displayed as quickly as possible to prevent danger.

I once saw Hugues, my husband's nephew, in a flash meeting with a car accident. So,

I advised him not to drive and should stay home that night. He agreed with me, so I was happy. But a close friend came with a car and invited him to go somewhere. That night, I dreamed of him inside the car, wounded. His head was bathed in blood. In fact, their vehicle hit a large pole and the broken lamppost came through the roof of their car.

I wonder why my young daughter had precisely the same dream that night. Upon awakening, we immediately called Claudie, Hugues's mother, to find out if he was still in bed. She said Hugues had not slept at home. We were all in panic. We called the police and the hospitals. It turned out that Hugues was in the hospital, seriously wounded but alive. Surprisingly, the friend who drove the vehicle was not injured.

Oh my Lord Jesus Christ, please forgive me to ask this: Why I sometimes had the sense and dream of the upcoming events when, in fact, I couldn't prevent it?

Life can be challenging even in my husband's homeland. I persevered with trying to live life according to God's plan. I am blessed with a wealth of wisdom. I learned a new language, and despite some challenges, I acquired a good professional job. My husband and I built a new home with comforts, and we raised our family - a treasure that keeps us strongly bound to each together, even amidst the hardships of life.

At times I thought I have perhaps been punished because of my reticence, doubts, and anger to a mysterious man who appeared in the jeepney that I was riding in Butuan in February 1980. He spoke to me in a parable which was quite hard to understand at the time. It was as if he knew me and who I would chose for my husband; who was he who had dared to interfere in my life? This question persisted in my mind for more than three decades.

I only know now who he was, as I discovered while writing this memoir. It took me many long years to understand that he was an angel or the messenger of God.

Today, when I think of all the adventures I have lived through, some of which could have been fatal, I know I have been rescued sometimes "in extremis" by the "divine hand." I sometimes thought that, maybe, my destiny was already written since my birth – or even maybe before I was conceived.

I strove to survive while battling against a life threatening experiences such as: when the boat was about to capsize in the middle of a storm in the Pacific Ocean; a near plane-crash; being crushed by the crowd in panic during Pope John Paul II's visit to Manila in 1981; and I was kidnapped in Cebu, but managed to escape from a network of criminals, among other difficult situations.

I've realised, God never left me.

Paradise on Earth 1956-1961

I spent a happy childhood in my mother's land, in the beautiful natural environment of Mabini, in Cabadbaran, Agusan del Norte, where I experienced my first intangible connection with the Holy Spirit. It was also the place where I experienced my first premonition dream at the age of five, and where I enjoyed schooling rich with religious and spiritual guidance. Every day I counted my powerful blessings.

A few days after Nolwen's birth, we left our house in New Asia, Butuan City for Mabini, to live with my grandmother (Nanay Pantay). It is about 29 kilometres (driving distance) from Butuan, my birthplace.

During the first night, Dan, Nelly, and I all slept together on the wooden floor of our living room, under a wide mosquito net made of cotton in a purple-red colour, while baby Nolwen was with Mama on their bed. The night was so quiet. Unlike in Butuan, we did not hear cars, motorcycle, and lorries in the street. Instead, we heard some high-pitched songs and squeals of birds that I had never known before. Another sound early in the morning that woke me was the *tok-ko*. I had never heard the sound before, Nanay said it was a giant lizard. There were so many animals in this Mabini environment: goats, pigs, cats, dogs, and we had a chicken coop in our large backyard. Behind the house were the goats in their shelter, cows in the open field near the valley behind the bamboos and the carabaos wallowed in their puddles. Nanay's house was surrounded by a variety of medicinal plants and several fruit trees. At the end of the yard were the thick groves of giant bamboo trees, and a clear stream running from a small valley. For me, it was a real paradise.

Nanay's place was just a few meters from the paved road, which had a narrow stony walking path alongside. But instead of hearing vehicles on the road during the day, horses would pass every now and then, pulling a *caratella* or *kalesa* [small carts on two or four wheels driven by one person]. Only a few people owned a kalesa in our barrio. Most people walked downtown. For them, time did not matter when they were not working on their farms.

I did not know whether the people living in Mabini ever realized how lucky they were. I was stupefied seeing my new environment full of attractive nature celebrating God's creation. How grateful I was to have had the opportunity to experience the magical surroundings of that magnificent world. I immediately loved Mabini, and I quickly adjusted to the way of life. I was warmly welcomed by the other children, who were very friendly and showed curiosity to meet a little girl like me. Our relationships became deep and more vigorous every day. I loved their simplicity, and they talked to me full of sincerity and innocence. I was entertained by their simple ways of living, showing me their home-made toys, their means of recreation, and it seemed to me that they had everything they needed in that beautiful little world. I was fortunate to be a part of Mabini, now becoming a big, prosperous and joyful city. Later it was a place that had gave me many advantages in life, for me, a true paradise on earth. I have these memories of that lovely place, preserving the idea of my happy childhood. It was a place full of space and freedom with the beauty of nature, a position which was good for my health and was surely an ideal place for me to live and grow.

The spring water was everywhere, often flowing directly from the hillside. It provided sustainable irrigation for the farmers. The abundant spring water supplied unlimited supplies of safe drinking and cooking water; people used it without cravings or worries, all due to the power of nature. Artesian wells flowed permanently day and night, providing water free to all people. Waters formed into streams, nourishing the bamboo groves, which grew on both sides just at the edge of our backyard. The bamboo grew so high and dense we used to take the shoots with us to eat and sometimes to sell. Mabini possessed rich soil which helped all the vegetation grow healthy. Modern technology, industrialization, and commercialization did not yet exist in Mabini, so the air was clean and there was little pollution.

The farmers worked with carabaos; they could plough the different fields of rice, corn, sugar cane, pineapple, banana plantations and so on, with little risk of thirst or starvation. Other natural resources like streams, rivers, lakes, and farmland were all abundant in Mabini. Despite their daily hard labour, empowered by a healthy environment, the working animals remained strong and well.

People did not experience many illnesses, despite the fact that they only practiced natural medicine. For centuries, they relied on natural techniques and herbal remedies to treat illnesses and to heal injuries. They cured the sick and fought disease by using medicinal plants and trees, for example boiling the bark of a tree to drink like a tea to cure diarrhoea; this had an unusually bitter taste. I cried when Nanay forced me to drink a full glass of this "tea" once when I was ill. But potent medicine that it was, I was cured almost immediately, although I never wanted to taste it again. Everything from the common cold to life-threatening conditions such as cancer, diabetes, high blood pressure and heart disease were successfully treated without modern medical equipment. I was privileged to witness my elders cure illnesses using these types of natural remedies. Once, I saw the improvement of the health of my neighbour, who was suffering from broken bones, and my brother Dan's broken arm. I watched Nanay use the sap of a leaf of the tree as eye-drops; she proudly never wore a pair of eyeglasses throughout her long life, not for reading or for long-distance. Two of my grandmother's great aunts, who were fans of natural techniques and legal medicines, were said to have lived to the age of 135 years old.

Most women in our barrio used herbal extracts from plants and trees. They used coconut milk as hair shampoo, and papaya leaves for cleaning the skin. Nature provided our ancestors with sufficient food and shelter. There was no modernization, but people were happy and contented with what they had, and improved their lives in the ways that they could. Indeed, they gained significant benefits from nature, as they lived a green lifestyle, which was probably the main reason for their longevity. We had never thought of using industrial or chemical products such as fertilizers or insecticides.

Houses were seldom closed or locked, people left their homes with windows and entrance doors wide open. I had never heard the fear of robbers, kidnappers or rapists either. Parents allowed their children, roaming freely outdoors. For me, that felt like true freedom. Everyone respected other people's rights and responsibilities. As a child, I was free to move around our barrio and downtown without fear, as everyone knew everyone, and each one was responsible for the others. Despite the absence of telephones and radios, news would spread quickly in the neighbourhood.

Dan and I spent much of our time playing outside as soon as we finished our daily assigned chores. We did not have toys bought from the shops, but we used to make them by ourselves with what we found in nature, such as wood, stones, tree stalks, lianas, abaca fibres, rubber and string. I was so busy it kept me happy, my mind nourished with the magnificent gifts of our natural environment.

I was surprised one day when Tatay came to ask me what toy I wanted. I immediately answered that I wanted to ride a horse. He made me a wooden horse that swung like a rocking chair, and had an air chamber made out of ancient bicycle tyre that made horse sounds when deflated, like a balloon. I played with it from the age of 5 to 7 years old. I used to pretend like I was galloping, even though it was only swinging back and forth. To let my horse whinny, I pressed the rubber balloon attached on top of the head. It made two different sounds: when I pressed it deeply, I heard the voice of my horse neighing of happiness while galloping; when I pressed it lightly, to hear the relaxing sound of horse hooves, walking. The toy was painted with the red sap from a tree leaf, which I called the magic tree because it provided us with a kind of paint without harmful chemicals. For me, my wooden horse was better than playing with any plastic baby doll. I imagined that I was a cowboy, wearing a straw hat that my uncle had made, held in place by two fine threads that I could tie around my neck like a ribbon. Thus the hat was not at risk of blowing away in the wind. Tatay also made Dan a wooden lorry and tractor. Tatay used the tree's sticky sap as glue to join together all the pieces of the tractor and lorry. Dan habitually filled them both with flying insects that he caught from the green fields, like grasshoppers and dragonflies. In my eyes, Tatay was an artist.

Mystical Experiences

A mysterious white dove - 1957

Before dawn, I was suddenly awakened by a weird noise that captured my full attention. It was as if there was wild wind, roaring thunder and lightning flashed with a sound of strong water cascade dropping altogether into our living room, yet, there was no water. It felt like sunrays and moonlight simultaneously entered at home, I was surprised to witness this in the early morning hours, with incredible bright white lights remaining. But it was still dark outside, and all our windows and doors were closed. Only five years old, I was confused. Where did all those lights came from?

It was amazing. I was curious and wanted to go out from the mosquito net to understand what it was. No one else was awake to see it. There was a big ball of bright white light moving towards me. I wanted to wake up my mother and grandmother to have them witness the phenomenon, but I was unable to speak or move. I watched this ball of light. I was kneeling in a half-seated position, and I waited. It was so beautiful, as if I was watching a magnificent film.

Silence reigned; I heard only my own heartbeats and my own breath as the light came closer to me, a white ball of light transforming into white rays. I could start to distinguish the shape of a head, but it was difficult while the bright light covered its whole body. Out emerged a white dove bathed in shimmering light that glittered, spread, and sprinkled throughout the bedroom. My head felt full of new knowledge but without the power to express it. I was overwhelmed with joy, observing the white light expanding in our house, coming in the door ... it was a magnificent white dove.

I wondered where it came from. I waited excitedly as it moved closer. My heart pounded intensely fast, but still, I couldn't move. I wanted to shout to call it nearer to me, as I was eager to touch it; but the closer it came, the slower its movements became and the bright white light gradually diminished.

When it was approaching me, I heard a length of sound somewhat like it was tapping its beak to a microphone, creating an echo.. What I knew was that the white dove entered into my room, and came closer to me, reaching in front of me, but it looked so tired. The glittering bird stopped walking and faced me. For a brief moment, we both stared at each other.

It was as if I were being analyzed, and I could do nothing but wait. I felt I was alone in the house with the presence of that white dove, and for a while I couldn't move.

Eventually I raised up the mosquito net, but the beautiful white dove had disappeared. I wondered where it had gone. I searched for it everywhere in the house, in vain. However, I held onto an unusual feeling of joy. After that visit, I was both so happy and, at the same time, tormented with curiosity. I kept on asking myself, why did it appear to me? Would I be able to see it again in the coming days?

I was full of confusion when it disappeared and full of hope at the same time; maybe next time it wouldn't disappear. I kept on checking around the home. I sometimes woke up at dawn to see whether the magnificent white dove would visit me again, but it was in vain. All my thoughts were with the beautiful dove, and I was sure that nothing could compare to those brilliant white rays that I saw that day.

Nanay was still asleep in her bed next to mine in the same room, and I woke her up to inform her about the visit of the glittering white dove. I described it repeatedly to Nanay and to my Mama, and they both answered at the same time. "Oh, so lucky of you, Bebe. What a privilege! You have seen the Holy Spirit." They said it together as if singing in chorus. Then they both made a sign of a cross, the same manner when we prayed. But it was not the answer I had expected from them. My curiosity remained unanswered. At the age of five, I was too young to understand what they told me and what they wanted to explain. Every time I see a picture of a white dove, it reminds me of the most beautiful sparkling white dove who appeared to me, which remained with me in spirit throughout my childhood.

Ever since that day, strange phenomena have occurred in my life. Had I got spiritual connection after the visit of the white sparkling dove at home?

The killer lightning: a premonition dream that came true

I recovered from the wound, a small piece of sharp bamboo pierced to my right knee. I was holding the ropes tied to the three small goats and I was pulled by them when they ran so fast frightened by the rain. I fell into a sharp bamboo stick. The pain disappeared so that I could walked again as usual. I would whine when my mother refused to take me with her. I was fed-up and bored of being alone at home, lonely almost every day. Although I had loved to stay with Nanay, I also couldn't avoid thinking about my father. Why was he always away from us? Why didn't we join him in Butuan City and live with him? I was upset but I didn't know why.

Mama said I started having premonition dreams and nightmares when I was four years old. I also had nightmares during the day. Nanay once said I was five years old when several premonitory dreams occurred while we were in Mabini. All I knew was that I was not attending school yet, but I could never forget my tremendous nightmare during my afternoon nap about the roaring and deafening thunder together with a strong electric lightning bolt. Here is the dream:

The white clouds were carried away by the wind and suddenly became dark and heavy, the temperature rose. Dark clouds pretended to go, and the sky returned clear; now, the dark clouds were gone but quickly replaced by even darker clouds, the scene was being repeated. Clouds and winds were turning around the sky. The whirlwind was fast approaching, and coming closer. I wondered what would make it stop. After a while, the road was empty and clean, no more leaves flying over, no more vehicles passing by, nobody was crossing, no people walking along the sidewalks. There were no more kalesa nor horses. Oh no, the strong wind was back, the trees were whistling, the branches were crackling, breaking, banging one another while the leaves were blown and disappeared.

Then everything stopped turning. The surroundings were now in total silence, except my own breath.

The goats stopped bleating, cats and dogs returned to their niches, all the animals around the house were resting silently. The wind ceased blowing, the hens stopped their cackling, and the cocks stopped crowing. Only the sound of overpowering silence remained.

Suddenly, thunder rumbled through the sky, with a boom boom! It was like an intense bomb explosion with the powerful dizzying electrical lightning crossing Mabini, hitting the houses and trees around our house. The coconut trees burned badly; some coconut trees stood half-tall, but most of them burned down to just ash.

A carabao and a young rider were struck by lightning. Both fell to the ground, burnt! I screamed loudly until my voice gave out. My heart pounded so fast that I could hardly breathe.

Nanay shook me repeatedly, and I awoke sweating profusely, lost and couldn't tell if it was a dream or real. The roaring of angry thunder refused to leave my ears. I could hardly stop crying, feeling anguish as the thunder had seemed so real, so vivid, and scary. It took me some time to realize where I was.

"It was just a bad nightmare," said Nanay, holding me safe. My fears remained as I had difficulty describing the dream to her. The thunder and lightning scene was stuck in my brain and I cried again.

"Bebe, don't be afraid, your dream is finished, so try to forget it," she tried soothing me. "I am with you, try to relax. Breathe deeply and forget about that nightmare," she said repeatedly.

Although Nanay soothed my fears, anxiety remained, I could not find peace or calm. She gave me an infusion to drink with some leaves floating in the glass. The smell was comforting. Nanay watched me. Despite the bitter taste I drank it all, slowly. I felt better afterwards.

I went to the balcony to see the bright sun, with no wind blowing, but I was not entirely convinced. I don't know how long I remained sitting on the bench, observing the environment. At the same time, Nanay was busy arranging all the breakable materials such as the wardrobe, mirrors, cabinets, and cupboards with glass doors, and especially her beautifully designed Spanish porcelain dishes. I did not dare to ask her why she turned them upside-down and covered them all with white sheets. I observed her expression: She was sure of what she was doing. My curiosity grew while she covered all those things to protect them against the dust, but I remained silent. Were we going out somewhere, I wondered?

Mama came home with little Nolwen, asking me if everything was alright. Nanay went to the yard where there were plenty of banana flowers blooming. She harvested two red-purple banana blossoms; she chopped them finely and cooked them like cabbage, mixed with beef stew and some condiments. We had an excellent dinner, but I only ate small a portion of it. The nightmare had stolen my appetite.

The banana flower produced a violet-colored sap, staining my white teeth. There was no toothpaste, so I rub my teeth with some salt. I took a massive water cup from the jar full of spring water, and rinsed. As I looked to the mirror, my teeth returned white again. Nanay used to say: "We can live without anything, as nature has provided everything for us. Just look around, and you'll see that you have everything you need to live."

We saw such a beautiful sunset that day that I wanted it to stay longer. But Nanay said, "Tonight, we must sleep earlier, and don't forget to drink the tea I prepared for you Bebe. It will help you sleep soundly." I just wanted to sink into dreamless sleep where no nightmare would disrupt me.

"Do you want to sleep with me?" she asked.

"No, thank you," I said. I entered into the mosquito net of my younger brother, while Mama slept with my little sisters Nelly and Nolwen.

Although I had a sound sleep, I did not feel like leaving bed the next morning. A noise outside woke me. People were calling out as if something was wrong? I hopped out of bed and found myself all alone in the house. Where were they? I dashed to the balcony, and I was shocked by seeing the same picture of my dream the previous afternoon!

The trauma I had felt during my previous nightmare came back! "Oh no! It is impossible! It's the same landscape that happened in my dream!" I sobbed, but nobody was there to ease my tension. I prayed that the man I saw on the back of the carabao who got hurt in my dream was not in real life.

From our balcony, I saw the coconut trees in front of our house, all burnt. The fire was gone by then, leaving the bottom of the burnt trees smoking. There was no rain, but the morning's humid fog had stopped the burning of trees and houses. The neighbouring houses further down the road were partially burnt too. Some still stood, but many had lost their roof.

Crying again, I wanted to shout, but I had lost my voice. I was shocked by what I saw. I checked whether I was fully awake. I felt pain when I pinch my skin and hit my face. I confirmed I was no longer dreaming. How did all these things happened, and I did not hear a thing?

Are my visions and dreams prophetic gifts of the holy spirit?

Had I slept soundly the whole night, slipping into a kind of trance? I did not even hear the lighting storm which occurred at dawn. My nightmare became real. Suddenly a heavy rain fell, and my family ran back home. But no one spoke to me about the thunder and lightning. They were all in shock too.

I went to the yard after the rain. The smell of burning ash was gone, and I was glad to see that some trees were still standing, despite their shallow roots. I saw coffee and cacao plants, with thick foliage and branches normally covered with bundles of crimson red fruits. They had lost much of their foliage, but they survived; maybe because they were shorter than other the trees. The *lanzones, tambis,* mango, papaya, and even the banana trees had also suffered from the storm with the tops and most branches burnt. They surely wouldn't bear fruits for a long time. However, it was reassuring to know that banana trees can quickly recover. A giant clumping tropical herb was cut and left in large clusters as they grew. Perhaps those trees were also protected by another group of thick giant bamboo plants whose leaves were partially singes but still stood proudly. I also wondered why the bamboos had resisted from the lightning bolt. Maybe because they could swing?

 Did I think that maybe the bamboos had covered our house too, not to be struck by the lightning?

I was only five years old, probably too young to comprehend, but this hypothesis keeps repeating in my mind. I wonder why those houses in front of our home were all burned except ours? Was it like a miracle?

I thought there must be a scientific answer.

About 200 meters from our backyard stood a group of strong thick giant bamboo trees that grew along the stream; in a very short amount of time they reached 1,250 feet high, more or less. When you went near them, they looked like forest.

Those irresistible bamboo treats were part of my childhood. I loved to eat bamboo shoots. I like the way Mama cooks them, and although they can have a bitter taste, they become delicious when mixed with other ingredients like coconut milk or spices. I was also grateful to them for protecting our home against the lightning bolt. This hypothesis was being repeated all the time in my little head.

Two days later, Nanay learned that a young man and his carabao both died after being struck by lightning that day. Sadly, the young man was a student of medicine, whose parents were old farmers. They said they had sold all their land to pay for the expenses of their one and only child's studies. The story made me feel so sad and helpless. If he had not awakened at dawn, and brought his carabao to the usual place where they would have rested after ploughing the rice-fields, perhaps both would still have been alive. I did not know his parents, but it was said that they were too old to work; they had no more carabao, and no more son to care for them.

Now I knew the reason why Nanay had covered all those breakable things with a thin white cloth. She knew that my dream would happen. She had let me drink the tea she had prepared for me, which permitted me to sleep undisturbed, and not been interrupted by the murderous storm.

It was incredible seeing those bamboo groves thickly clumped on both sides of the stream, which could also be seen from the neighbourhood's backyard. I understood they grew as long as there was a water barrier. After the lightning bolt, most inhabitants in

Mabini used the matured bamboo trees to rebuild their houses, fences and furniture by freely helping each other. People cut them into different shapes and sizes. They even use them as tubes and water pipes. They transported the bundles of cut bamboos using their *balsahan* [a bamboo water raft drawn by a carabao] while others used a *carromata* [a light two-wheeled, box-like vehicle usually drawn by a single pony, carabao or horse]. The bamboo rhizomes have remarkable ways of surviving cuts and sending up shoots again with powerful growth.

With one person on each end, they carried water with a five-meter-long bamboo stick balanced over their shoulders, filled with spring water to drink. Everyone helped one another without complaining. They rebuilt their homes in good moods and were satisfied with their labour.

Was the Good Spirit illuminating my way home?

One evening in 1959, when I was seven, I heard Yoyo Supri and Yoyo Vicente saying they were going to use a *baroto* [slim boat] to cross the big river during the full moon. Nanay carried a fishing net that she had repaired with a nylon thread, checking several times to ensure no holes remained.

I was so curious to know how people could bring home plenty of fish, shrimps, and crabs by fishing during the night. I stood on a stool to unlock the door, and silently ran to the stairs, trying not to wake Mama and my siblings, who were still deeply asleep.

I dashed through the forest to catch up with them, hiding from time to time behind the trees so as to keep them unaware of my presence. I reached the river side and waited, but nobody was there. I saw it was low tide, by watching stones visible through the crystal water. The river was divided into two. I crossed the smaller branch, hoping to find them, but I was too small to cross the wider part of the river. I had not learned to swim and was too afraid to continue. They were gone, by boat.

I realized I would be stranded when the high tide returned if I stayed and waited for them. I hurried to go back on my way, frustrated.

To go home, I walked across a thick forest filled with coconut trees. It was so scary in the dark, and I shivered. Several thick clouds covered the moon. I prayed it would shine again to light my way back. I thought I was being punished for being so curious.

I suddenly heard a hissing sound as if the wind blew above my head. I felt encouraged to look up high, and I noticed some lights were glowing above me. When I looked where the bright light came from, I saw the coconut trees in line, like their leaves were on fire. They were like lighted torches hanging high along my path. When the clouds lifted, the moon shined through again. I decided to trace my way back to the river to see the burning leaves again. I stared up for I don't know how long to the highest top of the coconut trees, and I was stupefied to see that all the leaves were still whole and not even a single leaf been burnt through. Was it supernatural?

I kept wondering who made the fire that had illuminated along my way?

How could I relate this strange phenomenon to Nanay? It would be either that she would believe me, or maybe she would just ignore it. If the people with her heard about my experience, they would probably think I was just silly or kidding. Although Nanay knew that I sometimes saw and heard things that others couldn't, she would surely punish me and prevent me from going out from the house to play with other children, if she learned that I followed her to the river in the middle of the night. Nobody could tell me what had really happened, so I preferred to keep it to myself. Believe me, it was not fun for a child like me, thinking like an adult, trying to find the answer to these mystical experiences. I kept coming back to the same question.

Why do I hear and see things that others can't?

One day, Yoyo Supri brought me with him when he went fishing in the middle of the sea, during the day. Along our way to the sea, he was on the back of his carabao that pulled the *cart* (a light two-wheeled wooden vehicle) I was riding, full of materials for fishing. We had a long way to go before we reached the place on the shore where his small fishing boat was kept. He said that it took him six months to make his boat out of wood and bamboo. He had carefully made it himself out a tree. He had made a roof out of palm trees, which offered us a good amount of shade against the rays of the sun. Using colored sap from different trees, he made mixtures of paints in dark browns and blacks. There was no engine on the boat, only wooden paddles. To provides stability, he fitted the boat with two bamboo out-riggers that offered extra support on the rough seas.

That day, the sea was calm. He caught several small and big shrimp with his fishing net. He showed me how to eat the fine shrimps with tuba vinegar in a small wooden bowl that he also made. The fresh shrimp had a sweet taste when eaten with the fine coconut-vinegar that he had made as well. At first, I hesitated to eat them, but they were so delicious once dipped into the vinegar that I had ate so much. I enjoyed watching my uncle throwing his fishing net repeatedly unto the sea and pulled it back full of big and small fish. The big fish *sinugba* (grilled fish) smelled so good, cooked on top of the charcoal of coconut shells, we've got a delicious dinner. I even drank some drops of tuba; Nolwen drank much more than me, and fell asleep quickly.

While eating, I talked to my uncle about my mystical experience of seeing the several burning coconut leaves like torches in line, which helped me find my way back home that night. I asked him if he had seen the same weird experience that haunted me:

"Why did those burning coconut leaves remain fresh and green, in spite of the blaze?" I asked. "Who built the fire?"

"It was probably some spirit who was playing with you," he said. "You should thank the good spirit for loving you," he said looking at me tenderly. I supposed he was not joking, as he did not even smile, but I thought he was pleased. Did he already know I was seeing things that others did not?

"I thought the spirits already knew that I was so thankful, but how would I know if they were really good spirits? Was the good spirit illuminating my way?" I asked starring at him.

He replied with another question: "Were you afraid?"

"No, not at all," I said. " I felt thankful that they guided me and lit my way."

"So, they were good spirits, but if you do it again, the spirits won't help you anymore," he said firmly. "Don't you know that I was with Nanay?" he lifted his eyebrows facing me. "If I'd had known that you had followed us, I would have surely strictly driven you back home," he said, in a warning to me.

We had lot of conversations over the years. One thing that had caught my attention was that he always became more serious when talking about his fields of crops and plantations and all that he sowed. He worked with all his energy to obtain good harvest of the principal crops, such as rice and corn.

"Where was your son, to help you? I asked him.

"You know very well who and where my son is," he answered staring at me.

"I don't know who your son is," I said, wondering.

"You know him, I saw you once on his shoulders putting your hands around his neck," he said.

"Ahh, you mean Manoy Gunding? I did not know he is your son. I heard the elders telling stories that Manoy Gunding was brought to Manila by a beautiful woman and left him after when he finds some job."

"My son is not living with me, and he is not interested in working as a farmer," Yoyo Supri said with melancholy.

Every day, at dawn rain or shine, Yoyo Supri harvested *tuba*, coconut red wine and distributed it to the stores. He earned money this way. We heard him cleaning and tapping the container each day. For me, it created a nice rhythmic sound. He owned lot of coconut trees and harvested several gallons of tuba every day and brought some home. I loved drinking it when it was still fresh and sweet, but it had sour taste after it had been saved two days as it became a *bahal,* traditional Filipino palm wine made from fermented coconut or nipa palm sap. That is the way that a lot of Filipinos love to drink it.

Yoyo Supri's spirit

In a dream: *I saw Yoyo Supri in his bed with his blood coming out from his nose*, and I awoke.

I refused to accept that he could die because he promised me a visit to his coconut trees and said he would teach me how to climb. I wanted to tell Nanay at once early that morning, but she was still snoring. I sprinted to see Yoyo Supri myself in his house and I met his companion running on my way. She said something about informing Nanay, but I didn't properly hear. I continued running. I already knew what she would tell me anyway. And there, Yoyo Supri was alone at home, on his bed, with blood coming out from his nose.

I was angry with him, as he left before fulfilling his promise to me. Before the people came to take care of his corpse, I climbed to his bed and sat on his stomach. I shook him, and I said: "You have failed to keep your promise." I wait awhile to see if he would open his eyes but he was really dead, and I sobbed. They said he died of high blood pressure.

The day after his burial, at dawn, I heard the tapping of the coconut tree blossoms. I hopped out from bed, dashing to the staircase, to see who was harvesting tuba. I darted to the first coconut tree not so far from our yard and I looked up to the top of the tree, but nobody was there, but the tapping continued. I went to the next tree and still nobody.

"Yoyo, Yoyo," I called him, and the noise vanished. I stayed a short moment, hoping that someone would come down from the tree, but I waited in vain. I returned home and informed Mama and Nanay what happened. They only shrugged.

I remained silent frustrated and continued asking myself: Why was it they did not hear anything?

It seems to me that they believed what I said. I contemplated and asked in my prayers for Yoyo Supri to let them hear next time. I noticed that Mama did not go down the stairway in the early morning. I heard her talking to our neighbour who came to play sungka with her.

"I love Manoy Supri and I had fun hearing his jokes. He was for me a joker, but you didn't often see him smiling. He was someone who chuckled, jesting with a serious look, but now that he is dead, I am afraid that he will touch my legs when I am going down the stairs," said Mama.

A few nights earlier, we were already lying down under the mosquito net, while I saw Yoyo Supri roaming around us. I did not pay attention because I knew that he had loved us very much, and that he used to check whether everyone was home before he returned to his own house, which was only walking distance away. But in my little brain I was asking myself: How it could be possible for a dead person to walk around like a living one, while his embalmed body was lying inside his coffin? When I told Mama about it, she did not argue with me, and I knew she had seen him also. She was reluctant to discuss about it and remained silent. But in a way I understood her fears.

At dawn the next day, I heard again the tapping of the coconut tree for morning tuba. When I told Mama about it, she was furious. She was fearful with goose bumps. We asked ourselves: Who was tapping his coconut trees if it was not Yoyo Supri? While I was sure it was him doing it because I sensed it, and I couldn't prove it.

The third early morning after the burial, there was another tapping in the coconut tree near our house, and this time both Nanay and Mama heard the sounds, which lasted longer than before. I was happy and satisfied that day, as Yoyo Supri answered my request. But we did not have any tuba anymore for a long time. Since then, I kept in mind that if I prayed heartily and earnestly for the fulfillment of our prayers, they would be answered, although sometimes it took time.

One week passed after his burial, and Mama went to visit his house to clean. There she saw her brother's spirit, sitting on his favourite chair near the window, facing towards his plantations in the fields where he had laboured. Watching him so sad, Mama forgot her fears. She told him that he must not be worried about them, as there would be someone who could take care of the planted crops, and that there could still be a good season with an excellent harvest. Then Yoyo Supri's ghost disappeared.

My Schooling Interrupted – 1961

All those beautiful childhood experiences and my schooling in the private school ended brutally in May I never had expected that I would be forced to interrupt studying so early.

"Bebe, your Mama is expecting a baby," Tatay said. "She will surely need you while I am working far away, but I will do my best to bring you all with me to Butuan soon. Can I count on you?"

"Of course, Tatay, but I can only help during the evening as I am in school during the day." I answered with hesitation while staring at my father's eyes. I had sensed that his decision was definite. Mama was pregnant, but we did not yet know that she was carrying two babies.

"Bebe, listen to me please, this is what I am telling you. You should not be enrolled in school this coming June, because Mama will have the baby in September. If you are enrolled in June and stop schooling in September, your teachers won't be happy, and you wouldn't be either. You can still catch-up with the other children later, because you went straight to first grade at five years old," he said decisively.

I was shocked by what I heard, but I did not dare to object. In my thoughts, I wondered how Tatay could decide to stop my schooling, when he knew very well that I loved going to school, even though I had to wake up so early and walk several kilometres. I would be missing the school programmes, the dance presentations, the classes, and all my classmates. His decision thwarted my ambitions, and for me, it was terrible to miss my studies, even just for a single year.

When he asked me to stop my schooling, he seemed to be asking me not to breathe for a little while. Could I cope? I was very sensitive, and I craved approval, affection and understanding. The difficult idea made me think over the schooling in years past. I tried to remember all the teachers I had known in Candelaria Institute: for kindergarten, it was Madame Toyay; for Grade 1, Sister Maria; for Grade 2, Miss Ventillo; and Grade 3, Mrs. Caldavero.

I allowed my mind to wander. What else could I do? I cried without a single tear. I yelled voicelessly, my breast tightened, and my heart bled. That day I hated my parents. I realized how hard it was to be the eldest in the family.

"Don't you know that I am almost nine years old?" I managed to ask.

"Yes, I know," he sighed.

"Could you please buy me some books? Books from school so that I can study at home? And some novels of Barbara Cartland or a detective story by Agatha Christie?" I asked him firmly.

"Bebe, you're too young to read those," he said.

"You don't know me at all! I am old enough to understand what is written in those books," I answered back, but with respect.

I felt guilty giving my father an ultimatum, but maybe I was too sensitive and paranoid. It was my way to get him to understand that stopping schooling for a year was an extreme sacrifice for me.

I waited impatiently for my books, so much that one week seemed an eternity. After three weeks, I had finally obtained two books: a famous story of a girl living in a college dormitory with a detested land lady, and one advanced mathematics book for higher grade levels. Tears fell when I touched those books.

Elizabeth, a girl from the fourth grade and whose father was a calesa driver, used to come home to our house to show me their homework in mathematics and literature. For writing paper, I hid old calendars offered by one of the Chinese stores in the town. I used the empty backs of the pages for mathematics lessons and started thinking about obtaining some other paper to continue writing and solving mathematical problems shown in the book.

Nanay picked and cooked some bamboo shoots. She also picked some ripe sarabia banana bundles to be fried as banana-barbecues for me to sell. Through this, I earned some pesos that I used to buy paper, notebooks, pencils, and some crayons for drawing. I marketed my wares using a loud voice, inviting everyone to buy my products. It was quite a difficult task, but I was happy when someone approached me with a smile. I also received compliments and encouragement, so I could be enormously proud and happy of what I accomplished that day. All was sold, and I could buy the materials I needed for my home-studies. This auto-education process helped me forget that I was not anymore in the school classroom.

However, when Mama brought me with her for her pre-natal check-up in the puericulture centre, I heard the midwife informing her that she was expecting twin babies. I was full of joy when I heard that news, that I had forgotten my disappointment to stop schooling. Mama would surely need me, even more so now that we knew she was carrying two babies in her womb.

This phrase kept repeating in my head: two babies in her womb. It was beautiful. Before Tatay left for Butuan to return to work, I reassured him that yes, I would help Mama take care of the babies.

One early fine and exceptional morning, Mama requested me to go to Elizabeth's house and ask her father Juancho to drive me with his kalesa to town, to ask the midwife to come urgently. It was time for Mama to have the babies. Manoy Gunding went to Butuan to tell Tatay that the babies were coming. Dan's job was to fill up the jar with spring water and to not forget to transfer the goats to the green field then bring them to their home place before the rain comes. Each one of us had fulfilled our responsibility, and it was so exciting!

Amelie and Ashley's Birth

The sun was generously shining that Friday morning. I felt as if the birds were also incredibly happy singing around our house. I arrived home with Annie, the midwife. Nanay had boiled water and had sterilized all the accessories and maternity equipment, while Mama was already impatient to start labour. I stayed at our wooden gate covered with scented white flower, the sampaguita, and I was so proud to tell people, especially to the children who were passing by, about the coming of the twin babies. We were still waiting for Tatay when I heard a cute baby's voice quickly followed by the second one. The midwife was busy with the first baby, but she was immediately followed by the second; I heard her exclaim, "oh please wait, baby!"

I was so excited to see them, but I was prohibited from entering the room. When Nanay went out, she left the door opened. Annie washed and dressed the newborns: two baby girls. I saw Ashley, who had a shining scalp with very fine hair, and Amelie had already thick dark hair.

The midwife praising their health and congratulating Mama. She was blessed with a healthy and smooth labour. I learned that Amelie was born breech: she came out with legs out first. It had been a risky delivery, but Mama delivered them both without difficulty. Ashley was born with her head down. Thus, Amelie and Ashley were born at home in Mabini, Cabadbaran Agusan del Norte, in September 1961. They have the Zodiac sign of Virgo. They are twins but do not bear much resemblance to each other: Amelie has a round head while Ashley had a semi-sharp shaped head.

Bottle time

Becoming a second mother at the age of nine, I treated them like my own babies and felt responsible for them. They were my highest concern and priority. I asked God to give them excellent health and a bright future.

I concentrated for a whole year to take care of them, feeling sleepy during the day, unable to read my books as I took charge of preparing their bottles. I understood that when they cried at night, it was because they were calling for their milk. When Mama gave her breast milk to Ashley, I was also giving the bottle to Amelie and vice-versa. Breastfeeding is perfect, but almost impossible to provide simultaneously to two babies at the same time. I enjoyed helping Mama take care of the twin babies, but after a few weeks, I started to become fed-up and tired.

I wanted to skip the monotony by reading books or magazines, but I felt so sleepy during the day. I have forgotten that I was just nine years old. I should have been playing outside with other children, but I was really busy like an adult. The twins cried at the same time, so I endured sleepless nights. It was so difficult to get up to prepare the bottle when I had been deeply asleep. Mama and I agreed that she would wake me up to prepare the baby's bottle even at night. I had to learn how to avoid being stuck in negative thinking about my situation, so I changed my perception by daydreaming. While writing this memoir, I realized that this might have been the time when I had started to feel a kind of depression unknowingly, because the only distraction I could have had would be to return to normal life, was to school, and that was not an option.

The best baby-soother

There was no colorful crib mobile at home for the newborn babies. But I was rocking and soothing them to sleep in a *duyan*, a cloth hammock. Large wooden posts at my grandmother's house reached the ceiling, and we used to tie a rope to these posts and attach their makeshift hammock. The duyan became the twins' best baby-soother.

During the day, especially in the afternoon, I placed them in their duyan, and I lay between them while singing songs and swinging them lightly to get them to sleep faster, one at my left and the other to my right. The rocking movement allowed them to feel reassured in a comforting and convenient environment.

Sometimes they remained awake for a time. They liked listening to my singing, and they cried when I stopped. I knew that the twins wanted to hear me sing, but most of the time, I became so sleepy that my eyes were closing before theirs, and I could not sing anymore. Yet the twins sometimes reacted as fussy babies as they have grew a bit older; they remained awake, so I was obliged to sing again and continue humming. It was my fault as I let them build a habit. Although I sometimes did not remember the words of the songs, I just kept on singing. It was so reassuring that they did not mind about the missing words anyway, until they finally closed their eyes. I loved watching them while they slept, and thanks to the duyan, their sleep was prolonged. This also gave me some little time to have a short nap as well, to help me recover from the lack of sleep during the night. The duyan probably help my baby sisters' heads to develop an excellent, rounded shape, as they were not sleeping on a flat mattress during the day. At the same time, my head is flat and not symmetric, because Mama said that I had always loved to sleep with pillows under my head since I was a baby.

When the weather was good, Mama placed the sizeable rectangular table under the morning sun near the foot of our stairs facing the northeast, so she could put the newly bathed babies on that table in the healthy rays of the sun. The twins soaked in the sun's gentle glow from 7 to 9 am, to enable them to absorb vitamin D and calcium during their early childhood. The sunbathing became like a ritual every morning. And the babies were soothed by the rays of the sun, leading them to sleep deeply after that early morning rite.

The baby twins' characters

Both were lovely babies, and each one had her character and personality, distinct from the other. I learned their emotions: Ashley was fragile and not a happy baby. She often cried gently, much more than Amelie. I tried to understand why. They used to have a short sleep in the morning and a long nap in the afternoon. I wondered whether baby Ashley felt sick, in some kind of pain or physical distress, or if she was just bored when she cried. It was a pity that the babies never expressed what they felt except by crying (and laughing, when they got a bit older). I know that hunger, fear, and the need to sleep made the babies cry. But Ashley had a moody temperament, so that she cried even after taking her bottle; perhaps she had some tummy pain or something. She was not comfortable most of the time, and she called out when she had hiccups. She only smiled when I was dancing in front of her. Then I understood that she loved dancing.

Meanwhile, even though Amelie was only a baby, I noticed that she was independent and self-assured. While awake in her duyan, Amelie remained quiet and played, and of course she also used to cry when feeling hungry. But I spent more time soothing Ashley than her. I kept on yawning while I lay down between two on the duyan as I was often feeling sleepy before them. When I felt someone touching me, it was baby Amelie, who tried to go out from her duyan. I wondered how she did it, but she was able to stand inside her duyan. Whereas with Ashley, she immediately cried when she woke up from her nap.

When Ashley cried, I immediately knew she wanted me to take her in my arms; while Amelie in the meantime would be busy crawling and sitting down while observing her twin and looking around curiously. Ashley tended to cling to me, more than she did to our mother.

At times, I believed that Amelie had a strong sense of telepathy: she showed anger and frustration to Ashley by looking straight into her sister's eyes, then Ashley began to cry. I believed that Ashley might be afraid of her twin. They talked to themselves in front of the mirror that was in Nanay's closet. It was even funny sometimes because Amelie did not want Ashley to tap the mirror, so she stared in Ashley's eyes, and Ashley would stop tapping the mirror, but she'd cry. To change the ambiance, I would dance in front of them, and Ashley would finally laughed while Amelie remained silent.

The Flood in Butuan 1961- 1962

In the end, Mama wanted to return to Butuan with Tatay. Before we move back, Nanay repeatedly warned me not to go near the riverbank and not to go down to the river. She said she would have had loved to keep me with her in Cabadbaran.

Two months after the birth of the twins in September, we returned to Butuan in November to be with Tatay. Mama's elder half-sister, Modesta, was married to Anatalio Palma, who came from Tubigon, Bohol - the same town as Tatay. They owned a newly built two-storey wooden house near the riverbank of Agusan river. Tatay renovated the first floor and added more rooms to accommodate us: there were Dan, Nelly, Nolwen, Ashley, Amelie, and me. My parents rented the space, thus it became our new home where I celebrated my tenth birthday in January 1962.

The house had a balcony, and during weekends or holidays we enjoyed watching the happenings in and along the riverside. I could never forget the view of Manoy Gunding, with two beautiful women and sometimes more. I really don't know where those women came from, but both of them wanted to ride with him in his speedboat, arguing who would go first. At that time, Manoy was working with a logging company, and usually visited us by boat. On another day, a different woman would be with him. He roamed around the river with the speedboat, going back and forth, leaving huge waves behind him while my younger siblings and I watched from the balcony. I wondered how Manoy could manage to navigate the speedboat with all those women chasing him? He had no time to join my younger siblings and me anymore. I started to resent him.

Even though the river was not so large at that time, a lot of speed boats came. Dan was fond of swimming. One day, he and his friends crossed the river and reached the other side of the riverbank with his clothes held by his hand over his head. He put on his dry clothes as soon as he reached the other side of riverbank. I observed them enviously, as I did not know how to swim.

One time, heavy rains continued for three days. Floodwaters were rising all around. Tatay built a platform and a small bridge to join the stairs to the balcony where we could see so many things being carried off by the current on the river like watching a thrilling film. We saw several broken small houses, logs, uprooted whole trunks and branches of trees, and so on, all swiftly taken by the water. In fact, it was as if we were also in the river floating, because the water had covered the ground. One thing that broke my heart was a small wooden house in which half of the roof was collapsing; some parts of it started to disperse, the woods began separating from each other. The worst thing was that there were people inside that small house. A mother was screaming for help, and a baby was crying as they were quickly carried by the swollen river. I could imagine the baby's feelings, frightened by the cries of his or her mother. Upon seeing them, I felt as if I'd shrunk while feeling the pain, and guilt, of being unable to help them. I prayed there would be a boat and people who could save them.

A dead body

At the time of the floods, I still had not recovered from a sad event in the river two weeks earlier. There was the annual fiesta celebration in Mahogany that day. A small *baroto* [a dugout boat made and used for fishing and transportation] with three men on board came from Mahogany, who attended an annual fiesta.

My friends and I watched them arriving at the riverbank. Two friends were waiting for them, also wanting to go to Mahogany. But the three men on board were drunk, and did not want to come out of the boat. Instead, they all crossed the river to go to Mahogany, and with all five men on board. The small baroto can accommodate only three riders. We heard them arguing and punching each another, because two men really needed to get off. The boat started to turn as if it was carried by a whirlwind. Then they calmed down, and begged each other to get out, but only one had left the baroto. They continued arguing as the second man insisted on staying, the boat jerked. Two men used the paddles, and the others stroked the water with their hands to go faster. Although it was inevitable, we were all surprised to see when the baroto capsized in the middle of the river. They were all in the water, and the boat was lost underwater. We watched three men swimming to the riverbank. Sadly, one of the drunk ones disappeared under the surface of the river. Everyone looked for him in vain.

Two days later, a man yelled. "There is something strange floating behind the logs in the river." Quickly, a group of curious people flocked to the riverbank while we, the children, hopped up to the balcony and watched. The dead body was already in a state of decomposition; it had expanded like a balloon ready to burst, and people were afraid to touch it. The unbearable smell of the corpse was carried by the wind. We all pulled our shirts and blouses to cover our nostrils to prevent us from smelling the odour of that corpse. It was a sad and disturbing scene. The men had been all so excited to attend the fiesta celebration in Mahogany, but it ended in tragedy.

Nanay dying while Butuan was in flood

It rained every day all over Butuan and Agusan del Norte. The excessive rain had lasted for several days, causing the Agusan River to overflow. The floods of 1961 and 1962 created many more victims than the flood of December 1960. Usually, the Agusan River's water overflowed the riverbanks twice a year. Several people suffered losses of their homes, materials, and others had lost their jobs. Food became scarce, and a lot of children grew sick. Classes and work were suspended in both the private sector and in government. All the streets in Butuan were flooded, and other roads had waters that rose up to four metres high. To distinguish the streets, you need to look through those houses or buildings in lines along the roadsides. Only Magsaysay bridge was not underwater. The stores were closed while others were trading in their barotos, which became the main means of transportation. Most people were traveling by using rafts that they personally built from pieces of lumber, like the way Tatay had made ours.

I was not yet enrolled in the Elementary School during the flood of 1962 which lasted more than two months. It was not only Butuan and Agusan that were flooded, but throughout the region of Mindanao.

At first, the flood receded, but then it started to rise up again because of the continuous rain. Then we heard the news from family in Cabadbaran that Nanay died the night before (March 21, 1962); it had been too difficult for them to get the word to us before, because of the flood. The next day was the burial. Despite all the difficulties in organizing our departure, my parents did everything they could to reach Cabadbaran to attend my grandmother's funeral.

Tatay asked for help from a friend driving a *lantsa*, a strong boat capable of resisting the river's strong current, usually used for pulling a group of logs in the Agusan River coming from upper Agusan del Sur. Early in the next morning, two lantsa were there, standing by in the river in front of our house waiting for us. All of us: my parents, Dan, Nelly, Nolwen, the baby twins, me, Modesta (as we called her, Mama Moding), our cousins Domingo Palma, and Manoy Gunding were ready to go. Only Domingo's father, Anatalio Palma, was left at home living in the house's upper part (second floor). My father had also hired two small wooden baroto to fetch us from our house's entrance door to reach the lantsa. The flood was getting high. We tried not to fall into the water while walking to a small temporary platform that Tatay had constructed, in front of our entrance. I still have pictures in my mind of our embarkation to the lantsa that day. I was in-charge of remembering the baby twins' needs, including their bottles. As children, we were all excited about the unexpected travel during the flood. At the same time, we were so sad knowing that our grandmother had passed away. I would have loved to have a hug before she left, but then, it was too late.

Baby Amelie and Ashley remained silent. They were fortunate not to sense the sadness in our hearts; everyone else was quiet. I prayed that we could arrive at Cababdbaran safely before Nanay was buried, to be able to say goodbye, despite the difficulties. Mama remained silent; she didn't say a word. After we learned that Nanay died, she was coming to terms with the idea that she would never see her mother again. Everyone was so quiet, even the driver of the lantsa. We only heard the motor. It seemed to me that our travel was not to spend holidays but to bring us back to Magallanes, the delta, mouth between the river and the sea. The travel was not finished then, as we still needed to go down from the boat and take a jeep that took us three hours to arrive to bring the whole family from Magallanes to Cabadbaran though it's going at top speed. It was already organized that from Magallanes, we would all go to the cemetery directly. However, I had to stay with the babies in Nanay's house.

Nanay's spirit visited us

My family were still in the cemetery, or maybe while they were on their way home, and I prepared the babies' bottles. Suddenly, I smelled the odor of tobacco. I looked towards the entrance door, thinking that someone probably arrived before the others. Perhaps they preferred to stay and rest in the *descanso*. But the odor came from the balcony. There, I saw Nanay in one of her beautiful Spanish dresses, sitting in her favorite rocking chair. She was looking far away, with her face in silhouette. I wanted to get closer to her and touch her. But she disappeared before I could reach her, leaving behind her a slight fog of tobacco smoke spreading over my head. I remained standing there until the smoke dissipated and completely disappeared. I stayed a while in the balcony and talked to her. I knew she was still there listening to me.

"Nanay, I am sorry not to see you before you left to the other side," I said. "But I miss you. I know you can hear me because of your tobacco odor." I don't know how long I remained in front of her rocking chair, but I knew she was there. I wanted to keep talking, but the twins started to cry, calling for their milk.

I attempted to tell Mama that Nanay had come for short visit, just with the twins and me. But she remained remorsefully silent. She looked so tired. I was afraid of bothering her. I told her again before we went to bed about grandmother's visit. However, Mama seemed deaf to my story. The family stayed in Nanay's house until the ninth day of prayers. Tatay returned to Butuan before us to see if the flood was over; he would need to gather our belongings and fix anything broken, in the mess we left behind.

Inside the mosquito net, Nolwen, who was four years old, talked with someone, and she called out, "Nanay." When Mama heard Nolwen calling her late mother, she at once hid Nolwen with her under the blanket. Mama was intensely afraid; for me there was no reason to hide like that, as I was convinced that grandmother's spirit would never harm anybody. I waited for Nanay to reappear again, in vain.

Two days after was Mama's birthday, and she did not cook something special. I remembered that she used to make a *biko,* a sweet rice cake. It was made of coconut milk, brown sugar, and glutinous rice; we all also adored *suman,* a rice cake cooked by steaming, made from glutinous rice cooked in coconut milk, often wrapped in banana leaves or with coconut leaves. However, Mama was never the same since Nanay's death. Her eyes were filled with deep sadness, and it was like Mama was not fully there. At the funeral and in the days following, Mama experienced a lot of remorse; she acknowledged the hurt and the consequences of her failing to take care of her dear mother. Regrets had never come before, and it was so painful for her, as we can never bring back the past.

I have this memory: I thought back to when Nanay asked me whether I would have liked to stay with her and continue my studies in Cabadbaran. I said yes without hesitation, but we were overruled. We were both a bit bewildered because we couldn't decide without my parent's consent. I, too, had deep sadness at Nanay's death, but much less than my mother. Nanay had always been surrounded by family. And yet, the day that she had really needed us, there was nobody by her side. No one helped her, no one brought her to the hospital, and she died alone in her house. The neighbours had been wondering why the windows were closed during the day. They discovered the rigid body of my dear grandmother.

While I was busy at home with the babies that day of the funeral, many things came to my mind. I remembered one time when Mama had a significant dispute with Nanay. Mama brought me with her, taking the bus during the night. I was so sleepy, but Mama kept on checking on me to see whether I was alright. She even checked my breathing. She was probably scared to be blamed if I grew ill or stressed, as Nanay told her not to bring me.

Nanay's spirit was not the first one to have visited the family. Purification (Inse Puri), was Nanay's elder sister, who died in Mama Dominga's arms. Forty days of novena prayers were held, and we attended the prayers every night. One night, Mama did not feel like going to prayers and that night, Inse Puri's spirit visited us in the bedroom. Nolwen saw our great-aunt and was talking to Inse Puri, Mama hurriedly took Nolwen in her arms and sprinted to Inse's house to attend her prayers. I felt the fear of my Mama, while I waited for Inse Puri to reappear again, in vain. I found it so lovely when ghost comes to visit, and I believed that the ghost wouldn't harm me. This time, as we were staying in Nanay's house, I wondered how Mama would react if ever her mother's spirit appeared in front of her? I know that she dreamed of Nanay many times, but I don't think she had seen her mother's spirit in front of her. I likewise believed that a good spirits would not appear to you if they knew that you had the tendency to be afraid. This is maybe why a good spirit sometimes only comes to you in the form of a dream, often just before you wake up in the morning.

We returned to Butuan when Amelie and Ashley were three-months old, too young to remember Nanay's face. In my view, this is one of the reasons why Nanay's spirit visited us the day of her burial.

Returning to school

In June 1962, a long-awaited moment came. Three of us were enrolled for the first time at Bading Elementary School: Dan, age nine was in Grade 3; Nelly, seven years old was in Grade 1, and at the age of ten, I was in Grade 4.

One time, it heavily rained every day for five days. That day, our classes ended in the morning. We received an alert concerning the coming flood. We were told to be vigilant and should go home directly, especially for those living along the riverbanks like us. I reached home so hungry while the river water had started flowing throughout Butuan. Anxiety invaded me and I was distraught when I found nobody at home while the strong current of water was already running under our elevated ground floor. The deluge has risen so rapidly.

Once I opened our entrance door I was shocked to see drops of fresh blood everywhere on the floor. It made me dizzy. Anguish numbed me throughout my body so that I could hardly move. Where were they? Who was wounded? I followed the blood traces that reached the stairways, which had begun to fade because of the rain. I continued walking until outside the house and thought of asking the neighbours why there were drops of blood on the floor, and where's my family, but I fainted on my way.

I was awakened surrounded by children and the neighbours on the higher ground where the water had not yet reached. Nang Pening, was asking me to open my mouth and told me to swallow the food in the spoon that she was inserting into my mouth. We were all soaked by the rain and the flood water. They said baby Ashley, who was only a eight months old, had fallen onto the ground, entirely covered with river water. Luckily, she was not carried by the current. She was crying excessively, so Dan was dancing with her in his arms, trying to calm her down. She was so nervous that she had kept on jerking and gesticulating until she slipped out of Dan's arms. She hit her head on the ground, was wounded, and bled. Thank God, she was not carried away by the water current and did not drown.

Near-Death Experience and Out-of-Body Sensations

Are near-death experiences viewed today as they were in biblical times? Is it possible to be separated from our physical body and yet remain alive and totally aware? Is it a widely accepted phenomenon? For me the process of dying begun and has religious and spiritual interpretation. Is my out of body experience common to others? These questions haunt my mind.

Our house stood about 800 meters away from the riverbank of the Agusan River – the longest river in Mindanao, and the third-largest in the country. Many speed boats and giant cargo ships often stopped over for several days as they waited for goods and cargo to be loaded. The boats carried a lot of different products of the Philippines, such as bananas, pineapples, coconuts, and other fruits. Most of the cargo was cut lumber in various sizes that were all carefully piled up to seven metres high along the pier. The labourers for the lumber shipyards worked day and night to earn a living to feed their families. The ship's hoist that picked up the cargo along the pier made a terrible noise that prevented us from sleeping when it was operated at night..

1962. At the age of 10, I did the household chores at home: such as cooking, washing the dishes, and taking care of the twins. One Saturday morning in June 1962, Mama went to the market leaving Ashley and Amelie, just 9 months old, with me, while Nelly was in school and Nolwen was with Mama. She instructed me before they left to wash the dishes, and then to clean the rags after cleaning the house while the babies slept.

I sang to little Amelie and Ashley, to help them get sleep faster. Then I heard my friends outside shouting excitedly, "It's time to go! It's time to go!"

My little sisters were asleep at last! As for me, it was time to join my friends. The weather was so hot that swimming was the best way to handle the heat. However, I thought that I might not join them, as I didn't know how to swim very well.

Early on, Agusan River was quite a small river, wherein only small boats were coming and stayed overnights along the riverside, before the cargo ships and the port. Then some businesses moved in. On the other side of the river, a sawmill called Mahogany released black smog and vapor through a long round metal tube pointing to the sky. Mahogany derived its name from the prestigious wood of the same name, and became the name of their district. Through the years, the Agusan river became now broad and deep polluted with the gasoline and crude oil from big boats and cargo ships, as well as the garbage thrown by the people on the river, and people living nearby.

Despite all this, and stupid I was, I decided to go down to the river. It was low tide, water current was getting stronger. More and more ships were coming in, created big waves that had cut at the riverbank. I was full of stress looking to the riverbank, eroded, and polluted.

I went down the muddy slope, alert in my movements, as I gripped the grasses, even though they would have been too weak to prevent me from falling. I found myself standing on an enormous log pile tied together by massive cables and spikes. At first, I watched some children competing as to how long they could hold their breath and stay under the water. I myself had inhaled and exhaled air several times while they were still under the surface.

There was a considerable number of cargo and passenger ships that had landed in the port since the night. Despite the crew's warning, a lot of children enjoyed diving from the top of the vessels. Children were prohibited from going up to the ship's top deck, but some of them persisted. Adults too climbed up to the roof – about seven meters high – and dived down to the water. Children about my age, also enjoyed diving from the logs floating in the river. I believed they were firmly joined together by the iron-headed nails or spikes. At one point, one person gave a signal, then all participants of the contest threw themselves in together into the deep water. I enjoyed watching them, and was a bit envious of their fun. I had almost forgotten that I was supposed to be washing the rags, which was my principal reason why I came to the river. I rub them with soap marked "Perla."

Meanwhile, one big ship followed by a lantsa and three speedboats passed one after the other, making big waves in their wake. Suddenly, I was shaken by the big waves, while people in the water were yelling for help. The yellow round basin filled with our dirty rags fell and disappeared into the water. There were sounds of bouncing, banging, and crackling all around me; the logs were rubbing against each other.

Oh no! The iron-cables were breaking one after the other. The logs separated and scattered everywhere, and I found myself lying upside-down, grasping one of the logs against my face, chest and stomach while trying to hold on to the log with my legs. I used all my muscles and strength, but the log was so wide that I could not get my arms around it tightly. The log was bouncing and banging against other logs again and again. The other children and the adults behind me were shouting, "Bebe jump now!"

" I didn't know how to swim," I yelled.

"Come on, jump, jump! Then we can help you! Otherwise you will be carried by the current!" Men were shouting instructions and waving their hands to help me to see them.

I was about to jump, but it was too late. I was violently ejected far down into the water. I panicked. Every time I opened my eyes, I saw the vast logs around my head. I was terrified. I swam as strongly as I could, but it was more and more difficult for me to reach the surface. I was carried away by the strong current. I tried to fight my way back and reach the surface, to call for help. Finally, my head came out of the water, and I could see our house and my friends getting smaller and further away, so small in the distance. The current became much stronger. The other children continued waving their hands and calling to me, until I did not hear them anymore.

Several logs surrounded me, and suddenly I felt a hard bang over my head, which pushed me back underwater. I was struck by one of those logs and felt dizzy, exhausted, and helpless. I swallowed water, tried not to breathe it in, then my ears felt the pressure and my eyes hurt too. I tried to keep my eyes open to see what was going on around me. I was desperate while splashing with my head bobbling, while I struggled to float.

I struggled to reach the surface again, but my strenght abandoned me. I did not know how long I had been in the water, or if I was dying, but it was better not to know. So I ultimately submitted myself to God. I prayed: "Please God, you know very well that I struggled to help myself but failed. I beg you to forgive me for coming to the river without my parents' permission, but please help me if You want." In my mind, my surroundings were no longer the river water, but a great mysterious world with an incredible beauty. I even said to myself: "If this is always the way when we die, there is no need to fear death."

I suddenly felt incredibly wondrous and relieved from fear, pain, and worries. I felt an unending heavenly love and peace. I felt someone carry me up in a floating sensation, with angels singing holy chants all dressed in white.. I was admiring an atmosphere entirely surrounded by wonderful emmanating white light, and all was white around me. I felt tremendous, beaming with a mighty love, feeling warmly protected in a peaceful, restful place. Heavenly voices were singing continuously, more beautiful than I had ever heard before, more even than during our church's chants. It was so beautiful, beyond words. I had never felt so amazingly good of all my life. Oh my God, I was in heaven, heaven is real

Then I saw my spiritual body floating over my body and over the heads of the children. I could see and hear everything that was being said and done. My body was lying down on the small balcony of our house, surrounded by children and neighbours, some of them were crying. I touched my mother's shoulder, who was bending down towards my body, and I wanted to ask her forgiveness for losing the basin in the river. I touched some of the children too, but they all ignored me. At that very moment, I did not really understand why I was separated from my body. I was full of worry, feeling like nobody cared for me. I felt sad looking to my body lying on the floor, not beautiful, then everyone focused their eyes to it. They did not even look at me floating above their heads. I felt lost, confused, and frustrated.

I saw Nanay in front of me. I did not expect to encounter her, but everything seemingly occurred naturally. I asked her forgiveness for disobeying her orders to not go down to the river. She had passed away and been buried a few months before but she was there with me alive, comforting me, standing in front of me, and was telling me that everything will be fine. She said I had to go home because my mother still needed me, as she was waiting for my brother and a new younger sister to come. But I felt sad when she disappeared. My grandmother had been present, but quickly she left me alone with a troubled mind full of questions. I was confused and disoriented. Then

I heard the children asking me to come back. "Please open your eyes," they said. Some were crying.

I came back to myself, not in the riverbank. I was there lying in my physical body on the small balcony at home. I wanted to tell the children that I was alright. I felt strange but fully alive. I did not really understand what happened to me. I saw people focusing their eyes on me. Then I suddenly found myself alone while I heard an extraordinary, pleasant sound of a man whispering to my ears.

"It is your second life," he said, with a tender voice so close to me that I had to look around, but nobody was with me. That voice impressed me tremendously. And until now, I still kept on wondering if that inimitable voice, was it the whisper of God? How I wish to see His face.

I heard the children come closer to me again. They were announcing to one another "Bebe is alive!" It took me years to understand. As I grew older, I realized I had experienced a profound near-death experience, a glimpse of heaven, and I have been to the "other Side," where I encountered my late grandmother who told me to return home.

I was brought back to myself, and I was not feeling happy, feeling dizzy, sick and lost. For two days after, I felt strong pains. Part of me regretted my choice. I would have liked to have asked my grandmother to bring me with her instead. Unluckily, in the days after, I suffered from side effects and troubles. I became irritable because of abdominal swelling, bloating, and indigestion, eardrum troubles, and dermatological problems.

I can remember the man who came to our house every day to clean my stomach with a long transparent tube in plastic, a kind of hose or a "syringe." used to suction out the dirty water I had swallowed. One end was going down to the basin that was placed on the floor. The second end was inserted into my anus, and I could not see how he had manoeuvred, I heard the water that came out from my stomach that goes to the basin. From that time, I suffered an intense phobia of the deep water. I kept myself from seeing the river and the sea for several years afterwards.

The whisper said this is my second chance for life, but I wondered what my mission on earth was. Indeed, I sometimes felt the need for someone who could reveal my core purpose in life. I prayed to God to enlighten my mind and spirit, and now I understand while writing this memoir: Ever since after the visit of the Holy Spirit when I was a young child, and after I have seen a portion of heaven during my drowning when I was ten, strange phenomena have occurred in my life.

Claustrophobia

I only started to understand when I began to write after Tatay's death, that I have a condition called claustrophobia, the consequence from my drowning experience. For many years I refused to admit it. In fact, I still feel panic when I am in a small room or narrow space. I feel like I am suffocating if I wear tight-necked clothing, and with age, my anxiety has increased. I preferred climbing in the stairways until the 20th floor, rather than using the lift. I tried to ignore it for many years, even refusing to see a doctor if the waiting room was too small and crowded.

The worst example of when claustrophobia was triggered in me in later life was when I had a breast cancer diagnosis in 2013. Mammograms were not enough for the diagnosis. I underwent screening, biopsy, and a chest X-ray. I yelled like a young child when I learned that they would put me inside a tunnel-like machine to be examined by scans and by MRI, in addition to the radiology. The panic made me almost crazy, so that my medical appointments were all postponed.

Before my drowning episode, I could hide under the chairs and even inside dark holes to play without being scared. I did not tell anybody in my family at the time, because being the eldest of eight siblings, I was supposed to be the model for the others. My parents gave me the privelege of leadership of the family. I did not want them to criticize my uncontrollable shortcomings. But every time I tried to hide this fault of mine, the more I experienced claustrophobia. In many instances, I panicked or fainted.

In any case, I had obeyed Nanay to come back to myself, but I regretted it. If only she had asked me to go with her, I would have followed her willingly. Still, she said I needed to return home, talking about a coming brother and sister, but how could she know it? This question kept being repeated in my mind. But she did not explain the gaps of years that would be between the children. As a child, I did not really understand what she was telling me.

Almost a year later, my younger brother Melchor was born on my birthday in January 1964.

Remembering the experience: Until now, I am still intrigued as I really don't know how long I was unconscious in the water. For whoever saved me, climbing up the slippery slope of the riverbank would have been challenging. I forgot to ask Tatay how long he ran going back home, carrying me in his arms.

I am as well impressed by my memory of being out of my body experience, and the episode of my grandmother's presence. No matter what, I obeyed Nanay. I could never forget the sensation of being protected, as if I was being carried by angels. I can recall the overwhelming feeling of extreme peacefulness and serenity. It was a beautiful environment, full of pure and intense light, surrounded by magnificent chants and magical sound of music. Religious people told me, "God gives you the privelege to see a portion of heaven." At my young age, I did not know how to explain to my family that I saw my body lying down on the floor. I communicated with my deceased grandmother from the "other side?"

In fact, I informed my father two days after my drowning that Nanay was present, but he had just answered me, "Oh, you were probably dreaming."

"No, I was not dreaming of her at all, as I was not asleep," I said to him insistently. "I nearly drowned in the river, remember? But Nanay was there talking to me. She even told me that I had to return home because Mama will surely need me with a brother coming, then a sister." I could not fully express what I had experienced. No matter what I said, my father remained stunned upon hearing me, but that was all. I was left upset, frustrated, confused, and disoriented as usual; nobody had been able to explain to me about the appearance of my grandmother at the time. Luckily, though I had waited a long time, as I grew older, I finally understood everything with the help of religious people.

I had a short stay with Mama in May 2017, three days after my father's burial. I had a conversation with her inside the *bahay-kubo* [a rest-house made of bamboo with a nipa hut]. I asked her in front of my younger sister Nelly, about the presence of Nanay Pantay when I nearly drowned and was unconscious. It was an out-of-body experience, I tried to explain.

When I talked to her about the river's happenings, she asked me whether Nanay had invited me to follow and stay with her. I answered her that Nanay did not ask me anything, but she told me about the coming of a brother, then a sister, and she requested me to go home. It seems to me that my mother was not interested at all in my drowning. Perhaps she just preferred not to remember how hard it was for her. She seemed evasive. I understood that she did not wish to continue our conversation about this topic. The expression on Mama's face led me to think about her childhood experiences. She never knew how to express well herself, but I felt that she had things she could tell, many more than she wanted to reveal. I know she was still grieving like all of us, but I needed to get answers to the questions that ran around in my head. At that time, I did not know yet that I would write a memoir.

Mama told me about a time when she was brought to the hospital unconscious when she collapsed, maybe due to fatigue or missed meals. There, she also had the experience of seeing her late mother. She, too, had seen the "other side." She said her mother had asked her to go with her, but she's so much devoted for her husband, and she chosed to stay; then Nanay disappeared. But when I asked her to tell me more about my drowning and about Nanay, she answered: "No need to talk about all that, as I might have a nightmare again." And that was all. Communication sometimes was lacking in our family.

One time, a few years after my near-death experiences, Mama was working hard. She was feeling stressed the whole day as she was the principal host of Manoy Gunding's marriage in 1965. After the wedding celebration, she was bleeding heavily. She was brought to the hospital in Butuan City, but she had miscarried a baby. At the time, I was 13 years old, but I remembered what my Nanay had said that I would have another younger sister. Then I thought that Mama had probably lost a baby girl, and maybe I would no longer have that extra younger sister.

However, four years after Melchor's birth, Imelda was born in June 1968. So, what my late grandmother predicted came to be. Had I ever asked how did she know? I was always thinking that if I had not had my exhilarating mystical experience in the Agusan river, I would not have had seen my grandmother in the afterlife, and she had not predicted the coming of Melchor and Imelda.

Can all spirits predict someone's situation and the future?

Life as A Schoolgirl 1962-1980

Life in Butuan was utterly different from that of Cabadbaran. Grandmother was no longer there, nor Manoy Gunding to console me. He was working in a logging company in Agusan del Sur, quite far from where we lived.

Before the beginning of our morning classes, every pupil needed to be in line while singing the National Anthem in Tagalog entitled, *Lupang Hinirang* [Land of the Morning] It was different than at the Candelaria Institute, where we used to pray first. Then, facing our Philippine national flag that was raised in the middle of our school, we sang our National Anthem hymn in English, before going to our respective classrooms.

During the School Day celebration, Dan, Nolwen, and I had participated in the programme of activities and performances. Dan recited a poem; Nolwen joined in the singing contest and won the first place. I was so proud of her, while I participated in the contemporary dance show.

"Your brother Dan usually refuses to participate in the classroom discussion," Mrs. Sanchez, his teacher, said. "He usually remains silent on his seat. However, this time I have given him a task to recite a poem on stage during the school program in front of the parents, classmates, and friends. I am sure that at eight years old, he could recite it perfectly if he wanted to. But he needs to be convinced, and maybe you know how to persuade him," she said with enthusiasm. Despite everything, she seemed convinced of Dan's potential.

I could not find words to answer her, because I was skeptical of my brother's capabilities. Then I remembered his notebooks full of drawings of airplanes. I really wondered where he kept his lessons and homework. Now, he needed to study the poem to recite it. I reminded him that he wouldn't get nervous in front of the audience if he memorized it very well. Then he would gain a higher grade in class.

On performance day, we were all surprised. Dan recited his poem on stage with great expression and immense skill. In fact, I had not expected that he would recite his poem fluently without mistakes. He was well applauded by the audience. It was a pity that Tatay was not present during the programme, because he was not able to get away from work; he should have been there to watch his son and to see how excellent he was.

"I observed my son, discretely," Mama said later. "He was memorizing the poem at home behind his bedroom door one day before the school day celebration, speaking in an incredibly soft voice. He was too shy to let everyone know that he would finally seriously recite the poem, that his teacher trusted him with such a poem," she said proudly. We were all proud of him.

While I was putting on my costume behind the stage with the other dancers, I glanced at the audience by peeping between two curtains. I wished that Dan would watch me dancing the contemporary dance, but he was already catching up with the giant dragonflies again.

As I shared earlier, things changed abruptly when my brother Dan was born in December of the same year as me. On reflection, I lost some of my childhood at the age of 11 months; I only had ten months of my parents' full attention. I admittedly turned into a sad child longing and needing more of my parents' love and affection. These feelings welled up during my teenage years.

In many ways, I was blessed to be the eldest of eight children: we were six girls and two boys. I had a lot of fun watching my seven siblings grow up. Most of the time, my parents were more demanding of me than of my younger brothers and sisters. So, I had to be smart, a positive role model, a natural leader, and an example of perfection in all matters, especially in decision making. The latter was the most difficult to handle, making me act much older than my age. Though I may probably have high intelligence that I got from my parents, a high IQ alone is not enough to be a practical and hands-on teacher to my younger siblings. It was a challenging role for a young child to perform well. It was never an option for me to leave them behind and to mingle with children of my age, to just play and have some fun without responsibilities. Instead, I was obliged to work and stay put, acting like a respectable small adult. Sometimes. I shaped myself in how to behave, thinking about my responsibilities more than taking care of myself. My family knew that all their concerns were and would always be my problem, as the eldest.

I was deprived of the wonders of the natural environment that I had experienced in Cabadbaran once we moved back to Butuan. My school days and adolescence were full of humiliation and torments that I hid deep inside me. The school building was built in a previously swampy area of palm trees. It was then filled in with sawdust of cut-woods called "siren", tiny particles of wood produced during the processing and handling of timber. The siren had been deposited for been many years by the New Asia sawmill and the East Mindanao sawmills.

My elementary school ground was plagued with ultra-fine dust particles; this caused me respiratory problems. I developed a skin allergy. At that time, we did not have masks for children. Mama usually placed a handkerchief with a pin at the upper part of my dress just below my chin, so I could cover my nose when the wind blew with dust. I could not help thinking of my grandmother, who always found the right remedy for treating me with medicinal plants; unfortunately, she was no longer with us.

The Philippines at that time did not have a good social welfare system. There was no social protection for all; only the well-off families could access a health insurance system. In any case, I hated those three years of schooling (Grades 4, 5, and 6) in Bading Elementary School, due to the environment. During the recess period, I often was upset about my allergies and hid in the comfort-room, so I won't be exposed to the sun while other children enjoyed playing. I remember fainting outside, and then going back to the classroom, but the teacher who did not understand my situation grew angry at me.

I hated myself. I was fed-up with my allergies, hated the place, and even hated my parents for sending me to that school. I would have loved to have returned to Candelaria Institute in Cabadbaran, where there was no sawdust, and there were plenty of trees around the school with shade that protected children from the sun. Sometimes, my classmates mocked when they saw me scratching. I cried so many times while I was walking home. I sobbed when I thought no one could see. I regretted coming back after my near-death experience. Nanay should have had not told me to go back, I thought. I still heard someone telling me that it was my second life, but I felt like this life was full of hatred. I thought that God had abandoned me.

Despite all my troubles, I studied hard, so that my grades were the highest among my classmates in Grade 6. But I felt unwelcome in that class and they looked at me with disdain when I got the highest grade in the examinations. I was supposed to be the Valedictorian, but my classmates' parents protested because, according to them, I studied in Bading for only three years, whereas the others had been there since Grade 1. I did not understand because, for me, seniority had nothing to do with my grades. What was worst was that, during their meeting, the committee headed by the principal, was asking my parents to donate a *lechon* (a whole roasted pork dish). I was silently seething of anger. My parents could not satisfy their demand, and I was nominated as Salutatorian instead. It cannot be right that the Valedictorian had lower final grades than the Salutatorian.

Let me recall my schooling in Bading. I was disgusted almost immediately knowing there was no strict discipline regarding the languages, and my classmates were not speaking proper English. Frustrated, I did not improve my pronunciation. I thought it was a useful language. Somehow, they looked at me strangely, like an alien from another planet. I agree that "The language we speak shapes the way we think," as stated by Lera Boroditsky, a cognitive scientist and professor in the fields of language and cognition. Now I felt lost. I held lots of words silent in my mind, and said less and less. I was devastated, and I regretted leaving my previous school, the Candelaria Institute in Cabadbaran.

Fast learners: the crack section

The following year was decisive. I was enrolled at Urios High School, the private Catholic high school in Butuan City. As a Salutatorian, I was half-scholar. Urios granted me 100% free tuition, not the matriculation and miscellaneous expenses or book allowance, unfortunately. At that time scholarship was limited.

I had to work during the two months of vacation in April and May. I worked as a salesgirl in a department store whose owners were Turkish, and I waitressed on weekends in the Busa Restaurant, just behind Busa Store. I spent my salary on buying books (although some were borrowed). I also paid for cloth for my uniform, a white blouse and blue skirt, made by a dressmaker, and I bought a new pair of shoes. What I lacked was the money for daily transportation, money for the canteen, snacks, and all the miscellaneous expenses, such as a new dress or suits for dance, sports, school representation during the annual junior high school programs, etc. I was quite sure that I was the only girl that came from a low-income family. And God knows how my parents suffered; during weekends, I was also working as a babysitter to our neighbours, yet after classes, I had to return home walking three kilometres to save money. I can't count of how many times I attended examinations on an empty stomach.

There were six sections: from A to F, and I belonged to section A, which was considered "the crack section" or the fast-learner section. I was amazed that among 31 students, 20 were Valedictorian, and only 11 were salutatorians. Most of them came from outside Butuan City: Gingoog, Buenavista, Nasipit, Carmen, Agusan del Sur, Cabadbaran, Ampayon, Surigao, and so on. Most of my classmates lived in a boarding house near Urios, and their parents belonged to a well-off family working in Agusan's timber industry. The selection for academic full-scholarship could only be taken from our section, and that we must maintain the final grade from flat 1.0 to 1.25 to be selected. At the end of the school year, I was granted general average of 1.3 (which was below what was needed). Catastrophic! I lost my qualification for the academic scholarship, a great deception. In retrospect, if I had been able to study comfortably without having to work during weekends, with enough food to eat and no concerns about poverty, I would have had undoubtedly been one of the full academic scholars.

My parents couldn't afford to let me continue my studies the following year; it made me feel sick. And I couldn't let myself to just be a babysitter for the rest of my life. My job was to bring a child to the Chinese school and stay in the classroom as they took their classes. In that time I had the chance to read books and learn. However, I missed the opportunity to learn the Chinese language because I was quite stubborn; at the time I was not interested in talking or writing the Chinese language. Now I regret that choice so much. I could have been trilingual. Speaking different languages would have been so helpful when searching for a job, especially in the commercial domain, when we come into contact with so many different nationalities and foreigners.

I worked as a salesgirl again, but I was bored when there were no customers in the store. It was not a job that would improve my life, and what I earned was not enough to really help my parents, not even enough for me to have a little money for myself. The department store closed, and I returned to being a babysitter again. I was fed up taking care of our neighbours' children.

Segundino's wife, Sabel, visited us and invited me to visit their place in Surigao. Without hesitation, I went with her. I did not ask permission from my parents, but they did not prevent me from going. They knew very well that I was very eager to change my environment. Segundino and Sabel had a three year old girl and a baby boy. Manoy Gunding was often absent from working in logging. He was lodging somewhere in Tandag or Surigao del Sur. In the beginning, everything was going fine. However, two weeks after I arrived, I was alone with the children, and sometimes Nang Sabel did not come home at night. She said she went to visit her husband, but it left me in an awkward position, as we lived with her elderly father. I thought that he was not happy to see me living in his house. I came with Nang Sabel for change, but not to be again a baby sitter.

One evening there was a serenade outside the house. I did not appreciate it; not because the singers were older than me, but because they woke me. Sabel's father opened the windows, and the songs became even louder. He forced me to watch them, but I remained in the bedroom, not going outside. The elderly father grew angry with me. I did not know those people who came to see me. I understood later that it was their custom and tradition to welcome any new arrival to the village. Three weeks passed, I started to get bored taking care of the young children, with Manoy Gunding not there. I had not seen him since I came to live with Nang Sabel. I wanted to go back home to Butuan, but I did not have a single cent to cover the transportation expenses.

Jazz instructor and dressmaking (1967)

One day I bought a bottle of kerosine for the lamp and I met Adriana, the daughter of the store owner. She was three years older than me, a high school student in Surigao del Norte. She invited me to watch their school program and attend to their evening party.

We had danced a lot of the cha-cha, boogie woogie, rock n' roll in the style of Elvis Presley. At 15 years old, I enjoyed dancing without shame as I knew that nobody knew me, and no younger siblings were watching me. The celebration went until three in the morning. Afterwards, Adriana brought me home with her, and I slept in her bedroom. Adriana's grandmother was so caring who reminded me of Nanay Pantay. She said I could stay with her unique granddaughter during the school vacation if I wanted.

Lilly, a teacher who saw me dancing, asked me to teach modern dance to her pupils of eight and nine years old, for a performance the following month, and invited me to stay in her house. She said the same dancers would open the program during the fiesta celebration in their town. I did not promise anything, as I knew I would go back home to Butuan when Manoy Gunding came back, but he was not there for almost four months.

Thus I became the instructor for Jazz lessons for 12 pupils, mixed classes of boys and girls. I was overwhelmed with their enthusiasm for dancing, and they learned jazz very well and fast. However, it took me such a long time to convince their parents to understand that their children needed to follow my instructions, to move their bodies graciously without hesitation, according to the beautiful music that Adriana and I had chosen. They were fabulous. I was surprised by our success during the dance presentation. I cried for joy while peeping between curtains on the backstage, watching the children dancing with the choreography I have invented. The audience were excited and applauded enthusiastically. During the fiesta celebration, perhaps because of my long hair, they chosed me to act as a mother of a young princess during the theatre presentation, *the pageant*. I humbly admit that I became famous in their town, just for a short period.

On the other side of the road, just in front of Adriana's house, was a tailoring and dressmaking shop. I had applied as a working student: meaning, I would learn dressmaking while working from 9:30 in the morning to 5:00 in the evening, with a 1-hour break for lunch. Unbelievable, I was accepted. I did not have to pay anything, but I did not get paid either. Still I was happy to assist them sew the hemlines of trousers and dresses for customers, in addition to my lessons on how to sew and to cut out patterns for dresses.

Adriana returned to school and Lilly, living next to the dressmaking shop, insisted on inviting me to stay in her house while waiting for Manoy Gunding to return. In the beginning I had a delema: shall I stay with Adriana or with Lily? Their hospitality touched my heart. I choosed Lily because her house is next to the tailoring/dressmaking. She was so kind too and I was giving jazz dance lessons to her pupils. After ten days, the shop's owner offered me some pieces of coloured plain cloth. I was able to sew my skirt and blouse, a pair of pajamas, and a full dress. I felt the immense emotion, unables to hold my tears when I started laying the newspaper sheet out on the table and cut out the patterns for my puffed-sleeved blouse and full skirted-skirts.

In the evening, I continued teaching jazz lessons. The parents brought their children to Lilly's house, where I felt at home. I was touched by their kindness.

One night, I was suffering from toothache, and the mother of Lilly's husband's gave me a kind of tea to drink that provided relief. She also gave me a massage from my head to my back that helped me to relax, and she cooked soft-red rice for me. She wore spanish dress: Kimona and long wide skirt, reminded me again of my Nanay Pantay. I was stunned: She was not my grandmother but she talked and cared for me like Nanay did. "Bebe, don't worry, the tea you drank will help you relieve from pain," she said as she continues massaging my head, neck and shoulder. It was as if my grandmother was resurrected. I was so thankful to God for providing me someone to take care of me in moments of pain.

However, Nang Sabel was not happy that I did not return to her place in the middle of the rice fields. This was mainly because of my allergies, and because I was scared of her father. I had almost forgotten my desire to go back home to my parents, when Manoy Gunding reappeared to bring me back home to Butuan.

On the bus, I could not stop crying, so much that Manoy Gunding thought I was sick. I realized how I had loved my almost four-months stay in that place, where I learned cutting patterns and sewing dresses. I was about to start to learn how to sew menswear when Manoy came early that morning. I had a heavy heart leaving, as I did not get a chance to say goodbye to my friend Adriana; she attended her classes that day. But I had to return home to see my own family in Butuan. I had waited for Manoy for so long, enough time to love the place and the people in Surigao. I did not hear any more about his reasons because I kept on crying, and this was always my problem: when I cry, I can't talk at the same time. I sobbed like a young child. I was happy anyway with my bag full of dresses I personally sewed.

While on the bus, I suddenly remembered that before I came to Surigao, I posted in the letter-box of the radio station of Butuan DXGM, a short story of my family, my life wherein I had expressed my feelings and emotions, and my passion of dance. Their radio host had been reading life stories during their story program. However, I did not know if it was well-written, or whether it had even been read. Anyway, nobody in my family could guess that it was my story because I used an alias, Sandra.

The dance contest

There was a dance contest every Sunday afternoon, where the boys came to ask you to be their partner, and you would dance according to the music. In Butuan I had succeeded in escaping from the house for two Sundays in a row. My mother would have never allowed me to go, but my father already understood that I would go to participate in the dance, and he did not prevent me from going. One time he saw me dancing the boogie or rock n roll style of Elvis Presley alone in my room, holding a rope as my partner, while listening to the radio announcing the dance contest. The rope was tied to masonry nails firmly hammered to the thick wooden wall. After that, I knew that Tatay understood my passion for dancing.

The competitors were officially practicing their dance many times in a week with their partners. My case was different as I had no partner. But I won second place, dancing the cha-cha and boogie-woogie with a partner I didn't know at the DXGM radio station. These were the dances had made me famous in Surigao. I realized how busy I was with activities for those four months in Surigao, but I could never stop thinking about how good I felt when I was dancing. I had come to Surigao with a brown paper bag full of clothes and without a single cent. I returned to Butuan still with no money, but with a traveling bag offered by the tailoring shop, full of new clothes that I sewed myself. As a girl who loved to dance, I was proud and happy with my accomplishments.

But then I cried again because when school re-started, and I was not enrolled. I should finish my studies to help my parents. I regretted being away from my family for the four months; in my absence a lot of things had happened. I saw my father with his beard and long hair, pale and thinner than when I left. My mother looked exhausted too, but they never blamed me of being selfish when I went to Surigao. No one could imagine how I felt guilty for not helping my parents financially during my absence, when they needed me most.

The Sawmill Explodes

The New Asia Sawmill & Lumber Company exploded while I was not with my family. The entire two buildings burnt, and also the materials and pieces of machinery used to cut the raw logs. Only a few stocked lumbered woods deposited outside the building, and the logs on the river remained intact.

The sawmill was the livelihood of 90 percent of the population. Workers and office employees lost their jobs. The whole barangay was in mourning. The inhabitants lost their jobs and their hopes. The students were striving to pursue their studies, yet most of them had stopped attending school entirely. New Asia became an abandoned area. The stores closed, one after the other. Sick people who had no means for medication or hospitalization died. The sawmill was never rebuilt, and the trade left. The remaining inhabitants had no choice but to struggle to survive.

The story is a personal one for our family. Tatay worked there, and we were used to the sounds of the sawmill operations. I was told the story of Tatay's experience:

On the day of the explosion, Tatay wanted to enter the building to check something, but it was hard to find the right key. He was still checking one by one the keys on the keychain, when he heard a terrifying sound, like thunder. Several flashes of lightning struck the building, and light bulbs burst. One burning light bulb dropped into the barrels full of reserved crude oil, which was used for running the machinery for cutting the logs into smaller pieces. In just a few seconds, the fire was out of control, ravaging everything in its path. The sawmill compound was left a pile of charred ashes, the buildings disappeared.

Boom! The explosion had immense power, and blasted Tatay far away from the building; he was left stunned, but alive. If he had found the right key, he would have been inside the building and probably would not have survived from the detonation. It had not rained for several weeks, so everything was bone dry. The explosion was luckily followed by rain, which prevented the fire from travelling further towards people's homes. The fire trucks arrived, but all the buildings were already gone. Tatay remained working as the security guard for few months until all the sawmill stocks were sold.

The guardhouse that Tatay had constructed farther from the sawmill building that was very close to the riverbank was not burn. It was almost as high as a coconut tree behind and served as his station. He had been the head of the Company's Security Guard, and most of the time he worked the night shift. He could see around the company compound, and make sure there was nothing unusual going on. I had been there once or twice, bringing his snacks for the night. He had a wide view and remained alert, overlooking the logs floating in Agusan river tied with strong cables; they danced with the waves when ships and speed boats passed by.

When Anatalio left, Francisco replaced him. He had done his job with all his heart. He had been an outstanding employee, well appreciated by his employers and loved by his co-workers. He had assumed essential and dangerous responsibilities. He patrolled and inspected property against fire, theft, vandalism, and all illegal activity. He checked the logs, counting them from his post before he went downstairs to check the full area of the sawmill. There, he would conduct security checks in the interior and outside of the building, count the numbers of electric light bulbs to be replaced, and write comprehensive reports outlining what he had observed while on patrol. He climbed up and down the 50 steps of the guardhouse's wooden stairs with his long and heavy shot-gun, the leather strap slung across his shoulder. He had loved his job, and now, it was gone. He undeniably suffered a strong psychological shock, that remained with him for some time.

However, a few weeks later, a baby girl was born. She was named Imelda. Because I was working as a babysitter to our neighbours, I could not take care of my youngest sister. The twins had started going to school at the age of seven. They were a bit behind, I knew, but they directly enrolled into Grade 1 in the same grade school of Dan, Nelly, Nolwen and me.

Tatay reminding me to write

One day, Tatay sat beside me and faced me with peculiar look. "Did you send a life-story to the radio station called DXGM?" he asked me with a particular tone that led me to understand he was almost sure it was me.

I answered him with another question: "How did you know it was me?

"I am your father, and the story was unique because it talked about our own family experiences. There was a cash award, but nobody had claimed for it because it was for Sandra," he said in a low voice. His remarks with disappointment hit me. I realized I was wrong to use an alias. But honestly, I did not expect that my story would be chosen to win a prize, because there were so many contestants. If I had known, I would have had not gone to Surigao with Nang Sabel. Then maybe, I could have claimed my award in cash. Despite Tatay's disappointment, communicating with him was enjoyable, and he possessed the best quality of comprehension, broad minded and precise in all matters. You could guess his emotions through his facial expression, full of feelings towards the topic.

"If you wish, you can always write again and can tell more, because our life story is not finished, and more experiences are to come," he said and sighed. My heart ached. I was so sorry that it was too late to claim the prize.

On the other hand, I was delighted to learn that my story has been read by DXGM radio station and heard by their followers. I would have liked to have heard how it was read by the radio commentator. Meanwhile, while writing this memoir, I was reminded again of how Tatay wanted me to write. I sometimes thought: Was Tatay predicting me unconsciously I would write books one day?

So, my dear Tatay, I am here to fill in the gaps that dementia stole from your mind. Even if I am not yet a confirmed author, I promise you that this memoir will leave a legacy of living history for the generations to come. Thus, your memories will remain alive for always.

I could never forget the day when I submitted my first article to *Urian*, the Urios Journal, which inspired me to write. Tatay had just finished fetching water from the artesian well and filled our jar, which kept the drinking water fresh while I was doing my assignment. As soon as I put down my pen, he came near me and I guessed he wanted to talk about something. He never disturbed me when I was writing, but I did not know he was waiting.

"I heard you have sent your article and was published in *Urian*," he said in an odd tone. "It was well done. I'm proud of you, but don't you know that Luisa did not believe it was yours?" Luisa was the advisor of editorial activities in Urios university, known for her toughness. Tatay was clearly not entirely comfortable, but at the same time, I saw his facial reaction, that he wanted to talk even though he was sighing with bitterness. Maybe he had heard some angry reaction.

I answered him with questions: "Why do you think that? What do you mean?"

But right away, Tatay asked me to forget what he said and I insisted. "They cannot believe you because we are poor." That statement broke my heart, and I sensed Tatay was more affected than me. The bitterness in his heart could never be fully removed. I prayed that someday we would be both healed.

I wanted to visit Luisa in her home to ask for an explanation, but I was not sure it would be a good idea to engage in a discussion that might have led us to an argument. Luisa was almost the same age as my mother, and I respected her immensely. She lived across the street from my godfather's house. She came from a well-off family, living in a big house that was constructed along the same road as ours. At Urios University, I asked her colleagues where I can find her, but I learned she was at home; she had filed sick leave. I abandoned the idea of seeing her and tried to forget the whole thing. But this case is preying on my mind today, October 10, my father's birthday, so I feel the need to say this again:

Tatay, despite our poverty, I have had many successes that depended not on financial wealth but through the wisdom I inherited from you.

To raise a family of eight children without a permanent job was incredibly difficult. One job he did was going door-to-door to sell the nipa wine [*lacsoy*], harvested and distilled in Babag. Babag was where his friends once generously helped him to hide when he had eloped with Mama, who fell pregnant with me before they were ready yet to get married, while Dominga's family was furiously searching for them. Tatay had gathered some wood that was left behind after the sawmill's explosion. He cut them with an axe, placed them inside the *kariton* [a cart with three wheels], and sold them to the people who need wood to light the fire in their stove. He pushed the kariton all day long until there was nothing left. Thus, he could give Amelie and Ashley some centavos for their *baon* – coins to be spent at school to buy some drinks or biscuits for snacks during recess. Tatay never stayed at home without earning.

When Imelda was born in 1968, our family had a very hard time. Poverty entered the portals of our home. I understood why Nanay Pantay wanted me to go back home after my near-drowning, yet if she had invited me to go with her, I would have had followed. But she had told me that my mother would surely need me, and that was the truth. As the eldest of eight siblings, it was my duty to help my parents earn money. To allow me to earn more, my employer entrusted me with increasing responsibilities. In addition to being a babysitter, I also did the household chores. This interrupted my college studies and prevented me from experiencing real teenage life. But at least I wouldn't have a troubled conscience, because I was helping my parents financially. I continued hoping that I would someday finish my studies.

Tatay said that before I was born, he worked as a labourer. He carried the lumber on his shoulders. He was a hard worker, always ready to sacrifice for the good of his family. When he married Dominga, he became a company guard at the New Asia Sawmill and Lumber Company. I remember that while he worked as a guard during the night, and he also worked as an electrician and maintenance in-charge during the day. He repaired some defected electric wiring and lights, which was sometimes was so dangerous because he did not have the excellent materials that we have today. He was absolutely security conscientious. I was proud of him. Tatay was born in October 1931. He was officially retired in the year 1991 at the age of 60 and was receiving his small monthly pension from the Philippine social security system. He continued taking on the tasks of being a security guard and maintenance crew in his own home, even during his final days at the age of 86.

Part-time job

I stopped working as babysitter to our neighbours, the Chinese family. I pursued my high school studies by attending evening classes while working during the day as babysitter to my godmother's daughters (and a baby); then to a couple who were both professors from Butuan City Colleges. After one year, I worked with another family living in Caltex near to my parent's house this time, until I graduated high school as Valedictorian in Butuan City Colleges. I had also accomplished two semesters of the Citizen's Army Training in March 1975.

The next year, I was so happy in returning to Urios College, enrolled as academic scholar. A one-semester, "on-the-job training," was a part of my two-year secretarial science course. I had to work during the day, and attended classes in the evening. It was not easy. As a secretarial student, I had to undergo office training. I was trained as a clerk steno-typist in the office of Attorney Gonzales-Espinoza Law office for three days a week for one semester. At the end of the first month, I received a kind of transportation allowance. For the other two days, I had to report to work as an insurance councilor agent as my part-time job with an insurance company called Filipino Life Insurance Saving's Plan. The main office was located on Marcos Calo street, just near the Magsaysay bridge. I went door-to-door visiting prospective clients to try to persuade them to buy insurance policies. What I received was a commission out from the insurance sold, but it was the kind of job that scared me because I didn't want to be liable for any little thing that could go wrong.

My lost paradise

One early morning I went to Cabadbaran to canvass new insurance clients. I wanted to surround myself with my cousins, the Beray family, Ramon's younger siblings, and his parents, to explain to them about insurance without pressuring them to subscribe. My main objective was to see them, as I had not seen them after Nanay's death.

I was shocked to discover how Mabini had changed. It was not any more the Mabini I knew. I did not find any trace of the artesian well that flowed with fresh spring-water all the time, or where long streams ran, where bamboo grooves grew; at this time, all the surroundings were dry. The beautiful giant coconut trees were getting old, leaves withered and dying. There were no more plantations, the inhabitants had neglected the land and left. The Mabini that I knew was a graveyard. I was chilled, seeing that sad landscape.

My grandmother's house and trees surrounding it had disappeared. Even all the houses along the road were gone. I felt the severe pain of nostalgia and melancholy. Luckily, my cousin Ramon was there holding my hand. He was three or four years older than me, and treated me like his younger sister. He had surely understood the great pain of losing the paradise I loved during my early childhood. Although Ramon and I were cousins, their neighbours believed that we were probably engaged as lovers because we were so close to each other. Unable to control my emotions, I had to hide my face, preventing Ramon from seeing my tears. I had lost my paradise! My pain was unbearable.

Ramon tried to cheer me up, and he found a remedy to boost and distract my mind by inviting me to see his friends at a place where the coconut trees were in bloom. We walked under the trees very far from the roads. I was welcomed by two charming young guys, who looked at me and smiled. One of them quickly climbed high up to the top of the coconut tree and picked some young green coconuts. The second guy broke them into halves, and we drank the sweet and refreshing juice. The young coconut meat that we usually called *butong* or *buko* was undeniably so delicious. We poured the fresh coconut water into a big gallon, mixed it with condensed milk, and put in the white fleshy, gelatinous, and creamy parts of the coconut. It was my favorite snack and a special meal for that hot day. I did not feel hungry again until the following day. That enjoyable moment had helped me forget for a while, the melancholy of my lost paradise.

The next day, I had some breathtaking experiences when canvassing insurance near and around Mount Mayapay, which had now became an important tourist spot. In 1974-1975, canvassing was one of the most effective means to gain new clients. One day I went there in the early afternoon, smartly dressed up, hoping to gain respect and convince people to buy insurance contracts. I hired a tricycle to get there, but the end of the road was destroyed, it was covered with thick mud and swamps. No tricycle could use this road, the driver left me. Despite this I continued walking. It was the first time I had gone to that place, and that experience was something that no one would enjoy. Trapped by the heavy rain, while my umbrella was blown away by the wind. My pair of sandals broke and then got stuck in the mud, so I had to continue walking and barefooted. It would have been better to have come with a raincoat and a pair of boots. The sky was getting so dark, there was not a single source of light. I did not see any houses and no more vehicles to bring me back home. While walking along that difficult, slippery way, I was already thinking about how I was going to go back home. I did not know that the village was far from the road. After long hours of walking, a man on a carabao pulling a *balsahan*, a two wheeled cart, saw me. He brought me to his house made out of bamboo with nipa palms roof. The man was also thoroughly drenched like me.

" What had been such an exciting purpose that had brought you to our place wearing clothes like rich people living in the city?" He asked. I did not know what to answer, and he remained silent after that. I understood that he was not happy when he learned that I was an insurance agent, and I wondered what had made him feel bitter about insurance.

I realized that my attire was not appropriate when canvassing people living a simple life, with basic bamboo houses with nipa huts in the village. But maybe I was not in the right area, I wondered. The little house was located on top of a small hill surrounded by coconut trees. There were some pigs, chicken and a carabao. I was obliged to ask to spend the night with them, and there was no means to tell my parents that I would not be home that evening, or tell them that I was safe.

The man's wife was kind and gentle, but she didn't speak to me the way I had expected. She lent me her robe for the night, and she dried my clothes and hung them above their stove full of burning branches of the coconut tree and the charcoal of coconut shells. She was too shy and she gave me the best of their light cotton blankets and a small pillow for the night. I wanted to go back home early in the morning without trying to sell any insurance, but I needed to explain to them about my mission, although I was hesitant at the beginning.

The roosters crowed under the house many times until dawn. I spent a sleepless night, despite the silence and country air. The rain had stopped, and they took me in the balsahan again and brought me to the nearest road, which was different from yesterday's road. I had to take a very long walk with my broken sandal that became my slipper that exhausted me. On my way home, I persevered with some canvassing, finally convinced three people to buy the insurance and I brought three valid insurance pass-books to the office.

I was so worried about the people who had subscribed to my insurance. I wondered how they could come to the office to claim if they needed to. The poor people were so courageous; they really needed and deserved more consideration, respect, and assistance in case of accidents or death which is covered by their insurance.

Now that I live in France, far from the Philippines, I still think of my responsibility to them as I know how difficult is to earn a living. The insurance company had used me to connect directly with them. Despite my compassion, I had abandoned them. I felt the guilt. My conscience, full of contradiction, continuously tormented me with remorse.

Another time, I went to Babag, a small district of Butuan with the Nipa Wine Distillery. They produced a local wine made from Nipa sap, the *lacsoy*, a local whisky. Canvassing insurance customers in Barangay Babag was also one way to visit my parents' old friends. Babag was a place where I learned the story of their elopement, and how they had to hide from Mama's family before I was born.

Performing house-to-house canvassing selling insurance is a good way to also play a psychologist's role for people. You learn to understand as they express in their own words their hardships and worries. Many times, they were so endearing that I forgot my mission, and I stopped trying to persuade them about life insurance services. Canvassing insurance clients was not my priority anymore, because I was so touched by those gentle and loving people living there. They entertained and welcomed me joyfully like a relative. I was so impressed with their enthusiasm of seeing me back after long years. They were all more than kind and gentle, which made me feel at home. I stayed one night with them. The grandmother, whom my mother called "Manay Paz," was like my parents' second parents. They told me about my parent's life while I was still in my mother's womb. I was born in Poyohon, which became the New Asia district derived from the New Asia Sawmill. When I was a newborn baby, we stayed in Babag while my parents were still waiting to find their own house to live in. Later, they transferred to the house near the sawmill entrance gate, where my father was working.

I understood why my parents were delighted when I told them that I was going to Babag. Their faces were illuminated with joy; they knew that in Babag, I would be safe.

A few months later, I became a regular employee as a secretary in the Gonzalez-Espinosa Law Office, where I started to receive a small salary and I was compensated with rich office experience and bilingual knowledge, honing with the updated technical secretarial skills. Meanwhile, I got an interview from a Reserved Officer Training Corps officer after passing the practical exam. I resigned after 18 months from the law office.

On the same year, I finished my two-year course and earned my Diploma in Secretarial Science. I likewise received the Certificate of Merit and Distinction and awarded for Outstanding Academic Performance during the school year 1976-1977. Urios College was now called Father Saturnino Urios University (FSUU).

A few weeks after, I started a new job as casual Secretary/civilian employee of the Philippine Army, assigned in the ROTC office in the city of Butuan.

Living Under Martial Law 1972-1981

On that hot rainy afternoon I was typing with the old typewritter the list of teachers and their high school students from the different secondary schools in Agusan del Norte. I was fascinated by my new challenging responsibilities, but after one month, I did not receive my salary. The Commander said it was delayed, as it took time, and promised that I would have the two salaries together on the second month. But two months passed, and still I did not receive anything, so I had to go to Cagayan de Oro to claim for it.

I confided my problem to the Dean of Student Affairs in Urios. I asked him if I should stop my studies, as I couldn't pay the tuition if I had no salary. He convinced me not to stop, and promised he would look into my case. ROTC office is also a part of Urios University. I temporarily stopped working in the ROTC office while waiting for my salary as a casual employee and my appointment from the Minister of National Defense before to become a regular civilian employee of the Philippine Army. Sir Kimilat hired me as his student assistant. I was proud working with him, no salary but my tuition fees were fully paid for the whole semester.

Ferdinand Marcos declared martial law on September 21, 1972. One of the Presidential Decrees, it was to implement the Reserve Officer Training Corps, (ROTC) and the

Women's Army Training Corps (WATC), a compulsory course to all students of any baccalaureate degree course or technical vocational course in public or private educational institutions were obliged to undergo the military training for two semesters. This is why both civilian and military administration was born, the famous 'ROTC Office' in Butuan City.

Voucher and payroll

I finally received my appointment as a regular civilian employee of the 4th Infantry Division, Philippine Army, and I was also appointed as a Reservist-Lieutenant of the Philippine Army, to be called up in time of war as signed by the Secretary of National Defence: General Juan Ponce Enrile. But the processing of my voucher was delayed, I had to follow-up personally to see what the trouble was. At that time, not all roads were cemented. I took an eight-hour bus ride to the Philippine Army Headquarters in Cagayan de Oro City, to claim my first and second salary from the finance department.

I was shocked to discover my voucher intact inside a folder tied with an elastic ribbon on top of the Officer-in-Charges' desk: It was not processed!

They said I could go home but I could not bring with me a pay cheque because my voucher was incomplete; they were waiting for a missing document which had not been submitted by my Commander. I was so mad, trying coping with the stress of the lack of pay, while standing in front of the desk of the Lieutenant, then a Captain, and the last the General, trying to find out how I could obtain my salary on time.

Although I was welcome by a Major in his residence near Cagayan de Oro Philippine Army Headquarters, I spent a sleepless night. Instead of returning home to Butuan, I returned to the finance department early in the morning. I was sent from one building to another, confronting their varied reactions. Sometimes it felt unbearable, but I persevered; my motivation was my salary. After a long struggle, I finally returned to Butuan on the third day with my check.

Although I had been deceived and disgusted with their administrative procedure for salary payments, I was proud to have been one of the civilian employees in the Army. I learned many things. The civilian employees working there were all amazed at my approach; they said they had not seen any civilian employees who had dared to argue and interrogate the military officers. They were surprised by the way I pushed them to do their job, in order to achieve my objective.

I was quite hesitant and timid at first, but later on I really insisted. I did not want to miss my classes one day more. I had human rights as a civilian and was protected by the law, although I was afraid that they would chase me out, or that I would faint when facing the General. On the last day, I told the civilian and military officers that I wouldn't be going home without my pay cheque. I was starving and had suffered enough working without receiving a single cent. I still had an eight-hour bus journey ahead of me, on difficult unpaved roads. I knew that there was only one ROTC Office throughout Agusan del Sur, and Agusan del Norte. All their reports go through my office. I was alone as a civilian employee, working in the ROTC office in Butuan, surrounded by military officers and also civilian students. I was not affiliated in the Army general headquarters, but I did my job rigorously, and I deserved to receive my salary regularly.

I did not regret going to the Camp Evangelista headquarters in the end, because I met the responsible military officers in the finance department. Thanks to the time spent there, I learned all the advantages I could claim, such as: hazardous allowance, clothing, and transportation allowance, aside from my monthly salary.

As agreed with the Dean of Student Affairs, Sir Kimilat, I stopped working as his student assistant upon receiving my official appointment.

After that, I undertook various missions to Cagayan, and also going with my Commander to the secondary schools where the Citizen's Army training tactical inspections were held. All the instructors of the first year of secondary schools became a civilian Commander of the citizen's military training to their students, where a tactical inspection was obligatory. After these inspections, most of the time we came back to the ROTC office at night-time especially when we went to two or more secondary schools in different directions on the same day. Sometimes the school community celebrated a surprise welcome party in honour of our Commander, with us as principal guests in the evening; and it was hard to refuse their invitation to stay for a night, when rooms were already duly reserved for each of us: our Commander, a Lieutenant, a Sergeant, one ROTC officer, and myself.

But it was problematic for my evening classes and homework. My grades were falling. I was at risk of losing my scholarship. I had to pay my tuition the following semesters. I didn't have any vacation because I also attended classes during the school holidays to complete the four-year course in commerce or business administration and management.

I had even stopped attending the piano and organ lessons that I loved, even though I had fully paid for the whole semester. What a waste. Most of the time, important work in the office reached me just when it was the time for me to leave the office. I had to abandon my Spanish lessons too, because it was my earliest class, and I was often late, which I regretted so much.

An accident in a dream that proved to be true

When Martial Law was declared in 1972, all first-year students enrolled in colleges and universities were obliged to attend citizen's military training: the ROTC for men and WATC for women. I was in-charge of the enrolment for all Urios ROTC College students. All the teachers in the secondary schools in the entire Agusan del Sur, and Agusan del Norte needed to submit to our office the list of the students enrolled in private and government secondary schools.

My mission: The military government had no budget, they said. So I had to solicit honourable sponsors to donate trophies as a reward to the first and the second winners of the Citizen's Military Training tactical inspection, held in the secondary and high schools throughout Butuan City and Agusan del Sur. My mission for fundraising was challenging. I sometimes had to insist to ask companies to donate, which was humiliating. Some places were walking distance from my office while others were not and I had no car of my own. But one day I obtained honourable donors of trophies from the bank managers: one for the first winner, and one for the second. My mission was fully accomplished.

In the office, I was surrounded by military men, but I had a student assistant and also a WATC cadet working with me. Civil-military relations was one of my responsibilities, and I was writing the speech for our Commander to give to the public in English. After that, he told me to write an article to submit to our daily journal or magazine. He happened to find me in the office late one evening writing my reports, but I was also writing my feasibility studies as one of the requirements for commerce graduating students, using the modern but noisy typewriter. He said I should write a memoir, and I answered him that I was still too young to write one, and that was not my priority. I had no time to do that on top of being a student in the evening and working full time during the day. I hope to see Major Referente someday to inform him that I have written my memoir now, at last.

Another mission: There was a regional oration contest held in Camp Evangelista Headquarters, Cagayan de Oro, and each Infantry Division was required to participate. My mission was to organize a request to Dr. Juanito Lao, Urios President, informing him that Elia L., our student WATC officer, had been chosen to be our candidate to represent Urios and 4ID Philippine Army. On behalf of my Commander and Urios President, I organized a meeting with Sir Kimilat to obtain the transportation and meals allowance. I requested an English professor who could provide one oratorical piece and an instruction for Elia. I spent one hour a day to support Elia for the performance, reminding her of the manner and expressions of the speech, as the professor had only shown her once. Elia memorized it and practiced in front of me, and I made her some suggestions.

While waiting for her turn, Elia was so stressed, and I was too. I hid behind the curtain backstage and persuaded her not to abandon it, that she must show to the public that she was determined to win. As soon as she had finished delivering her speech, she ran to me for a hug. We both cried and the tension in our shoulders eased to have been through to that event luckily with success. Our collaboration was rewarded, as she won the second place, and we could both be proud. The first winner was a young guy from Zamboanga del Sur who had only one point more than Elia. There were only two female participants out of the total of 16 competitors.

The following day was a Saturday. I did not go with Sergeant Cabaraban and others in a military jeep, because a few nights previously, I saw an accident with a jeep in a dream. So I decided not to go back home to Butuan with them, and tried to convince Elia to come with me by bus the next day. However, she decided to go home in the military jeep, as she thought it would be faster than the bus.

I wished that she had listened to me. Perhaps I should have been more insistent and told her about my dream. On the bus home, I had a short sleep and I dreamed again:

The military jeep was rolling fast down to the lower side part of the road. Elia tried to escape but was crawling and could not get out from the jeep. I felt suffocated for her.

It scared me so much that I almost shouted, inside the bus. It was impossible to call her as there's no cellular phone yet. That dream wouldn't let me go, Elia was my concern. I reported to my office earlier that Monday morning and planned to go to Bancasi 4th Infantry Division, Philippine Army to ask our commandant about Elia, the Master Sgt Cabaraban, and the young Sgt, the driver. Elia appeared in the office with a bandage around her head, and we hugged again. I was so relieved to see her.

The accident in my dream came true. "The jeep was running uphill when the driver lost control. The car rolled thumbling upside down many times down to the slope while we were trapped inside," Elia recalled.

"Don't worry Sarah, despite our accident, everyone was safe, although I had got some bruises in my forehead," she reassured me. But We were all shocked and saddened the following day when we learned that the driver was brought to hospital because of severe headache, and he died there due to cerebral haemorrhage. The Sargent had just been married, and his wife was pregnant. It was so sad.

My first and last hangover

I was like a mother to all the girls who were undergoing the WATC, and I developed a strong affection for them, especially to Elia and Laila. From time to time, a military officer, a Major from the headquarters of Philippine Army from Camp Evangelista, came to visit the 4ID in Bancasi. Major Referente and Captain Rara were accustomed to ask me to gather some interested ROTC and WATC to come with us to the discotheque to dance in honour of our guests. Elia and Laila assisted me to ask permission from the the girls' landlady of the dormitory that was located few meters from the Urios University campus. It was not the first time I asked permission from their landlady, and I had an excellent reputation for always bringing back the girls safely.

The girls and I enjoyed disco dancing our guests, although the men drank a lot of beer. We formed a circle on the dance floor, and one dancer had to stay at the middle to show a dance, then everyone would follow their moves which was sometimes inimitable. It was fun.

I had never appreciated the taste of beer, but that night I drank several glasses because I was so thirsty with all the dancing. I emptied my glass every time I returned to my seat, and they always refilled it. I was obviously drunk, and feeling nauseous.

Once I stepped out from the jeep, the neighbours looked from their windows to satisfy their curiosity. I waved my hand to greet them, but I did not know anymore if I was saying goodnight or good morning. I had a mild headache and dizziness, and it was hard to concentrate.

My feet shuffled as I walked, trying to reach our entrance door, and I wondered if I should knock; instead, I squatted on the floor leaning my back at the door that opened widely.

Tatay was there waiting for me. "You smell of cigarettes," he said. It's funny he did not say I was drunk. I don't smoke, but most of the dancers did. I collapsed. Tatay caught me before I fell to the floor.

He helped me climb the stairs, and I slumped to my bed. Luckily, everyone else was sleeping including my mother; if she had seen me in that state, I would have surely received an interminable sermon. I vomited through the window. It felt as if my stomach was turning upside down. I closed my eyes, and it felt as if the roof and walls were turning all around me. In few hours, it was the time to go to work, but I did not go that day. I was severely sick the whole day. What a nightmare!

I had no idea how someone could ever drink several bottles of beer everyday without being sick. I said to myself: this was my first and last hangover. I decided never to drink beer again, no matter what.

ROTC Cadet's presentation of their Queen

I was a civilian employee, and was also a student. As Chairman of Student's Day programme, I encouraged the ROTC cadets to present a show: The Queen's Coronation. As usual, Elia and Laila were there. All ROTC participants had learned and reviewed their own tricky scripts, where they had shown smoothly more in physical actions than words. Our group had assigned a tall man, handsome and smiling in the play, a joker to play the part of the Queen.

Prompt attendance was obligatory. Costumes and technical attires as well as the accessories were checked one by one, and had to be perfect. We did the make-up for our "Queen" in my office, I gave some lessons to him as to how to walk as royalty. We had so much fun while doing the rehearsals and everyone was so cooperative that we had experienced immense satisfaction. It was a great success, as we won first place in the competition.

I delivered a short opening speech. I kept it quick so that the audience would not get bored while their faces were all on me. They were so impatient. When I announced that we were presenting the Queen's Coronation, the audience became serious and silent.

They were not aware that our Queen was a young man, and with his make-up you could not recognize him. And when the audience saw our queen walking like a fashion model along the aisle with his royal partner, they exploded. They were so enthusiastic with their admiration for the performance. There was roaring applause. I was so proud of the actors. It was as if the delirious audience threatened to blow out the whole stadium with the excess of their joyful exuberance. I can still see the image of the Queen's make-up, done by Laila and Elia. It was perfectly gay and funny. Everyone was overflowing with laughter even just watching the happy face of the Queen, and her respective servants. I could never forget that show. Student life was agreeable and memorable. How I miss those college days!

Support the soccer team – my other mission

Someone knocked three times consecutively at the office door. A Sergeant from Camp Evangelista appeared. He looked around for a quick inspection. A second officer, a Major came-in, followed by our Commandant Major Referente. But it was the time for my evening classes.

I report to my office at 8 a.m. and my Spanish lessons started at 17h15 but I went there late as usual. After my classes, I went back to the office and found several soldiers, all soccer players representing the 4th Infantry Division, Philippine Army. Their guide and coach was Major Pacana, whom I had met during my salary claim in Camp Evangelista. We were both delighted meeting again. The officers lodged in the Camp of Bancasi and the soccer team slept in the building where my office was located. That made it easy for them to visit Butuan.

My Commander assigned me a mission: first, to solicit sponsors for meals for the soccer players during their stay in Butuan. Second, to request a doctor and nurses from the Health Office who could be called upon in case of casualties. Believe me, these were not easy tasks. I missed all my first evening classes through the whole week, though my mission was fully accomplished.

I went to several restaurant owners, asking if they could provide meals to the players for five days, and different canteens for their snacks. I solicited the Mayor, the Governor, bank managers, people with department stores and the Chinese enterprises in Butuan. There was no money involved, but I was so happy in the end because I had developed a professional feeling of solidarity, sympathy, friendship and cooperation with all those people I had solicited. I had to handle the schedules for the different restaurants' services. Some restaurants served two days of meals, others more. Some made sandwiches and non-alcoholic drinks for snacks. All the soccer players ate their three meals regularly every day, for free, during their stay in Butuan. I received appreciations, I was proud of myself. It was a true success.

I was always present during the games, cheering them on as one of their loyal fans. They were rewarded with a trophy, but they unluckily did not win the top award. What was important was that they represented the Philippine Army from Camp Evangelista Headquarters, Cagayan de Oro City.

I rode with them in the Army truck from the office to the stadium, but I experienced some trouble: for someone of my height, the truck was too high to get in and out. Someone always lent me their arm. I was so pleased with their courtesy. They all behaved like they were my elder brothers. We used to sing all together in the truck, and I had a nice feeling of being protected. I loved their company, even for only few days.

Another nice thing from that mission was that while I was recruiting some sponsors, I met the different bank managers and discussed my chances of being employed in banking someday.

The alpha sigma phi fraternity/sorority

Marianne, a charming young woman who had also studied in Urios, was my friend and neighbour. I was touched and somewhat proud when she asked me to join to their student organization, the Alpha Sigma Phi Fraternity/Sorority. I joined them because for me, she set an example. However, I grew to dislike the organization, due to the violent attitudes in some of their members and traditions.

My desire to be part of that organization was fading, but it became too late to back out. I particularly hated the *bizutage* [hazing] which was used as a way for older students to exercise power over younger ones which included "rituals." These were forced challenges, psychological manipulation, often with harassment, abuse and/or humiliation to initiate a person into the group.

I it was a pity, I survived their hazing! What would have had happened to me if I had left the ceremony area without undergoing the initiation? This question remained running around my mind to this day. It is not a matter of being afraid of the initiation, but because I observed they became unreasonable; if I had left, others might have followed me, and I would have been blamed. I would have been known as a quitter, or a loser, and I was almost sure that as a university student, I would have had to live with a bad reputation that would surely torment me. I prayed that the hazing would finish soon and maybe I could forget it. Needless to say, joining them was not the best decision I made.

After you passed all the hazing, you became a member of that college student organisation. Signals and codes were inflicted to us to confirm that we were an Alpha Sigma Phi member, and communication sometimes required passwords or a special style of whistle and shaking hands. They also insisted on a tattoo on the right hand to see you are a member while shaking hands. [The tattoo is permanently etched in the skin, a symbol with three points]. It was not so painful but my skin swelled up, and the three dark blue points joined together and became blurred due to the infection. Nobody heard me complaining about it, though, because I did not want my parents to get involved or be concerned.

Much later, during my visit to my parents in Butuan in 1984 (after I'd moved to France), I wanted to visit Marianne to ask her about the rituals and bizutage. Instead, I met Madam Juana Montilla, the adopted mother of Marianne. She said that Marianne died after delivering her baby girl. I was surprised, because I had seen her in a dream, so pretty and smiling. I was almost sure she had a happy crossing over, and Madame Juana was delighted to hearing it. "I presumed that Marianne was happy to see to her baby before passing away," she said.

In France, many years later, my husband declared that the three-points tattoo near my right thumb was a Masonic sign. The Masons had the ambition to take over the world. What annoyed me most is that for some people, like the anarchists, the tattoo of three points means an insult to the police. So I always wanted to have it removed.

One day in university, Mr Kimilat, the Dean of Student Affairs, asked me to join the oration contest. I was eager to join, and I even planned to write my own speech, but I did not have enough time to prepare because I was working during the day. And I was tired out from activities from the Alpha Sigma Phi programme. After a bit of time, I did manage to write my own speech or oration, and Mr Kimilat was there when I delivered it in front of an audience. He seemed to appreciate my performance delivery. I thought about submitting it to *the Urian*, Urios' official journal, but articles I had sent previously had been lost. Still, I kept trying and I submitted my speech to the student editorial team, but maybe it was also lost; it was not published either. I didn't know why it would have been rejected. In fact, it only mentioned positive ideas and happy events. I had offended no one. In any case, I was discouraged from submitting any other articles or poems. I thought maybe someone was set against me and jealous. I was however surprised when my nephew James, who was not yet born when I was a student in Urios 1976-1980, informed me later that he had read some of my poems and articles I had submitted when he was a student in Urios, in the years when I was already living in France. I really wonder why I was not able to read them.

I had endeavoured to convince myself to write about that student organization and their "rituals", but I did not have enough courage or inspiration. In any case, it might have done more harm than good. I still wonder what was the real purpose of the Alpha Sigma Phi; was it honour and a sense of belonging? I would have preferred to prepare the students for success after college in a different way. At the beginning, I thought that they were a group of intellectuals, but I was confused. I regretted being a member.

One night, to sleep I was wearing a long T-shirt, which covered my legs only just below my knees. My parents were so surprised and upset when they discovered the bruises on my hips and buttocks from the hazing. I was too tired to answer their questions, as the initiation had made me exhausted of fatigue. I never wanted my parents to see me like that.

If I could share all that I have observed: the so called "Lady" and "Lord" who directed the initiations and hit us with a wooden paddle, causing mental anguish, humiliating us because it was funny for them, traumatizing us, and ordering us to do evil and undesirable acts. What was their purpose? To form an organization where the elders take advantage of the weaknesses of the younger ones? My experience did not certainly build a team spirit. I prayed that no one in my family would have to undergo all those stupid initiations just to become part of a group. I was disgusted and angry with myself for having agreed to join.

Hazing for me is a violation of human rights. It had an impact on schooling, because some of the students were dropping out. There were also psychological consequences. Unfortunately, many victims, like me, did not dare to speak about it for fear of reprisals. During student days, I was always chosen as student teacher in the class, and I wanted to encourage all the students to refuse the recruiters to join to any student organisation. But I chose to stay silent to avoid me answering difficult questions. Bizutage and hazing are dangerous; they should not be allowed in universities anymore.

Would I have been condemned if I had spoken up?

Financial hurdles as a self-supporting student 1969-80

Remembering my past: They were turbulent times, my unbearable dark days while I was a self-supporting student. How I wished I could have found a job which provided a good salary and other incentives. I sometimes thought that God had forsaken me.

Dark clouds added my sadness, I had been feeling out of control. I was particularly hopeless, tired, and fed-up with all the hardships I had to endure. Instead of sprinting home before the evening fell, I found myself on the Magsaysay bridge over the Agusan river, far from home. There was not a single boat, not even a barquero in his baroto under the bridge. Eyes closed, I ended up on the parapet wall of the bridge and the reflections of the river water lit up the bridge. During rush hour after work lots of passenger jeeps passed at high speed; so no one would notice me.

As I thought of jumping from that bridge, the buzzing noise attacked my ears, and head, as if my angel was there struggling to save me was fighting against the evil and I started to get scared. I suddenly heard footsteps approaching so close to me. I was surprised to see Brenda, my schoolmate, as by hazard she passed by. The devil has gone, Brenda has thwarted his plan. My angel won! I was save from mortal sin.

Brenda did not ask me why I was on the bridge. I sobbed silently, and she respected my silence as we walked. I met her mother, and her younger sisters for the first time, who seemed kind and generous. It was the first time I wanted to end my life, I was ashamed of my faibless. I asked God for forgiveness.

To go back home from Baan, I took a baroto to traverse the river. I suddenly remember my near-drowning when I was ten. Afterwards, I jolt even when glancing to the river, whereas now the river was so inviting, I was not afraid anymore if the baroto should sink, nor to get drown in the river, and I thought of jumping into the water again, and same time I thought of my family. I am the eldest of eight siblings and my parents needed me. But how can I help them when I still had more than a year to finish my business studies? My mind was still wandering so I was startled when the barquero called to me to tell me we had arrived, and I could disembark. I was lost far away in my deep thoughts.

"Give me your hand, I will help you not to get wet," he said. He placed the small flat plank at the edge of his boat to help me go down unto the dry part of the riverside.

I walked another hour to reach home. Along my way there were small stores still open, where drunkards were singing with a glass of tuba or bottle of beer in their hands. I could smell their bad alcohol-tinted breath. I was afraid they would block my way.

It was past midnight when I reached home. Everyone was in bed except Tatay. He stared at me, as he must have understood I had passed a bad evening. He inhaled deeply and sighed. I could read the questions in his eyes, but he did not say anything. He was always waiting up for me, everytime I got home very late. Tatay, I am so sorry for that.

Despite all the hardship, I persevered and pursued my studies, and I managed the difficulties in working full-time during the day and studying full-time in the evening. I worked hard to motivate myself every day to find energy. A secretarial job would not be enough to provide the resources and skills for a better life.

I was in Urios for my first year high school as half-scholar and stop. Next, I was a working student where I attended evening classes in a private secondary school- Butuan City Colleges, where I have graduated from high school as Valedictorian. From there I obtained a diploma of Citizen's Army Training (CAT), the compulsory military training for a year during the Martial Law period. I then successfully passed the amended National College Entrance Examination (NCEE) in 1975 a prerequisite at that time for admission to any professional degree program.

After a long struggle, I finally finished the four-year course in Commerce, and graduated the Diploma of Bachelor of Science in Commerce major in Business Management in Urios. I had a lot to be proud of.

Graduation Day

One most awaited moment came, at last. With an old Spanish sewing machine, I made my own gown in brilliant plain satin in apricot colour, that I wore under my graduation gown. A few days before the ceremony, all the graduates were instructed to be photographed wearing that customary black matte graduation gowns, the long flowing robes with hood and caps over our standard formal attire. Universities made it compulsory for university students to wear these gowns: a symbol of all the hard work that we had undertaken. The hood came in different colours, representing the college and degree that we obtained. We were instructed on how it was supposed to be worn, how to pose with the cap and which side of our head that the cord should hang, that was significant.

Our photos were posted in the *Veritas*, a book solely for the graduates. For me, it was a valuable souvenir, and I even brought it with me when I moved to France in October 1981. From time to time I quickly glance at it with a little nostalgia, thinking of all the sleepless nights, effort, and sacrifices, but also the laughter, friendship and betrayal, heartbreaks, and deception, and all the adventures and problems I had to overcome during my studies.

It also makes me think about my parents: they attended my graduation ceremony and wore their best clothes. I had bought a piece of cloth for Mama from Gaisano department store in Cagayan de Oro, and she asked her dressmaker for her gown to fit perfectly, so she would feel at ease, as she was not used to this kind of event. She couldn't refuse to attend my graduation. For me, it marked the end of an era, one of the most memorable and special events in my life.

In 1980, former President Marcos signed a decree which was used by authorities as deterrent against bomb threats. There were bomb attacks in Butuan; luckily, they were not so serious. We were all busy preparing for the graduation, while Urios University had received a bomb threat that something would explode during the graduation ceremony. So the Urios President, changed the date of our graduation, and although our school had taken the bomb threat seriously, our ceremony was not annulled for the second time. Our graduation was not held in Urios University stadium, but in the Saint Joseph Cathedral located near Urios university that was only announced by FSUU president at the last minute. The holy mass was held for this, praying for our safety.

The Cathedral was full of graduates, parents, relatives, and friends. Meanwhile, I had heard that the church was also a potential target for bombs, but it was not announced to the public to avoid panic, especially as the ceremony had already started. I was thinking that as soon as I was called and received my diploma, I would immediately go out from the church with my whole family, but that would probably have been too difficult because of the crowd. The space became too small to accommodate all the family and friends of the graduates, so most of the friends stayed outside on the benches in the garden of the Cathedral. The crowds reached up to Rizal Park, more than 200 meters away.

While I was waiting impatiently for my turn to be called, sitting with my co-graduates on the bench of the Cathedral, my anxiety and nervousness grew. I prayed that no bomb would explode. I was profusely sweating and could barely breathe while my thoughts were with my whole family inside the Cathedral, except my brother Dan. I almost jumped when I heard my name called at last. My parents had helped me fix my hood and cap to make it correctly in place before, and I felt like I was hovering, flying up to the sky as I marched nearer to the altar to receive my diploma. The front of the altar had become the stage of the ceremony. The crowd's cheers augmented while I shook hands with President Dr. Juanito A. Lao, the Dean of Academic Affairs Mrs. S. Rosales, the Dean of Commerce, Mrs. Yecyec, and the College Registrar Mr. F. Itao. I am mentioning their names as I liked and admired them. I have these wonderful memories of my Alma Matter, and I experienced overwhelming emotions that I had never felt before – pride, nostalgia, and relief mixed together. For a little while, I forgot the threat of the bomb in the cathedral.

The ceremony was brief but had finished safely. There were different authorities in civilian attire: Philippine Constabulary, Philippine Army, and the local police had surrounded the place discretely. A bomb was found by the special authority experts of detecting explosives, but there was no explosion either in Urios University or near the Cathedral. God was with us on that memorable occasion. He blessed us with a wonderful graduation day. It was one of the most memorable moments of my lifetime.

It is not every day that we can have a chance to celebrate a momentous celebration. After the ceremony, I was so happy to see all my family and some friends waiting for me. And for the very first time, we all went to the shop of photos and we made some poses in front of the photographers to mark and save our memories of my graduation day.

On my reflection, it is quite amazing that I started my kindergarten and primary classes in a private Catholic school, the Candelaria Institute, that stood just near the church or the Cathedral of Senora Candelaria in Cabadbaran. And despite hardship and poverty, I successfully finished my high school, and university studies in the private Catholic university in Butuan that was also near the church, and moreover, our graduation ceremony was not held near the church, but inside the house of God, the St. Joseph Cathedral of Butuan City, instead of the stadium of Father Saturnino Urios University because of the bomb threats.

Now I realized that wherever I was, God was always present, and had guided me through along. He has my eternal gratitude.

All my endeavours were rewarded with a simple life, but one full of achievements and accomplishments. I acquired my university diplomas in March 1980, the next year I married a man I loved, who shares my religion, and we pursued a new life together in France.

Conflicting and invalid identity

After my graduation, I had a dilemma: working in the bank in Butuan, or going abroad. I was called for an interview in one of the bank in Butuan whose manager was one of the trophy donors that I have sollicited while working in the ROTC office. He said I could start the next Monday as a teller. But I did not go. My thought was to learn the French language and had always an intense desire to travel abroad, so that I had decided to start processing my papers.

I was asked to file for police clearance, one of the requirements before going abroad. This was so that the National Bureau of Investigation could check whether you had a criminal record. There was no NBI in Butuan, so I went to Cagayan de Oro City, and eight-hour bus ride from Butuan.

While filling in the form I was surprised to discover for the first time that my real first name that was written in my birth certificate was Baltazara. I was in a dilemma as to which name I should write in the form, Sarah or Baltazara? In the end I wrote Baltazara. I joined the copies of my *cedula* [a community tax certificate] my identification card, and my student card with picture (as if I would study abroad) and I immediately presented the package to the officer in charge. And I waited. But my request was not granted. They said I have invalid identity papers. I had to go back to Butuan with empty hands.

Why did they enroll me in school with a different name? I had to start from the beginning. I was instructed to go to the City Court of Justice in Butuan with my parents to sign a "Joint Affidavit of Correction" stating that my birth was duly registered in the local civil registrar, and that my parents were my legitimate parents, that Sarah or Baltazara is their daughter, the only one and the same person and so on. In January 1981, I went back to Cagayan de Oro with all the necessary papers, and I finally got home with my police clearance at last! All effort, travels and endless queueing were been rewarded.

It was easier to process my first Philippine passport, as I just showed my birth certificate and the NBI clearance. But I was in trouble again: my identity card, and student card was Sarah as my first name, I showed them my Joint Affidavit of Correction to avoid complications to finally acquire my first Philippine Passport. However, they printed my two first names together: Baltazara Serohijos, in the first line, and Sarah R. Serohijos to the second. What an ordeal!

Another nice thing from that mission was that while I was recruiting some sponsors, I met the different bank managers and discussed my chances of being employed in banking someday.

My Younger Siblings

How Dan survived a stabbing

Dan was very attractive to girls. He was "fond of *barkadas*" [peer group going together]. He was always a good looking teenager, dressing well and spending most of his time with his peers and barkadas; he needed his independence and privacy. He was not interested in pursuing his studies or even going to high school. He seldom spoke up, being a shy of boy, but lot of girls had crushes on him, until he became romantically involved.

1970. One evening, he arrived late in front of our house with his hands pressing against his stomach. He was pale, and he vomited blood before he reached our door. He fell to the ground unconscious, having lost a lot of blood. The police later said he was stabbed with six-inch ice-pick by one of his barkadas who slipped away quickly, and nobody knew who or why. Despite the witnesses' declarations, the police unluckily lost the perpetrator.

Dan was brought to Butuan Hospital after he was stabbed. It turned out to have been a rival who wooing the same girl. Dan's physical state gave us so many worries and we feared for his life. It made even more financial troubles to our entire family, at a time when Tatay had no permanent job after the New Asia explosion.

The stabbing had penetrated his liver, damaging it so much that his skin and the whites of his eyes turned a yellowish colour. He also had lost so much blood. A family friend, Rudy, was found to have compatible blood with my brother, and so he willingly donated blood to help. My sister Nelly was working in Torralba department store at that time and was of great help. She convinced all the workers in the company, those who had the same blood type as Dan, to donate their blood. This probably saved Dan's life. However, we also needed to have the money to buy all the prescribed medicines. I was furious and wondered why public hospitals in the Philippines couldn't supply medicines to their patients who were tenuously between life and death.

The doctor operated on him for four hours, and then came to inform us Dan was in coma. We were told that if he woke within 24 hours, he could be saved. We feared for his life.

That night was so long; we were all counting the hours in anguish. Everyone in our family thought we were going to lose him, but he woke two days later.

"He is so lucky to have survived despite the deep wound that damaged his liver. It's like a miracle," said the doctor.

It was scary to see him so sick and immobilised. Both his arms were held in place for the IVs: one arm had his dextrose; the other had blood transfusing, but I was not able to look because of my phobia. He also had a plastic drainage tube used in surgery from his stomach into a bottle to facilitate the discharge of fluids. That day, in addition to the costly blood tests, the doctor made several prescriptions of medicines to prevent infection. We needed to buy additional bottles of dextrose to combat low blood sugar, and to supply him with appropriate food. Dan couldn't eat solid foods before or after his operation. We had to run on foot to the pharmacy, far from the hospital, as we had no vehicle of our own. Worries took over us every day as we searched for some financial support to obtain the medicines he badly needed, and we were all exhausted.

I begged for help from my professors and fellow students, and I had collected a small amount of money to contribute for medicines and the hospitalisation. Nelly, who had a steady job, contributed as much as she could for the hospitalisation expenses. Thanks to her fellow workers in Torralba enterprise, Dan obtained enough blood to replace what he had lost.

We took shifts day and night to take care of Dan in the hospital, and I saw how he suffered from his wound. He had difficulty speaking. He gave me signals with his eyes when he needed something, as he could not move by himself. He had a drainage tube. He was shaking from the pain, his lips trembled, and I observed his eyes became dull and yellowish and also his skin. "It was due to his wounded liver and that Dan needed special foods. If his liver recovered normal function, he would survive." Said the doctor.

A member of the family needed to be there at all times for when he asked to move his pillow to the left or to the right; we needed to help him change positions as he wished, changing his clothes, drinking water through a straw, wiping away his sweat, and moistening his lips. We needed to lean in close, with our ear to his mouth to understand what he said. I kept on praying that our endurance will last as long as he needed.

We all looked like the living dead. My parents, Nelly, and I forgot to prepare meals for ourselves, and couldn't eat when we were on guard for Dan, losing our appetites from a mixture of the medicine's odour and the dirty environment. Sometimes friends prepared food and we tried to eat. The hot weather without air conditioning and no circulation of the air, made the hospital feel suffocating, even in the hallway. I was sad to see that the place was unsafe and not sanitary. Germs were present everywhere and made us feel ill, like we were swimming against the current, as we were exposed to germs and viruses. I prayed that Dan would leave the hospital soon, healed.

Many times I missed my classes or attended them but with severe headaches due to lack of sleep. It didn't help that Dan was not the only patient in the room; it held four patients with four different problems. The room felt very small when the patient's families came in to look after them. One of the other patients was a gunshot victim. I heard him cry in agony. Three calibre bullets pierced his spine and his lungs, and he died in the hospital. Another patient died the second day while I was present. He had occupied the top of the bunk bed, also in agony the whole night. The patient in the bed underneath had a high fever and died the next day. That room was hell.

Before Dan was discharged, I heard his proud doctor talking to his colleagues while smoking cigarettes. "Only the stabbed patient survived in that hospital room, Dan Serohijos. I did not expect him to survive the wounds that had damaged his liver. It is like a miracle. He is so lucky to live a second life," he said loudly so everyone could hear.

Dan is married, but has no job – 1973

Dan stayed two weeks in the hospital and had three months of convalescence at home. He had a fast recovery, but he said sometimes the scar from the deep wound hurt him when he moved. When he started to walk normally, he went to Cabadbaran to look for a job. He did not find one.

One day, Dan came back home with his Chinese girlfriend, Betsy to my parents' home, and she stayed with us from 1973 until 1975. When my parents realised they were very much in love and inseparable, a civil wedding ceremony was held in Cabadbaran in 1974. Thus, they became husband and wife when they were both 21 years old and jobless, which increased the financial difficulties in our family. Tatay Eco never said anything against the couple who stayed with us. Tatay continued working hard with his occasional jobs, never complaining as he always had a big heart. Meanwhile, Mama continued taking care of everyone, hand washing and ironing the clothes, preparing the meals. I could tell that, like any other parent, they would have liked for Dan to find a job. However, without a diploma, looking for a job was always an endless back and forth struggle.

We had limited space at home of eight children, and the arrival of Dan's wife made us all uncomfortable. Dan and Betsy were like a cat and dog; they often argued and fought loud yelling fights that everyone could hear. Our family environment became physically and mentally unsafe.

One evening I went home from work as usual, on a day when I didn't attend evening classes. But as soon as I reached the entrance to our house, a flying object nearly struck my head. Luckily, I saw it just before, but I was not able to catch it, so it fell to the floor and broke. Betsy was yelling at my brother. She was very anxious and nervous much of the time. In retrospect, they were both very young and not emotionally stable or mature enough to manage a healthy relationship. They were only silent when deeply sleeping and they quarrelled almost every day, even in the middle of the night. They did not bring joy and laughter to our family; in fact, their presence was difficult to take. That situation made me lose my temper, and I was about to drive them away from home for the number of times when I was awakened by the noise of their repeated arguments at night.

Dan was alone in the lounge. It gave me a chance to talk to him before I left for work that morning, Being the eldest, I could insist on a face to face conversation with him.

"Dan, your wife will surely have a baby soon. You must look for a job and have your own home to live. You should raise your family with dignity and become a proud parent, be a stable head of your family who can provide for the needs of your own family," I said clearly.

Dan did not utter a word, but I felt relieved. It was so hard for me know how and when to tell him, and I had emptied my aching heart. My parents did not dare to tell him the truth, but that morning although it was not easy, I did it and I prayed that he would understand my objective. I knew he was not happy to be told frankly our views, because my parents were not able to tell him directly how they felt. I felt bad for my father, who put all his efforts into feeding the whole family, but having a big heart was not enough; we needed to be realistic.

Three months later, Dan had found a tricycle to drive, and started work picking up passengers like a taxi. He earned enough money for them to move to Ong Yiu District, where they rented a small house. Since then, we did not hear from them until their first son, Carter, was born in January 1975.

Dan is accused and put in jail – 1976

One day Tatay suddenly appeared in my office, terrified and sweating. He said he walked so fast from home. "Dan did not return home last night because he was detained in jail, under the custody at Butuan police station," he said, short of breath. That news gave him so much pain.

"I will look for help from the Army if necessary," I said, "but first I must check myself if he is still in the police station to know what are the charges against him." I tried to reassure him. "Tay please don't worry; I will do my best to find a solution."

Visiting him in jail, I was shocked to see my brother with his hands and feet cuffed with an iron-chains and his mouth was bleeding. I sensed torture or mistreatment because the police wanted Dan to confess to the crime as a drug dealer.

Dan had not seen me yet. I talked to the police in charge, and he said there were two accusations filed against my brother. "Madame, first he was dealing drugs, and second, he tried to run from the police."

I answered him quickly: "Sir, if you have the proof, please give me a written detailed statement of the accusation in full, signed by your supervisor. For my part, I will ask my superior in the Philippine Army to look into this case, for there will be surely some investigations."

I was about to leave when he said: "Ma'am, the Philippine Army has nothing to do with this case," he said.

"That was maybe the case as of yesterday, but now the case is under the military because Dan is my brother, and I work with the Philippine Army. He must be out by this evening sir. Now I will inform them about the detention of my brother." I was bluffing, hoping it didn't show.

Before I left from the police station, I went to see my brother and he said that the accusations against him were not true. "I am innocent, but I was scared, so I attempted to escape. I had never met my passenger before, and I did not know he was carrying around illegal drugs." He said it with such melancholy. Staring into his eyes, I felt he spoke the truth.

Another police officer came to me and said: "If Dan is innocent, then he will be set free."

I answered him: "I am hoping for his freedom very soon sir. He has been hit and his lips are still bleeding, and he cannot even wipe it away because he's tied up like a criminal. He doesn't deserve to be tortured because I know he is innocent." Then I hurriedly left because I did not want the police to see me crying. It was so hard for me to see my brother handcuffed at the hands and feet, with iron-chains like a monster. That's when I realised how much I love him.

Dan is set free

That evening I attended my evening classes in Urios, but I did not succeed in chasing my brother from my mind; it was impossible to concentrate in class. I wanted to visit the police station again to see if Dan was still there, but strangely after the class, my intuition told me to go home right away.

Dan was home with his wife and my parents sitting on the sofa. I was so relieved. The following day, in my office, Bonifacio Lim, our ROTC cadet officer from Cabadbaran informed me that he was the owner of the tricycle that Dan was driving. He had signed a paper as a witness in favour of my brother. He added that if he had known that Dan was my brother, he would have surely rung the police immediately to call for him be released earlier. I wondered if Betsy had known that I went to the police station to ask for Dan's liberation. What was important for me was that my brother was released. Dan and Tatay knew of what I have done for his freedom. But until now, I could never forget the image of Dan's handcuffed hands and feet with iron chains. I still feel the pain like a pinching of my heart. I would never allow anybody in my family to be treated that way, never again.

Tatay was so shocked from the event that he remained silent. I did not dare to talk to him about it. I did not want to annoy him although I knew that his state of solicitude had gradually lifted. My parents were made vulnerable by the shock and fear of losing their son. I confide to this memoir that my mother preferred Dan to me, but it didn't change the way I felt about him. I always loved him

Dan's family life

Little Carter, my first nephew, was followed by Dave, born in July 1978, and the two boys were often at my parents' house. This was because when Dan was driving, Betsy would ride with him at the back of the motorcycle. I often wondered why she could not afford to stay at home and take care of their boys while Dan was working. I dared to ask Mama why were they leaving the children with her so often.

Mama answered: "It doesn't matter Sarah; the boys behave well anyway." But Mama was so busy all day long that she could not find time to rest. She had us eight children and instead of having a good time, she still had to take care of the little boys.

"No Mama, it is not a matter of behaving, but what you are doing doesn't help Dan and Betsy understand that although they are young, they should grow up and become responsible parents." Since my childhood, Mama always covered the faults of my brother and continued to do so, even when he was grown up. He should have had work during the day and finished his studies at night, like me, and thus obtained a diploma before starting a family of his own. Dan never helped our parents financially and with his dominating wife, he became a puppet being manipulated as *under de saya* [under a woman's dress] – meaning, a man cowering to a woman. Dan loved his wife so much that what his wife said became a law.

One day, Betsy appeared at our home. She said she felt the pain in her belly. I saw her in pain. Mama and I had a feeling that a baby would come. Mama became the midwife. I heard the baby cry; I saw her with the baby already in her arms. It was as easy as that: the baby came out from her mother's womb without too much labour. I thought I was hallucinating. But I had suddenly thought that riding the tricycle was maybe the reason why Betsy's baby delivery had been so smooth and fast as that. They called the baby, Sheila, born in October 1979.

Dan went back to school and earned his college diploma while I was already settled in France. He resigned as bodyguard to the Mayor, and worked in the Auditor's Office as someone who checks construction materials. Two years later, Betsy and Dan were able to build their own house. He resigned from his job and opened his own business. He had one van, bought by bank credit; Dan used it to pick up private passengers by appointment. He hired a driver, and his business was flourishing.

They have three children: Carter, Dave, and Sheila. Carter became a Pastor. He has two sons: Kyle and Christopher, who both earned degrees in Commerce and in Architecture, respectively. Dave had two girls: Hansel and Kylie. Sheila got married and has a son, who was born in Thailand while she was working there as a teacher.

Nelly

My sister Nelly, born in August 1955, was three years younger than me. She was anxious since her early childhood, insecure and emotional, but also affectionate and undemanding. She worried about everything and would cry easily, not knowing how to function in an unexpected new situation. The worst was when she felt like everyone disliked her. But I understood her as I maybe cry easily, like her.

Mama once described her this way: "Nelly can easily climb to any high post in the house. Sometimes I thought a cat from the neighbour had entered the house and climbed up to the ceiling. I was surprised to see Nelly above my head. I wondered how she did it. The other day it was very funny to see her climbing like a cat, and she was just behind the cat of our neighbours that scurried fast to the ceiling before her," said Mama, laughing.

I was reminded of what Tatay told me once: "When I was a young boy, I sometimes climbed to the ceiling of the church when there were fights between barkadas. One time I needed to stay there the whole day to hide," he had said laughing. So Nelly loves to climb, like Tatay Eco.

Nelly was a competent salesgirl in Torralba Expo, working in their textile department store in Butuan from 1971 until 1982. She also helped our parents financially. In 1984 she married to Ciriaco Dela Pena in a civil wedding in January 1984. Their church wedding was held nearly a decade later on December 18, 1993 in Davao where her husband worked. Our parents were present during their church wedding ceremony. The new couple had no vices and saved their money to open a "Sari-Sari Store", a type of convenience store. It was a one fluorishing stop shop that sells what families commonly needed, and provided them with extra support alongside Ciriaco's salary.

What would you do when you sensed the person you were hugging would die young, leaving his whole family behind him? When I hugged Ciriaco, on a visit in 2002, I sensed the surroundings of melancholy. I wanted to deny the feeling of losing him, because for me his death would be so premature, and maybe I was wrong. I prayed that it would not happen. He was so good, and Nelly was so lucky to have him as husband. It was so hard for me to realise that a good person is often called before their time.

I didn't tell my sister about that sensation and emotion. Ciriaco welcomed me in their home, so smiling and kind. He rushed to the market and was a good cook, so we had a nice lunch and dinner together; that was my only visit to them in Davao in 2002 just before I proceeded to Butuan. It was also the last time I saw Nelly's husband. Seven years later, Ciriaco died of acute lymphocytic leukaemia in April 2009.

Nelly tried to overcome the grief of her husband's death. Losing a partner is utterly devastating and difficult to bear. However, she was lucky to receive the retirement pay of her late husband and their newly built house was finished completely. Their daughter Heidi graduated in Computer Science from the University of the Philippines, and is now married blessed with a boy, born in December 2018. Heidi's younger brother Gil, was born in May 1989, and has now graduated with a degree in Hotel/Restaurant and Management from Davao Central College. He got married in October 2020.

Nolwen

Nolwen was born in January 1957 in Butuan City. She was a healthy and pretty baby, with large nut-shelled coloured eyes, and curly hair. She was very different from Nelly, Amelie, Ashley, Imelda, and me; her hair was not dark but light brown, and we all loved it. It was a bit of a pity that it became darker later. She still was very beautiful as she grew older.

As a teenager, Nolwen was not interested in continuing her studies, even though she had several chances to do so. She worked as a waitress in the Roxan restaurant and looked very beautiful in her uniform. She met several men who were attracted to her beauty.

She enrolled in the technical school of typing, but she failed to finish. She made me her enemy when I asked her to keep studying to be able to get a better job, like in an office.

She met Teddy, a man working in a prosperous logging company and they got married in January 1983 in Cabadbaran City. In 1984, she was working as a casher in a big department store located near the Crown Theatre in Butuan, but she did not carry and her husband was laid off from his job; their livelihood was severely affected while Nolwen was pregnant to her second son, James.

Of her children, Nolwen's son Ricardo had tasted drugs that had damaged his brain. He resigned from his job in a bank, and is still living with his parents until now, March 2021.

Our current president Rodrigo Duterte's priority mission is: "To protect Philippines from illegal drugs and criminality; and to fight against corruption." This was his election platform when he successfully ran for President in June 2016. I pray that he will be successful in clearing ruthless drug traffickers and dealers from the Philippines. I was conscious that protecting the future of our youth today, and future generations, can be always a hazardous mission. So far, he is the first Philippine President who had the courage to declare a "war against drugs."

Nolwen's other son, James, was very different from his elder brother. He had concentrated on his studies as a full scholar at Urios University. He finished his course as *Summa Cum Laude*, and got married to Johanna immediately after he graduated in March 2012. They are blessed with two children, both born in Pasig City, a suburb of Manila. James found his first job in Manila, and has always been a responsible father and son, taking care of his own family, and his unending support to his parents, and his elder brother, Ricardo.

Amelie and Ashley

One beautiful sunny morning, no single cloud in the sky, Amelie and Ashley, were born at home in Cabadbaran, Agusan del Norte on Friday, the 1st of September 1961.

I was only nine years old when my schooling was interrupted to help Mama to take care of them. I shouldered much responsibility early, so I learned to break the monotony of tedious daily activities, with little moments like this when I enjoyed being with them.

One day, I placed a mat on the floor and put the twins on it, and I gave them a kind of game. I placed two colorful calendar pages – one showed a girl dancing and a mother cooking; the second showed pictures of beautiful houses with an airplane on top of the houses. Then I tapped a glass to call them to me, and they both crawled forward. Amelie arrived first, looking at the two pictures, and she had chosen the beautiful houses with the plane above and she sat down on it. I took it from her and put it back on the mat. She was not happy, but she did not cry. Ashley, who arrived after her sister, chose the girl dancing with a mother cooking, and she pointed her fingers at it and smiled, while Amelie took back the paper with houses and played with it.

I had almost forgotten that lovely moment. Now that I am writing this memoir, all those pictures have remained inscribed in my brain are coming into focus again. I believed that those experiences are now showing the signs of the twins' choices and personalities. Regarding their favorite colours: Ashley loved pink, purple, or red, while Amelie loved darker colours, but also liked sky blue.

One particular thing about Ashley was that she never argued with Amelie. When she wanted to take something from Amelie's hand, she would tap the thing slightly while looking straight to Amelie's eyes, then she waited for Amelie to give it to her. Amelie acted differently. When she wanted to take something from Ashley's hand, she also first stared into Ashley's eyes. But simultaneously, she would take the thing from Ashley. Ashley would cry and run to me because she could not refuse to her sister.

Years later, I understood why Ashley was weaker and less happy than her twin sister Amelie. Mama was accustomed to smoking tobacco, even while pregnant, it had damaged Ashley's health, from her time in the womb to the first days as a small baby. Baby Ashley had absorbed some nicotine and carbon monoxide instead of oxygen and nutrients. It's a little like forcing a baby to breathe through a narrow pipe. Mama was also an asthmatic child because Nanay smoked tobacco. I observed how Nanay prepared a broadleaf that she rolled-up before she smoke it. It was a vice that had passed from ancestors down to my mother's generation.

During the high school studies, Ashley enrolled in the compulsory Citizen's Military Training and learned the principal theories but with her problem of Asthma, she was exempted during the basic physical military exercises or drilling and the Tactical Inspection which ranged from the unpleasant to the brutal, and obliged to follow the military discipline and punishment. We sometimes experienced a rough time during the tactical inspection. Suppose you are told not to be immobile during unbearable waiting. In that case, you must not move even under the heat of the sun at 50 degrees centigrade at noon, and always alert of whatever command ordered by your commanding officer not to receive the punishment. Luckily, Ashley did not endure all that.

However, she persevered in her studies and successfully graduated the secretarial course despite all. Ashley is a diligent and persevering worker who enjoys doing a job well, finishing what is being started. She works best with her hands and physical strength, usually slowly and deliberately, and without pressure. Otherwise, she could become frustrated and thwarted in her efforts. But she had a strong driving force in creative endeavours like innovative design and inventiveness. She had acquired technical knowledge in a beauty parlour: make-ups, haircuts, manicuring, and pedicuring; she can create new ideas like inventing unique jewellery style, and most significantly, the talents of baking cakes or cooking recipes. I'm so proud of her.

Ashley also loves traveling and mostly loves dancing for fun. I admire her ways of facing life. Now at 59 years, Ashley enjoys the finer things in life. She lives happy and healthy with her lovely family.

Nevertheless, Amelie was so lucky that she was not affected by the tobacco while she was still in our mother's womb. She was always more alert, keen, and she detested defeat more than anyone. Those personality traits continued throughout her life. Amelie is less smiling than her twins. She usually talks brief, precise, and hid her worries and fears perhaps just not to bother anyone but she could also be funny at times. She possessed a brave and confident character, ever since she was a baby although I knew she had her own fears and worries. She had a strong personality: courageous, independent, and determined to manage her own life. Her attitude made her strong enough to face obstacles, trials and to confront any potential adversity with success, even without seeking assistance from her elders. She could not be easily swayed, especially when she believed that she had made the right decision.

In high school, she was a Citizen's Military Training Officer; she had undergone and had coped up the military drilling on the hot sunny day over 50 degrees centigrade. Wow, anyway, this was my impression when I was doing the routine and my military training during my high school days. She was even much pretty with her uniform. And as cadet officer, she had rendered more drill practices in the field than the other cadets to be acquainted with the command orders. Like any other cadet officers, she also gave punishments and asked more than the push-ups or sitting in the air for those late on the drill. She was well respected as an excellent officer and an exceptional leader, and of course, I was so proud of her.

Like anyone, Amelie loves beautiful houses, and conducts transactions of sale, purchase, rental or subletting of real estate of her own properties. She was able to resist stress and responsiveness, and coped the environmental and tax regulations like a real estate agent.

We can also rely on Amelie's talents of organizing travels. It's thanks to her that we: Ashley, me, Amelie, Corinne and her, had visited in 2015, the three marvellous tourists spots in the Philippines, like Baguio, known as the summer capital of the Philippines; the Boracay beach resort with white sand; and the Villa Escudero with their warm welcome, their locale delicious foods, and ferric waterfalls.

Melchor

My brother Melchor was born on my birthday, the day of the Epiphany celebration, in January 1964. It was raining hard when he experienced his first day on earth, and that day I was attending my Grade 5 elementary classes at Bading Elementary school, a school that I hated. I had realised that day that my grandmother had been totally accurate. She predicted the coming of my younger brother.

During his high school days, Melchor encountered several trials. One day he asked me to provide him some pocket money, which was quite normal; then he said that he couldn't continue going to high school this way. He had some projects, and he could not submit them to his instructor if he did not have enough money to buy the materials. It was so painful to hear his worries. But I reminded him that to reach the goal of success, he must be prepared to undergo some sacrifices. I said I wished I could support his studies, but I was also still striving for my own education. What could I do? Later I heard that due to peer pressure from his barkadas he tasted smoking marijuana, a drug that could damage the brain. He had no intention to continue smoking, fortunately.

I have settled in France when Melchor met a young woman who was also born on his birthday, and mine too. Lordelina was a college student and the niece of my parents' neighbour, whose new house was constructed just beside my parents' old house in Sintos. With my parents' support, they celebrated their civil wedding ceremony on August 24, 1989. They were both very much in love, but unfortunately they were unemployed for many months. That must have been very hard. My parents continued to make sacrifices, the monthly support that they received from us abroad was never enough, without Tatay having a permanent income. It reminded me again of the situation of when Dan and his wife Betsy lived with them. With my parents' encouragement Lordelina finished her course successfully aand graduated in March 1990. She found a job almost immediately after graduation.

The new couple had encountered some trials. Melchor was often drunk, and that made his character and behaviour deteriorate who became dangerous to his wife and to his daughters when drunk. He used to drink with his barkadas and returned home wildly angry and unreasonable that made their life became unbearable. At that time, Melchor's true love was alcohol.

With a little sacrifice and perseverance, and with the help of Lordelina who was so patient with him, Melchor recovered from alcoholism. They had two daughters: Ivy Rose was born in December 1991; and Anmelord in June 1990.

Later, both Melchor and his wife found good jobs in the town of Esperanza, Agusan del Sur: Lordelina in the Department of Social Welfare and Development (DSWD), while Melchor worked as a private bodyguard for the Mayor. He took the job that Dan had done, as Dan was then setting up his own business. Melchor resigned later and joined the Task Force as a traffic enforcer; while Lordelina was transferred to Human Resources Admin. Melchor and Lordelina are now grandparents. Ivy Rose and Annemelord both married and became lovely mothers: As of now, Ivy has one daughter, Aleckxia. Annemelord has one daughter, Laureen born in June 2009, and one little boy, Josiah, born in June 2020.

Imelda

Imelda was born in June 1968. Time passed by swiftly. She's my youngest sister, also had to undergo the Citizen's Military Training as an officer, and had memorable experiences during her high school days. She studied brilliantly and graduated with a Bachelor of Science in Economics in March 1990 from Father Saturnino Urios University. I was so proud of her. During Student Day she actively participated in games like volleyball, and her team was often the winner. She also played strategy games like chess, and won.

She revealed in me in 2018, some of her childhood and adult experiences. For me, her fascinating life story meritted to be written.

Years later, she became a young missionary. She travelled abroad: to New York in 1999 and 2001; China in 2000; Canada in 2001; Brazil in 2002; Thailand from 2004-2005 and 2007; Indonesia 1996-1998, and 2004-2005; Australia in 2011, and some other places.

When I visited the Philippines in 2015, we had a wonderful family reunion, I sensed that there was something particular with Imee's personality and this sensation became stronger after I attended Tatay's burial in May 2017. But I did not dare to ask her, because we were grieving.

The call from God

Imelda recalls her experiences:

"The call from God started during my early childhood. I was proud to obtain excellent records in Catechism through Ma'am Juana. Starting from five to seven years old, Tatay used to carry me in his arms walking to Ma'am Juana's house to let me attend Catechism with other children in New Asia. Ma'am Juana held classes in her residence which was wide enough to accommodate hundreds of children. Between the ages of eight and nine, I was trained by her. I started leading Flores de Mayo in San Vicente Chapel. I became the only leader for the whole barangay. I taught Catechism to the children when Ma'am Juana was sick. I went around the entire barangay telling the kids about the coming Flores de Mayo. I cleaned the chapel and prepared the flowers ahead of time. My leaderships lasted for three years. I was happy of what I had accomplished." She said proudly.

Imelda had learned theological lessons through Catechisms, and in turn she taught it to the children. In my view, she had learned the Catechism by doing God's work. Unknowingly, she had started fulfilling her mission as a Christian during her early childhood, in retelling and interpreting the biblical story. She was born when our lives were hard. She was baptized and nurtured in the Christian Catholic faith. Imelda, when asked about her childhood experiences, said:

" I had experienced forced labour as well. I was a babysitter to our neighbour's children just to earn some allowance for schooling, transportation, and school materials when I was between six and ten years old. Mama's menopause and poverty made her so irritable, a hard time for me. I was told by our parents to go to the store to buy goods with "credit" for our food. I would bring these scraps of paper that said we would be "good for" the money later. I prayed while walking that the store owners would allow us to obtain some canned goods. I was so ashamed and shy to show the papers which indicated the list of goods we needed, I usually asked myself: How could we pay all this? One time when it had been raining hard, which lasted several days, the Agusan River flooded throughout New Asia and all over the Butuan City. Usually, a flood lasted only from two to five days, but this time it lasted a month, which paralysed our daily activities. However we used that opportunity to obtain more things for free, and sometimes pretended to have fun and a feeling of satisfaction. During the flood, lots of fish and shrimps were carried by the current. Together with our parents, we walked into the water catching them, but we did not own any fishing nets or rods. So we used our old mosquito net, which was so helpful, and we returned home with fish and shrimps, thus having good meals. But in my childhood, I did not begrudge or feel bitter to our parents," said Imelda.

Our hardship in life became more difficult when the sawmill burst due to thunder and lightning, and luckily Tatay had survived from explosion, he was protected by God." I recalled to her.

Detained in China

She was very courageous in adventuring in China in January and February 2000. To my mind, she was very lucky that she was not imprisoned for long time because I know that the Chinese Communist government can be terribly strict and ruthless with the strangers, especially if they came to distribute bibles and tracks.

She said: "My team was the first to be detained. I was so lucky to have been able to escape with my interpreter and hid the remaining bibles with the help of the other two Chinese friends. When my team's interrogation stopped, I was called, and answered the interrogations on my turn. I was detained for one day without food or drink; I was not even allowed to use their toilet because of the crime of giving away bibles. They inspected our hotel. If ever they had found out that I had still bibles in my possession stored somewhere, I would have had been in prison for 21 years or more."

When I asked her what was her feeling during the interrogation, she only said:

"I did not feel any fear. I only trusted the Lord. I know He wouldn't leave me; He was always there whenever I was in danger."

Terrorist attack – 2001

There was a terrorist's attack on the twin towers of the World Trade Center in New York on September 11, 2001. Imelda was in New York, and I was terribly worried for her. I was following the news in the television the whole night, watching the devil's deeds. The twin towers exploded after being hit by planes and had no survivors. So terrifying!

I was only relieved when I received two calls from my sisters in Australia at 4 a.m. Paris time. They said that Imelda, was already in Atlanta at the time of the attack. Imelda was safe. Thanks God!

While writing this memoir, I asked Imelda about her flight from New York and where was she during the terrorists' attacked, and she explained:

"It could have been different. I was about to book that flight that was used by the terrorists, while I was looking at the flight schedule from Boston to Atlanta; but God was leading me not to take the plane. The flight that the terrorists used left Boston in the morning, while my flight from Atlanta to New York was the day after the attack. I was in New York together with my companions in our community praying for New York and the people. We were serving the police, as well as firemen and other volunteers to make their tasks easier to perform. And I was already in Atlanta when Amelie was able to contact me. God had protected us not to be in New York during the terrorist's attack."

She recalled: "I started my missionary/priesthood work in 1995. I sensed my call in the early 1990s to do Christian missions after my studies. I was officially declared a pastor in 2015."

A divine gift for humanity's sake

November 2013. In my view, Imelda received the divine gift to better serve humanity after the devastating typhoon hit the Philippines. The storm was called Haiyan by Europeans, and called as Super Typhoon Yolanda by people living in the Philippines. I asked Imelda about her experiences as a missionary and her work as a pastor. So, through our messages, she told to me her story:

> "Days after the typhoon, I cried while praying as I felt pain and compassion. I was praying again and again and wished I could help the victims and their families. But how? We did not have funds for that. Then that week, I dreamed about money with specific amount, but I did not pay attention to it because for me it was just a dream.
>
> That same week, I opened Facebook and read a particular message from someone who said he wanted to help Haiyan's victims and asked how he could send the money. He did not tell me the amount he could send, and I did not tell him how much we need to help the victims. But the money that he sent me was exactly the same amount as what I had seen in my dream.
>
> We were able to go to Leyte together with another team. We distributed bottles of water, clothes, generator machines for electricity, and many other supplies. I visited Leyte three times. We were sharing and preaching God's word in Palo-Leyte, the place where thousands of people had died, thousands of houses were destroyed, and all in the surroundings were devastated, nothing was left. But some unhappy people threw stones at us."

Super Typhoon Haiyan/Yolanda was one of the strongest tropical cyclones ever recorded in the history of the Philippines.

Until now, Imelda remain unmarried. She said: "With God alone, I am happy and contented."

My Love Life 1979-1981

My friends and I, often went to meet up to discuss our activities and views about the day in the Farmacia Rosita in Butuan, managed by Francing a family friend who was older than me. She was a charming pretty woman, the younger sister of Yoyo Supri's wife, the aunt of Segundino. Francing's mother lived in Mabini, Cabadbaran, the same hometown as Nanay Pantay.

I happened to buy some medicines one day in that pharmacy and met Francing who seemed familiar to me: she looked like her mother. She said she had seen me when I was a young child. She considered me as a relative and asked me to come after 5 p.m. to introduce me to all her colleagues: Jenny, Alicia, Juvy, Linda, and Naima. We all became friends. I also met: Kandy and Nora, who were both teachers; Minda and Yolanda, students who were used to going to that pharmacy after their college classes; and Rachel, who was more than sixty years old and the owner of another pharmacy.

Most of us had letters from our pen pals all over the world, except Rachel who served as our audience and advisor. Each one of us opened our letters from our pen-pals abroad; we shared comments, compared their photos and postcards, and discussed how and what to say to them in writing and by phone. It was fun.

Here is the story: A young professor who was getting married gave me the address of her pen pal from United States. She said she had no more time to write him. She also gave me a list of people who desired meeting friends through correspondence from different countries that she took from the magazines and newspapers. I wrote to all of them. Three weeks later, I was so excited to receive letters from different countries in Europe, the United States, Russia, Australia and so on. I did not expect they would all answer me quickly. I distributed some of them to my friends from Farmacia Rosita. They were all more excited than me.

One day, I received a letter from my pen pal from Germany called Friedrich, who was five years older than me, and was a young dentist. He said he wanted to see my parents and would ask their blessing to marry me, and then he would bring me to Germany. At first I thought he was not serious, but this time he insisted asking me of when I could fetch him from Manila International Airport and what were the pre-requirements for him to bring for marriage.

Ohlala! I was in panic and scared. I wasn't sure if we were well suited for each other. He was much taller than me, and loved playing basketball. I learned through letters about him, that he was a kind, gentle man, who was understanding, loved horse riding, and also camping and traveling in a caravan. However, I told him I hated camping because of the mosquitoes and the heat, and I didn't know if I would like staying in the caravan. I felt unsafe to think about marriage to a foreigner, as I lacked confidence in myself due to my inferiority complex. I did not feel strong enough to confront anyone or to be an equal with someone in order to be bound in matrimony. I was afraid to encounter problems regarding the language, behaviour, personal interests, food, culture, religion, etcetera. Once I gave his letter to another girl, he did not hear from him anymore.

Later, I distributed all my pen pals to the girls who were interested in marrying a foreigner. But I was always pleased to help them when they needed me. I'd always been thrilled to be of service, especially when it came to speaking English even on the phone.

Anyway, in 1980 Francing got married to her another pen pal, Bim, an American aircraft pilot from the United States. They got two sons. Kandy, a teacher from Agusan High School, got married in the same year to Gustave, from Chicago. I had a nice moment attending their lovely church wedding celebration in Butuan.

Meeting Lionel

In August 1979 I met Lionel in Farmacia Rosita, on a Friday early evening. Francing and Kandy were still in Butuan. After enjoying eating the fresh watermelon, Francing was doing card readings seriously, but just for fun for me when Lionel, a tall man, slim and elegant, walked into the pharmacy for the first time. He wore khaki coloured trousers, a long-sleeved shirt and a hat of the same cloth and colour. He was with a tourist guide in Butuan who went by the nickname "Boy," a musician and Francing's friend and former classmate. Meanwhile, the girls entertained him and poor Lionel did not know anymore to whom he was supposed to answer. The card reading was finished. I rose up from my chair while stretching my arms, I had been on the chair for more than an hour. I'd forgotten Lionel was still there.

Boy introduced him to me. Lionel so smiling, wore thick old-fashioned glasses. His skin was red and peeling off; it must have been due to sunburn because he said he had stayed on top of a boat in the sun the whole day. He talked about his long travels from France, then from Manila to Cebu, then from Surigao to Nasipit by boat, and finally he took a passenger jeepney from Nasipit to Butuan. It was a long, long trip but all he said was: "You are my sweet reward Sarah, my divine providence after such travel."

I did not understand what he really meant, but I liked his French accent which was so different from the other foreigners I met in Butuan. I was used to hearing the American and Australian accents, even though they were sometimes hard to understand. Lionel spoke English fluently. He said he practiced English in Ireland.

It was getting dark and some of the girls invited Lionel to join them for a dance at the discotheque, knowing that they were not that fond of going to the disco. I was thinking that maybe they were only joking after all.

Lionel said: "Why not? But Sarah should come with us." I was surprised to hear it. I said it was late, and I needed to go home, and that I was feeling worn out and hungry. I had to wake-up early the next morning to work. I was still a student and I had taken an examination at Urios university that afternoon. If God was willing, I would graduate the next year, March 1980, I told him.

Lionel continued telling me about himself and Boy, while the other girls said goodbye. The three salesgirls in the Farmacia Rosita enjoyed trying to convince Boy to go to the disco while Lionel asked me to help him find a nice restaurant in the city. Finally, Minda, Boy, Lionel, and I went together to dine at the Narra Hotel Restaurant, one of the best restaurants in the city at that time. Then we finally went altogether to the Discothèque called Magada.

In the middle of the dance floor Minda and Boy enjoyed dancing together. From time to time, they glanced at Lionel and me. We danced the slow steps, no matter what the music was, and I was guiding him as he was not really dancing at all. He took some steps forward then some steps back, and sometimes he stepped on my feet. Despite the loud music, I could tell that he spoke English very well. He told me again that he had practiced speaking English in North Ireland every summer vacation, except that year. But he did not tell me that he had a fiancée over there. Instead, he said that he wished he could bring me to France, but I ignored it because for me, France was at the edge of the world. It would have been impossible for me to reach there by my own expense.

The next day, Saturday morning, I was working and Lionel came to visit me in my office with his camera. He enjoyed taking the photos of the cadets and vice-versa. After our lunch together, he asked me if he could visit my parents and introduce himself to them. I remember they were all there: my parents, small Dave, Ashley, Amelie, and Melchor, but Dan and Carter were absent. Tatay and Amelie spoke in English to Lionel while my mother remained silently smiling. Then I learned that our neighbours thought that Lionel was my pen-pal.

He said he loves to travel across Asia. He was invited by his younger brother Fabien who was working in Japan and married a Japanese woman. But Lionel planned to go to South Korea first. However, he had changed his mind because of his British pen pal named Margaret, living in England, who had a Chinese pen pal named Shou-Ling who worked as a cashier in the Chinese store called Butuan Wings Hardware in Butuan. It became his pretext for coming to the Philippines. Margaret asked Lionel to bring her presents (a small package) to Shou-Ling, which enabled him to have a travel destination and an opportunity to meet the Chinese woman. But Lionel had no idea at all where Butuan was located. He had thought that it was just a suburb of Manila. He learned later that Butuan was in the northside of Mindanao. Some people tried to dissuade him, saying that Mindanao was not a safe place to travel because of the Muslim rebels who had spread troubles around the region.

He was astonished when he learned that he had to take a boat to Butuan, and he had never taken a boat in all his life. But he was excited to take it. He took the ticket for 3rd class for a ship which carried freight and passengers from Manila to Surigao. It made plenty of stopovers over three days traveling on the Pacific Ocean. He was not even aware that for the

3rd class tickets, there were no meals included. He noticed inside the boat that people were bringing their own foods. Luckily, he was invited by the people in the 2nd class to their table and they offered him good meals. While he was telling me his experiences, he made some jokes to allay my anxiety, thus we continued our lengthy conversation.

"Oh, don't worry," he said. "The good spirit is always with me so I can never be hungry, and my guardian angel is always there to protect me. Let me tell you, it was a blessing that my pen pal Margaret had asked me to bring her presents to Shou-ling, otherwise I would have had not come to Butuan. And to come to Philippines was one of my dangerous adventures, but meeting you is a divine providence," he said, smilingly as usual. He kept repeating that his guardian angel was always protecting him, especially at the midst of danger.

He journeyed with a man named Ben, who he met onboard. Ben had plenty of relatives living throughout Butuan and Tungao. Lionel met so many people, including Miss Mendez who gave him a hand-made green mat with her name woven into it, as their reminder of their meeting, in the hopes that Lionel would come back to marry her. Both Lionel and Ben stayed one week in the house of Ben's sister. Lionel left Tungao and returned to the Ambassador Hotel in Butuan not far from my office, while Ben returned to his family in Sani-Sani Island near Surigao.

Lionel waited until much later, once we were settled in France, to tell me his full experience in the Philippines. He said while having meals in the Hotel's restaurant, he met the musician who called himself Boy, who was living in Obrero, a purok [village] just next to that of my parents, and offered his services as a tourist guide to Lionel anywhere he wanted to go. It was a kind offer, so they went together first to Boy's grandfather who owned a large farm. It was far away from other farms, with diverse plantings, including several species of banana, coffee, and other crops. Then they visited the gold-mines, owned by a Presbyterian family, where Lionel had a lot of interesting conversations. They met people along their way who worked along the river in search of gold. They used sieves to separate the small stones and the gold embedded in the sand and gravel.

From there, they continued walking everywhere in Butuan until late in the evening and by chance, they had reached Villa Kananga, the neighbouring barangay near Sintos Subdivision where my parents lived. The following day Lionel went a long walk all alone around Butuan. He explored the city until he reached the barrio of San Vicente, where people were waiting for their priest to arrive. It was believed in the Philippines that foreign priests were often balding. So when Lionel who was slightly balding reached their barangay, the people were so happy and welcomed him as a priest.

Here's the story: "I was there standing at the midst of people forming a circle around me. I was so surprised and wondered, upon seeing their enthusiasm, why had they surrounded me like that? They thought I was the priest. But when people learned that I was not the priest they were waiting for, the women in Villa Kananga surrounded me much closer, became so excited wanting to introduce me to their daughters to marry. Suddenly, I was in trouble because I did not know how to answer to all those mothers who wanted me. I felt strange the way they asked me to marry their daughters, and they even prevented me from walking away," He explained. But Lionel never told me until much later how he was asked to marry those young women. He continued: "Even Boy, asked me to marry his younger sister, who was a 28-year old teacher. I was wondering how those girls had dared to ask a stranger like me to marry them. Just like that. For me, to get married is a serious matter," said Lionel raising his eyebrows. I did not dare to answer him, I was afraid to utter some prejudicial words against my fellow Filipinos.

Lionel wanted to know me, so he prolonged his stay in Butuan. He said it was a pity that he met me when he was about to leave for Manila. He had wished to go to Japan or Korea and maybe we could go together. I answered him that I must first graduate in March the next year (1980). He left for Manila the next day and said he will still stay for three days in the capital before leaving for France.

Our initial meeting led us to become friends and to a kind of mutual understanding. After he left, we continued to exchange our different ideas and interests through letters and through cassettes. He left his cassette recorder for me to listen all what he sent. We became like pen pals. He told me about his voyages throughout Europe but he was more interested in Asia, while I was so interested in Europe and all his travels around the world. For me, it was fantastic to listen his cassettes with his voice telling different stories and music from France. I learn lot of things better than reading a long letter; as you cannot write everything on paper.

However, despite our regular communication, I missed an important detail regarding his next visit to Philippines. When he said that he was coming the next summer, I thought it would be in August 1981, (two years after our meeting) but I was confused. Lionel came back to visit me in Butuan City in the last week of July 1980. His last cassette telling me was delayed, so that I had only received it when I returned home from Manila. He said that unlike his first travel in Butuan in 1979 where he was a simple messenger, this time his main purpose was expressly to see me back.

Six months later, I met an Australian, Jason, in February 1980 at the Farmacia Rosita, the same place I met Lionel. He was a friend of Liam Brown, Naima's pen pal.

We had exchanges of jokes and life stories were revealing, but one thing that caught my attention was how Jason looked at me, that had made me feel uncomfortable that I slid to the edge of my seat. I had tried to evade his glances, but he always found funny topics that everyone enjoyed and drew attention to himself. He gazed up at me, and his smile completely disarmed me. I did not know anything about him early on, although he seemed like a good guy, a decent man and a gentleman. He said he was a Director of the Post Office in New South Wales. But I was skeptical about what was the real story, as I learned later that he was divorced. He said he never missed the chance to travel outside Australia every year during holidays.

Did I feel love for Jason?

In July 1980, the two Australians (Jason and Liam) came back to Butuan. Liam and Naima wanted to make an official announcement about their engagement, and their plan to get married. Naima asked me to go with them to the Australian Embassy in Manila as her chaperone to assist them in registering their marriage application and applying for their marriage publication; this is one of the requirements or protocols in the Philippines before getting married to a foreigner. However, they needed to first undergo an interview with the Australian Embassy Officer.

Meanwhile, during my 8-day short-stay with them in Manila, waiting for the result of their interviews, Jason courted me vigorously. I started to feel love and affection grow for him, which me to accept his proposal of marriage. I thought I would never get bored with him. I learned to laugh more, which was rare, as I was usually very serious. I felt that he was sincere when he asked me to marry him; he said he loved me since the first time he saw me in Farmacia Rosita. I was a little embarrassed in front of everyone when he knelt down in Luneta Park. I didn't know the customs and traditions yet. It was the first time that someone had asked me to marry them. I accepted his marriage proposal, because I felt marvelously good and serene when I was with him, although I wasn't sure whether I was really in love with him. He never tried to bully me nor sway my decision. What I knew was that he loved me, and for me, that was the most important thing.

Jason became more attentive to me once we became engaged, while he remained a kind gentleman. I enjoyed his company full of lovely and thoughtful conversation. We seemed to be always on the same wavelength. I felt comfortable and confident with him at my side even inside the taxi, and I did not need to ask him where we would go. We were visiting places that Naima and I never had the chance to see before. Naima and Liam were in a second taxi behind following ours. However, Naima and I had a kind of pact: we promised we would never separate no matter what, but when we could not all fit in the taxi together, it contradicted our alliance.

One beautiful Saturday morning we visited the Pagsanjan Falls, also known as Cavinti Falls. It is one of the famous waterfalls and tourist attractions in the Philippines, located in Laguna. I did not realize that we would take a long river trip in a dugout canoe before reaching the waterfall. Four of us took the boats, and we put our hands under the waterfall, which was cool and exciting, and we were completely soaked. It was exhilarating. However, I felt sorry for the boatmen. It was probably exhausting for them to push our boats against the current of the water while we four remained sitting inside.

I was relieved later when a young boatman told me, with a beautiful smile showing me his well lines white teeth, that they were proud of their skills to maneuver the boats through the narrow rocks every day, and that they did not feel the fatigue anymore. He added: "especially when the tourists are generous," which made me laugh. He was hilarious. I admired his enthusiasm for serving us, and for that I was ready to thank him more than he asked; Jason was so generous, I knew that the boatman would be well compensated. And if everyone was like him, no one could be annoyed, and business would always be a success. Sometimes the bottom of the boat struck the stony surface under the waters, and the boatman had to make extra effort showing me his grimace while pushing our boat against the current of the water came from the cascade or falls. In my mind, their efforts made us experience an unforgettable journey.

Jason whispered to me: "I wouldn't allow people to see your breasts exposed under your wet clothes." Jason and Liam had bought us beautiful blouses, quite loose for me and Naima, which were suitable to cover our soaked bodies. I was touched by this caring gesture. Now I had then understood why they had disappeared after our dinner the night before.

I had thought that perhaps they were disappointed with Naima and me because we had not accepted their invitation to go swimming with them that evening, though the hotel's swimming pool was so inviting. I learned later that they had suspected us that we did not know how to swim, so they were very careful so that Naima and I didn't fall into the Pagsanjan Waterfalls. But as chance would have it, Naima and I both had our monthly visitor. The men showed us two bathing suits not for the waterfalls, but for swimming privately in the hotel's pool.

During our promenade in the Luneta parc, Naima and I were still recalling about our boat ride the previous day when thunder rumbled in the sky with electrical white lightning followed by heavy rain. We sprinted back to the hotel and glanced behind to see whether Liam and Jason were following us. We were surprised to see them dancing, jumping, running, and singing excitedly under the rain like young kids. While watching them behaving this way, we were wondering: are they not a bit crazy in Australia? They even invited us to join them, but I found it too silly. They continued running around in circles in front of the hotel; they sometimes lifted their feet higher one at a time, marching like soldiers during a parade and jumping while shaking the rain from their hands.

"The rain in Australia is so cold that nobody would want to stay under the heavy raindrops," they said. My curiosity increased. Naima and I were also like children as we ran into the hotel hall across the reception counter. We were even afraid that we might get tempted to join them, mostly because they could be so persuasive. I was quite embarrassed when they entered the hall to catch us, soaked. They tried again to convince us to go dancing with them under the rain, while the young employees at the reception desk were watching us curiously; they would have thought the Australians were behaving like crazy boys.

On the fifth day of our stay in Manila, we were still waiting for the results of Naima and Liam's application for marriage, while I accepted Jason's invitation to apply ourselves. We filled in the forms of application for marriage too. However, I was hesitant because we didn't know each other very well yet. I found myself facing the Australian Embassy officer who had conducted our oral interviews privately, and made the publication of our marriage on the same day. Strangely, I was stupefied to find that our application was approved even before Naima and Liam. Jason said he showed the document as proof of the termination of his previous marriage. Everything was moving so fast, and it was so easy for Jason and me. I answered all the questions and riddles for which items were sometimes tricky to answer, because the Australian officer was digging up our private and personal information.

The following day, I was surprised to see Lionel in Luneta park, in the middle of Luneta park. It was a shock, to say the least. I did not know yet that he was already in Butuan, but how come that I was seeing him walking in the garden in Manila? He was far from me, and didn't turn around. And suddenly he disappeared. I was feeling very confused, my mind was troubled. Perhaps I was hallucinating?

We visited several tourist spots in Manila, but I don't remember any of them anymore. Every evening we dined in the best restaurants, where they served a generous selection of Filipino favorite and delicious dishes. The restaurants had beautiful and mouthwatering buffets of selected roasted fish and shrimps, *lapu-lapu* [a reddish-coloured fish named after Cebu's legendary chieftain, Asia's most sought-after reef fish] steamed or broiled in soy, and clams, lobsters, and fresh seaweed. We enjoyed dining while watching the staff do different performances, such as Filipino folklore, modern dance, and some comedy sketches. We came back to the hotel at 2 a.m.

That morning, Jason wondered why I was sad. He handed me my return ticket for my flight to Butuan. He said that it was an open ticket so that I could choose any date for my flight. I was sitting on a park bench, realizing I was so lucky to be in Manila without spending a single cent. But I was very pre-occupied with what date I would choose for my flight, although I knew that there was only one flight in the morning from Manila to Butuan. My mind was in a million miles away wandering hectically, asking myself whether I should return to Butuan now, or later.

The next afternoon, I saw Lionel again, and this time he was there in front of me; he took off his hat, then he raised his right hand and saluted me like an Army officer, then quickly he left.

I was not sick or hungry. I was just tired, and this vivid vision with Lionel kept repeating in front of my eyes. I was not anymore asking myself if I was hallucinating or not; instead, it was a matter of interrogating myself about what would be the sense and the consequences of those visions.

I was feeling good that evening. The fresh air breeze touched my cheeks, and I did not even notice that Jason came and sat down on the bench next to me. He moved closer, reaching to me to remind me of his infinite love. He gives me a gentle smile and held me passionately on his breast while asking me why I was melancholy; once again he shared me some jokes, and he suddenly lifted me with his hands under my arms and turned like spinning top and said: "Come on baby, show me your smile."

" It is a nice day today, while you are strangely pale," he said. He caressed my head, moving his fingers through my hair. He kissed me on my forehead, my temples, my cheeks, and he kissed my lips tenderly. He was my gentle fiancé. He deserved to be loved and to be respected. How could I tell him that I was seeing visions of Lionel? He did not know anything about Lionel, why should I tell him? I did not know how I would say it to him. The torment had invaded my being.

The next day, we had a splendid journey. Naima and I had a promenade together while our fiancés were just behind us. I saw Lionel for the third time, walking across the park at approximately 10 meters away from us; like before he quickly disappeared.

I abruptly stopped walking, planting my feet on the ground. Naima frowned, wondering what was wrong with me.

"Why are you acting weird?" Her eyes narrow in on me. "Are you alright?" I nod my head twice so fast. "Absolutely fine," I said.

I couldn't tell her about Lionel, as she would have said I was hallucinating. I was thinking about how to tell her without being taken as a fool. I did not dare, afraid of the consequences. Luckily, Jason and Liam were having a gripping discussion that they did not notice my confusing reaction. Seeing him repeatedly so vividly in the park disturbed me seriously: Was that vision a kind of an alert informing or preventing me not to accept Jason's proposal? But was it too late? I had already accepted Jason, and we had even published with the Australian Embassy the planned date of our marriage, February 1981.

I did not know it, but Lionel was at that time in Butuan, looking for me in my office, but he did not find me, of course. During our first meeting in August 1979, we did not have enough time to know each other because we met when it was close to the time for him to leave. This time, in the beginning of August 1980, he was already in Butuan and I was in Manila, and weren't Lionel and I just friends? But how come that I had a kind of pre-sentiments that something would bind me to him? A severe headache attacked me, as I did not know how to resolve my conflicting feelings.

I learned that there was discrepancy and conflicting information during Naima and Liam's interviews that had caused delays in the completion of the necessary formalities for their marriage license. They were obliged to remain in Manila for another couple of days until the publication of their future marriage and Naima still needed me as her chaperone. I was so sorry about that. But I did not dare to have allowed myself to stay more days with them. In contrast, I felt a strong urge to return home to Butuan, though I did not know why. Perhaps because of so much of work would be waiting for me, after being away from my office for eight days. It would indeed prove to be hard for me to catch-up on the huge piles of work stranded on my desk.

Life is sometimes cruel and complicated. I had been dreaming of travelling in different beautiful places in the Philippines, but I had many financial difficulties. With Jason, I could finally travel for free, but still, I could not fully enjoy it. On the other hand, I was asking myself, did I really feel in love for Jason?

The air conditioner catches fire

That night, Naima and I were half-asleep when we heard people knocking at our door. We were both hesitant to open it, but the knocking was urgent. As soon as the door was opened, Jason and Liam both rushed inside our room nervously while telling us something, but we did not understand as they spoke so fast and at the same time.

At first, I thought they were doing a naughty trick to prevent me from going back to Butuan at dawn, and I was mad because I needed to sleep. But then a hotel employee informed us that the air conditioner in their room had caught fire, so they needed to move to another place. We allowed them to enter our room. I finally understood why they were so nervous and afraid, like young kids.

There were two sofas facing the window of our room. Liam was with Naima on their couch, and Jason was with me in ours. Naima was always looking at me, perhaps to remind me of our pact, that we said we would never allow the men to stay in our bedroom. So, we remained wisely on the sofas while waiting for their room to be ready. Though Naima and I were the same age, I was her chaperone, and it was my duty to take care of her, and ensure that our pact was fully respected.

Thirty minutes later, the hotel employee said all of their belongings had been transferred to their new room. Us girls were relieved, hoping we could return to bed and sleep. But before they left our room, Jason asked if he could cuddle me, and this time, our embrace lasted longer. I tried to prevent myself from falling too deeply into the emotion. I was afraid Jason wouldn't leave our room.

Jason and I had also agreed a covenant that he must not touch me before marriage. I was grateful he had successfully respected our understanding. But for the first time, he kissed me on my lips deeply, and I was helpless to stop him. He said it was so hard for him to let me go home to Butuan without him. I listened to him with apprehension as he tried to convince me again to stay more days in Manila, to allow us to get to know each other better. I was scared that my emotions would be carried away, slipping out of our promise. I felt sorry for him. But I also felt that if he had loved me the way he said he did, he could surely wait.

I hated seeing myself at the mirror showing smudges under my eyes. I had spent sleepless nights thinking of my engagement to Jason. We had talked a lot about him and his previous marriage. He said that he left his house to his ex-wife. They had once had beautiful moments together, but life had separated them, and the divorce was difficult. He said that he had not expected to fall in love again, but he found new love with me and couldn't afford to let me go. I didn' find a word to answer him.

At 3:30 a.m., Naima, Liam, and Jason brought me to the domestic airport in Manila to catch my flight at 5:00 a.m. for Butuan. Our farewell was short and intensely passionate. Jason hugged me firmly, holding back emotion as his lips trembled. I did not know any more how many times and how long we kissed, and it hurt to say goodbye, but I resisted the pull to stay with him. I felt an immense pain in leaving him and I cried. It was a real goodbye. It felt like my heart bled, and my chest had tightened. I sensed that Jason and I would not see each other again. I even started to miss him. I did not understand my feelings. I was happy that I became his fiancée, but I was also sad at the same time. I cried on the plane. My thoughts were full of images of Lionel, who appeared in visions. But my fiancé, who was undeniably kind and gentle, respected my choice to go back to Butuan before he could. I felt a strong guilt that pursued me everywhere.

My travel was smooth and reached Butuan safely. Tired of the early travel that morning, I was hoping to recover with some sleep. I was about to lie down when I heard my younger sister, Amelie, calling excitedly our mother: "Mama, Mama, Lionel is here. My tricycle is waiting, I can't stay. I must go back now to Urios to attend the rest of my classes," she explained. She did not know that I was back from Manila, as she had not entered the house, but maybe she saw me at the window. I didn't have the chance to ask her.

The story I heard later was that Lionel had not found me at my office. He said he even went to the Bangcasi PA Headquarters to see Major Reference, whom he met the previous year, but the Major was not in his office either. Lionel was looking for me the whole morning and luckily, some ROTC cadets were there in my office who informed him that I had a sister at Urios. Lionel remembered Amelie, and they went together to my parent's place.

I glanced at the window wondering about of Amelie's excitement, and saw Lionel coming up to the house. Why did he come without telling me? In his letters, he said he was coming back next August, meaning summer 1981. I was really confused.

Then I realized that if I had known that Lionel was going to arrive that month, I would have stayed in Butuan, and I would not have had this experience of traveling to Manila with Liam, Naima, and Jason. I was somehow grateful that fate changed the course of my life. That experience would indeed remain etched in my heart.

Lionel was searching me in Butuan, and amazingly, I was also seeing him in the park. But that was not the reason why my mind was shaken. The fact was that he was wearing the same suit as I saw in my vision in Luneta Park, Manila. He wore a white shirt and navy-blue trousers. Upon looking at him through my bedroom window, my heart was beating unusually strongly, which I never felt with Jason. I quickly understood that I was in love with him. I hastily told my mother that I was in love with Lionel.

Mama frowns, she rolled her lips flat and shrugged her shoulders. "So that's it? You went to Manila as a chaperone to Naima, and you came back home as a fiancée to an Australian. Now you are in love with a French. What should you do now, Sarah?" Mama said rising her eye brows.

I was frozen, thinking of my new feelings. I answered: "I don't know, Mama, what should I do?" Mama shakes her head and exhaled: "I met Lionel last year, then today, but not Jason yet."

Meanwhile Lionel was in our living room waiting for me. This time, I felt so nervous, whereas the previous year, everything was different as I was just felt serene and was so comfortable with him at dinner and in the discotheque too while my friends from Farmacia Rosita were teasing me with their peculiar look. I did not feel anything special towards him then. While now, his smile seemed so precious.

My heart was overwhelmed beating a hundreds miles per minute, I didn't find a word to say hello. He stood tall and we stared at each other for I don't know how long, and I felt faint when he took my hands getting all clammy and frozen, and I worried he would notice. I had not felt anything like this with Jason. I had sensed that Lionel had incredible thoughts and contagious emotions, maybe stronger than mine. But our spirits were deeply communicating and soon I forgot my environment. When he started to talk, I heard him as if his voice and words were like a breeze, with music in my ears.

I was awakened from that intense emotion when Mama interrupted to ask me if Lionel would like to have lunch with us. But we both preferred to take our lunch outside that day, to spend time alone and maybe come to understand our new found feelings reciprocally.

I spent sleepless nights later, thinking about my planned marriage to Jason, scheduled for February or March 1981 and my new feelings towards Lionel. Did he not tell me he was once engaged to Irene from Northern Ireland? Meanwhile, he had proposed to marry me through his letters that I received every week, and now he is with me.

Would I tell him that finally, I love him too? Oh, God can You help me? I asked. Should I report to Lionel that, yes, I love him too, but I will marry Jason?

Furthermore, Jason wanted to meet my parents in February. He was longing to talk to them about celebrating our engagement and our future marriage ceremony that would be held in Butuan City. He had a civil wedding with his first wife, but he agreed to celebrate our marriage in the church, although I was still skeptical whether the Catholic Church would allow us to do so, because he was a divorced man. I continued to seek help from God to ease my mind and help me make the right decision about which path to take.

How could I tell Jason that I wanted to renounce our engagement? There was no way to do it without hurting him. Should I inform Lionel that I loved him, but I was already engaged to Jason? Should I marry Jason anyways? These questions kept on repeating themselves in my head.

In the ROTC Office

I found it difficult to concentrate on performing my essential functions at work, even though my role was vital to the overall effectiveness of our office. My mind was in trouble, incapable of accomplishing any specified task. So I informed my superiors: our Commander, and the Assistant Commander, along with some other colleagues, about my situation. I revealed to them that I was engaged to marry Jason, but I was in love with Lionel. For the moment, I couldn't stay in the office, as I was afraid that as soon as Jason was back from Manila, he would try to find me there. I had no idea how he would react once he knew that I had changed my mind. I was ashamed of myself, but I needed time. For me, it was just not the time to see Jason. He would be arriving soon from Manila with Naima and Liam, and there was a chance he could meet Lionel. In the meantime, I needed to find a way to prevent them from seeing each other. Otherwise, I didn't know what the reactions would be between them, and mine as well.

It was so challenging to inform my friends in the pharmacy about the arrival of Lionel, as there were no cell phones yet. They already knew that Jason and I were engaged, but they did not know that Lionel was coming for me that year, so they were all surprised when they saw me with him. They informed me that Jason was arriving at Butuan that evening with Naima and Liam. They had finally published their forthcoming marriage by the Australian Embassy and would get married soon.

The guilt gnaws at me

Jason was always so gentle and lovely to me, and I couldn't let him suffer. So I did not dare to see him. He didn't know yet that I was in love with Lionel. I was too weak and ashamed to tell him that I was not the good woman he described to his mother; she had even called me from Australia, informing me of her joy when she learned that her son would soon be remarried. I could not imagine what her feelings and reactions would be when she received back the necklace and pendant that she had sent to me as a gift. I felt shameful guilt towards my friends in Farmacia Rosita, as I still didn't know how to inform Jason that I was breaking our engagement. I would always have this guilt that gnaws inside me.

My commander, Major Reference, was so understanding. He signed my request to extend my vacation- leave, allowing me to settle down my personal problems knowing that both Jason and Lionel were in Butuan. I was in anguish. I kept on asking myself, should I tell Lionel that I was already committed to Jason? Meanwhile, I was not sure yet, that if I broke my engagement with Jason, would Lionel still want to marry me? Would he change his mind? Oh, God, help me.

That early evening after work, Lionel fetched me from my office and took our dinner in the restaurant. He repeatedly said: "I came back to see you, Sarah, because I can't live without you." I accepted his proposal, and it was not a hasty decision because I realized I loved him truly.

The next day he informed my parents about his intention to marry me, and asked for their blessing; then, he would come back to celebrate our marriage the following year, 1981.

After our lunch in the restaurant, I went with him in the parc of the capitol. I informed him about me and Jason; that we were engaged but nothing had happened between us except some lovely kisses. Jason had respected our arrangement not to touch me. Lionel did not say anything at first. In fact, I was worried with his long silence. He was in deep contemplation. Then he said he would take a long walk that day while I returned to work.

I said to myself at least the hardest thing was now over. But I cried in my office. I cried the whole night. It was the most horrible painful feelings I ever had in my whole life. I truly loved him. For a moment I was thinking that he would never want to see me again. How could I cope now?

I was happily surprised when I found Lionel in my office. I had passed a sleepless night and I came in late that morning. But he was there standing before me, timidely smiling. My heart pumped so fast again.

Discreetly he whispered: "I love you Sarah. I can't live without you." I hugged him barely in front of the ROTC cadets present in my office. Thank God, it was a great relief!

We immediately left the office and went to see my previous employers, Attorney Gonzalez and his associates Attorney Espinoza, in their law office in Marcos Calo street, where I once worked as a Secretary when I was still a secretarial student. I needed their help as lawyers. They said they were delighted to meet a French person for the first time.

In front of Lionel, I asked them, "Sirs, do we have the right to change our mind regarding marriage?"

"Of course, Sarah, we have the right to change our mind," Attorney Gonzalez said in front of Attorney Espinoza. In that floor there were two offices: one for Atty Gonzales and the second for Atty Espinoza with one common secretary.

"Alright, Sarah, please explain so that I will know how I could help you," Atty Gonzalez said with enthusiasme. I did not know where to start, though I felt some relief upon hearing about my legal rights. He said they would take all the necessary steps to annul my marriage to Jason and stop the publication by sending a telegram or Telex and a letter to the Australian Embassy with their stamp and signatures. I was so lucky to have known them, and Attorney Jose Gonzales, a good lawyer, who acted like a father to me. He was there when I needed his help.

When Jason arrived in Butuan from Manila in the evening, Lionel and I were in Cabadbaran visiting the birthplace of Nanay and Mama. We returned to Butuan the next afternoon, but Jason and Liam had left for Australia early in the morning. They had stayed in Manila much longer than expected, so that they had to leave for Australia on the morning after bringing Naima back home. Naima frowned with piercing eyes as she stared at me. She was undeniably so angry with me.

Jason can't forgive me

In January 1981, I finally wrote a brief, informative letter to Jason. I could feel his pain while writing it. I sent it to him in Australia, asking him for his forgiveness; it was so hard to find the words to explain, while trying not to hurt him. However, I did not wait for his response. I knew it could bring him much pain to write. I did not know how to ease my conscience.

I was planning to take a boat to Manila for language lessons, but before I left at the end of January 1981, I visited my friends in Farmacia Rosita one last time. I tried to assure them that Jason would not come for me, because I sent him my letter of renunciation for marriage and the publication was already annulled in the Australian Embassy in Manila. They couldn't believe I did it.

They all frowned and contradicted me by their grim facial expressions. Despite their negative reactions, I handed to them another letter for Jason, where I explained that it was impossible for me to marry him as I was not sure of my feelings. But I had not told him about Lionel and me.

They said Jason would be coming back to Butuan with Liam in February as planned, and they gave me the name of the hotel in Manila, where they would be checking in. February was also the month that Jason was supposed to see my parents for our engagement, ask for their blessing, and fix the date of our marriage ceremony. My friends who, partially, did not agree with my decision, reminded me that Jason was definitely coming back to the Philippines to marry me before December 1981. I could not say anything. My throat tightened. I admit that I still felt the pinch of guilt in my heart and knot of stress in my stomach when I thought of Jason. I hoped that one day, he could grant me his forgiveness after all.

Jason did come back to Butuan in February 1981. And when he learned that I was already in Manila to study the French language while waiting for Lionel, who was coming back in August for our marriage, he became so angry. My friends said: "Sarah, Jason smashed all the gifts that he had brought for your family, like the bottles of wine for your parents and perfumes for your sisters in front of the crowd at Farmacia Rosita." He was truly hurt and very mad at me. I had already annulled our marriage officially with the Australian Embassy in Manila, and I had written to him. As I was sure that he had received my letter to his home address, why did he still insist on coming to marry me? I would have had liked to tell him face to face of my renunciation, but distance and time did not allow it, not even by the phone. I was again in trouble. Although I regretted it so much, I still felt his pain.

Back in 1980, while I was in the pharmacy, I spotted Nora seemed to be in love at first sight with Jason, despite the fact that he was interested in me. So, I was sure that she would be so happy if Jason and her could become much closer. Maybe he would forgive me if he fell in love with her. Unconsciously, Nora was showing to me her uncontrollable attraction and her intense emotions, her eyes sparkled while being near Jason. To my mind, they could develop a romantic relationship.

I learned that Nora had been waiting in Farmacia Rosita when Jason appeared in February 1981. She observed how Jason was hurt and angry with me. She did her best to console him, and they became friends. Time passed, and they grew closer. Later I was happy to hear that they were officially engaged. They went to the Australian Embassy in Manila in October 1981, to publish their upcoming marriage. By chance, I was still in Manila that month of October.

Nora and Jason were in the hotel in Manila and were filing an application for their future marriage in the Australian embassy. Before leaving for France, I phoned Nora to tell her that I would be leaving at the end of that month, and she invited me to come to their hotel restaurant to have a meal together. However, I discovered that Nora wasn't confident talking about Jason, because she saw him looking at my photo and maybe she was jealous. She wanted me to ask Jason to give me back my ID photo that was taken for the Australian Embassy, which he kept in his wallet. I had already forgotten about that picture. For Nora, once my image disappeared from his wallet, he could surely forgive me and finally forget me for good.

I took her advice at face value and I hastily went to their hotel. But Jason did not want to leave their room. He did not even come down to the restaurant to eat. I presumed he was still profoundly hurt that he did not want to see me again. I could not take back my photo, and I did not eat anything from their restaurant. I said sorry to Nora, and I wished her a happy marriage, then I left. Fundamentally, it was better this way because I don't know what my reaction would have been, seeing Jason face to face.

Once I had settled in France in October 1981, I heard that Nora and Jason were married, living in Australia and she was pregnant. But unfortunately, they were not happy in their marriage. Jason spent his time drinking, and maybe I was one of the causes: was his heart still broken over me? Did he hate me? I was tormented with remorse.

Nora wanted to return to the Philippines, and she would have probably given birth to her first baby in Butuan, but Jason did not allow her to go. Nora had no choice but to stay in Australia with her husband. Later, my friends from pharmacy said that Nora had wanted to come back to the Philippines to stay. However, she discovered that she was expecting her second baby boy, so again, she remained in Australia, and that was the last news I heard.

Meanwhile, the Farmacia Rosita went closed. I did not hear from them anymore except Alicia, who got married and lived in Sweden. We phoned each other from time to time. Her elder sister Linda was also married and lived with her husband in Wisconsin, USA. Alicia said: "Nora and Jason were separated, and this time Nora needed to go back to the Philippines with her two sons." Today, I still wonder whether Nora's plan to return to Butuan was realized.

For time to time, during meditation, I also wonder, what would have been my life if I had married Jason? I had often had imagined settling in Australia or USA, but my destiny brought me to Europe.

Was it the will of God that I became Lionel's wife and settled in France?

Was My Life Planned Before I Was Born?

Before I traveled to France, I met a pastor in Butuan in 1979, who warned me to avoid venturing in any large body of deep water, and that I should abstain from joining in with crowds. But I only ignored his predictions because, I thought it was natural and inevitable that I would be on water or in a crowd. I had mystical experiences, but also discomfort, anxiety and depression, before and after my marriage, and faced many hurdles, but I continued to struggle to overcome them.

Upon contemplating my whole life, now at 69, I often have this feeling that my life was planned out in advance, even before I was conceived. It was as if many things had already been decided. And I have unforgettable experiences: my nightmare that came true when I was only a young child; I nearly drowned, and came back after having a glimpse of heaven and the other world. And I had many other difficult experiences and visions that I describe below. But the image of the Holy Spirit remains in my brain. I have seen heaven when I was nearly drown and I was only a child of ten; did it come to tell me I should pass trials on earth before to go to heaven for good?

I often had this feeling that someone or a kind of dark force was trying to block my path, and that I would have to face trials before reaching my goal. On the other hand, I also have endless gratitude to those Divine hands who always saved me. Sometimes my faith in

God was shakened but deep in me I know God had never left me.

The Datu who stabbed the tricycle driver

One night in Butuan, on my way home after my evening classes in 1980, I hailed a tricycle without any other passenger on board. We were barely on our way when the tricycle was stopped by a stout, short man who planted himself in the middle of the road, intent on forcing the driver to stop. In the tricycle's headlights, I spotted something hanging from his shoulder, crescent-shaped and wrapped in brown paper, with a string or cord. I glanced at the man's face and stiffened, sensing he was dangerous. I pretended indifference, not wanting him to know that I was afraid of him, but I was acutely aware that my home was still some distance away.

The tricycle jerked and leaned to one side when the man dropped himself onto the seat behind me. I sensed his agitation and it made me even more uncomfortable. I looked away when the man focused his eyes on me, seated closer to the driver who was to the left of me. He ordered the driver to go to Langihan first.

The driver shook his head. "Sorry, sir, but my other passenger came before you, and she is going to New Asia. We will drop her first in New Asia, and then I will drive you to Langihan after that, sir."

"No!" the man ordered, harshly. "You must bring me first to Langihan." I recognized the dialect and the accent as belonging to the Manobo tribe of Agusan del Sur.

I knew the dialect all too well because I was once an interpreter for weekend conferences to the American businessman, Bob Gilbert, who hired men from Agusan del Sur, where most of them were the Manobo, working in the forest. They dealt with different hardwoods like narra wood, mahogany, and kamagong.

The driver glanced at me and I looked away. Slowly, hesitantly, he turned and headed towards Langihan. The man, enraged, shouted for him to drive faster. I was terrified, and briefly contemplated asking the driver to stop and let me out, but the road to Langihan was dark, scary, and sparsely inhabited.

When the driver reached the destination, the man turned and glared at me, and for a moment I thought he was going to strike me. Instead, he disembarked and before either of us could react, he pulled out a billhook machete and stabbed the driver in the stomach. The driver fell to the ground with an odd splashing sound. I looked in horror to see the driver's blood gushing in a torrent. I wanted to run, but for an instant my feet were frozen.

The man looked down at the driver with a mixture of contempt and satisfaction as he yanked the curved machete free, dripping with blood.

I went crazy. Then fears provided me with the energy to jump out from the tricycle. I screamed for help voiceless, scared that the perpetrator would stab me too. As christian, it's my responsibility to assist a person in danger or victim from possible death. He was vomiting so much blood, I had to turn my head away. But I left him alone on the ground, in excruciating pain drenched by his own blood. I was in a dilemma. Despite his agony in fetus position, I had to run away to find help along the dark road not knowing which way to follow. It was like following a trail I couldn't see. I darted to the first store half closed, screaming loudly for help to save the driver's life.

By chance, a man in the store was a policeman in simple civilian attire. He caught me just before I fainted. I woke me up smelling a chemical solution below my nostrils. I immediately informed him of the wounded driver, describing the Manobo with his machete. The policeman's wife gave me a glass of hot milk to drink while she made interrogations like a police officer too. I was delighted to find out that she was the Aunt of a friend, and former high school classmate. I informed her I had lost all my notebooks and the book I was carrying, including my purse.

The police officer came back at almost midnight. He put on his uniform and said: "I found the wounded driver unconscious emptied by his blood, was carried by a group of tricycle drivers to the hospital. They took off their T-shirts and pressed them against the wound of the driver. His injuries are believed to be life-threatening," he said, staring at me.

"I also found the Manobo surrounded by another group of drivers," he exhaled "The profound solidarity of the drivers was amazing, had prevented the culprit from escaping. He will be put in jail for his criminal and barbaric act." Although I was devastated, I almost felt relieved for the driver.

"Sarah, you must go with me to the police precinct station to identify the dangerous Manobo," the policeman ordered. "Your testimony is crucial. You should confirm if he is the same man who stabbed the tricycle driver with his machete," he said firmly. I was sweating profusely, scared at the thought of seeing the Manobo again.

"You have nothing to be scared of now because the suspect is in jail but still under investigation," said the policeman. "

I hopped unto the policeman's motorcycle gripping around his waist not to fall off. I closed my eyes and felt as if my face was being hit by a swarm of flying insects as the motorcycle speeds forward. I had no experience in riding like this without helmet to protect my head. The wind lifted my hair and my college uniform flapping in the air, (skirt and blouse) while my sandals were slipping. But we reached the police precinct station safely.

The Manobo without his machete, standing handcuffed with the policemen at his sides. Despite the distance at about six meters, I shuddered when he looked at me though my escort helped me ease my fears. I had to stay in the police station for more than two hours which seemed an eternity. Tthey were typing up my declaration. It to wait for the police to bring me back home while it was already past 2:00 a.m.

They found my notebooks and my book but not my wallet. As I was escorted home by the police, all our neighbours were intrigued and wondered what crime had happened. I was surprised to see my parents still awake, worried waiting for me, wordless, but tried to hide their fears. Were they informed by he police about the stabbing? Did Reynaldo Calo, a policeman and our neighbour, had reassured them that I was held in the police's rightful hands only to identify an aggressor to bring him to justice before I could go back home?

I learned that the assailant was the Datu or Filipino chieftain, the head of the Manobo tribe living along the village hillside beyond the town of Prosperidad, Agusan del Sur. He belonged to a well-off family in their tribe. This Datu was well known for his abuse of power. His family occupied the land near the Agusan River. He owned several hectares of land with several plantations.

At first, I categorically refused when Reynaldo, the police and my escort, asked me to be present during the first hearing. Scared to meet the Datu again, I did not wish for the members of his tribe to see me and feel vengeful. However, for the sake of the wounded driver, it was my duty to attend the trial, being the sole witness of the crime. I had to testify about on how the Datu carried out his barbaric act and he needed to be condemned for that and pay all the hospitalization expenses and indemnities. I was escorted by police anyway. The hearing had lasted the whole day from 8:30 in the morning. I did not stay to hear the verdict, as it was delivered in the evening, as I had to attend my evening classes.

I wanted to visit him in the hospital and to reassure his family off my sincere moral support. His wound was so deep that it had also damaged his intestines and liver. He was unconscious when he had reached the hospital and was still unconscious after the surgery. He was in critical condition and fell into a coma from which he did not awake for eight days. It reminded me of when my brother Dan was stabbed with an ice pick, not by his passenger, but by his rival.

In January 1981, a day before I left Butuan for Manila, someone knocked at the door. A woman came up to me, smiling and very determined to talk to me. She was the wife of the driver that had been stabbed the year before. What a coincidence; it was a chance that she came to see me that day, she would have missed me. She said due to the severity of her husband's wounds, he had stayed for 45 days in the hospital. He did not drive for more than a year.

She handed me a basket made of straw and abaca fibre, full of eggs and exotic fruits. I was deeply touched by her sincere gesture.

"My husband received the visit of two women in the hospital while I was there," she said. "But that was not a mere visit of courtesy; it was to intimidate us. The two women were the wives of the Datu who tried to convince us to remove our complaint so that their husband would be freed from prison. But the Datu deserved to be in prison, and I hope he learned a lesson," she said firmly.

The Datu paid all the hospital expenses, medications, and some indemnities until thre driver could go back to drive again to earn for their living. But no one could compensate for the driver's suffering and his wife's pain that he caused them. The driver had survived. God is good.

Four years later, Lionel and I spent our holiday in Butuan in 1984 and I was again a passenger in a tricycle. I took some coins from my wallet to pay the driver when I suddenly heard him said, "Ma'am, there's no need." He smiled at me, and I wondered what he meant. He continued saying: "There's no need, Ma'am, you are Ma'am Sarah? Dan's sister?" When our eyes met, I recognized him even though he looked a little stronger than the first time I saw him when I was his passenger in 1980. He was the wounded driver who was stabbed in front of me by the Datu. I had never expected to meet him back after four years.

I agree with what the French poet Charles Baudelaire said: "To a child who is fond of maps and engravings, the universe is the size of his immense hunger. Ah! how vast is the world in the light of a lamp! In memory's eyes how small the world is!"

However, the scene is still fresh in my mind, and it enters my nightmares from time to time. Still now, I cannot bear to see a sharp sword, a bolo and any type of machete, not even the point of a sharp knife. Every time I am in a store where they are sold, I have to turn my head. I only have a simple kitchen knife at home to cut the thin sliced meat, fish, and vegetables, and a small bread knife used to slice the cake, bread, butter and cheese. I can't bear seeing my own blood during a blood test. I am scared to see a child wounded, and blood flowing, like I did that night. Thanks to writing this memoir, I now understand where all my phobias of blood and knives come from.

My brief encounter with a mysterious passenger

At the end of February 1980 I had attended my last exam in business law before graduating in March. I did well to recall the answers, and I was confident that I would have good results, despite the fatigue from work. My empty stomach rumbled. I had to hail a passenger tricycle to return home, but not one was vacant.

A jeepney without passenger stopped just in front of me with a driver who looked about 40 years old, haggard and slim. He invited me to ride, saying he was going to Obrero, a barrio near to our home. At first, I was hesitant because I was alone. Despite my reluctance, I found myself inside the jeepney.

He said: "You are so lucky, Ma'am, I am going to Obrero, and I can drop you in New Asia," then he drove so fast that it scared me. I wondered if there was a law enforcing speed limits in Butuan. The jeepney ran at full speed, wind blew my hair in all directions. It felt like the pressure of air was pinching my face. There were many buildings along the way in line, and crowds of people, including students along the sidewalk waiting for a tricycle to bring them back home, but the driver did not stop to let them ride. Meanwhile, I was still in the middle of my dilemma about who I should marry. I went back and forth, asking myself repeatedly Lionel or Jason?

Feeling scared, I asked the driver to stop to let me get down from his jeepney. It seemed that he was deaf or pretending not to hear me. There were two seats facing each other: Suddenly, I saw a man seated at the end of the bench near the jeepney's entrance door, while I sat at the end of the other seat, near to the driver. I wondered, how was he able to get inside the vehicle? When the jeep did not stop at all, and the driver drove so fast, how come he was able to come aboard?

The mysterious passenger was a simple man, good looking, relaxed, and did not say a word at first. But when he stared at me, focusing on my eyes, it was like I was like magnetized and couldn't look away. He communicated with me telepathically, and vice versa. With mouth closed, he spoke to me in a low voice that was quite comforting. He indicated to me that there was something spiritually good about Lionel. I heard his voice clearly; he talked in a parable saying that Lionel was a nice guy and had promising visions. He said something would happened about Lionel's eyes, but it would be all right. That was what I understood, anyway. Then with a quick wink, he disappeared in the same manner as he appeared, leaving me alone sitting in the jeep, stupefied and confused. I glanced outside the jeepney in case I could see him, but no one was on the road.

I wondered who this man was, how he knew Lionel, and why was he telling me about Lionel's vision? I was thinking that he did not want me to ask him any questions. Perhaps, that was the ultimate reason why he had just disappeared, leaving my mind full with no answers.

I wanted to ask the driver about the mysterious man, but I was afraid he would think I was insane or hallucinating. I kept on asking myself how that strange man had known Lionel. Why was he in favour of Lionel when I'd never met him before? Who was he to tell me who to choose? I thought perhaps that the driver was also hypnotized by the mysterious passenger; was that the reason why he refused to pick up any one else on the way to Obrero?

The jeepney kept running so fast. Along the sidewalks, I recognized some people, students waiting for a ride bound to Obrero living not far from where I lived, so I asked the driver if he could let them ride too. But he categorically refused to stop.

While the jeepney was running, I continued to wonder how that mysterious man had entered the jeep and how he disappeared, as the jeepney never stopped. I finally asked the driver. " Have you seen the man in your jeep? He only shook his head. I was afraid he would think I was crazy, but it didn't matter. Then the driver stopped his jeepney at the sidewalk just in front of my parents' home. I had thrown one last glance at the jeepney, in case I would see the mysterious man again. While the driver drove away without asking me to pay.

Now I recalled and contemplated: his voice was somewhat unusual. I heard his voice from far away, and yet he was near to me in the jeepney sitting on the bench just in front of mine. I was surprised, but not scared. It was a strange feeling, hard to describe. One thing that impressed me tremendously was the way he spoke: he was confident and spoke of knowledge of certainty while staring at me and I could not quit his eyes, and he left the jeep the way he came.

I would always remember, after our first meeting in August 1979, Lionel was supposed to fetch me from my office, but he did not come. After work I went to his hotel near my office but I learned from the receptionist that he was not back, so I waited in the hotel feeling uncomfortable, praying that nothing had happened to him. There were lot of rebels who were kidnapping foreigners to earn money this way, and some victims were killed. Later, Lionel said that he had gone for a long walk with his friend Boy, and they encountered thunder and heavy rains. He came back to the hotel with his clothes and shoes drenched and invited me to enter his room. While he was rummaging through his suitcase searching for clothes, I took his soaked shoes to clean. Nolwen, my younger sister, appeared behind me. She said she did not find me in my office and the Sergeant informed her that Lionel had not come. The hotel was on her way home, so she went to see if Lionel was back. She saw me washing Lionel's shoes and said: ""So you wash Lionel's shoes in the lavabo to remove all the sticky mud?" She frowned facing me. "He is not your husband," she said, with disdain.

I answered: "I wonder why, but since I met him, I have always felt responsible for him and I couldn't duck the responsibility, even though we were just friends. There was a kind of spiritual telepathy connection that happened between us but hard to explain. I wonder about it myself." I tried to explain to Nolwen, but she seemed to ignore my answer. I went home with Lionel and Nolwen. It was the first time that Lionel stayed over night at my parent's house.

A treacherous journey from Butuan to Manila

The French language sounds like music to me. As soon as I first heard Lionel speaking French, I wanted to learn it as soon as I graduate my course in Commerce but I did not know yet when or how. Before he returned to France in September 1979, he advised me to learn French which was not taught in Butuan. I had to gather the financial means to go to Alliance Française in Manila. Another inconvenience was that I knew no one in Manila, and knew of nowhere affordable to stay. Lionel said that he would be so pleased to hear me speaking French during his next visit in the Philippines, so I could presume he was planning to come back.

The next year, in March 1980, I graduated and obtained my diploma in Commerce majoring in Business Administration. I really wanted to study the French language at that point, but I did not know yet how.

In December that year, my friend, Sally from Magallanes, working as a civilian employee in the Butuan Philippine Constabulary Administration, had just married a German, U. Johannsen. She said she needed to first stay in Manila for at least six months to learn the basics of the German language before to join her husband in Germany. She told me that if ever I was interested to learning French, I also could stay in Manila. She assured me to help me to find a student room in a boarding house there. It was an exciting opportunity and lovely of her to offer me assistance to find a place to live. It was a golden opportunity.

I was delighted to receive a letter from her saying that her Aunt in Manila, had trustworthy friends who owned and managed a student boarding house. If I would come, she could make a reservation for me before January 1981. She said vacancies were limited, I should confirm to her as soon as possible. The enrolment in Alliance Française had already started, and fortunately the school made an extension of welcoming the new students until the end of January 1981.

I felt positive about it, so I seized this rare opportunity. Lionel relied on me to give him my new address in Manila as soon as I had one. Nevertheless, I forgot to tell him that I would take a boat instead of traveling by plane. For me, the ship was cheaper, although it would take us a long time – three days – to arrive, and I had never been on board such a big boat as the ones that go to Manila. There were famous big cargo shipping lines at that time, which made ship trip from Butuan to Manila only once a week. I tried not to miss it, to get enrolled and attend classes before February.

Onboard, I discovered that I had seasickness, but I tried to pretend to be all right. However, my face betrayed the facts. I was sick and it was impossible to eat properly for three days, although I tried. After swallowing something, I would quickly vomit it up. I was fully dehydrated. In addition to this, a sea storm caught us in the middle of the Pacific Ocean just before we reached Manila. I wondered why we were out on the sea; the travel should have been postponed. Or perhaps the Captain had failed to properly consult the weather forecast before sailing. This experience is hard to forget:

The boat fought against the strong winds and huge waves of the ocean, struggling not to capsize. We all tried to save ourselves, and yet, we were not provided with lifejackets. I was in anguish, and regretted not taking the plane. The water entered the boat and swept our things away from us. Darkness engulfed us, and I did not know anymore whether it was the day or night. We were all soaked. The water was everywhere in the boat, while the wind continued blowing hard, and the giant waves continued bringing our boat with them. At the time, I did not recognize anymore whether we were facing the sky or underwater. We the passengers tried our best to keep our balance while the boat tilted badly and sometimes had big problems regaining equilibrium. Terror stayed with us all day long, and we spent scary nights, feeling hopeless.

It was for me a deliverance when our boat finally reached Manila's port. However, my friend Sally was not there and I couldn't call her from the boat. The weather returned to normal, and it was sunny and hot as if to comfort us after our horrible ordeal. But without Sally, anguish invaded me again, fearing that nobody else could take me to a place to live in metro Manila. I had no more energy, was starved, alone, vulnerable, and hopeless. I stopped thinking of Lionel and my family, I even stopped thinking about the future. My head was heavy and empty. I left everything to God.

Suddenly, a woman spoke to me, a blessing in disguise! I did not recognize her at first. She was my professor in Theology at Urios University from 1978 to 1979. She took me to her residence in Cubao, Quezon City, about 50 kilometers from the port. I did not expect that anyone would recognize me, but she was there on the boat with us. She let me shower and restored me with good food, which gave me strength. Thank God, He sent me an angel! She saved me from starvation. My faith in God grew with an endless gratitude. In my hour of need I always found someone to help me, even amid fears and the thunder of torments of hopelessness. I phoned Sally. She came to fetch me from Mrs. Balmocena's residence and brought me to the Sampaloc boarding house that she had rented for me. Once again, I had endured trials before reaching my goal. But "All's well that ends well," wrote William Shakespeare.

Sally said she came twice on two consecutive days to fetch me, but our boat was still battling against the storm in the middle of the ocean, struggling not to capsize or sink.

Thus my life as a student in Manila began. I studied French at the Alliance Française in Makati, Manila, and also enrolled at the same time in driving school. I learned how to cross streets with heavy traffic and obtained an official international driving license. Sally stayed for five days with me in the boarding house, and we talked about my hazardous ship travel. She found me so skinny and still I had sleepless nights and a lack of appetite, so she brought me to a doctor working in the University of Santo Thomas.

"I was so worried and spent sleepless nights when I learned that your boat was struggling against the storm," she said. "I was afraid that I would never see you again, although I kept hoping," she said embracing me. She had a funny way of telling me sad stories, and so we spent our days with laughter. She was expecting her first baby; her husband was coming back to Manila to bring her to Germany. Sally was inspired by Lady Diana Spencer, who got married that year (1981) to Charles, the Prince of Wales, the eldest son of Queen Elizabeth II in the UK. Thus Sally named her baby, Diane. And Sally's husband called their baby, Princess Diane.

The crowds around Pope John Paul II's visit

The Pope's official visit to the Philippines in February 1981 remains engraved in my heart. He was met at Manila International Airport by Manila Archbishop Jaime Cardinal Sin and President Ferdinand Marcos, who had lifted martial law ahead of the visit. The Pope was impressed with the warm welcome given by the University of Santo Thomas (UST), the oldest and the largest Catholic University of the Philippines.

Benita, the niece of the landlady of the boarding house went with me to the UST campus to see the Pope on that sunny day of February 18, 1981. Several road intersections were closed to traffic for security reasons. Afraid to miss the bus, we sprinted to reach the jeepney terminal. Then we had almost an hour's drive by the jeepney, because the vehicles were not allowed to park near the UST. We had to walk about 30 minutes, as there was massive traffic everywhere and so many people on the streets. It was impossible to walk at a normal pace.

We were surprised to see many people already lined up outside the UST campus entrance in the early morning. The trash cans were already full of garbage. Many even took a light breakfast in the grounds to find a convenient place to see the Pope. Others had spent the night on campus in a queue in order to occupy the best places. To be sure not to miss the Pope, we joined the queue against a metallic barrier or fence near the road where the Pope in his special vehicle was supposed to pass. I no longer remember how long we stayed in that line that continued to grow. But knowing that it was probably our only chance to experience a once-in-a-lifetime historical event, I was thrilled to personally bear witness and pay respect to the Pope, time did not matter.

Despite the sun, we persevered sitting on the ground with umbrellas and some hats in different forms on the people's heads, protecting their eyes with various styles and colours of sunglasses. Benita and I did the same, so we were protected from the searing heat of midday. We remained silent to preserve some strength before the arrival of the Pope, finding out that he was delayed. The UST campus was by then filled with masses of people from the three significant regions of the Philippines: Luzon, Visayas, and Mindanao. We were all there, ready to pay homages to Pope John Paul II.

When it was announced that the Pope was arriving, in the queue we all kneeled to say a short and relatively fast prayer. Then we stood up to cheer and welcomed him.

The crowds started jostling when the Pope approached the entrance gate of the campus. The police guards blew their horns and whistles, instructing people to calm down. Benita and I stood up, putting our hands on the fence while the people started getting so close to us that we could smell their underarm odors and perspiration.

Once the Pope's car came near, the crowd became hysterical and uncontrollable. There was so much pushing to try to approach the Pope. He came down from his car and started shaking people's hands. The police were unable to withstand the pressure of the crowd and were overwhelmed.

I looked up to the face of the Pope. Our eyes met, and I could feel his Holiness. I was about to grasp his holy hand when suddenly the fence broke, and I was knocked down. I was savagely crushed and trampled by the crowd behind me. The people were like a troop of elephants running across us. We had been waiting for long hours, all for one brief blessed moment, and yet I was not able to touch his holy hands. For me, he was a Saint. After our eyes met, he became a part of me. But with the barrier collapsed, and the crowd was walking on it, the group continued to crush me. (I said the evil was there again to prevent me from holding the Pope's hands). Then I heard Benita calling my name before I fainted.

I awoke at dawn on a military hospital bed, where an Army officer was sitting down on a chair beside me. He told me at once that he was a doctor and that I was in the Philippine Army Hospital. My head was aching, and I felt pain all over my body. I noticed the curtain behind the doctor. I understood I was not alone in that hospital room. He took something from the front pocket of his uniform, he pressed the button, and another doctor came; he was a Captain who was probably their head doctor. He said they were happy to see me awake, as they had been waiting the whole night. He said that I was lucky as the radiology result showed that no bones were broken, but I had some serious bruising throughout my body. I did not know I was examined. Although they reassured me that I could go out soon, they said I should stay 24 hours in the hospital for observation.

The Army officer asked me what had happened. I told him that I only spent a brief moment with Pope John Paul II, when the crowd went hysterical, and the barriers fell, and I was crushed.

The bottle of Dextrose on an IV into my arm, and I did not know what treatments I received in the army hospital, but I was feeling very sleepy. I was not able to finish my statement to the officer.

Benita and her cousin Helen came to visit me with Sally in the hospital. They showed me my torn-off clothes, with broken and unusable blue sandals, the umbrella totally torn off, and my handbag almost empty which had lost its handles. I thought that the Army had also looked at my identity card, my badge as civilian employee of the Philippine Army, and my student card, which I had forgotten to take back as I was forgetful. I had to go home to our boarding house without them. I would have like to go back to the Army hospital in Quezon City, but it was too far from where we lived, and it would have taken more time and expenses.

Benita, Sally, and all my co-boarders said that I was fortunate to have encountered the Pope in Manila and to have survived, as there were people who died in the crowd but the media had never publicized the number. And although I was unhappy about the crowd preventing me from grasping Pope Jean Paul II's holy hand, I had the lasting memory of seeing him in front of me, when his eyes met mine.

Before going to France, I remember that pastor who once had advised me to avoid the crowd and the ocean while I was still in the Philippines. So there was my boat, nearly capsizing on the Pacific Ocean, and I had my adventure in the huge crowd and could have died during the visit of the Pope. So I can almost believe that I was already predestined to live all these adventures. I sensed once again that my life was already written, because I am powerless to change it.

I would never forget the whisper in my ears on a tender voice when I was awoken in our small balcony at home who said: "It is your second life." So I have this conviction that my life was planned out even before I was born. After my near-drowning, I was living a blessed second life, which was nourished with a substantial variety of trials and hurdles, ever since my accident in the Agusan river in 1962.

Lionel Comes Back for Marriage

One day I was hanging out in bed, on a day when I didn't have French classes in Alliance Française in Manila. But I hopped up when I heard the postman pronouncing my name for his morning delivery. My co-boarders who were mostly students who treated me like their auntie were even more excited than me.

"Wow, another letter for you Ate Sarah," they would say, enviously. I received Lionel's letters almost every day, and it was very moving. It blew my mind.

Lionel came to Philippines for the third time in 1981, and it was so different from the previous two years as this time he came to marry me. I was full of intense emotions and feeling overwhelmed. Everything felt different around me. I didn't know how to express it. I had not known that I was capable of feeling this difficult mix of emotions: anxiety and happiness together, but also some questions lingered in my mind. What if I came to regret my decision? I knew he was not perfect, and neither was I. No matter what, I yearned to see him again and to reaffirm that the love for him was real, and different than anything I had felt before.

My friends were also excited to meet him. They were counting the days until the date of his arrival. Benita and I went together straight to the Remil Apartel (the hotel where you can also cook) to make him a reservation. It was a well-furnished hotel-apartment which include fully equipped kitchen with modern facilities, including an efficient electric hood that absorbed the smell of any cooked foods. We had everything we would need. The wide lounge had two comfortable armchairs, two sofas and everything for our comforts, a large bedroom with two windows and a king-sized bed. There was also a spacious bathroom with granite tiles, and the best services from the hotel employees. The only drawback were the sounds from the busy road, and I found it quite noisy at night.

Unfortunately, before I could see Lionel in person, there was a challenge; he had to have an operation on his left eye in May 1981 just three months before the date of our marriage. Lionel said he could never forget that day; it was also was the day of the presidential election in France. I did not hear from him for 10 days. When he asked me as to whether I would still have the intention to marry him: I said yes, no matter what. Deep in my heart I couldn't deny how much I loved him. Then I remember what the mysterious man in the jeepney told me; I now understood what he said.

Despite everything, Lionel came on the 3rd of August 1981. Two nieces of my landlady, accompanied me with enthusiasm to fetch Lionel from Ninoy Aquino International Airport. Luckily for me, the other girls were working. They would have had all wanted to go with me. In truth, I would have preferred to welcome Lionel by myself as he arrived, so I could concentrate on him alone.

Civil wedding in Manila

My stay in Manila was a beautiful experience that had lasted only for a short period of six months, but had been busy with hectic activities: I attended French classes three times a week, along with obtaining my driver's licence. I drove the car with my monitor back and forth between Cubao, Quezon City and Makati. I was always writing letters to Lionel, and I took up crocheting during my free time, making him a full bed cover before he reached Manila.

We learned that it was possible to get married in Manila. Thus, we held a civil wedding solemnized by the City Judge of the City Court of Manila, on August 17, 1981, witnessed by Atty. Maramba and Mrs. Rilioraza, my landlady.

Everything was going smoothly although we were so stressed because of the heavy traffic in Metro Manila in going to the Hall of the Court of Justice. We celebrated our union in a favorite restaurant with our godparents. Lionel and I had been impressed by the Filipina Administrative Secretary who spoke French fluently in the French Embassy. At that time, my French was mediocre, and I was longing to soon speak French fluently like Madame Zapanta. The French Ambassador, Monsieur Albert Treca, warmly welcomed us and gave Lionel an extension to his visa by 10 days. This was welcome but it was not enough for the fulfillment of the obligatory requirements demanded by the Catholic Church.

Ship voyage back to Butuan

We've planned to get married in the church in Butuan surrounded by my family, although I was skeptical that Lionel could stay long enough as his visa would expire in 15 days, despite the extension granted by the French Embassy. We had waited more than two weeks before our civil marriage in Manila, and waited another week for the remaining necessary papers from the French Embassy to be presented for a church wedding, hopefully in France.

I wondered how we could bring all the things, particularly the food. I had bought a lot of goods for cooking, such as rice, fruit, and vegetables like ampalaya and eggplant, vegetable oil, flour, sugar, butter, eggs, bottles of fruit juice etc. They would be good for at least eight days. I even bought some *sab-a banana* to be fried as I really love to eat *maruya*, but I had cooked only few of these things, as Lionel and I were always out visiting different places in Manila. We took long walks everyday around the city and around Manila Bay. We took our meals in the restaurant and usually went home late at night to the hotel, tired and worn out. We left some of those goods in the hotel. We wanted to give them to cleaning ladies, but they refused to accept them, although I was quite sure they needed them; they said it was prohibited by the hotel and the could lose their jobs. I then decided to bring those to my family in Butuan.

With a roll of strong string. Lionel tied each carton with abaca fibre forming a rope for a handle to make easier to carry. We packed all those things for us to take to Butuan by boat, as we couldn't bring the cartons to the plane. We had a cabin with two beds, and everything was alright by then. But there were no boats to bring us directly to Butuan without stopping over in Cebu. We would be venturing down to Cebu, then transfer onto another boat that would bring us to Butuan. I was feeling reassured so that I already had bought two tickets for the ship, although I couldn't forget my dark experience of January 1981 when the boat hit the tropical storm. That time I came to Manila by boat because it was cheaper compared to the plane ticket; but this time was different because Lionel was with me.

At the dock, two porters installed our cartons and baggage altogether inside the big trolley and brought them directly to our cabin. Our journey in the boat from Manila to Cebu was excellent. No sea sickness this time. The ocean was gently calm. We stayed in a private cabin with all our stuff. I was happy to find a comfortable room, a double-sized bed already made up with bedsheets and blankets, and small round table with two wooden chairs. We ordered our dinner in our cabin. Everything was going well. We visited the open veranda of the boat, and breathed the fresh air smelling of sea water. We stayed almost two hours observing the half-moon and bright stars in the sky. The weather was good, humid, and hot. A drunk man sang with his guitar swallowing the song's words, prevented us from sleep earlier. Other passengers asked him to stop singing but he yelled at them.

We both slept soundly past dawn. We were awakened with slight motions of the sea around eight in the morning, and we were hungry. I had a small pack of chocolate powder and coffee in my bag. I ordered a thermos of hot water and a teapot of hot milk, and we ate the croissants that I had kept in my bag. That was the only meal we had got for the whole day and night.

Porters and The Kidnappers

Our boat had a stop-over in Cebu and were obliged to transfer to another boat that would bring us to Butuan. But there was no good organization in the port.

We were counting all our baggage when suddenly three different men were handling our cartons and baggage, and they carried them away from us. My husband was surprised when porters were grabbing our luggage from our hands, they were like hungry wolves flocked into their foods. Everyone wanted to carry our personal belongings. One porter was already on the way to the other boat for Butuan running away far from us carrying our two cartons, the second was carrying my luggage and the third carried Lionel's luggage who again wanted to carry Lionel's hand luggage. In fact, those baggage could be carried in only one trolley like what we had in Manila.

Meanwhile, Lionel was holding firmly to his personal luggage when he was accosted by the porters. They grabbed at the bags by grasping the handle, and it broke. Their ferocity, like animals, scared me; they persisted arguing with us in loud, violent voices. And despite our firm refusal that they should not carry our personal belongings, as we were capable of carrying them by ourselves, they successfully prevented us from taking hold of them. They were even arguing who could be the first one to carry our luggage. I had never expected that things can be happened this way. Lionel was fully overwhelmed to the porters and I was embarrassed by their wild attitude.

I looked around the area and confirmed that Lionel was the only foreigner present that day, so he was preyed upon by wild porters. At the midst of this exasperation, I was angry with our Philippine government for failing to enforce laws and regulations to improve the methods of welcoming foreigners. They needed to educate and professionalize porters, so that they would attract the tourists to come to Philippines, instead of terrifying them.

Lionel burst out with anger and his face turned red while staring at me. I could not find a way to evade his angry glances. I felt a horrible discomfort. I was ashamed of the reality, ashamed why people in my own country and of my own race acted in that way; I was ashamed that those porters were targeting him, were disrespectful and out of control. Because of anger, I can no longer think efficiently. Lionel's attitude seemed to have greatly changed. Perhaps he was showing me the real Lionel when he got angry. We were just newlyweds, but I wondered whether I could remain his wife longer if this situation would happen again.

Fears invaded me, I was wondering how I could explain to my husband to convince him that he needed to just trust the porters, then it would be alright; that the porters would be hopefully waiting for us with all our things. What made him terribly mad was the incontestable wild behavior of the men. Lionel stared at me and said furiously: "What did your bloody government do with their political powers to dare to allow their savage porters to treat a stranger like me in your country?" What he said had hurt me. It was an insult but also the truth.

On the way to the boat, Lionel did not say a word. I continued walking and he just followed me, still angry. The temperature was more than 39 degrees under the heat of the sun luckily Lionel loved a hot climate. While my perspiration was dripping from my whole body, sweaty hands moistened my bag, and my clothes stuck to my skin. The salty taste of sweat dropped onto my lips. Sweat stung my eyes and prevented me from seeing Lionel's face, protected by his hat. I could hardly breathe, being affected by the dust and lack of fresh air; I should have had a hat like him. I was wiping my face with my small handkerchief from my pocket and tied my long hair back with my wet handkerchief.

I was thirsty but no bottle of water to drink. I felt dizzy. I was about to fall, though I tried to breathe in, despite the polluted hot air around. As if a hairdryer blowing hot air to my head. My intestines thumbling upside down and I wanted to release the congestion of gas and stress in my stomach to prevent me from fainting. At the same time I had a ringing sound in my ears. Cold sweat covered my face and despite the heat of the sun I felt chilled; my vision became blurred. I bent down to my knees and I fell to the ground but remained conscious. I vomited while pressing hard on my stomach, until the pain had gradually disappeared. Then I felt a little better.

I did not know anymore where Lionel was. But I was quite reassured that my handbag was still on my shoulder that I intentionally crossed over across my breast from left shoulder to the right side of my waist. I glanced farther ahead again but crowds of people blocked my view. Some children yelled, others cried looking for their mothers, and some wooden trollies filled with baggage had prevented me to see further to check if Lionel was still on the wharf.

Suddenly, a man said: "You are looking for the Americano?" He thought that Lionel was an American. "Oh yes please," I said smiling at him.

"There, he is standing in front of the boat," he said pointing. I sprinted towards Lionel not to make him wait much longer. I wondered how long he was standing in the same place without moving, I even forgot about the porters.

I wondered if he had noticed that I was sick or perhaps he just ignored me. Anyway, he waited for me. We walked on the flat ironed-metal small passarella with metal chain as security handrail at the middle to secure the passengers going in and out from the boat. There was also an iron flat metal as security border that prevented the passengers from falling into the water.

We had requested a private cabin, but we were frustrated when the crew said it did not exist on that boat from Cebu to Butuan. However, we were relieved to find the porters waiting for us to get them paid. Our tickets did not mention any bed numbers, so we could just choose the right place for us. However, I was unhappy to see some people lying down uncomfortably on top of their baggage, instead of lying on a bed.

I understood there were not enough beds for all the passengers. It worried me. Anguish took over and I was unable how to think clearly. Was it legal to allow all those people on board? I was hoping that the cargo-ship was not over loaded. Then again, I remembered the incident of January 1981.

I closed my eyes, searching for some relief. I spent energy to convince myself to stay strong. I said to myself: "Be brave Sarah. You can manage it. Remain calm and think positively of your objective and help yourself. It is not the right time to faint or fall. Take back your spirit and breathe deeply." Then I began to recover.

After that experience, I developed a phobia: whenever I see baggage and porters together, no matter where: it is either porter in the airport or porters in the port, it triggers in me a wave of cultural shock. I feel invaded with panic, discomfort, and insecurity that leads my mind and thoughts into complete paralysis. Sometimes I search for a place to hide or someone to comfort me, but at the same time I need to be alone, away from the trigger, or feeling the nausea preventing me to eat.

With our bad experience with the porters during our transfer, I was already thinking of our eventual arrival in Butuan dock. I went down from the ship to send a telegram to my parents to inform them that we were arriving Butuan the following morning. I reminded Lionel not to leave the bed to ensure that nobody would take our stuff by mistake.

It took me 35 minutes walking and I excitedly hurried up my pace once I spotted the sign announcing, "Telegram here." There was nobody inside, but I had to wait. A man in his 50s appeared, wearing old fashioned eye glasses which fell to the tip of his nose. He bent his head to stare at me and then raised his head when glancing to the form I was filling in. My mind kept on telling me to hurry up and leave the place urgently, as I had a feeling of imminent danger approaching. I tried writing my text correctly, while the pen was sliding in my sweaty fingers. I was nervous and all my thoughts were to rejoin my husband in the ship. I knew he was so impatient to reach Butuan to be away from the boat. I prayed he won't be worried of my absence. The images of the wild porters refused to leave my head; I had read the evil in their face. And I suddenly felt very uncomfortable, sensing danger around me.

My fear was not diminished. Kidnappers, disguised as gentlemen, were there waiting for me ready to trap me. Forty years had passed since this incident, but the uncomfortable feeling of fear resurfaces while writing my kidnapping experiences; strong emotions and anger remain palpable until today, which is sometimes too difficult to cope.

I looked around, trying to guess which way to take to go back to the boat. I briefly thought of buying sandwiches for lunch. But a man appeared facing me, looking almost elegant with well-trimmed moustache, wearing a white T-shirt and a pair of dark jeans. He greeted me with a smile.

"Hello Ma'am, I was in the boat, Escaño Lines, like you," he said blocking my way. I continued walking and he stayed to my right.

"We have enough time to take our lunch in the restaurant before going back to the boat," he said, insisting.

"Thank you, mister. But I need to go back to the boat," I said, and stepped forward pretending not to be scared. However, a second man wearing sunglasses, taller than the first, with bulging muscles in his biceps, appeared at my left side. I scanned their faces. They were band of gangsters. My fears grew as I was trapped between them. They said they were friends, and that they needed take the same Butuan ship as me. They insisted that we still had three hours before departure, which was true. But I was not duped to believe that he was going to Butuan. Not at all.

They became so talkative trying to bully me, which augmented my fears. I did not know them and their manner of talking showed me they were Cebuano and Ilonggo, living in Cebu; it meant they knew every corner of Cebu Island while I had never been there before. They kept on talking stupid and non-sensensical topics. I sped up my pace trying to get rid of them, and by the time I started to run away from them, quickly, a third bandit appeared behind me pressing a knife against my back. I was scared stiff and bewildered when a jeepney without passengers appeared in front of us. They held my arms and forced me to get inside. I begged them, in vain, to let me go. Anguish invaded me while my thoughts were with my husband on the ship.

The first man mocked me with a devilish grin, saying that his friend was only joking so I had no reason to be afraid. I glanced quickly to the other jeep behind to see if some passengers could see me and understand that I needed urgent assistance. I wanted to yell to get their attention, but the man placed his hand on my head. He looked at me fixedly and pushed me into the jeep on the bench until I was sitting next to the driver. I noticed two other men with the driver, but I was unable to see their faces.

The driver drove the jeepney very fast; I could no longer read the signs with the names of the streets. I did not know where I was; all I knew was that we were getting further from the boat. I was captured by six men including the driver. I prayed that someone would rescue me.

Traumatized, I couldn't hold back my tears. My sunglasses fell down my slippery nose, wet with tears, and the sweat had never dried, despite the increasing pace of the jeepney. I thought about how there were six men against me. I needed to absolutely find a trick on how to escape from abductors. But how?

Every time I moved, the man pressed the knife to my back that touched my spine; the pain became unbearable. I tried to glance again to the jeepney behind, to see if other accomplices were following us. I planned to jump to the moving jeep beside ours. Unluckily, the men at my side held firmly my arms while pressing me back, which prevented me from turning my head. My plan to escape was doomed to fail. Oh my Lord Jesus Christ, please rescue me.

Being vigilant to the man holding my left arm, I noticed his tick: his left eyelid moved, and he always scratched his head leaving only one hand that was holding my arm. I thought of using that single second to kick him and run away. When I moved to stand, the third man pushed my head down again. He got up and blocked the entrance door. How could I escape now?

He ordered the driver to speed up, which had now gone about two kilometres from the telegraphic centre. But I did not know anymore the time or how far we were from our ship. I was so worried that the ship would leave the port without me, hoping that Lionel could cope with the worry. I knew he loved me, and I loved. him. I remained strong for him and prayed God would help us both. I needed a strategy to achieve my plan to escape from those cursed bandits. I was so scared that I couldn't think clearly anymore. I sobbed inside.

The jeepney stopped suddenly, pushing our heads together so I could smell the sweat and breath of the kidnappers on either side of me, which made me feel nauseous. The man who sat with the driver went down. He entered the jeep and stayed standing at the entrance, now there were two men blocking the door, while the driver remained silent and my chance of escaping became more and more remote. I was losing my energy and tried to save my strength, waiting for the right time to fight against them. The next steps were horrible, because they placed my hands at my back, tied with strong tape, and put tape over my mouth too. Although it freaked me out, I remained steady, pretending to be calm while keeping alert and thinking about how to attack them and flee.

The fifth man remained sitting with the driver. The jeepney stopped in front of a house which had windows all covered with strong iron bars. I refused to climb the staircase, but it was impossible to escape. I was warned not to make any noise, but I yelled for help under the tape. One man carried me nervously on his shoulder to the first floor and threw me onto the couch. They ordered me not to move otherwise they would kill me. It was like a nightmare. I was asking God that no matter what would happen to me, Lionel must be able to return back home to France safely.

Four bandits stayed around me. I felt hopeless and stopped praying to God. One of them took off the tape brutally from over my mouth and said: "If you don't stop crying, we will cover your head." They were playing poker and asked me to participate. I answered them that honestly I did not know anything about playing cards, but they insisted and laughed at me.

One of them opened one bottle of beer and ordered me to drink it: "Poor girl you must be thirsty now," he said with a horrendous look. I pretended to drink, and they were all laughing. They played cards with money and they talked in Ilonggo, a kind of dialect that I didn't understand very well. They continued laughing and mocking me. I felt the boiling blood rising to my face.

They told me to give them 100 pesos. I opened my bag with difficulty because my hands were tied, but I was surprised; there was not a single peso left. They had already taken all the money from my handbag; only Lionel's watch with a broken band was left. There, I finally understood why they had always laughed mocking at me. I was begging them to let me go now. Why did they still need to keep me with them?

One of them removed the tape around my hands and instructed me to follow him in how to play with the cards. I answered again that I didn't know how to play, and they became very nervous. I did not understand why they burst out in laughter. One man came back with more bottles of beers, several packets of peanuts and cigarettes, reminding his companions to drink their beers afterwards. After what? I really did not know why and what they had to do before drinking.

I kept this episode of my life secret for 40 years now, and still I am reluctant to write these lines because it reminds me of my shock and terror: Five men wanted to rape me! I was petrified, full of apprehension upon hearing their evil words and seeing their perversity and sexual hunger.

My tears and stickened perspsiration augmented while facing a horrible scene. My anxiety heightened when one of them pulled me roughly against him. He pasted a new tape over my mouth, took off his trousers and touched me all over my body. I was so angry, my blood roared in my ears. When I tried to move away he became wild while the others were impatiently watching behind him. He ordered me not to move or I would be tied up, while he was telling his accomplices to wait for their turn. I felt as if I was losing my mind feeling the terror of their devilish desire. All the while, I was thinking of how I could defend myself against all those monstres.

I left my destiny to God, as I was helpless against them. Despite it being 40 years ago, the trauma I felt remains palpable even now. My hand shakes while writing these lines.

The men were distracted when someone yelled loudly in their dialect from downstairs. Everyone started to panic; one man quickly went downstairs, then another followed him, leaving three men around me. The noises downstairs became louder. They were fighting, arguing in a language I didn't understand.

Suddenly, the door opened wide, and the fifth man reappeared with his t-shirt stained red and a knife in his hand dripping with blood.

"The driver did not obey so I killed him," he said as he approached me. I was frozen stiff. Suddenly my fears awakened my defensive instincts. I sprinted, tumbling over the sofa while the three men were still seated. When they stood up, I kicked them violently though I felt the pain in my legs. But the men were all on the floor. My versatile *bakya*, my wooden sandal, was probably very painful when it hit their bodies. I threw the unopened bottles of beers towards them, which broke after they struck, and the knife fell to the floor. They were all surprised and I did not really know how I did it. I was surprised myself too, or maybe I remembered all tricks from judo-karate I learned long ago for self-defence. Perhaps they had never expected me to be capable of defending myself.

I recovered my lost hope. I darted towards the opened door, but one bastard followed me. I kicked him twice or more that hit his privates first, and he groaned with the pain; I dashed past him out of the door and hastily jumped over the staircase and fled. I ran as fast as I could while yelling for help.

"Help me! Please call the police! Help! Kidnappers are after me, please call the police!" I yelled repeatedly. I continued running further not along the road, but behind the houses, across the uncultivated fields, and I heard some people from their windows.

"What happened?" they asked curiously.

My pace decreased when my versatile bakya became slippery, moistened by the wet grasses. "Kidnappers are following me, please call the police!" I said, and I hurried up my pace to hide behind the trees. I heard a jeepney and I felt breathless. I jumped over the shrubs and bushes, sometimes crossing small roads when I did not have the choice. I tried to avoid the roads as I thought they might take the jeepney to trap me. I kept on running, not knowing where to go. I stumbled on the harsh bumpy ground, and on the roots gripping the ground, but I stood up again and kept running. I didn't know how long, but my fears gave me the energy and strength to run. I continued running until my legs felt numb.

Then after a point my chest tightened, and my strength started to abandon me. I fell on my knees. I heard the sound of drums in my ears. I tried to resist, but the surroundings darkened. I fainted.

Escape, police and investigation

I found myself lying on the ground near the roadside full of thick grass and stones. I was surrounded by curious people and among them were the police. All their faces were watching me.

"Miss, wake up," they said. Their voices sounded like drums in my ears while I smelled something strong in my nostrils and I awoke. My hair and clothes were wet. Someone said they poured fresh water on to my face to wake me up. My sunglasses had disappeared. A woman gave me a glass of water to drink, and a clean handkerchief to wipe my face. She told me that her young son was taking a walk with his dog and found me unconscious. I learned later that she was the wife of the policeman in uniform who questioned me, surrounded by those curious people. But I was incapable of saying a word. It took me some seconds to remember what had happened, where I was and why I was there.

Then I revealed to the police the atrocities of the kidnappers, describing their appearance and the house where they brought me. Among the crowd, a man said: "Ahh, I know some of those men; some of my friends who are now living abroad were also their victims." The police asked the man to ride in his car and identify the kidnappers at the police station, but he was hesitant. "But Sir, today is my day off," he whispered. I understood that he was also a police sergeant in civilian attire.

The police insisted on bringing me to the police station of Cebu City to file a complaint against the six kidnapers and identify them. But all my thoughts were with Lionel. I kept on begging him to inform my husband that I am alright now and safe, that the police needed to contact the Captain of the boat at once before it would be too late. I needed him to tell them not to let the boat leave the dock without me. I was not sure whether the police were really aware of my worries, as he did not even ask the name of my husband.

So I told him: "Well Sir, I will go with you to the police station, but you must promise me that you will bring me to the boat before it leaves at 6:30 in the evening." I really insisted.

"Yes Ma'am, don't worry," he finally answered. He talked to his radio with a high antenna. He made reports, probably to his Chief, and gave some orders to his subordinates then we left in the police patrol jeep.

As the car speeds forward, I was so impatience to reach to the police station, but there was a lot of traffic, many vehicles and red lights along our way. The siren was on, but our journey to the police station was far too long as we spent more than an hour which seemed an eternity, and increased my nervousness. Lionel was in danger of leaving without me, and I felt his worries of my long absence. Unable to hold back my emotions, I sobbed again.

"The crew of the boat is now aware of the problem and extended the maximum of 1 hour and 45 minutes for the departure," said the chief. I asked the Sergeant to read my declaration of complaint that he typed. They were using a very old typewriter. He read it, but I did not sign because it was not complete. My demand to give me back my money was not indicated; they failed to mention it, so I went to see their Chief, but he was not anymore in his office. I found him in the next office seated comfortably with a telephone in his hand and at this point, I was determined to ask him for an explanation.

"Sir, I must get back the money. I won't go back to my boat without it," I insisted. He was surprised to see me again. He'd thought I was gone. He pretended to forget that I did not live in Cebu. I reminded him that I needed to catch a boat where my husband is waiting.

"Ma'am if you will take back your money, Ma'am, the kidnappers will have another victim as we would be obliged to let them free. You should leave it here as proof of their culpability and they will be judged," he answered firmly. But I did not agree to that blackmail. I argued, and started to get upset with the whole situation.

"Sir, have you forgotten they had kidnapped me? They should be judged and be condemned for that," I said. He did not answer. It was getting complicated that I felt the hot blood rushing up to my head, and I felt dizzy and weak. I was bursting with anger and same time I tried to control my emotions.

"Sir, I have no time to wait for the hearing and the judgement. My husband and I will use that money for our marriage celebration and will leave soon for France. Please allow me to use your telephone and I will call my Commander in the 4th Infantry Division in Bancasi or the Secretary of National Defense, General Juan Ponce Enrile in the General Headquarters of the Philippine Army in Manila; they will surely take care of your problem of how to condemn the kidnapers and put them in jail for a long period of time. May I mention your name?" I declared while staring to his uniform and his name plate. I prayed he was convinced.

He remained silent for a while. Maybe he did not expect of my reaction. I tried to make him understand indirectly that my parents, who had surely received my telegram, would have already contacted the Philippine Army, and would come to his office for investigation. I showed to him my identity papers, and told him to verify if he wishes and I gave him the name of my superiors in the Philippine Army assigned in Bancasi, and in the headquarters of the Philippine Army in Camp Evangelista.

I asked him if he needed the name of the Commander of the Philippine Constabulary in Butuan.

He answered by shaking his head, remained silent for a while, then he told me to wait. When he came back, he asked me to follow him and this time, we both entered his office. There, I found the Sergeant who brought me in his car, seated on the chair in front of their chief. I was sure he had checked all the evidence because he finally gave me back the remaining money. I requested him to allow me to say goodbye to the kidnappers as I was full of questions over them. "I knew where they are," I said.

There, I stood in front of the kidnappers staring into their eyes without saying a word. This time, they did not laugh or mock at me anymore; they stood like beaten dogs. The police had hit them to return the entire amount of money that they took from my bag. But the bandits said they had partied, and they bought drinks like beer, whiskey, and cigarettes, peanuts etc. It was weird, I almost felt sorry for them, but I was thinking of the other victims, and they should be punished for that.

They were begging me to grant them my pardon, but they had cruelly humiliated and freaked me out; they would have raped me if they hadn't been interrupted. They did not deserve my pardon. I left my husband in the ship worried of my absence, and I experienced unbearable fears and anguishes. At that time, I did not know yet that my husband had also been attacked by their colleagues, and they were all complicit.

"Now you must pay all your debts not only to me but to all your victims," I told them before I left. The Sergeant did not say a word. I followed him to his car with a noisy engine where another Sergeant in civil attire was already comfortable in his seat. We rode for more than an hour in silence.

I was relieved I was able to express myself without fear to the Chief of the police who was well-known for his toughness.

"Nobody talked to him the way you did," said the Sergeant. I was so tired and at the end of my energy. I was crying, and that was my problem. I easily cried. I was meditating and I kept on praying to God to keep Lionel safe despite all, and to not let the boat depart before I could join him on board.

The two policemen remained silent, so that we had only heard the bizarre sound of the car's engine. Despite that noise, I recognized the siren of the boat's warning of departure, so loud that I heard it from far distance.

"It's our boat!" I said, yelling with stress while my heart pounded. I stopped crying but I became so nervous again, afraid that the boat would leave without me. I asked them to please speed up and get there before the boat can leave the port.

"Madame, please calm down, the jeep is at maximum speed and it's so dangerous. We must be very careful not to hit any people," they said.

The car was zigzagging along the road amidst heavy traffic, while keeping vigilant that no vehicles will cross us or crash. I was so tense and fearful that I closed my eyes while praying for everyone's safety. Finally, the car had stopped just about 20 meters in front of the boat. I did not have enough time to bid goodbye to the Sergeants. I jumped out of the jeep and sprinted to the boat which was preparing for departure. My anxieties grew when they had started to lower the mooring. I was really afraid that the passarella would be completely removed, and I would be left behind. I was incapable to hold back my emotions that I cried of joy upon walking to the metal gateway that brought me inside the ship.

I thanked God for bringing me in on time; and this time, I waved my hands to the Sergeants waiting in the harbour.

Knowing that the bandits were in prison, I had no regret of coming to the police station. I had taken back most of the money, and the police brought me to dock where the boat was launching. The departure was delayed for more than two hours because the Captain and the crew were waiting for me. I felt an endless gratitude to God.

Bandits attack Lionel

I found my husband in the same place where I had left him. Lionel was sitting on his bed, weary with his head hanging down and an iron chain in his hand. He seemed terribly angry and though I felt sad, I was happy to have found him.

I sat beside him and told him at once that I had been kidnapped and was brought to an empty house guarded by iron bars, but he did not answer. He didn't even bother to look at me. I did not really know if he had understood what I said, but I felt his pain. He must have been very worried to my disappearance. I would have loved to hear his thoughts at that very moment. He was so quiet, and I began to cry again. How I needed him this time. I wanted to throw myself into a hug with him and find comfort. I was disappointed, but at the same time I understood what he had experienced. He turned his head away from me when I started to talk. I felt his sorrows gnawing at me.

Several questions battled in my head. Did he lose his trust in me? I decided not to bother him anymore and let him rest. We did not eat our lunch, although I was sure he was hungry, I regretted being unable to buy something to eat for dinner, when I was kidnapped.

I removed all our belongings I had placed on my bed and put them all on the floor. I contemplated sitting on my bed, and when I turned my head, Sister Cecilia, my cousin, was also on the boat sitting on her bed. I was so happy to see her; I knew everything would be fine now. I joined her with sigh of relief. I confided in her everything about what had happened that day, my fears against the savage porters and their wild behaviour, the evil kidnappers that needed to be punished, the challenging escape, the interrogations by the police, my fear of missing the boat, and worrying about Lionel alone on the ship that might have left without me. Those events were very hard to cope with, all on the same day. Now I needed to convince my husband to forget those trials, although it would be hard. Sister Cecille was like my guardian angel. She calmed my anxieties and we talked until midnight. She said I must banish those dark experiences from my head and concentrate on expressing my love and compassion to my husband, as he had maybe also experienced anguish and worries during my absence.

I tried to rest and empty my mind. I was exhausted and the night seemed to sympathize with me. Even the sea tried to help by offering slight waves, but I did not sleep a wink all night. I had an unhappy state of mind regarding my husband. I needed him to bring me some comfort and vice-versa; that would lead us to find a feeling of inner peace and happiness despite everything. But his silence hurt me.

Did he sleep? We had not eaten lunch nor or dinner; I was very sorry for that. The boat did not offer anything. It was not mealtime, but we were hungry. I went to the kitchen bar and asked for a cup of hot milk. They only gave me hot water but I drank it. We talked about my kidnapping and my husband's reaction, and he offered me a coffee. I never drink coffee, so I brought it to Lionel. He drank it without hesitation, as he was terribly hungry. I was ashamed of those undesirable events done by my compatriots. I was ashamed because they were my fellowmen, and ashamed of the police system in my own country. I did not even know yet at that time that Lionel had difficulties with his heart. Nobody knew about his congenital heart problems, not even his mother. He did not know yet himself that he had been born with problems.

At five in the morning, most passengers were taking their breakfast sitting on their bed or eating around the table. I went near the kitchen and asked the staff if we could have a little breakfast.

"Yes of course," they said, "show me your ticket."

I told him that because of the kidnapping I lost all my papers. He gave me a cup of hot milk this time and two slices of American bread and some butter for me and Lionel. Sister Cecille said she had taken her lunch before she came to the boat, and one cup of coffee in the morning was enough, so she gave Lionel the extra two slices of bread and drank the small cup of coffee. But I knew he needed a big cup of coffee every morning. I remember when he said: "With a big bowl of coffee I could go around the world." I handed a little money to the cook and he gave me a second small cup of coffee for Lionel, and a piece of red banana for me, so I was satisfied.

Lionel speaks to me, at last

Lionel felt better after the light breakfast. I talked to him again about the kidnapping and this time he listened to me. Now I learned that he had not understood that I was kidnapped.

"How were you able to escape from the kidnappers?" he asked. I told him almost everything and he took a long profound breath of relief. Then he talked of his terrible worries and fears; he recounted what happened during my absence, still in state of anger. He said:

"I was surrounded by thugs from the mafia who wanted me to leave my bed and remove the things on your bed," he said repeatedly. His expression proved me his fears, that being without me at his side on the boat was something that no one would wish to experience.

"I wondered what you had been doing. Your long absence worried me, and I did not know how I could have helped you," he added with immense emotion. How I had these feelings of pain for him! He pulled me close against his chest, and I felt his powerful love.

He was traumatized. He said: "A few moments after you left, two men asked me to move from my bed and remove all the things you left on your bed. They wanted me to transfer the baggage to another place. They had been stalking me, but I remained seated, and I told them that was the bed for my wife."

"Perhaps they just wanted to take the baggage," I said.

"They left after I showed them that I could defend myself with a metal chain I brought on my travels, for emergencies. I thought they had gone. But they came back and sat on my bed and they insisted on telling me to leave the belongings. I told them that I would call for the police, making as if I could kick them with my strong pair of boots, and they left again."

He continued, "They came back a third time to urged me again to go away from my bed, but I remained sitting and I told them firmly, showing again the chain and my strong pair of boots, warning them not to insist anymore. All the other passengers were watching us. The three men finally left for good. I was determined to hit them if ever they ever came back, but I did not know what would happen next," he said sadly.

He had finally expressed his fears and anger while he embraced me, followed by a long sigh of bliss. Lionel's life had been in danger, because he had received a shock when he was confronted alone by the threatening bandits. He had tackled his fear and he had resisted. Life had been cruel to both of us that day. But God had saved us.

It was my turn to explain again to him calmly all the horrible circumstances I had endured after I have sent the telegram. Knowing that the band of kidnappers were in prison I did not regret coming to the police station. Despite all the problems, I had taken back most of the money they'd stolen, and although I had insisted, the police were kind enough in the end to bring me to the dock where the boat was leaving. I said, "I was especially happy to find you in the same place where I had left you. The boat's departure was delayed for more than two hours to allow us to be reunited. And sister Cecilia had helped me alleviated my pains."

But I had started to wonder along my thoughts: What evil wanted to block our pathway that prevented us to be happy? I had this impression of taking one step forward and two steps back. I sometimes thought that the closer I am to God, the more evils are after me.

"We'll try to forget our past difficulties, and together we will concentrate planning ahead our future," Lionel said serenely.

I promised myself that I would never again have a stopover in Cebu. Whenever I see a jeepney, it reminds me of the day I was kidnapped. It triggers in me painful memories and anguish which still is hard to overcome today.

These questions continue to haunt my mind:

After Lionel told the bandits that the second bed was mine, why did they persist in asking Lionel to leave his bed and remove all the luggage? What did they really want?

Why did the fifth man kill the driver with his knife? Did he really kill him?

When I arrived in the precinct, the four kidnappers were already in jail. How did the police know that they were my kidnapers?

I did not see the driver again. Why was he separated from the four? Who was he?

Why was it that only after I told the Chief of police to contact the officers of the Philippine Army, he gave me back the money that the kidnapers had taken from my bag?

While writing this memoir, I remembered that before I left the precinct, the police informed me that one of my kidnappers was known to be very dangerous; he had been condemned before for the crime of rape but was released from prison recently. I was shocked. He was re-offending with me; why had he been released from jail? I still have flash backs of palpable trauma that reappear in my nightmares. As if an electric shock stinging me bringing me back to that moment 40 years ago everytime I met unknown people in the street grouping together going to my direction, while I'm all alone.

We finally reach Butuan

Tatay received the telegram I sent from Cebu before I was trapped by the kidnappers. I was so happy to see him with my brother Dan, waiting for us. The boat was still preparing to reach the dock, so I waved my hands to let them know that Lionel and I were in the boat. We were not bothered by the porters in Butuan. Tatay and my brother took good care of all our stuff. We had finally reached our destination, Butuan City, my hometown. Now it was different because Lionel and I were married. My parents were so happy seeing us back home safely after all. I did not tell them yet about my kidnapping; I did not want to spoil our reunion.

Everyone was excited at home, and I realised how much I loved my parents and my younger siblings. I was thinking that I would be leaving them again soon, to follow my husband to

France. I prayed I would be able to cope with missing them, and this time it would be for several long years.

We stayed in the Narra Hotel, located in a quiet place in Butuan, just a half a kilometer from my parents' place, but we spent most of our time with them during the day. It was nice to see all the furniture made in narra wood. Narra tree is the national tree of the Philippines. I had visited the Narra Hotel in Bading when Sally invited me for lunch before they left for Manila. I was also present during their wedding reception held in the Narra Restaurant in Butuan in 1980, and they stayed in the Narra Hotel in Bading for several weeks after.

Lionel and I spent some extra time with my whole family for three days before we left for Manila. We had getting together at Tinago beach. Lionel still remembered our family gathering where he was present in 1979, 1980 then this year 1981. That family gathering on the beach was repeated in 1984, 1986, 1989 and 1993. I have endless gratitude to God for the continuous blessings He bestowed upon us.

The Scariest Landing

1981 was my first international travel, to joind my husband in France. On the plane, I listened with eyes closed to my favorite old songs. It was so relaxing that I was about to sleep, and I had forgotten about the blistering in my heels and swollen toes from my last days walking around Manila. Meanwhile, despite earphones blocking my ears, I was still alert to the announcements being made. The flight attendant said that we were approaching Bangkok airport, and we were requested to fasten our seatbelts. The engine's vibration hit my ears.

The plane suddenly quake with the weird noise of the engines before stopping. It became quiet, too quiet, only deafening sound of silence left, no one said a thing except my heart and my breathing ... then the plane dove straight downward banking sharply to the left first, then we sank to the right, as if it was a bird dropping with broken wings. I closed my eyes while gripping the armrest. The passengers screamed. I held my breath. We had no choice but to pray and wait. Then the engines restarted up, and the plane righted itself into its normal position. Everyone tried to get their breathing back to normal too. But quickly the plane tilted again for the descent, our heads tipped to the other side. I wondered how long we would remain in that position. The flight attendant with his trolley went quickly back to his post. Snacks were not distributed, and all the flight attendants remained seated, eyes closed.

When the plane returned to its normal position again, they reassured us that all was fine. So everybody was fairly calm for a couple of minutes. However, then the attendants instructed us to go into the brace position for an emergency landing.

A few minutes before landing, they were suddenly shouting again as loudly as they could: "Brace position! Heads down!" They repeated it over and over for I don't know how long. I was really scared, with my head bumps against the seat in front of me as the plane was descending in lateral position as if losing its balance. **Feeling so insecure, I thought that** maybe this would be my first and last international flight.

Naïve, I asked myself: Was this a normal way to land at Bangkok airport?

I tried to convince myself to remain calm. There were so many weird and scary sounds, and as if we were on top of a washing machine, shaking. It was likely to be a malfunction of the plane's engine, but there was no announcement from the pilot. Perhaps the crew was trying to prevent panic, but passengers were screaming loudly again. I was very afraid. When I dared to look behind me, I saw mothers praying with their holy rosary beads between their fingers. Others prayed louder: "Oh God, Jesus Mary mother of God..." Children and adults were screaming loudly above the engine's noise, some were vomiting, while baggage fell down from the racks and some hurt people.

The flight announcements said we were preparing for landing, and that we should all strictly adopt the brace position. We were ordered to remain calm, stay seated, and ensure our seatbelts were fastened. Meanwhile, the attendants did not seem at ease: one was running with his trolley, pushing it back to its post for the second time; another lifted the phone receiver, but he was not able to announce anything. I was sure that the plane had serious engine trouble.

Anguished, my thoughts were with my family in the Philippines and with Lionel in France. I thought that if God was willing to let me join my husband according to what He had planned for me, He would save me no matter what might happen next. I entrusted my life to Him, then I felt somewhat serene. I kept praying and waited.

The pilot and co-pilot surely did heroic efforts to manage to smoothly maneuver the aircraft despite the engine troubles. But I was still worried when the plane accelerate towards the ground at an extreme speed. The passengers are thrown forward as the engines roar to slow it down and it lands with a bump on runway. This time the engine refuse to slow down, I prayed that it would soon stop, I closed my eyes and continuing to hope. The plane pivots, with the weird cries of it's broken engine and with the tilting noise of the tyres as it bumps towards the runway and hits on the pavements.

I felt relieved in the end when the plane finally stopped. Hmmhahhh! a huge collective sigh of breaths from the passengers, including me of course echoed in the plane's atmosphere. That experience was almost unbearable, but surprisingly, nobody was physically injured. Through my window, I could see that we were surrounded by several fire trucks on the runway. At the bottom of the stairs, people wearing white vests waited for us, probably doctors and nurses, observing us gently and so smiling showing their dimples, others were nodding and applauding. I said to them: "What a strange way of welcoming us in Bangkok airport." I'll be always marked by that.

That was the scariest landing I've ever had experienced in Bangkok.

Struggle to reach France

First, we were told to stay in the waiting hall and wait for when the plane to be ready but I was not sure if we were supposed to board the same plane again?

What I had suspected came to pass: after about three hours, there was an announcement asking us to proceed to baggage claim, although that was not expected in our flight. We were supposed to claim our luggage only once we arrived at Paris Charles de Gaulle Airport. It was then confirmed that the plane had engine trouble and that we needed to wait until it was repaired. We were told to leave with all our stuff and take a shuttle that was waiting for us. We had to walk quite far, and I was suffering again, as I was wearing high heeled shoes. I should have had worn flat sandals, I was so stupid and stubborn. My feet were covered with blisters that started to burst. I was carrying a travelling bag on my right hand and my guitar in my left, then a handbag on my right shoulder. I waddled like a duck amidst the crowd of passengers, only relieved when we were finally seated in the shuttle.

Air France offered us rooms in the Hilton Hotel at a little past two o'clock in the morning local time. I was so thirsty, yet the counter offered us only cups of coffee that would trigger my nervousness. I had never drunk coffee because not only did I dislike the bitter taste, but I also did not want it to heighten my anxieties. This time, however, I felt obliged to drink it.

Room keys were distributed to more than 300 passengers. It took several minutes for me to realize that they were calling me: they were using my new married name, and I wasn't used to that yet! "Mrs. Tchermnykh" was called twice but badly pronounced. I waited to be sure, but when they said "Baltazara," there, I was now sure it was me. I was so happy that I was about to run to them, and this time I finally appreciate the uniqueness of my first name, whereas before I hated it.

I followed a good-looking young employee who moved my baggage with a trolley to my room. He had noticed me waddling uncomfortably. I smiled at him and then I took off my shoes and walked along corridor of the hotel, enjoying the feel of the thick, soft carpet until we reached the door to my room.

I was surprised. "Oh lala! Is this my room? It's so big for me alone. Are you sure you're not confused?" I asked. "Yes Ma'am, I'm sure this room is for you, it's written in the attendance log book," he answered and he read again my full name: "Mrs Baltazara Tchermnykh?"

As soon as he left, I jumped to the first bed, lay on my back while observing the beauty of the room, excellent quality bedding. I accidentally touched a button under the mattress and I was surprised when it started to shake. I had heard of waterbeds but had never seen one before. I touched another button to try to stop it, but the bed was waving vigorously. I jumped off the bed, it continued shaking and I was rattled as to how to use it correctly. I jumped to the second king sized bed, this one did not shake. Then I heard an announcement requesting us to be ready for breakfast at 7:30 a.m. in the dining hall. It was almost 4:00 a.m. and the bed was still moving. I rang, a man came to show me; it was so easy in fact. You just needed to press the button under the bottom of the bed, just the next to the one I had pressed. I felt so ignorant and stupid! I was ashame.

The room was for a couple, and I was alone with two bathrobes in two different colors: one light blue, and one white, hanging on the bathroom wall. There were two pairs of comfortable foam slippers matching the bathrobes. It would have been so nice if Lionel had been there with me. I did not feel serene lying alone in that wide bed for two. I did not remove my suit, as I was afraid that I would not be able to wake up at seven and I did not even touch my luggage. I wanted to be prepared just in case the plane needed me to be ready to fly at a moment's notice.

It was impossible to sleep. Did I have this monophobia, scared to be alone in that immense room? I wondered why it was given to me. I opened the fridge full of snacks. I took a pack of chocolate for a taste, and then I opened a small pack of peanuts, crisps, and a small bottle of mango juice. I even tasted a small bottle of wine, until I was feeling heavy and sick. The fridge was full and my small stomach too. At exactly seven in the morning someone knocked at the door and at the same time the announcement said that it was time to wake up and should prepare all our luggage before going down for breakfast. A Thai woman with well-coiffed dark hair, wearing white and red colored apron, entered my room. She calculated the cost of all the packs and beverages that I opened. I was shocked when she asked me to pay them. I was so ignorant! I thought that everything was pre-paid by Air France. She did not accept my pesos as she preferred dollars. I showed her 50 francs and she gave me back small coins of Thai money that was probably good for collection. I asked her to keep it, but she did not take it.

Of course, with all what I have taken from the fridge, I did not feel like eating for breakfast, but I joined the other passengers. I felt nauseous when I looked at athe food that was served on the table. The other Filipina passengers were discussing about their jobs. They said they were much more comfortable living and working as a servant in a wealthy home in Monaco, or as a one as a nurse to an elderly person, rather than living a life in the Philippines. They each had a free return tickets for vacation every year, and their work was easier than living on a family farm at home, doing backbreaking work from dawn to dusk.

I felt so guilty when they talked about their hotel rooms. Incredibly they were seven girls in one room because they did not want to be separated from each other: For four of them, it was their first travel in the foreign land, like me. They had not been comfortable, although one of them had successfully slept, but fell to the floor from their narrow bed. They did not mention if they had a round waterbed or massage bed like mine. I was terribly ashamed of myself knowing that I had been alone in that luxurious room.

Why did they give me such favour in that hotel? I didn't ask a big luxurious room for me alone?

I joind to their conversation but I didn't tell them about the size of my room. What I did say was that I was alone in my room, and that had I enjoyed tasting different beverages and pack of snacks from the minibar. I had just tasted them, and I was obliged to pay them, and yet I felt sick afterwards. It was not a matter of being greedy, but it was the nervousness of being all alone and the lack of sleep. They laughed at me, so much that one of them almost choked. They said in a choir: If you had managed to drink the whole bottle of wine, you might still be snoring and would have missed breakfast time. Worst of all, despite the delay, you could have missed our flight." And they laughed at me again. As they kept teasing me, I ended up laughing along with them.

I really thought we would be all going to the plane immediately after breakfast. But it was again a deception because the plane was not ready yet. We were instructed to go to the check-in desk with our luggage. Again my feet were swollen with blisters, despite new bandages and I did not get out any other pair of shoes. Once we went to the boarding waiting area, I took off the shoes and I made a long deep sigh of relief! After three more hours of waiting, boarding was finally announced mid-afternoon. And this time, we had a smooth flight to Paris, my final destination.

Arrival

The emotional discomfort during the trip all vanished at once when I saw the night-time sky above Paris Charles de Gaulle airport. It was incredibly beautiful, with sparkling lights glowing in different colours. It was so exciting to land, and I just couldn't believe that I had finally reached France, my final destination.

It was October 31, 1981. I felt an immense happiness once the plane touched the ground. My excitement grew, and all my thoughts were with Lionel. I was feeling serene, knowing he would be waiting for me and we would be soon together. I had eagerly awaited this moment, and as soon I felt the floor of the airport under my feet, the stress now gone, and I was blown away by a new emotion as I knew that it was the beginning of my new adventure together with my husband in a foreign land. I know that life had its ups and down and whether you are happy or not, you are obliged to accept it. Soon that Lionel would be at my side, everything would be alright, I hoped. But there was one more delay before we were reunited.

My guitar

I treasured my guitar that I bought in Manila, reminding me of singing with Chatou and the other girls from the lady's dormitory in Sampaloc. To avoid trouble with the other passengers and luggage, when we were boarding, the flight attendant had said that she would put my guitar in a safe place. She reassured me that as soon as we arrived in Paris, she would give me my guitar back before disembarking from the plane. But I had forgotten to ask her name, and I did not know where it was. She forgot to give it back, and this triggered my nervousness, so I was the last passenger to go down from the plane.

Ten minutes after landing I was still looking for her and waited naively. When I finally found her I immediately asked her for my guitar. My smile of relief has turned into a grimace when she gave me a long explanation of how she had already given it to me!

I answered to her with astonishment but firmly: "No Madam, you must be confused. You have surely given my guitar to someone else, to another woman. I am sorry to ask you again, but you must help me find my guitar. It was protected by an orange and black hard case. Do you remember now?" I said, impatiently.

I was angry with her and angry with myself, because I should have kept it with me in the overhead compartment. I had trusted her because she insisted. I remembered her face and her voice, the way she walked and her accent, so I was really sure that it was her who took my guitar. I should have taken her photo, then she could not deny it, but my camera was inside my luggage.

It took me another 10 minutes of waiting; another flight attendant came and said that she had noticed one guitar near the back seat behind the toilet.

What my guitar was been doing behind the toilet? It made me the last passenger to disembark from the plane, while Lionel and his family were wondering where I was; they said all Air France passengers from Bangkok had already left airport, and I still had to claim my luggage.

I glanced to the computer screen to see where I could find my baggage, but my flight was not listed anymore. There were people standing around the carousel, but they were not from my plane. I asked some people where was the information counter, but nobody could answer me in English.

I was lost and they all spoke French amazingly fast; I had only studied the basic level French language. I understood they were all in a hurry. It made me determined to study and achieve fluency in French. I continued walking farther and there, it was written in English just above the carousel which continued rolling with my baggage all alone: "Baggage claim here - Air France flight from Bangkok." At last! Thank God.

I was so excited to meet Lionel's family and was a little shocked to see 10 of them all there to fetch me from the Airport. I was flattered, but maybe due to all the excitement I almost couldn't talk to them. I was even hesitant to kiss Lionel the way we usually did, in front of them. However, I did understand what they told me, though they were of course speaking french.

I immediately recognized Irene, 18 years old, smiling inside the waiting hall. She was Lionel's niece, appearing even more beautiful than her photo. The others stood behind the wall of glass anxiously looking around. All my stress evaporated when I spotted Lionel standing behind the transparent door. He seemed more nervous and excited than I was. There were also Lionel's three sisters: Lydia, Claudie, and Ghislaine with their husbands: Bekka, Lydia's husband, and their daughter Camille; Pierre, Claudie's husband, and their children: Tatiana and Hugues.

They said a woman from my plane passed in front of them at the waiting area 25 minutes before me. She was taller than me, carrying a guitar, they thought that it could have been me. Tatiana, ten years old, with long blond hair and blue eyes, ran after her while calling out "Sarah!" But the woman didn't respond, leaving them frustrated.

"She did not even look at us; she walked straight to the man waiting for her," said Lydia. I was sorry to hear of their frustration when they realized it was not me.

The traditional French welcome

I could never forget my arrival at Charles de Gaulle airport. I was welcomed by ten members of Lionel's family with their traditional line of their kisses on both cheeks. I was not prepared; Lionel had failed to tell me what would happen. I stood frozen with surprise, as they each hugged me, and gave me four kisses on the cheeks, twice on each side: left- right- left-right. I got a total of 40 kisses from my new family. For me it was too much kissing this way: two kisses on each cheek! Luckily, Lionel had his own way of welcoming me, with intense emotion.

Once I got home, and over the following days, I got a severe stiff neck. It persisted for five days. I was unable to keep my head straight and too ashamed to tell them, not even to Lionel. It was hard pretending to keep my head upright. When I finally told them about it, they said it was due to the cold. They did not realise it was due to the plane ride and more of their kisses. In the airport, Claudie, covered my back with a warm vest as it was autumn in France, only about seven degrees centigrade. It was a big change of temperature, because when I left Bangkok it was more than 30 degrees.

In the airport I felt utterly overwhelmed with emotions with my new family-in-law in a new environment, so at first I did not notice the difference of temperature. We left the airport, and for me it felt like it was already past three o'clock in the morning. Charming Irene spoke to me in English timidly. She rode with us in the car that brought Lionel and me from the airport to our small apartment that Lionel had recently rented.

Lydia, Bekka and their three daughters, Irene, Camille and Leah, lived just next to Mama Huguette's house. Claudie, Pierre and their children, Tatiana and Hugues, lived on the other side. Our apartment was located in a private two-storey building in Stains, a little farther from them but still within walking distance.

Lionel said to me: "We must see my Mum very soon; she is expecting us this morning." I was thinking again about how many of them to welcome me, and that I needed to get used to their hugs and kisses.

I had dark circles under my eyes as I had not slept since the beginning of my travels, and again I was not able to sleep since I had landed in Paris. In fact, I was not ready to see anyone after my long and difficult travels. I am always grouchy when I don't get enough sleep, but I tried not to show them my mood swings that day.

I was so impressed and overwhelmed by the way they welcomed me. Lionel's mother, at the age of 73, was an extraordinary mother-in-law. I loved her on the spot. All those who met me in the airport came to her place the next day, and the kisses restarted again, and they were more this time. They were all living near around Mama Huguette in the same city called Stains, a suburb of the north of Paris. Only Sonia, another of Lionel's sisters, lived far from them – in Pontarlier, the northeast of France. Fabien, Lionel's brother, was the only one living abroad, in Japan. I met all of Lionel's sisters and brothers that were in the country: Sonia (the eldest), Nadia, Lydia, Claudie, Regine, Sylviane, Ghislaine were so warm to me right away. Of Lionel's two brothers, Serge also had blonde hair, and blue eyes. Even his eye lashes and eyebrows were blond. Fabien had dark hair, with a brown moustache, which seemed to me to be quite unusual. They were all very nice to me.

Houses were different from what I was used to. Paris is so beautiful. French food was different too, but I loved it all. At first, I did not feel like I was missing my family too much. However, when Lionel and I, and sometimes with my sisters-in-law and their children, visited the beautiful places in Paris, I was thinking how it would have been so wonderful to have my parents with us. Lionel showed me all the places I saw in the Paris magazine that he left in Butuan; my family would have loved to have seen all of that in person. That nostalgia was quite unbearable at times. Luckily, Lionel's mother was so nice to me, and also my sisters and brother in-laws, especially Serge. Sometimes Mama Huguette and Aunt Odette, her sister, came with us visiting Paris, and again I thought of my parents and my younger siblings.

Over the years, I learned about Lionel's family history. In Lionel's description, it is quite an unforgettable story, as he told me:

"My mother was born in 1908 in Paris from a family of four children, of which she was the eldest. There were three girls and one boy. She was ten years old at the end of the First World War and had a very specific memory of it: her father was fighting on the front line. Difficult circumstances followed the war, and she had to work in a laundry in Paris after her primary school. Married at the age of 19 to Alexandre Prosko, a Polish man, they had two children: Sonia and Sandine. Four years later, she found herself a widow after he died in hospital after a stomach operation.

A few years later, she married Lionide Tchermnykh, (my father) an officer of the White Army from a large family of the Russian nobility, himself from a family of seven children. Upon his arrival in France, he had to adapt courageously to a radical change of situation from his life in Russia before the civil war.

As for my mother, she had great courage too. She gave birth to eight more children, all born in Stains: seven girls and three boys. We were all born before and during the Second World War. Despite all the difficulties and dangers: such as bombing and street fighting, my parents managed to protect the family without physical damage. As the situation became critical, the authorities insisted for security reasons that my mother and all the children needed to be sent to live in an area near the Swiss border, while my father continued working in Paris. During these dark years, my parents made immense sacrifices to give everyone as much as they could, despite it being a time of food shortages. My parents loved all us children very much and thanks to all their sacrifices, we had a very happy and fulfilled childhood in a close-knit family, of which we remain nostalgic.

My mother had a passion for reading, literature and history that she passed on to me. I am largely self-taught. I have at home a lot of historical works but also geography, and astronomy as well as many Russian works, although alas, I do not understand the language. France and Russia have always been very close in the cultural field." Lionel explained with nostalgia.

My Life in France

When I was young in the Philippines, my grandmother and I went to church every Sunday. We walked the long kilometres to attend Holy Mass held in Latin. She rarely missed it. I loved to go with her, but I was still too young to walk several kilometres reliably, so sometimes we rode in a *tartanilla* or *caritela*, [a Cebuano term for a horse-drawn carriage with two wheels that was brought about by the Spanish conquest in the Philippines] particularly when we wanted to catch the first Mass.

Time moved by so quickly, and soon I found myself in France with fewer chances to practice Catholicism. Although I did regularly go to church.

I am proud to have been able to withstand difficulties and hurdles through my life with God's support. I have always been grateful for all the good blessings I receive from Him; His mercies are too many to count. I know life is a constant struggle. Many times, I felt lost and alone, although I continued to ask myself what might be my purpose in life. I would seek out his guidance and inspiration as I still am always learning who I am meant to be.

But nowadays I have decided to humbly entrust my life to Him. Spiritual experience has guided me to go straight ahead. It lightened my difficulties and has given me the strength to face life.

Our Church Wedding

In the Philippines, we ran out of time to have a traditional church wedding in front of my family. Lionel's visa was expiring, and despite the extension, 45 days was too short to make all the necessary arrangements and requirements of the church. So we held our religious marriage on December 14, 1981 in the Église de Notre Dame de l'Assomption, in France during winter, witnessed by Sonia, Lionel's eldest half-sister (the daughter of Huguette's first husband), and Serge, Lionel's elder brother. We would have liked to have celebrated our marriage in the springtime, but as most couples prefer a spring wedding, the waiting list was too long.

The first thing we had planned was to have a simple wedding to avoid extravagant expenses, and we did not regret that choice. No need of to choose bridesmaids and to get them to spend lot of money for dresses and matching shoes, nor choosing groomsmen to wear semi-formal evening suits. My wedding dress and white shoes had only been worn once. What was important was our marriage, the Holy Matrimony, and not just the wedding day. We all longed for a celebration focused on life, love, family, and friendship. The preparation and rendezvous with the priest was quite a bit longer than for our civil marriage in Manila. We attended seminars for several weeks before we could get married at the church. The priest also had a long waiting list of marriage celebrations to be held, so we were obliged to wait two months for our turn.

Everything was paid for in cash for our wedding to have no debts. As expected, we held our wedding reception at my mother in-law's house. It was a customary gathering among Lionel's family. More than 30 family members attended. We took some nice indoor photos, as it was too cold and snowing outside. It was my big day and I was a happy bride, but some of my thoughts were with my parents and my younger siblings in the Philippines. I regretted so much that my father was not there to walk me down the aisle where Lionel was waiting for me. I shared them some photos of my wedding day. I am sure they were delighted to see them.

I did not know if it was a normal custom for a French priest to visit a newlywed couple. A few days after our ceremony, Father Keller, our priest in Stains who had led our Holy Mass, made us a beautiful surprise. He visited us in our apartment, and spoke for awhile about various topics relating to Catholic spirituality and family. With his presence, our apartment felt blessed, and I was honoured. We discussed how Lionel and I had met the first time. I discovered that Lionel loved to talk about politics, while I never wanted to have an argument. I did not really feel like talking about our former President Ferdinand E. Marcos, whom I had once voted for. In the later years of his presidency I risked prison by marching in a rebellion parade when he turned out to be a dictator and brought corruption to my country. Instead, I would have liked to have spoken to the priest about the visit of the Holy Spirit at dawn when I was a young child. But I did not get the chance.

My first Christmas celebration in France was a whole romantic evening at home, far from family members. I drank a lot of champagne on Christmas Eve 1981 and I was not used to it. "You can't be sick with champagne," said Lionel. But I was drunk. I always remember that moment fondly.

I was hardly ever sick during my pregnancy. I did experience nausea, especially during the first three months. What was strange was that I had got quirky whims and wacky cravings. I have been known to eat several jars of pickles a day! Then the sweet and sour green mangoes like we have in the Philippines. I prohibited Lionel to touch the liver he bought from the market but I did not eat it either. Instead, for the full two months I grilled veal or liver every day inside the oven like a barbecue and let it turn brown until it looked like some kind of brown charcoal. Meanwhile, I breathed in the delicious smell, then I was no longer hungry for lunch. It was incredibly strange. What is even more bizarre is that Lysiane was born with a light grey big spot, like a piece of liver on her leg that remains until now. I always feel guilty when looking at it. I'm so sorry about that and I don't know how to get forgiven.

At two months pregnant I was so sensitive to odours of the different kinds of cheese that were grouped all together which made the smell too strong that I once fainted in the middle of the market.

Lysiane's Birth – 1982

I did not know how labour would be. I knew it was different for every woman. Worried about the elevator, we decided to go to the maternity ward early. I have this souvenir of my mother-in-law: On the fateful day, she waited for our car to pass in front of her house, through a small alley, on our way to the maternity ward. I could see her smiling by her window that faced the road. She threw me flying kisses and reassuring affectionate words: "Don't worry Sarah, it's nothing, everything will be fine." She was trying to reassure me, but the contractions were not yet there.

I had in mind the birth of my younger sisters, the twins Amelie and Ashley. I was there when Mama delivered them quickly and relatively painlessly. In my case, labour lasted 15 hours. My first contractions were like strong menstrual cramps and I thought I might collapse. The horrible cramps were a pounding pain that persisted. My whole body clutched. I growled. I knew that pain had a purpose. But it was almost unbearable that I had not able to eat my lunch and dinner, and my labouring dragged on for hours longer than expected.

Lysiane came just when her father entered the delivery room. I felt Lionel's hands caressing my face and my head was swamped with sweat. I had been in the "Labour Room" since 11:00 a.m. and my baby came naturally the next day without epidural injections in the maternity ward of l'Hôpital de la Fontaine in Saint Denis, 1:45 a.m. Monday, September 27, 1982.

Overwhelmed with joy, I forgot my pains once my baby was in my arms. She seemed soothed in the presence of her father. She weighed 3.75 kg and was 55 cm long with thick brown hair and dark eyes. Immediately after her first cry, she started sucking her thumb. My poor baby was so hungry because we both missed our meals. I was much hungrier after delivery, and I was so disappointed when they only gave me a small jar of yogurt and a glass of hot water to drink. I had to wait until 7:00 a.m. for breakfast. I was so hungry that I suffered a terrible headache. It was impossible to close my eyes. I said if my mother was there, she would surely have given me a cup of hot milk or a big bowl of delicious soup.

There was no bed for Lionel, so I sent him at home an hour afterwards. The rules were annoying, it was outrageous that a husband was not allowed to stay on the postnatal ward room following the birth of his child. Others said it would be disruptive especially if your husband was snoring and kept everyone awake. I had a traumatic birth requiring stitches. My baby and I stayed one week in the maternity ward.

Lionel's family members were all very kind to us. Lysiane was welcomed by the whole family, but I did not expect to see them the day of my baby's birth. I had not recovered yet from labour pains or a lack of sleep. I was startled by their visit. I was tired and not yet prepared to see them. They were all excited to see the baby. I heard them said: "The next one will be a boy, a Tchermnykh." I felt their profound disappointment. Lionel had two brothers:

Serge and Fabien, but unluckily neither of them had children.

However, I was happy to hear from Mama Huguette who said: "It's lovely to have a baby girl." What really mattered for me was that Lysiane was a healthy baby, who we already dearly loved so much. Lionel was overwhelmed and so impatient to hold her that he interrupted his family. Mama Huguette, Aunt Odette, Claudie, Pierre, Serge and Lydia came on the first day, then Irene came all the way from Bordeaux, the southwest of France, by train. Sonia, Lionel's eldest sister came from Pontarlier, in the eastern part of France, taking six hours by train and bus. Some people visited us the following day, and the others visited us at home, and so on. Lionel's family was quite big. We were lucky to have been granted an individual room in the maternity ward, which allowed us to accommodate all our visitors comfortably.

A few hours after Lysiane's birth, I discovered my full, swollen, engorged breasts. The swelling extended all the way to my armpit. Fever and terrible headaches had prevented me from getting the sleep I needed at night. I continued crying like a child not due to the pain, but because of nostalgia. I really wanted to have my mother at my side at that very moment.

At seven o'clock in the morning, just before taking the breakfast, a nurse, robuste, with a wide face and tall, came to wake me up. "Bonjour Madame Tchermnykh, we'll have to deflate your swollen breast," she said. She had trouble pronouncing our family name, although I was used to hearing it by now. She had a towel for me in one hand, and an antiseptic lotion on her second hand. I understood she did not trust me to go alone into the bathroom next to my room. Perhaps she had guessed that, like many women, I was afraid to use the toilet due to the stitches put in after labour; the area was particularly painful, and I was so stressed and afraid of tearing. The pain was close to unbearable when I pooed, despite the spoonful of olive oil I swallowed before taking meals. But I understood that showering would be good for my breast engorgement, so I obeyed her. I told her I can manage to have my shower alone, but she was insisted on me standing naked in front of her, and she turned on the shower with very hot water. I had really thought she was madly cruel.

She kept on saying, "come on keep going", while she poured boiling water on me, despite my screams. Tortured and naked, I was about to dash out the bathroom door, which exit was going directly to the hallway where other people could have seen me. It was awful to listen her croaky voice. She had probably smoked too many cigarettes from a young age. She ignored me when I said the water was too hot, and despite her robustness and heavy weight, I pushed her far from me. Surprised, her glasses fell to the tiles. Steam filled up the bathroom so that I could hardly see her. She bent down to pick up her glasses. I took that opportunity to shower her before stopping the water. She yelled and left the bathroom angry. She finally realized that the water was too hot. The pain of the stiches, prevented me to ran out of the bathroom from the very first jet of unbearably hot water. I felt humiliated as she talked to me so roughly, as if I was a villain or a naughty child. Meanwhile, I also sensed that she did not understand me. She made me angry so that I spoke to her in English, or in my maternal tongue -Visayan dialect, and that enraged her: "Madame, when you are in France you must speak French," she said repeatedly, pointing an angry finger towards me. My full breasts and throat were so red and painful afterwards that I needed another nurse to come and apply a cream to my burnt skin.

I was frustrated with my very rudimentary French ever since I first arrived France in October 1981. I felt ridiculous. I gave birth to Lysiane a year later; it was still too early for me to speak French fluently, as I'd stayed at home without the chance to attend lessons to learn to speak French properly. What I had learned from Alliance Française in Manila was literally only the basic lessons for beginners. It was rather difficult, though sometimes funny, in the class because my Belgian teacher only spoke in French; he could not write a complete sentence in English correctly. When he wanted to explain to us about our lessons, he made some drawings on the chalk board and expressed himself by signs or by actions. We were all like children in a kindergarten class.

My second teacher in the Philippines had been Vietnamese. She could speak English, but of course she had a Vietnamese accent that I brought with me to France. There were lot of Vietnamese refugees in France at the time. Lionel's family would gently laugh at me when they heard me speaking French with strong Vietnamese accent. Lionel said he would have had liked to hear me talking French with Visayan and Tagalog accents. This problem led me to develop a bit of an inferiority complex, so that I avoided speaking French except to my in-laws. They encouraged me to speak even with lot of mistakes, in order to improve and express myself; this allowed me to join in their conversations. It reminds me of the story of my father in-law who was Russian. Lionel told me that when his parents met for the first time and until the beginning of their married life, they communicated in broken French by using a dictionary and with actions, which was amusing.

I had always spoken to Lionel in English, and we continued in that vein. I spoke to my baby in English even when she was still in my womb, but also sometimes in Tagalog, which was pretty rusty, and sometimes with other dialects: Butuanon (my birthplace' dialect), Visayan or Cebuano, then Boholano, like Tatay. During my first two years in France, I had never met a Filipina whom I could talk to. I felt so lonely at home every time my husband was at work. At that time there was no computer, no fax, no cell phone nor internet to join or communicate to far-away family and friends abroad. There was a Minitel, but I for that I needed to go to the post office; I did not know how to use it alone by myself. What we had in our apartment was an iconic model of the 70s; a black retro phone with a rotating dial and an old-style mechanical ringtone.

Another nurse came to assist me in taking my shower; she persisted by saying the hot water would soften my swollen breasts due to the build-up of milk. Unlike the first nurse, this one was a more intelligent, with a gentle understanding of what I was going through.

The doctor visited me that morning together with a nurse who brought with her an interpreter to translate what I said. I had some pains I could only express in English and nobody could understand me, not even the doctor. They said I spoke English with strong American accent, and because of this I felt they detested me. But the French interpreter spoke very bad English, so that I could hardly understand her, and she had difficulty in understanding my French as well. I was desperate. They introduced me to another translator, a South African nurse. I was so relieved when she understood all of what I was telling her. At last! We had some funny conversations that made me feel calmer and happier. I could even tell her about my boiling shower.

I found it stressful every time my breast milk was pumped manually first, and then with an electric breast pump. That was to put my milk in a bottle to be stored in the freezer, so even when I was sleeping, a nurse could give my breast milk to my baby. I had never imagined that my two small breasts could manufacture so much milk; the flow of my milk gave me mastitis.

On Lysiane's first day she cried at dawn so loudly that it echoed all along the hallway. She was surely hungry, and I still couldn't give her my breasts that were so sore. I heard her somehow asking me to hurry up and feed her. She was lying on her stomach. I was stunned to see my newborn baby born at only four hours old; she seemed so determined. She swung her little body around, turning her head up to see me. She looked at me with an air of begging, and I had no resistance. I still had trouble walking due to my stitches, but I went fast to the kitchen. No one was there. I opened the refrigerator and found a bottle labelled "Lysiane" with her date of birth. I thawed it on the radiator near my bed. She emptied the whole thing. I let her burp then she quickly fell deeply asleep. She didn't cry for the whole morning. A nurse and an assistant came late to give her a bath, but she was still soundly sleeping. While they pumped my breast milk, they were wondering at how calm my baby was. Of course, they discovered later that I fed Lysiane before they came, and they pretended to be unhappy that I did their job.

I was so excited when the moment came to take her home. I couldn't wait! I wanted to be with my baby who looked so cute, dressed all in white and woolen clothes, paired with scarf, gloves, and a thick, soft woolen pair of shoes. My thoughts were bouncing around in so many directions: Now, no more torture with the hot showers. I would be able to give my breast milk normally, and would be thrilled to give bathe my baby by myself.

Before leaving the maternity ward, the nurses smiled at me and said: "Madame, we hope to see you back soon with your second baby."

I immediately replied: "No, I am sorry to contradict you, Mesdames, but I don't think I will be back."

They weren't listening, as they were so used to hearing praise and thanks from almost every mother who had their first baby. "Alright, we'll see then," they replied together in unison.

It was such a wonderful feeling to hold my baby in my arms, awake and alert; she understood we were going home. The month of October was the beginning of Autumn, and despite the cold breeze, I thought France looked so beautiful. Trees were changing colour all around the hospital and along the side of the road. The green was disappearing and there were red, yellow, orange, and dark brown leaves falling everywhere, blown by the wind along our way back home.

A travel of Lionel's astral body

Since I met Lionel, I quickly discovered something that I could hardly explain, about his spiritual side. I was really surprised by his unusual ability to spiritual travel and be in two places at once, a kind of "bilocation." This psychic experience started when I met him in 1979. I always remember that I had been shocked to see him standing in front of me in Luneta Park in Manila in 1980, when I was with the Australians and my friend Naima. Then I saw him walking across the park in Manila, when in fact, he was in Butuan at that time. I had even thought that he was still in France because I had misunderstood the information in his letters. The distance is considerable: it is 801 kms or 498 miles between Manila and Butuan, taking more than an hour by plane. The spiritual communication or the telepathy between us was quite strong, and yet we were not even engaged at that time. I did not know then that someday I would become his wife.

I also discovered his telepathic abilities and his spiritual travel had made him into a strong human being. He described it this way: "Time and distance do not matter, because when true love is present, the communication between two minds and hearts will always reach each other."

When I was still in the Philippines and he was in France, many times I happened to hear his voice calling me. It was twice a day, especially at dawn. I wrote to him about it in my letters, and he answered me that it was quite normal, because according to him he used to call to me, silently at night in France when he was in bed, before going to sleep. He called out to me early in the morning again as soon as he woke up, before starting to get ready for the office.

That experience led me to remember about the mysterious man who had suddenly appeared in front of me in the jeepney who communicated me mentally. The man who spoke of Lionel and his eyes, I always wondered, how did he know Lionel? He disappeared the same manner as he arrived, while the jeepney was going so fast and did not stop. I had really wondered, how come he was able to ride and get off that jeepney that never stopped?

I only told all this to Lionel much later, after the death of Tatay Eco, because my memories were resurfacing when I started to write this memoir. It was when I realized my father was no longer there for me, could never again listen to me and record my premonitions, dreams, precognitions, and visions. My father had been the witness to all my mystical experiences and adventures, which proved my spiritual sensitivity. He is not there anymore to give me any advice, though I do feel he is just here around me. Sometimes I wonder how we are be able to keep our memories so fresh in our minds. Anyway, my experience with my husband is lasting. Lionel, without knowing it, is capable of appearing onto the places he wants to go but hindrances, prevented him to do so. These moments were always important junctures, but they remained a rare occurrence.

Back to the time in the maternity ward: I gave birth to my baby in the maternity ward which was approximately seven kilometers away from our apartment, and approximately 15 kilometers from where Lionel worked. One day I saw him through the window walking towards the maternity ward and I waited for him, but he did not arrive. I was wondering why he did not come to my room. If only I had a telephone at that time, I would have had like to call him in his office, to alleviate my worries. He finally came to the maternity ward in the evening just before he returned home. We were so happy together that I did not talk to him about of what happened that afternoon, as I did not want to spoil the good feelings we shared, and he was so impatient to hold and hug our baby. I also was afraid that he would think I was sick or foolish. At that time, Lionel did not know yet all about my strange, mystical, or psychic experiences. I really did not know how to talk about them.

When the three of us (Lionel, the baby and me), were already installed at home, I told him of the times when I was in the hospital, after taking my lunch, I sometimes saw him at the window walking towards the maternity ward. I asked him why he did not come to my room.

He explained: " I wanted to come, but I was discouraged because the bus would take too long, and it would be frustrating not to be able to stay with enough time for the baby. So I decided to come only in the evening after work. After my lunch I usually took a short nap, sitting on my armchair in my office as usual. But my mind struggled between my desire to visit you in the maternity ward, at the same time I had thought it would be better to go in the evening before coming home."

He continued. " I was so lucky, I have a spacious office at the university which is like a small apartment. Aside from part of it that looks like a library, I have I another space separated by a thick wall where I eat lunch, and also a place where I can take a short nap in my armchair. I would close my eyes, but despite the comfort, it was hard to sleep deeply, because of my strong desire to visit you in the maternity ward." In my view, he did go into a quick, deep sleep while I saw him coming to the maternity ward in that early afternoon.

Once again, the only explanation that makes sense to me is that it was his Astral body that I had seen. Because of his eagerness to visit us, but a conflict in his mind as to whether or not he would have enough time, he wanted to be in two places at once. In the end, just his Astral body came to the maternity room to visit baby Lysiane and me. I found his ability to travel while sleeping just incredible. But all these things I kept to myself all these years, although I sometimes believe that Lionel had already detected his special ability to travel while sleeping.

At the age of five months, the baby was so irritable. She was crying, suffering from teething troubles and swollen gums, unable to sleep even at night. Lionel carried her around, doing his best to calm her and they both finally fell asleep together on the sofa. I was in my bed waiting for our baby to calm down and praying that she would sleep. Lysiane stopped crying, but Lionel did not come back to our room with her. However, his Astral body came. I saw him clearly at the door of our room. He pushed open the door and entered our bedroom without the baby. He looked at me for a moment and extended one hand as if he wanted to pull something from our bed.

I asked him what happened and what he wanted, but he did not answer. I raised my hands to reach him when he was about to touch me and I asked him again: "Lionel, you need something?" Still he did not answer. Again, I reached out to him, but I only touched emptiness. Our baby's bed was in our bedroom but empty, so I was wondering why he came without the baby. I hopped out the bed and went to the lounge, where I found him sleeping in the couch with Lysiane in his arms. I took a blanket from our room and covered them.

When the morning came, I asked him if he remembered something during their sleeping on the couch. He said: "I was afraid that baby Lysiane was feeling cold, so I held her tightly against my chest and I tried not to move, afraid that she might wake. I wanted to pick up a blanket from our bedroom to cover her, but it would have been a pity to disturb her."

So then, I understood that what I had seen in our bedroom was only Lionel's living Astral body, even though it seemed so vivid and real. He said that despite holding Lysiane in his arms, he finally had a good sleep and the baby did too, but he did not realize that I came to cover them. It was winter and despite the heater, we always preferred to be covered with a winter blanket while in bed. The blankets enabled them to have a prolonged sound sleep together.

Trip from France to the Philippines

August 1984 was our first visit to see my parents and my younger siblings in the Philippines since I settled in France three years before. My husband kept on telling Lysiane, aged 23 months, about our coming holiday to the Philippines, where she would meet her grandparents, aunties, uncles and cousins. Lysiane understood what we had been telling her, that she became excited too. We had planned our packing several weeks before our flight, thinking about bringing our little French girl to meet my parents for the first time. And I knew my parents were so excited to see their first granddaughter from France.

There was no direct flight from Paris Charles de Gaulle Airport to Manila at that time, which was only a half-hour drive from our home when there was no traffic. Instead, Pierre,

Lionel's brother-in-law, drove us to Orly airport, in the south of Paris, about a four hours' drive from home because of traffic jams.

Our baggage was checked-in and we waited for the boarding call. But there was no boarding, instead, we were informed that the plane had suffered a technical problem, so we needed to recover our baggage from the baggage dispatch area. Again! This remind me of my previous fearful experience when I had my scariest landing in Bangkok airport in October 1981. My anxieties came back.

Philippine Airlines drove us from the airport to a Hilton Hotel by shuttle. Despite the help of hotel porters, both of us had our hands full. Lionel carried the baby stroller and all of the stuff for the baby, while I carried the hand luggage because the hotel porters were too busy, with more than 300 flight passengers stranded. Lysiane held the hem of my blouse, but when we reached our floor, Lysiane was not with me anymore. I was scared for her security.

Then I heard her calling me: "Mama, Mama!" She was in the elevator going down to the ground floor. I rushed to the elevator while Lionel was looking for her down the corridors of the hotel. When I reached the ground floor, I heard Lysiane calling me again, but she was in an elevator that was going up, and the building had more than ten floors. Luckily, I finally found her with other people whose rooms were on the same floor of ours. Lionel and I were exhausted after the sort of "hide and seek", but fully relieved.

For dinner, the baby had eaten some rice with ground fish then a small piece of banana cake although she usually drank her bottle. Lionel enjoyed his order of duck confit. I ordered a *pansit*, a kind of noodle stir-fry with shrimp. The loudspeaker announced that we needed to be ready at 7:30 the next morning for our breakfast, ready for the departure, the plane could fly at any time. I started to feel excited for the trip. But the following morning, the plane was not ready. For a second night we were still in the Hilton Hotel. Every evening, the hotel would serve the *confit de canard* for all PAL passengers for the Philippines, which was good as Lionel enjoyed it, while I grew bored.

On the third day we were all requested to check -in again, to learn that our plane would not bring us to our destination as scheduled, but would first go to London Heathrow, and from there, we would transfer to another plane. They said Philippine Airlines would take care of transfering all our luggage. Although we were exhausted, we felt reassured. Travelling with a baby was not easy, and we still had two stops-overs (so two days stranded in the hotel, plus three days of travel) before we would reach Butuan.

On the plane we encountered another problem: Lysiane's bed box was too small. We asked the stewardess for a bigger one, but they said that it was the largest size, for a baby of two years. Lysiane was only 23 months old, but was very uncomfortable and cried in our arms. If we would have known, we would have purchased a seat for her. She had to lie down on the floor until she fell asleep.

As soon as we stepped out from the plane in Manila International airport, Lysiane collapsed while we were still on the staircase of the plane. Unfortunately, she did not bear the overwhelming heat and humidity in Manila. We rushed her to the nearest hospital by ambulance instead of going to the baggage claim area.

I was mad with the personnel of the hospital because, despite the urgency, they first demanded we pay and sign all the papers before Lysiane could be admitted. In France, the hospital would take care of the sick person first, before asking you to sign the papers and pay. Lysiane needed to eat and drink to recover from her dehydration, but there was no food for a child in that expensive hospital, and not even a bottle of water.

The Philippine hospitalization system and methods were indisputably mediocre. An IV was planted on the foot of our daughter, but it was not done correctly. Her foot swelled, and the volume was increasing; it was not normal. I went to see the Director of the hospital. But two strong men blocked my way and told me that it was not necessary to see their superior, but I insisted. I successfully reached him, I told him categorically: Sir, the care was not good enough, and my daughter's foot is swelling, which is not normal. I will ask for a refund of the hospitalisation fee." Then I went back to my daughter's side, and removed the IV by myself and went away from the hospital. Once we checked in to the hotel and dined in their restaurant, Lysiane's foot was not swollen anymore.

The following morning, we went to the airport to claim our baggage, but there was nothing. The employee told us to proceed to Butuan as scheduled, and they would send us our luggage through to Butuan airport, but two pieces of luggage did not arrive. It turned out that we had landed in Manila without our luggage: Lionel's luggage and mine were checked-in at Orly airport, but they were not with us on our plane. The report said: our luggage was transferred in London to a flight to Pakistan, while we were on board on our flight for Philippines! It was the error of the PAL, and possibly errors in labelling the bags. What a mess!

We spent one night in the Luneta hotel, Manila and the next morning we were on board a PAL flight to Cebu then finally onto Butuan Bangcasi airport.

My parents and all members of our family met us in the airport full of excitement. They were relieved to see us safe and well. Mama was so happy and overwhelmed to embrace her first granddaughter from France. My sisters wanted to take my baby unto their arms. At home, Dan and his two boys, Carter and Dave, were there too, while Melchor was so impatient to take

Lysiane with him. Lysiane was overwhelmed observing them too: she asked who were those people in front of her? They were all relieved from the anxiety about our travel because of the typhoon that had already started ravaging Luzon, then Cebu just after we left for Butuan. I was touched the way Tatay kissed Lysiane so tenderly, while she enjoyed caressing her grandfather's head.

On the same day of our arrival in Butuan we went to the PAL office to inform them about our missing luggage. I was more than delighted to see the assigned manager who was my former physics instructor, Mr. Miraballes, from my time at Butuan City Colleges. He took charge of our case, and made some inquiries with the head office in Manila. PAL gave us some money as our compensation so that Lionel and I were able to buy some clothes and things for the baby while waiting for our luggage. But they needed to find our bags, especially that there were gifts for my family and some important things for the baby. Our holiday would not be what we had planned because of our missing luggage.

Typhoon Maring

We reached Butuan safely and stayed in my parent's home. But that very evening of our arrival in Butuan, Typhoon Maring struck all over Philippines including Butuan City. Northern Luzon was the most affected, where many were made homeless and some people died. We're so worried, spending the whole night awake. I was afraid for my entire family's safety. Luckily Lysiane was too young to worry. Nobody was able to sleep that night except baby Lysiane. During the whole night, Lionel and I were kneeling and bent our heads to cover her from any dangerous material which was flying around. The strong wind stressed our roof. A huge branch of a coconut tree and other trees were lifted by the fierce wind and dropped straight onto our roof, crashing into the house. Most of our parent's stuff were destroyed while a lot was blown away. We covered ourselves with thick blankets and a piece of flat wood over our heads, and remained kneeling over our baby to protect her against any falling objects.

The wind shook the house; I was afraid that it would collapse together with my whole family. Tatay was checking to make sure that nobody was harmed. Mama was more nervous than us; I felt her terrible worries. We kept on praying that we would all survive. The typhoon lasted the whole night, and what we endured seemed never ending. The house remained standing but was basically destroyed.

In the morning, we were all exhausted but safe. I thanked God for saving us.

After the typhoon, heavy rain fell. The Agusan River overflowed not only throughout New Asia, but the whole City of Butuan was flooded. But when morning came, the weather was quite good despite the flood. Tatay made a paper-boat for Lysiane, so innocent. Not knowing the difficulties we endured, she enjoyed playing with her paper-boat floating in the water, accompanied by her uncle Melchor.

Seeing the flood around us, I suddenly remembered the events of my near-drowning. I wanted to ask Tatay, who was the person who saved me? But it was not the right time, because we were already preparing to move into an empty house in the Sintos subdivision. We had to evacuate from the New Asia district, and moved-in temporarily into an empty house in Sintos subdivision. It would hold all of us until my parent's house could be rebuilt. Lionel and I had bought a housing lot by instalments (at a distance, from Paris).

Tatay was so sad, but he remained quiet. I understood his feelings of melancholy and turmoil because we had to leave our home, one that he had rebuilt all by himself. I finally had a chance to ask about my near-drowning, and I learned from Tatay that a heavily pregnant woman named Zinas had caught my hair and had saved me from being carried away by the heavy strong current of the river that time so many years ago. I used to have long hair that reached down to my hips. It helped her to save me.

I would have had liked to meet Zinas and to thank her with all my heart for saving me, but it was too late. Nang Zinas died while giving birth to her baby. I was feeling like I would burst with sincere gratitude, but I had not been able to tell her anything before she died.

My father remembered more details, and said:

"I was working in the sawmill that day. Zinas was there to wash her dirty clothes, but they were all carried off by the water current. When everybody had given up on looking for you because of the strong current of the river, Zinas did not hesitate. She dived into the water with a strong determination to save you. She had been able to catch your long hair and pulled you up from the bottom of the river and reached to the surface, but struggled to climb up to the riverbank. And that was when I quickly jumped into the water and took you from Zinas' arms. We climbed up the slippery slope of the riverbank and reanimated you. Then I ran as fast as I could to reach home, carrying you all the way, followed by all the other children. I put you on the floor of our small balcony surrounded by the children and neighbours and reanimated you again."

The day after the typhoon, we went to the beach all together as usual, despite the past calamity. It was amazing to see those huge rocks stacked up almost as high as a coconut tree along the seashore. The people living nearby said that the waves of the hurricane carried those rocks to the shore from the depths of the sea. It was amazing how they were piled so high and well arranged by the sea water! More than 20 fishermen's houses which had stood near the shore had been carried away by the giant waves in the night; no one survived. So sad.

Mama took care of Lysiane, while Lionel and I went to the office of the Philippine Long Distance Telecommunications. We needed to reassure Lionel's family in France that we were all safe and sound despite the typhoon that was ravaging the country. There was damage in Manila, Cebu as well as Butuan. My parent's house was destroyed but God had saved us all.

However, that day the telephone communications from Philippines were not good. We went back to the PLDT office for a second time and luckily, we were able to talk to Lionel's mother this time to alleviate their fears and worries. I heard their anguish knowing that we were in Philippine Archipelago when the typhoon struck. Their worries disappeared when they heard from us.

They said they watched the news on television day and night, and were so upset when they learned that the typhoon was already in Philippines. They were so afraid that our plane had maybe been hit by the cyclone and crashed, because they had not heard from us since we left France. They knew that our connecting flight had a stopover in Manila and Cebu, but they did not know where we were.

Lionel explained to them: "When the typhoon had struck Manila, we were already in Cebu; when Cebu was struck, we were already in Butuan. We were very lucky that our flight had left from Cebu's airport just a few minutes before that the typhoon had struck Cebu City, as a lot of buildings and houses were completely destroyed, and the airport was closed soon after we took off. Our flight was the last one to fly from Cebu airport that day." God was with us.

Despite the fact that the typhoon struck and virtually destroyed my parents' house, the Lord spared us from danger repeatedly; our immense gratitude and faith in Him grows everyday.

That day, just before our transferring to Sintos subdivision, Sally, my friend who was living in Germany, came to visit her family in Magallanes. She visited us with her young daughter Diane. They arrived Philippines before the typhoon struct. I was so happy to see her again, but the gaiety of our conversation was spoiled when she talked about her mother in-law.

She said her husband was dependent on his mother for all decision-making. When she tried to change the situation, she realized that their marriage became fragile and they experienced a lot of conflict in their marriage. I was sorry for her. I was lucky to have Huguette as my mother-in-law. Before she returned to Germany, Sally visited us again, and this time in Sintos subdivision.

Our one month stay with my parents and my younger siblings was full of happiness despite the typhoon as we, Lionel, Lysiane and I were with them. I had been missing them all so much.

On the way to Bancasi airport, the jeepney was fully filled with my parents and all members of my family and this time, Sister Cecilia, our cousin was with us. We took a photo which I still have today. I always love to see this photo, which reminds me of my loving Tatay and Sister Cecilia, who are now departed. Mama Dominga was younger too. The photo reminds me of how big our family is: Dan and his family were there, Betsy, Carter and Dave; Nelly was there with her husband Ciriaco and their little daughter Heidi; there was Nolwen, her husband Teddy with their little boy Ricardo; my two younger sisters Amelie and Ashley; Melchor, and Imelda. They all came with us to the airport. I was so happy to have seen them all and I was still bidding them goodbye until through the plane window, my heart was aching with nostalgia. I did not know yet when we would be able to come back to see them again.

Our luggage saga continues

I am not a lawyer, and I had no experience about judiciary matters. I have only studied commercial law during my course in business management. I learned about the rights of customers, and as a customer of Philippine Airlines, we had the right to claim compensatory damages as a result of their poor performance for delivering our baggage, especially if we had suffered psychological effects. It was frustrating to beg PAL in London to find our two bags that were wrongly brought to another country. It definitely brought us down during the holiday.

As soon as we were back in France, we had to continuously chase the PAL office in London to find our luggage, and we needed to also send another reclamation letter which showed the sealed stamp and the signature of the lawyer that we hired. Even though I was the author of the letter with the precise information about our home address and phone number, we had still to pay an expensive honorarium to a lawyer for a simple signature and seal. However, it worked, because eventually PAL replied our letters of reclamation with a brief information after five months of humiliation and discomfort. We finally recovered our two bags and surprisingly, they were in a good state because they had not been opened, although they appeared to have severe scratches all around and had damaged locks. It was then the time that we discovered that our luggage had travelled from London to Pakistan instead of to the Philippines. As for our compensation, although they could not really fully recover all the damages we suffered psychologically, they offered us two return open tickets for free for our next travel to the Philippines. Fantastique! That cheered us up. We would have had liked to travel that next summer, but Lysiane had to have surgery on her eyes in June and July 1986.

Life in Paris

Lysiane started attending kindergarten classes at the age of three in September 1985. She had her first Solemn Communion in May 1994, together with her classmates in their private Catholic school, L'École Sainte Mary. Everyone in the family noticed her skills in art and drawing. She received a lot of appreciation and recognition in school. Her artwork was displayed around the school prominently. She often said that when she was tired she needed to draw, and her energy is renewed. We were all proud of her.

Her first year of kindergarten was interrupted by the problem of cataracts growing in both eyes. One day, she told me that there were some butterflies in her room. She played with a small rubber ball, but had a hard time catching it when I threw it to her. A week later, her teacher called me and asked about Lysiane's sight. The ophthalmologist confirmed that Lysiane had a congenital cataract blocking her vision in both eyes, despite being so young. It was a condition she inherited from her father, unfortunately. No one could imagine the anguish I was feeling, and the shock. At the time, I did not understand that cataracts are genetic. It was hard for me to accept that my baby would have to undergo surgery.

Her right eye was operated on in June, and the left eye in July 1986. She stayed in the hospital for two full months without a break. The intervention was successfully done by Professor Gaudric, eye cataract specialist and surgeon in the Intercommunal Hospital of Creteil. He transferred to Lariboisière Hospital in Paris and continued exercising his profession while being fully in charge of our daughter's eyes. Lysiane was his first baby patient he had operated at such a young age; the fact that it was a big success made him very famous professionally. We always thank God for being so good of saving our daughter's sight.

She was enrolled into a second year of kindergarten classes in September 1986, it was difficult at times because we had to bring her regularly to the doctor in Creteil then into Paris for the post operation check-ups. She had to endure many absences from class, particularly in the early months after the surgery.

My little girl had allergies to dust and animal hair. It was a pity because she had loved to caress pets like cats and dogs. And we did not allow people to enter our home with their dogs. She often had cough and colds, and sometimes she breathed as if she had astma, with wheeziness or shortness of breath. She took a medicine syrup before and after she entered her classroom. Luckily, those allergies stopped when she was about seven years old.

One day our friends Tessie and her husband from Paris came and we had lunch together at home. Lysiane did not finished her meal, so I gave her bottle with milk while Jean Jacques asked Lysiane: "How old are you?"

"I am six," she replied.

"And you still drink milk in the bottle?"

He was mocking my little girl and I was angry with him. It was my fault, because I was always worried if she ate less. I still remembered when she cried in the maternity ward, sucking her thumb because she was hungry. So I often offered a bottle of milk and she had loved it, although she was weaned off of sucking her thumb.

Lysiane ran to her room, humiliated. I was heartbroken for her. I followed her and found her hiding under her bed crying while her bottle was thrown into the corner of her room. Since then, Lysiane never took a bottle again. However, when her permanent teeth came in, she had misaligned teeth perhaps due to the sucking of bottle nipple for too long. It was again my fault. The orthodontist fitted her with braces that she wore for over a year.

We loved Lysiane so much and gave her everything she needed. When she was having her eye treatment, we went back and forth daily for two months, despite the roughly two hours' drive, from home to the Hospital Intercommunal de Creteil. Or we could take the bus, train (RER), and metro. We had to leave home at 6:00 a.m. and didn't come back home until late at night. We were not allowed to stay with the baby patients in their room. Nowadays, hospitals allow the mother or a father to have a bed in the child's room. I needed to be with her before her breakfast to assist her eating, because her two eyes were still obstructed by eye shields at that time. Procedure have changed and these days the ophthalmologist and surgeons use eye shields with transparent plastic windows, to let the patients see through.

I was overtired with my back-and-forth travel to the hospital, not missing a single day within two months. I did not even know I was pregnant, but I miscarried. I did not find time to rest. I had to concentrate on keeping watch on her so she would not bump or fall. It was impossible for me to look for a job. Once her eyesight recovered somewhat, my day was a little easier. I brought her to school in the morning and fetched her home for lunch, bringing her back to school for afternoon classes and fetching her home in the evening. I did this until she was almost nine years old.

Visit to the Philippines – 1986

We returned to the Philippines in December 1986 with our two free return tickets from PAL, and this time we had a much better travel experience. As usual, we went to the beach joyfully with my whole family together. The jeepney was so full that the conductor could hardly find a place for his hand to grasp at the entrance door of the jeepney. It was a kind of a family reunion held on the beach. Everyone was excited.

Tatay prepared the fish *kinilaw,* fish literally "eaten raw" but fully marinated with vinegar and spices in a preparation method native to the Philippines. Lionel loved it. There were fisherman roaming around the beach to sell their catch, and we had charcoal for grilling. All the members of my extended family were present (except those nieces and nephews who were not born yet in 1986). I have this endless gratitude to God. He had heard my prayers; my wish for the whole family to be united that day in Butuan. Often, Dan was absent during our family gatherings, but I was particularly happy this time because he and Tatay Eco were there.

Our five weeks' holiday in the Philippines was wonderful despite my worries for Lysiane's eyes because of the constant dust in Butuan. We returned to France happy and contented. But it did not last long. Life was constantly teasing us. Sometimes I wondered: How is it that our life is never smooth and easy? We met another intolerable surprise upon entering home in Stains.

I lose all trust in the neighbours

Before we left for Philippines we took some precautions: To prevent danger, we had switched off the electricity, and turned off the gas and heaters. We had cleaned and arranged everything at home, including covering all our furniture to protect from dust. Only the water was available to water the plants.

When we arrived home from our trip, we had a terrible surprise: As soon as we opened our door we were welcomed by a strange smell. I immediately knew that something was amiss. Everywhere was in a mess!

We felt like strangers in our own apartment and we immediately felt great distress. The electricity and the heater were on, the plants inside the apartment and in the terrace were all withered, faded, dried and thirsty, and many plants had died; they were not watered during our five weeks absence. The television was on. Our sofa crumpled and sweaty. I was furious to see wet clothes hanging in our bathroom. They had used our washing machine, and everything we had in our bathroom including our towels. They cooked in our kitchen without cleaning it, and the toilet was blocked. Even our reserved canned goods and other dried foods were consumed; soft drink cans littered the table, and some bottles of Lionel's collection of whiskey were open and drunk. Lysiane's toys and some books and one big dictionary disappeared. Our whole apartment was smelly and dirty. We wanted to call the police. But we contemplated: Our complaints would surely not be honoured by the police. Our testimony would be incoherent because we knew undeniably that the squatters and burglars were our neighbours. Sylvette and Jack lived just next door with their daughter.

We felt so stupid. Lionel and I naively trusted them with the key. We had really thought they were trustworthy neighbours. Their only job was to water the plants, yet they neglected to do even that. They squatted in our apartment with all the comforts for free while we were away. All our neighbours knew that we had a lot of plants, even inside the apartment, and mostly they were climbing plants; people even said I had a hanging garden in my dining hall and in the kitchen.

Sylvette and Jack offered services to water my plants. They said: "Nothing to worry about it Sarah, you can spend your vacation in peace. This is to thank you of providing us the fence for our whole terrace." They said it with a sweet smile. We were outraged to see they had taken advantage of our absence by squatting in our apartment and using everything we had at home for their benefit. Anger boiled up inside me. I was especially angry at myself for the absence of my clairvoyance. In fact, I usually had it. Why did it fail this time?

Our doorlock was not changed yet. The husband, rang our doorbell late in the evening. The key security trigger for door had prevented him from entering with the key. We did not see his wife and daughter. I hesitated to open the door because I was afraid that Lionel might hit him. It was not good for his heart to get angry like that. And I was afraid how Jack would react.

He gave us back our key. I looked straight to his eyes, but he just looked down and said: "I know you were coming back, so I opened the heater for you." I wanted to hit him; in fact, we did not tell them to what day we'll be back home. I demanded him to take away on the spot all their wet clothes they'd hung in our bathroom including our towels. I placed those clothes on our outside terrace table, but I did not want to get back our towels they had used. They should have hung it outside, for sure they did not want people to know they were squatting in our apartment. They kept the shutters remained closed with the lights on, so the consummation of the electricity, gas and water continued during our absence and the bills increased.

Lionel and I were so angry that we said few words. But I prayed never to see them again. We immediately changed the lock of our entrance door, and we bought new beds, mattresses, and beddings to try to forget that event.

I later learned from other neighbours that Sylvette and Jack were evicted from their apartment, so they stayed in ours. They were given just two days when they were not able to pay their rent. They had a 12-year-old daughter who seemed sweet, but was in trouble with drugs and delinquency. My trusting heart and naivety blinded me; I did not see all that before. Usually, I am clairvoyant. Because of the cataract, I was preoccupied with worries and looking after Lysiane. In the space of five weeks away from home, a lot had happened. I was always so kind to everyone, but it was now over.

I started being paranoid. I felt like we were being watched. I think it is linked with this experience with the untrustworthy neighbours. I felt like I could not trust any neighbours anymore, not even friends.

Just two days after, we were out to visit Aunt Odette at her home, as she had just been released from the hospital. There was thunder, strong winds, and heavy rains prevented us from reaching home sooner.

As soon as we opened our armored front door, we felt an unwelcome breeze. The carpets were wet, with traces of wet shoes still fresh. One window in our bedroom was broken, with pieces of broken glass scattered all over the floor. Anxiety and anger invaded us. I was so shaken and felt violated. We had been robbed!

Maybe the robber or robbers did not expect us to come back home early. The smell of someone's body and breath remained strong. The robber had entered through the window and escaped the same way. We were shocked. It took us some time to react before calling the police. Lysiane ran to her bedroom to see if her piggy bank that she had carefully hidden was still there.

I immediately sensed it was our old neighbour. I smelled the same odour when we arrived home from the Philippines. Lionel often told me that I had a very good sense of smell. "You should work with the police like a dog that detects drugs," he would joke with me. Also, Jack sprang to mind because he already knew everything we had at home, but we had no evidence to show to the police. We had an armoured door which was quite impossible to break. Instead, they broke our bedroom's insulated double glazed window. It was my fault, I did not close the shutter. They took our precious things, unused clothes, jewellery including personal belongings of my husband. He regretted of keeping them in good condition, and it happened that he was the same height and build as Jack. He said he waited for the best occasion to wear the nice clothes, but now it was too late, and they were gone. It was a good lesson to consider not to save up nice things without using them.

I likewise regretted of keeping all the beautiful clothes I bought from abroad and luxurious bedding, mostly were gifts from abroad, including unused kitchen utensils and other things in the original packaging. I had been saving save them for a special occasion too or when special visitors came. Unfortunately, we take withdrawn cash just that morning from the bank; it was taken too, which was not reimbursed by our insurance. Our jewellery was gone. The insurance agency demanded proof of ownership and receipts, but we did not have them anymore.

The robbers were surely attracted by my collection of expensive unopened perfume bottles, still wrapped in original packaging, and our VCR which was very trendy at that time, with many cassettes and movies that had been delivered only the day before. Only the neighbours next door could see who entered and out from our front door. Maybe they peeped behind their door through their keyhole. Our other neighbours who were living upstairs said they heard several heavy loud booms different from the sound of thunder, but they did not think to look out their window to see what it was, as there was thunder and heavy rains. Also, they did not know that we were not at home.

The next day, our neighbours next door were totally gone with all the things they took from us. New neighbours replaced them. I said to myself: "Be prudent now Sarah, don't trust any neighbours anymore. My generosity has to come to an end." Believe me, it was not simple to claim insurance especially when you could not provide a receipt for a stolen item such as a gift, or items of personal value. This experience led me to regret our choice to live on the ground floor of the building.

It is a pity that the money from our insurance company was just enough to install the security alarm and radar detectors. We were not able to replace the things that were taken. It is sad to know that we had to secure ourselves against an unsafe environment. Meanwhile, that experience triggered me a strong desire to buy an individual house surrounded by a high fence and gate, far from Stains. I did not know yet how or when, as I did not have a full-time job yet. I promised to myself to work hard. We started putting away savings with that in mind.

Despite my anxiousness about Lysiane's operation and development, I found that we could never let a child grow without physical activities. Like any normal child, she obviously needed to participate in some sports. One day we were bicycling in the Parc of La Courneuve. Lysiane was only about eight years old. We were roaming around the park when she suddenly changed direction and she did not return to our meeting point. Lionel was walking, far away from us on the other side of the immense Parc. I could not wait for him to return to meet us. Anguish took over and I heard two boys talking about the "flight Boeing 747" and the way they laughed, I guessed they were mocking someone. I took my bicycle and went after them, but then I saw Lysiane's bicycle down a small slope which was not a bicycle track for children. Further down there was a tree and Lysiane was just behind it. She had a small cut and bruise on her forehead. Luckily, I had brought a first aid kit that I kept inside my bicycle bag. She said she had been thrown from her bike and fell down, tumbling towards a small road, but luckily the young tree stopped her from going further down. The next weekend, we rode on a trike, a three-wheeled motorcycle with two wheels at the rear and a wheel at the front without motor. We roamed the full length of the park. This allowed us to have a relaxing ride while breathing the pure air. All motorized vehicles were prohibited from entering the park, so there was no pollution.

As Lysiane grew older, she experienced more sports like horse-riding, ice skating, roller skating, and she loved swimming. She obtained her *brevet de natation* [swimming certificate] during our summer vacation in Audenge, a suburb Bordeaux, in the south-west of France. I was proud to watch her being so confident in deep water.

We wanted a second child

Lysiane always asked for a brother or a sister. After her birth I had two pregnancies, but I miscarried both. I was left deeply affected. I tried different kinds of medications to help me to get pregnant again, but they failed.

One day, I was hoping for some good news, but I heard my doctor say "Now your uterus is neat and healthy. Madame, are you ready to have five babies?"

I was shocked by what I heard, and I felt paralyzed. It was as if a gong had struck between my ears, or a piece of bone was struck across my throat. My voice disappeared. The doctor continued explaining to me, but I became deaf, nervous, and felt like fainting. That news was so brutal and unfair. I walked off his office. I even forgot where I parked my car.

Five at once? I continued walking but unknowingly I was going back to the hospital while the medical secretary was looking for me. "Madame, the doctor had not yet finished examining you," she said.

I was there in front of him, wordless, what could I say. I knew that Lionel and I wanted to have another baby, but not five all at the same time. Another doctor came in front of me, a woman. "I am your psychiatrist," she introduced herself. I did not even understand why she was there. Anyway, she advised me to see her again later. I went home with several prescriptions for pills and an appointment, so I would probably see her back again.

One month passed. I decided not to have another baby anymore because I was scared that I would get pregnant with quintuplets. That day I started taking contraceptive pills.

I finally understood some of the reasons why I had experienced two miscarriages. The psychologist said my mind was poisoned by the different traumas: Lionel's eye operations, the discovery of his heart failure where the doctors said he would need to undergo heart surgery in the future, then Lysiane's eye operations at the age of three. Those factors created a state of permanent anxiety for me. I was excited with the idea of having baby, but at the same time I feared it. I did not look for a job because I was concentrating on taking care of Lionel and Lysiane, and at the same time I waited to another baby to come. "Family comes first," I told myself. Whereas now, I decided I did not want to be pregnant, not anymore. I only focused on looking for a job. However, I remembered when I told the midwives and nurses that I wouldn't be back in the maternity ward, as my mind was set against the nurse who pushed me into that boiling hot shower. Was I been punished for saying that?

The challenging period of adolescence

Lysiane remained our one and only child, our love was concentrated on her. She grew healthy and beautiful. There was no modern technology for hobbies like cellular phone, tablets or computers at that time. However, she loved drawing, painting, sculpting, and reading various books. She also enjoyed reading the magazines about science and nature. As she became teenager, she read less for some time and enjoyed music more. She used to compose her own songs with her own words, singing and recording them on cassettes, when there was no CD yet. She played badminton, or had fun with her friends and classmates putting on music in her room. Aside from biking, skating, and skiing, she enjoyed swimming, practices aikido (a martial art) but she didn't like dancing. To help her shape her life and career, we allowed her to travel with friends after she finished college at seventeen. Aside from UK they went to Spain, Italy, Portugal, then later to Madagascar, Greece, etc. In addition to French, she developed skills in language, speaking English, Spanish and Italian that improved as she grew older. And she loved baking cakes.

At the age of sixteen, we trusted her with a key and had instructed her not to let anybody enter to our apartment during our absence. But she had more and more suitors, from an early age, so this created problems.

One late evening, there were five or six boys of her age and older, all drinking beers in the parking lot near our terrace, and their group gradually became bigger and their noise increased. It was past midnight, most of them were drunk. They quarrelled, yelling and throwing their empty bottles onto our terrace, while demanding that Lysiane to go out. They were so aggressive like a group of bandits. Then they came so near to our window and entered in our terrace, despite the high fence. We were all scared, especially Lysiane.

We called the police asking them to clear away the revellers. Fortunately, we had already closed our window shutters, so they could not see us, but that meant that we were also not able to identify them. Their noise was unbearable, and it lasted the whole night and prevented us from sleeping. I really wondered whether the police came to disperse them. We did not hear any siren. What I knew was that the police only came when someone got hurt or died. I even suspecting the police were scared of these kids. In the morning, we found broken beer bottles all over the terrace, our chairs taken, and the table broken. We found all six chairs outside the terrace, junked in the corners of the parking, broken too.

At times, I worried that maybe my teenage daughter was depressed by being an only child, but it was so difficult to open a dialogue with her as she never told us what was wrong with her. I was sceptical when her father insisted that there was no problem. But as soon as she came home, she locked herself in her room. She would put on her music so loudly that she couldn't even hear us calling her. She is our one and only daughter, and we loved her so much. We provided her with everything she needed, except a little brother or sister.

Though I couldn't stand to have my daughter unhappy, I preferred to set some limits. I encouraged her to have a reciprocal, two-way, relationship with us, rather than a spoiled attitude. However, perhaps because we unconsciously spoiled her, she became a bit self-centred and preoccupied with her own needs. I refused to spoil her, but her father was always giving in to her. He never refused to give her what she asked for. He always said "Yes", even if I said "No", although I stood by my reasons. Lysiane became distant from me and preferred to ask her father instead. If we both refused to grant her request, she became a wild rebel. Our relationship became difficult. I was afraid she would become a spoiled adult.

One day, she showed unacceptable behaviour, with intense disobedience. She came home with a girl who was not a friend from her class. I believed that Lysiane did not know her well yet, and I had never met her either. But Lysiane allowed that girl to opened the door of our apartment and let another friend in; and there were other friends waiting outside. Despite Lysiane's attempt to refuse, those boys entered by climbing up to the fence of our terrace and walked in the open door to the kitchen. When I arrived home in the evening I smelt strange odour, and Lionel was at the front door with his sister Ghislaine. They stared at me strangely. I immediately understood that something was wrong. Ghislaine never came to our place in the evening and I was wondering, why was she there? Both Lionel and his sister remained silent for a while. This confirmed to me that something disagreeable had happened while I was still at work. At that time, I was still working in Paris which took me more time to reach home than Lionel.

It turned out that those who entered our apartment were drug addicts and drunkards searching for expensive or resalable items. They turned the mattress of our bed upside down and they poured a bottle of ketchup on it. It was shocking to see it, like red blood. Lot of things were scattered on the floor. Everywhere the house was in mess, so they were surely looking for cash; blankets and clothes which were well arranged in our cupboard were also stolen.

I found Lysiane safely in her bedroom with a girl older than her whom I had never seen before, and I immediately sensed that she was the source of the major problem. She said rudely to me that Lysiane was alright, but she was being neglected by her parents. Luckily Lionel did not hear. Who was she to tell me that? And when I asked my daughter who the girl was, she just said she was a friend. In fact, that friend had brought her bad influence into my home. The girl refused to go out from our place, not unless I called the police to come and investigate why she was with our daughter and why she had let her burglar friends entered into our home. I understood later that she was there to hide from someone; she used Lysiane's naivete to hide.

Many things were stolen and among them was Lionel's wedding ring which had been getting tight to his fingers during hot season, so he placed it on our night-table together with his newly bought watch which was still in its original box. Lionel's competition pistol together with its ammunition were taken, and we were obliged to report this to the police for security reasons. We cannot claim anything from our insurance because the entrance door was opened by that girl who refused to give us her name. She had so many friends and they were all in a hurry to enter at the same time. Our neighbours reported that those young delinquents were climbing through the fence, despite their warnings. That day our teenage daughter ignored all our rules and reminders for her safety. We had warned her not to allow anybody to enter at home during our absence, but she disobeyed us.

Another evening, I came home late and a group of young offenders or delinquents dispersed once I came close. I noticed several syringes littered on the ground just near the entrance of our building, which was so stressful. They were taking drugs, and that frightened me with the thought that the drug dealers were just probably the neighbours around us. We had to get our daughter away from them to protect her from harm. So we were obliged to look for a house to buy urgently, far away from Stains where the problems with drugs were growing. It was challenging to keep ourselves and our loved ones safe. Lysiane seemed to be vulnerable to influence.

We had a lot of difficulty looking for a home that would suit the three of us. Then one day, the real estate agents contacted us with an interesting proposal. They gave us the chance to build our future home, 35 kilometres away from our previous apartment. We could hardly wait. The construction took almost eight months, and we moved into our new home in Beaumont sur Oise in January 6, 2000, on my birthday. It was one of my most wonderful birthday gifts I ever had.

Pure visions while fully awake - a gift from God?

We were happier in our new home. Lysiane continued her high school studies at Charles de Foucauld, a private school in Paris. Being an adolescent, she gave us a lot of worries; not just her studies, but her friends seemed like disreputable types and bad acquaintances. Her adolescence period was becoming difficult. Trying to enforce rules or restrictions for security purposes had made her a rebel. Perhaps she was searching for personal freedom. She'd ignored our advice, and she got inexplicably angry at times, thus there was a lot of conflict at home.

Despite this, Lysiane successfully obtained her Diploma of Baccalaureate. She then entered in the University of Sorbonne in Paris in September 2001, taking the course of Arts Plastique, with a Cinema option.

An unexpected event happened at the beginning of summer, June 2001. One evening after work, Lionel and I were relaxing together on the sofa. I moved closer to his side and told him about my worries concerning our daughter, when I suddenly viewed an event in the future: It was a vision or premonition of some sort. At the start, I did not understand what I was seeing. The images were there in front of me, inside my eyes, or deeply in my brain, but I was not dreaming. Lionel and I were talking about our daughter when that vision occurred. I learned that seeing visions while awake can give me a kind of alert that can help us be better prepared, but not always. Even though the events occurred almost six months after my premonition, I was not completely prepared.

A weird feeling came over me, and it was hard to explain but everything stopped around me. I couldn't move but continued looking to those clear images as they seemed so vividly real. My eyes were closed while hearing the unusual sounds and same time familiar to me.

> *I saw a kind of tunnel, not dark nor full of lights. There were some pinkish particles floating, turning around something. I heard a noise like a drum, or the beating of a heart, two hearts, then an image came up... of a baby sucking its thumb, floating inside liquid going up like a silent cascade of water but the baby shows a shadow. Oh no, it was not a shadow. It was a second baby going up, following the first one. Then I understood that they were two babies turning inside a womb of a mother.*

I was stupefied. I realized it was a pure vision. I had kept on asking myself: Was it the vision from God? When the images went away, everything seemed normal again, I still felt devastated by what I saw. It changed my existence, and life was never the same. It worried me badly.

I tried to convince myself that they were not Lysiane's babies, as she was only 18 years old at the time, in her first year of university studies. I did not know how or when it would happen. I prayed God that if ever that vision did come true, I hoped it wouldn't happen right away. I was worried about how she would be able to finish her studies with two babies to take care of, but if she continued studying who would take care of the babies? How could I take care of them while working eight hours a day? What could I do so that this prediction could disappear? Could it be rebuked by my prayers? After long meditation, I asked God, that if ever it happens, would He be there to help us cope?

Days passed. While cleaning our house one day with the vacuum, I heard some young girls giggling, I stopped the vacuum and tried to concentrate on listening to giggling noise then I was thinking that Lysiane's babies will surely be two girls. That evening I told my husband that I heard young girls giggling around me.

He answered me with a question: "Aren't you afraid?"

"Not at all, they seem quite happy."

"So, let them stay," he said, probably as a joke.

At that very moment I was again thinking of telling him about the vision I had experienced, as we were talking about Lysiane's behavior and changing attitude, but I still had a feeling that it was not the right time. Perhaps I was afraid of what his reaction might be. Maybe he would ignore the vision or think it was absurd. Maybe he would think I'd lost my mind. He loved our daughter so much and it was surely hard for him to accept the idea that it was his always answering "Yes" to Lysiane's caprices that made her spoiled.

The next day we visited his mother, and I told her about hearing young girls playing around me.

She asked the same question, "were you afraid?"

"No Mama, they seem so happy giggling and their laughters tickle me."

I thought of calling my cousin, Sister Cecile, a nun in the Philippines. Perhaps she could help enlighten me and lift my heavy worries. But she was unreachable. I called on God to please send me his Holy Spirit and heal my mind.

This burden of not being able to talk to Lionel about that premonition led me to have many sleepless nights. I was almost sure that my vision concerned Lysiane, because she was our subject in our conversation that day. I kept on praying that those were not Lysiane's babies. But every time I thought of my daughter, the vision resurfaced. It stayed at the front of my mind, despite my attempts to deny it.

Weeks passed. I contemplated. I accepted the vision as a gift from the holy spirit. I also understood that perhaps everything had already been planned by the Highest? Perhaps He wanted me to be prepared and follow instructions according to His own will. But how could I announce it to Lionel who was undergoing treatment for heart troubles?

I always remembered when Doctor Charlier, his late cardiologist, advised me to be prudent; there were many things I had to not do for the health of my husband. Or was it maybe preferable to wait and see what would happen, without telling him about that vision. I was even thinking that it might not happen to our daughter, because I kept on praying that it wouldn't occur at all. She was only 18 years old. She deserved to finish her studies and find that good job that she was longing for. But at the midst of my wonderings, the memory of my vision persisted.

Lysiane continued her studies at the University of Sorbonne in Paris following her course in Arts Plastique with Cinema as option. Time passed quickly and soon, Christmas 2001 was approaching. To bring the spirit of Christmas home, the tree was decorated as usual to please our one and only daughter, and everything was ready for the celebration. However, when Lysiane came home, she went straight to her room and stayed awhile.

When she suddenly appeared in the lounge, she said: "Mama, you have over-decorated our house. Don't you know that I will celebrate Christmas with friends and am going to sleep at Lilibeth's house in Paris?"

I felt like a sharp knife was cutting my heart into pieces. "No, you did not tell me that" I said. "The food is ready to be served. Would you stay with us and taste them before going, what about that?" That very moment I felt slapped by reality. Lysiane was not a child anymore. She did not need me. On Christmas Eve, she preferred to stay with her friends rather than stay with her parents. Now, she was an adult. Evidently, we couldn't keep our child forever with us.

I can still remember when she told me that she was bored being with us; she was fed-up to celebrate her birthdays with his father's family around. She preferred to be with her friends, or with her classmates since their youngest school days. She also reminded us and listed all the activities that she was not allowed as a child: going to the beach with her friends because she was too young; not allowed to watch the concert of her favorite singers because of the dangers in the crowd; not to go to vacation by Youngs Colony despite being accompanied by the monitor and organizer because of the danger of kidnapping; we had even prevented her from going to McDonald's to avoid obesity.

My daughter was only nine when I started working full-time. Later I noticed her behaviour changed. It was true that we had always brought her with us during school vacations and other holidays. She said we were old fashioned and unsociable. She refused to understand that we wanted to protect her for her own good and for her life security. She grew up fast. All these facts were pounding my head and I felt the pain of being rejected. Now she needed distance and independence. But her dramatic changes of behavior drove me crazy. I realized how time went by so fast and yet I was not well-prepared for the painful changes.

As she had turned 19 years old in September that year, I had almost forgotten about my vision. Now for Christmas, she wore a new beautiful backless pink dress. She came to me and asked: "Mama, could you tie the ribbons at my back?"

While I was tying the ribbons, I experienced another clear vision as a sort of warning: I sensed that after midnight, she would become a mistress of a lover whom I had not met yet. I trembled. I went to my room to hide and cry. How could I prevent her from going to her Christmas party? I tried dissuading her, but she grew mad at me. I so hoped my prediction was wrong. But the same vision came to me again, and clearer this time.

I felt helpless. Anguish took over my mind. I sensed she was going to be the mother of her twin baby girls. What can a mother do for her adolescent daughter, pregnant? Oh God, I prayed. Will you help me in that whatever may happen, help me be able to handle it somehow. How could I support my daughter through the challenges that lay ahead?

As the days passed, she became irritable, nasty, and disobedient. One day she collapsed on the metro. Then few days after, she fainted on the tram and lost her papers for the second time: identity card, Visa card, student card, and so on. I was almost sure that this time she would know that something had changed in her. But perhaps she did not know yet, that she was on the way to her conception. For me, she was too young to be a mother. What would happen to her future?

I planned to have a heart-to-heart conversation with her, but I wondered if or how I could remain supportive of her. I was afraid I would be unable to control myself and my emotions in front of her. Maybe now would not be the right time to blame her and declare my disappointment. While I drove back home from work at the midst of traffic jams in the Paris ring road, so many questions battled in my head. But as her mother, I was scared to realize that she was pregnant. I asked myself whether I was ready to be a grandmother. It was surely a wonderful experience, but for me it was too soon. How could I overcome everything?

Was it my fault as I failed to stop of what I saw in my vision? I needed to find a way as to how to control my own emotions, to avoid an explosive confrontation between me and my daughter. To burst forth in anger would certainly not be healthy for any of us. I was anxious about her future: she should not quit university, but who would take care of the newborn babies? At the same time, I was more upset on how to deal with my emotions to inform Lionel about the situation of our teenage daughter. He should not burst into anger; it could prove fatal to his health. How would Lionel react upon knowing that his only daughter, only 19 and still a university student, was now pregnant?

I remember that at the age of 15 she said she wanted to have a baby very soon so that she wouldn't be alone anymore, but I took it for granted that she was kidding. When I did not have a job I was constantly with her. I even joined her school as a volunteer to accompany her class during their outings just to be with her during their visits to museums, excursion and sports such as ice skating, skiing, running, biking, pony riding etc. It was maybe hard for her to accept that I was not with her all the time anymore. But like her father, I had to work to earn a living and prepare for our future.

Many times, she said that I had failed. She said "Mama, unlike you, I will surely be successful to have plenty of children. And if by chance I only have one child, I will adopt other's children." She was full of enthusiasm. I did not know what to answer.

One evening, she returned home ill and was very nauseous. Our doctor examined her at home. He gave her two prescriptions: some tablets to take and a laboratory test to be done right away. Five days passed. I asked her if she had gone to the laboratory for the result. I was sure she knew the answer, but she did not tell us.

I was waiting for Lysiane to announce to me and her father that she would have a baby. That would become easier for me, rather than to tell Lionel myself that our daughter was pregnant. Although I was carrying this burden, I half-heartedly continued doing the daily activities as usual, pretending that everything was normal. But it was so difficult for me to concentrate on my work, because to get pregnant without a husband to serve as a father to her babies would be very complicated, especially that she was still studying.

I was using the vacuum cleaner when it suddenly made an unusual noise; it was a piece of envelope already opened, stuck in the suction. The paper inside showed the result of Lysiane's blood test: She was almost four weeks pregnant. But she still had not told me, and she was so evasive. I presumed that she intentionally left the result on top of the desk to let us see the result by ourselves. I felt guilty of not informing Lionel about my first premonition that Lysiane would have two babies. Now it became even more difficult to tell him.

Two days later, Lysiane called me at my office. She announced me excitedly that she was expecting a baby. She did not know yet she was carrying two. Although I already knew she was pregnant, I remained shocked not because of the babies, but because of her manner of announcing it to me. She was excited and it and seemed normal or simple for her. She seemed practically ready to accept all the responsibilities with all that it entailed, but I wondered if she could manage all alone by herself? She did not know that I was worried about how to tell her father. I told her that it might surely be difficult for all of us because she had not finished her studies yet, and to be a mother so early might ruin her life.

I remained asstonished when she answered: "Don't worry Mama, it is just a matter of organization then everything will be alright." She did not really realize the reality of what she said. I had even thought that she was probably scared to death to tell me that she was pregnant. But what I heard from her was an easy, optimistic version of the story. Again, I was wondering how I could tell all that to Lionel?

It was so hard for me to inform Lionel about Lysiane's new situation as he had heart troubles, and I still remembered his cardiologist who had instructed me to take some precautions, and not to worry or not to excite him suddenly. But I said to myself that tonight I had to tell him, and I hoped he would cope and have an appropriate conversation with our daughter. So, after our diner I had told him about Lysiane's pregnancy. He was shocked and so tensed that at first he did not say anything. He remained silent and grew pale. He would have had liked to talk to his daughter immediately, but Lysiane returned home late that night from university so we decided to talk to her early the next morning. It was perhaps better that way so that we could at least think clearly, to calm down on the first hand. It would allow us to have time to process this new information and prepare what to say without anger or conflict. It was always quite easy for the unhealthy emotion of anger to burst forth, and believe me I was terribly upset. We both remained awake the whole night as we both kept tossing and turning.

Lysiane stayed longer in her bed that morning. She had surely guessed that I had already told her father about her situation. I wondered if she had slept that night. I was almost sure that it would be too hard for her to tell him herself. She knew we love and trusted her, but she had disobeyed us. We had always emphasized the importance of her finishing her studies, and getting married before starting a family.

I sat on a chair in the corner of her room and was ready to listen to Lionel's views. I decided to let him talk first, while I kept praying that he would hold back his temper.

In a low but extremely tense voice, he asked Lysiane who was the father.

She did not answer right away; it was as if she was trying to find the right words.

Lionel asked her for the second time: "Can you tell us his name?"

Again, Lysiane did not answer.

Lionel's temper was about to burst, and mine too, but I remained silent, tensed, and I listened. I preferred not to interfere with Lionel. I was anxious that he might lose control. When Lysiane uttered the name of the father of her babies, her father turned red with rage. I came closer and stood between them. No more words came from Lionel nor from Lysiane, while I kept on praying that their difficult conversation would come to an end without trouble, or at least the first step towards healing could be over.

Lysiane did not want to tell him, and he was unemployed and not Catholic. But Lysiane would always be our daughter and there were still lot of things to be discussed for her and the preparations before the birth of the babies. I still did not tell Lionel about the two babies that I saw in my vision. To tell him such things at that moment would have been devastating to our relationship.

The atmosphere at home had drastically changed. I did not dare anymore to say a word to Lionel because I was afraid that things would turn into arguments. His shock and disappointment were overwhelming, so much that he did not say a word to me nor to our daughter. We became like perfect strangers at home. The shock penetrated us even when we were alone. We both had several sleepless nights and I wondered how long we could remain this way. I did not find any way as to how to improve the situation. I thought I wasn't a good mother to our daughter because I couldn't stop her from having babies before she finished her studies and before getting married.

Both of us felt guilty, but we could not take on all the responsibilities for the babies, and we needed to prepare their arrival whether we liked it or not. With God's help we could go through with it. On the other hand, when Lysiane announced to me that she would have a baby, I realized that she had really wanted to become a mother, although it was not as simple as she made it sound. She received the result of the third sonogram. She said that a shadow that was shown during the first and second examination was now confirmed: the shadow was a second baby. She was awfully happy and proud of carrying her two baby girls. She was overflowing with excitement.

Lionel, a practicing Christian and a devoted Catholic, had a hard time accepting the new situation of our daughter. He warned me categorically not to tell his family, not yet. I did not agree with him, but I obeyed. But after one week of long silence made me feel suffocated, not informing his sisters. So, I talked to my colleagues and friends at work and also to Lysiane's godmother, Irene. In May, Lysiane was five months pregnant and she was in a bad mood most of the time. Lysiane and I were like enemies. She was always lashing out at others.

I phoned my mother in the Philippines to tell her about my daughter's situation, and that she did not want to inform the father of her babies. And I also believed that my daughter was afraid that the father might try to take her babies, all those things were battling in my mind. I don't know, Lysiane did not confided me about the father.

I felt quite relieved to speak to my mother on the phone. I was astonished with her admirable attitude. In fact, I had even hesitated to inform her about my daughter's pregnancy because she was a devoted Catholic. I was overwhelmed that she had reacted so well to being a great-grandmother. She advised me to be careful with Lysiane, to avoid some arguments which could led her to miscarry her babies. And she added: "Lysiane is probably well prepared to be a mother because she will be 20 years in September." That statement from Mama made me felt quite relieved, as she reminded me that she had delivered me when she was not yet 19 years old. Lysiane would deliver her babies near her 20th birthday, more matured than when Mama delivered me.

Meanwhile, Mama informed me that my father was sick, and that he had been in bed for been several days. I went to Philippines that month, May 2002. I needed to see my father before I would be busy with the coming of the twins. Moreover, I was fed up of Lysiane's negative moods and irritability swirling around her pregnancy. The worst thing was that she and Lionel were not communicating at all. I was even afraid to open a conversation to my husband; my home was hell.

When I came back from the Philippines, our Bermuda garden were covered with long wild grasses which grew proudly during my absence. My plants had been abandoned. The flowers were not trimmed; they were thirsty and withered, others died. My garden looked so sad. But I was overwhelmed with joy upon knowing that my husband was reconciled to our daughter. It was the most beautiful gift of my returning home. I thanked God for how he reconciled my small family. He lighted my life with hopes, and my faith in Him grew.

Triumps Over The Trials

Sabrine and Typhaine

One Saturday morning, Lysiane and I went to buy some of the missing items needed for her babies: two cribs, one baby stroller for two, and two playpens. In the car, I announced to Lysiane that the coming Monday morning was my entrance examination for a new course I wanted to do. If I could pass the exams, I would be officially enrolled in University of Paris VIII. And although I had validated my university diplomas, I needed to pursue my studies to master English, to obtain a license to legally teach English in France.

Lysiane was delighted and she encouraged me to do it. She said, "Mama, I am sure you can pass the entrance examination and pursue your studies."

But while listening to my daughter, I had a strong feeling that she would go into labour sooner than the expected due date. I had a quick flash of a vision, showing the delivery room. I started praying that her giving birth would be easy and that the babies would be born healthy. I was panicking inside, but I tried not to let it rub off on my daughter, not to give her anxiety. Stop getting nervous Sarah, everything will be alright, I said to myself. I always remember back: Mama delivered her twins Amelie and Ashley so easily, at home. I entrusted ourselves to God.

September 27, 2002, on a Sunday evening, while we were taking our dinner, Lysiane called in a strange way and said: "Mama, look, the water is breaking! I can't help it!"

It took me a little time to realize that the babies were coming soon, too soon, three weeks before the due date. She said she did not feel any pains, but she couldn't move. I knew that she was carrying more than four kilos of babies in her womb, maybe too heavy for a mother to carry them for the first time in her life. When the ambulance came, Lysiane repeated that she couldn't stand, she could not move from her chair. The two medics from ambulance reassured her, told her not to get upset. I understood that she was already in labour. They carried her, still glued to her chair, into the ambulance.

I hurriedly drove my car to follow them. Lysiane was on a rolling bed surrounded with her obstetricians and gynaecologists. The doctor asked for Lysiane's papers. But Lysiane's suitcase was at home and my handbag too. Luckily, there were no police on the road as I drove faster than ever, and yet I did not have a single paper with me, not even a driving license. Although I was prepared because of my premonition dream and vision, I felt completely disoriented. In fact, I had known that the babies would come before their due date. But once the time arrived, becoming a grandmother at fifty was so overwhelming that I was nervous and excited at the same time.

At home, Lionel was sick. I was upset. I would take him to Georges Pompidou hospital in Paris tomorrow afternoon for his escheduled heart operation. He could not go with me to the maternity ward because he needed to rest that night. I almost forgot that I had to go back to the maternity hospital with Lysiane's papers and her suitcase for the babies. But I had to help Lionel first.

Lysiane had a caesarean delivery. Then quickly, a doctor went out delicately holding a baby girl and I followed them to the next room where babies were cleaned and dressed up; then the second baby followed. It was fabulous to see my little grandchildren, so fragile and so innocent. I am still incapable of fully describing my emotions that day. I was experiencing those happy moments, but I was all alone, no one to share with.

I would have had like to have shared the moment with someone, to express my feelings as a grandmother for the first time. I did not dare to call my sister-in laws from Stains, who were much older than Lionel and would have been asleep. And it was not easy to call my friends or office colleagues during the night. They were all living far from the maternity ward. Baby Sabrine was taken out first at 23h35 then followed by Typhaine at 23h37. They weighed a little more than two kilos each. And while they were washed by the nurses, I rushed to my daughter's room and congratulated her.

 I said, "your babies are cute and beautiful." She seemed tired but happy surrounded by good doctors, and I was quite reassured. As soon as I entered to the baby department, a nurse asked me to sit down unto the armchair that she had prepared and placed Sabrine and Typhaine in my arms. She took polaroid photos that I will always keep. The newly born babies were so small and fragile; I did not feel at ease, I was afraid they might slip from my arms.

I had not slept. That early morning as scheduled, I took and passed the entrance examination successfully in Paris VIII University. And with divine guidance, on the same day I would drove Lionel in the afternoon to Pompidou Hospital in Paris. Lionel had to undergo urgent heart surgery. It was his first time at that hospital famous for their good reputation in cardiac treatment. I was amazed when I realized that despite the birth of our grandchildren where I stayed so many hours in the maternity ward and my lack of sleep, I was not stressed nor worried. We reached the hospital smoothly safe and on time. I thought of Divine Providence. I continue to believe that all those things would happen as they should. I knew that that very moment that I needed to take care of my husband, my daughter, and my first two grandchildren all at the same time, while working fulltime, and studying in the evening. But I was awfully happy.

Lysiane was right when she told me in an enormously proud voice: " Mama, you have failed to give birth to your second baby, while I am proud of being a mother of my two girls, both born together, two at the same time." She kept on repeating that, and it reminds me of my grandmother. Nanay had given birth to twins twice, born during the Second World War. My mother did too. I did not give birth to twins, but now my daughter had twin daughters. It jumped over one generation. I experienced a strong and nurturing energy which I never knew before. I sometimes thought that I was invaded by a beautiful energy emanating from the universe. It is amazing that I can forget all the feelings of fatigue when I am with Sabrine and

Typhaine, perhaps because I love the babies so much. They are sort of a rejuvenating glow. I was quite amazed to have discovered this hidden energy that helped me in pursuing my new role as grandmother of my first two grandaughters.

Lionel's heart procedure - 2002

While Lysiane was still in the maternity hospital, Lionel had to have his first heart operation. At the time, I was working full time at the Medicines Agency. I had used much of my vacation days in attending classes in the University of Paris VIII. Still, with everything going on, I had many absences from my classes. It was absolutely impossible for me to go to four different directions each day and night: From Beaumont to Saint Denis, from there to Paris, then to the maternity ward in Beaumont sur Oise, then back home; the areas are quite far apart.

Each early morning, I went to the maternity ward with a thermos full of hot milk for Lysiane, and then drove 50 kilometers to reach my work. Luckily, there was no speed radar operating along the road at that time. At lunchtime I drove to the Hospital Pompidou in Paris to visit Lionel and stayed for an hour, then back to work in Saint Denis. I had no time to take my lunch, but I was not hungry anyway. Before going home from work, I visited first my husband in the hospital in Paris again, then to my daughter and her babies in the maternity ward in Beaumont sur Oise before I finally returned home at night. It became the routine.

Fifteen days after his heart intervention, Lionel was transferred to another hospital, l'Hôpital du Parc, in Taverny for his convalescence. During lunchtimes, I would help Lionel to walk around the park nearby to help him recover faster. I visited him again in the evening before going back to Beaumont to see Lysiane and the twins before going back home. But I was absent almost two weeks from my classes.

During my classes for the whole semester, my mind was divided between thinking of Lionel, Lysiane and the babies. I was happy to take care of them, particularly the babies. But it was impossible to undertake all these activities at the same time. So, I finished one semester then I stopped. I had still one and a half semesters to finish the course. But I was able to continue working professionally while taking care of the family.

As soon as Lysiane and the babies got out of the maternity ward, I took them directly to the Park Hospital to visit Lionel. I couldn't find the words for how to express my happiness while driving for the first time, with the two little angels in our car back seats. I was praying that our visit would help my husband to recover quickly. It was time he needed to think about his new life after the heart surgery, now that he was a grandfather. Lionel's face was full of hope and aspiration upon seeing his two newly born grandaughters. I was deeply touched by the manner Lionel tenderly caressed the two cute babies. He had forgotten for a while the pain of his newly operated chest, full of stitches and staples.

The babies at home

A midwife came to our house in the morning. For five consecutive days, she taught Lysiane how to take care of the babies while I was working. After two months, Lysiane was back to University while Lionel was still in Parc Hospital for his long convalescence. I took a leave from work for one week to help my daughter taking care of the babies and to organize everything.

Françoise, a mother of her friend, Lilibeth, who lived in Porte de Pantin, Paris nearer to Lysiane's university offered to help. She looked after the babies while I was working and taking care of Lionel. I left my cell phone on while attending classes in case of emergency. Normally I took the babies back home every evening before going home after work, or when I was not attending classes, but the traffic was so dense, and Paris was more than two hours' drive to our home and even more difficult with traffic jams. I had heart ache for the babies who were already travelling almost every day and Beaumont is quite far from Paris, so Lysiane stayed with Françoise in Paris for about one month, but Lionel and I continued fetching the babies from Françoise's every weekend and the holidays.

One-time Lysiane phoned me while I was in class. We were not supposed to leave our cell phone on while attending classes, but I was afraid to miss any important messages from my daughter. The whole day Lysiane was in the university which is far from where we lived; I worked during the day and attended classes in the evening, and I had to go to the Bibliothèque de France, the grand library in Paris, for my assignments on Saturdays.

I dropped some of my subjects because it was impossible for me to go to the library for my assignments every Saturday while the babies were at home, and I could not buy things for the babies or foods on Sundays, as all the stores were closed. So, I made the choice to leave the university after one semester to take care of the whole family. Maybe all that hectic scheduling was worth it, though.

Lionel's heart operation was successful. Sabrine and Typhaine were healthy and growing, and their mother continued going to the University of Sorbonne in Paris, and didn't miss out on her education. Those were my beautiful gifts.

Until now, I still can't imagine how I was able to do all those tasks everyday, going to four different places in four different directions far apart. But I was not worried about how to handle them. I had to simply to keep going, fulfilling my duty as a wife, a mother, and a grandmother. I am convinced that God was guiding me to triumph over the difficulties. Upon thinking it through, I again realize that I have never really been alone, because God was always there, with me. I have this endless gratitude to Him. Could I be able to face the most difficult trials and to gain victory through Jesus? Could I see heaven again and live eternal life with God?

Lionel's experience after heart surgery– 2002

Lionel had practiced recreational sports since childhood, such as skiing or bicycling. At home, he used the rowing machine for daily exercise, in addition to lots of walking. He adored the outdoors, and he actively participated in long walks accompanied by the members of social or cultural groups.

He said he had undergone several eye operations when he was young, and two eye surgeries just before our wedding. He experienced different chirurgical intervention and he said that the open-heart surgery was the most difficult experience he had ever known.

Lionel had problems of valves, heart failure (insufficiency mitral), and arterial damage. It resulted in him experiencing weakness, fatigue, and irregular heart rhythms. The cardiologist's diagnosis was that it was congenital, which required surgery and then extensive therapy and exercise after.

He had open-heart surgery on the 11th of September 2002 by Professor Latrimouille in Georges-Pompidou Hospital in Paris, one of the most reputable hospitals in Europe.

The day after the surgery, I saw him covered with antiseptic orange colour on his skin, a safety precaution to avoid infection. I felt pain, seeing his breast with skin pierced with metal staple-wires holding the wound closed; I could also see fine monofilament nylon thread stiches. The scar stretched from his chest to his navel.

Lionel told me about his experience during and after the surgery. He said:

"I was awakened with unbearable pain, with difficulty breathing perhaps because of the electrodes that were still connected to my heart. I only felt better after I had vomited. The surgeons were tapping my back, and massaging my entire body to improve the blood's circulation. But I fainted. I wasn't prepared for the stress, fear and nightmares that followed. But with the help of a clinical psychologist and cardiac rehabilitation, I slowly forged my path to recovery," he explained.

After Pompidou hospital, he spent the full two-month convalescence period in a hospital called *Hôpital de Parc de Taverny*. It was a public establishment that offered medical surveillance, re-education, and rehabilitation. Patients were provided with a place to recuperate and rehabilitate in a beautifully landscape – the wide parc. Every day I accompanied him walking at lunchtime. I always visited him twice a day to see his progress. He returned to work after four months away: two months in the hospitals and two months at home.

Meanwhile, Lysiane found an apartment in Livry Gargan, closer to Paris than where we live. As a student, she found a job as a tourist guide, so she was also earning while studying. That left little time for the girls because she was also working during Saturdays. Sunday was her only time to take a rest. Lionel and I continued keeping the little girls at home during weekends and holidays, and even during the week at times. Lionel and I took shifts to take care of the girls. I took 10 days vacation from work, then it was Lionel's turn to take his vacation leave; and we were altogether during our whole summer vacations. So, our grandchildren were nurtured by us in Beaumont sur Oise. And today, at the time of writing March 2021, Sabrine and Typhaine are eighteen years old, studying in universities in Paris.

The father claims his daughters

As we settled into the new life as grandparents, at first Lionel and I were both upset knowing that the twins' father, Mr. Rehibi, was not a Catholic like us. We were worried that it would create troubles and misunderstanding, incompatibility of traditions and culture, but we were wrong.

He had been living in Paris, did not know that he became a father. For some reason, Lysiane did not want him to give his name to their daughters. In the registrar office of Beaumont sur Oise, Lysiane registered the babies as Sabrine and Typhaine Tchermnykh. In the comments it was written "father unknown." She came back home satisfied. In her mind, all was fine.

But one day, the father reappeared, and he asserted his legal rights concerning the babies. This entailed a long legal procedure and a hard battle between them that lasted two years. The father won his case, and they were treated fairly by a family judge; the father had the right to visit and see his children. He obtained official documents from their registrar. Sabrine and Typhaine were 10 years old when their father got married and had two more children. Now, the girls usually spend some of their summer holidays together with their father, their half-brother and half-sisters.

Lysiane's Wedding

Sabrine and Typhaine were seven years old when their mother got married to B. Fontaine. She had met him while working at a social welfare centre. I was so excited, looking forward to the wedding celebration. But I was confronted with a bizarre sensation that I had to secretly fight against. I sensed that Lysiane's marriage wouldn't last long. I really wondered why that kept repeating in my head. I really hoped it was wrong. I was so tense even inside the church that I could hear my breathing and heart beats.

I was angry with myself of why I was feeling anxious, as if the wedding would be false? Chants were sung but I did not hear any sound, not even the sound of the organ, the people were singing but I heard no voices. Was it due to stress or something else? I felt strange, as if I was watching a silent film. It made me sad. What had really happened to me? I only learned later what was said when my friends showed me the videos they took during the ceremony.

What I recall: Lysiane stood on a rotating round platform trying on wedding dresses while I admired her. She looked so beautiful in those wedding dresses. She had had a third child, Vadim, with B. Fontaine and was happy to marry him. Two-month-old Vadim was in my arms. He was breastfed, and sometimes insisted on interrupting his mother as she tried to make a decision; it was difficult for me to advise her which one would be the best gown for her. She needed to choose the dress for herself, and not blame anyone else for her choice.

Lysiane put on on her wedding gown at home, assisted by her best friend. When I wanted to fix something on her dress, Lysiane said: "Mama, better not to touch my dress." As she wished, I did not touch her nor her dress that day. I wondered what superstitious belief she held. We had never talked about it, and I still don't know why until now.

Lysiane and B. Fontaine have two children: Vadim and Sasha. After seven years of marriage, they decided to divorce. As of today, March 2021, they are not divorced, but they live separately.

Vadim in my vision

Vadim was born in January 2009 in the maternity of Pavillons sous Bois. It was amazing to see him with the umbilical cord wrapped around his neck at birth. I can still recall that Lysiane had her final exposition of drawings in January 2009 in Paris, when Vadim was only few days old. As a baby, he loved to be carried and kept in motion. His father used to lift him up high and then bring him down to stop his crying.

He was already so sporty since his birth. From a young age, he was always an intelligent child, actively participating in the Boy Scout activities, games and sports in school and outdoors activities like swimming, snow skiing and athletics. He also enjoyed playing with Lego. He has strong enthusiasm for acting and theatre, and he especially loves art, drawing and painting like his parents. His father was a teacher in arts and crafts in a private high school.

As a grandmother, experiencing a vision is somewhat like watching the movie in the cinema or in the television. But to see events in the future is sometimes terribly worrying, especially when it concerns your own family.

One night I lay down on my bed earlier than usual, at about 8:30 pm. I was so tired. I tried to empty my head and close my eyes to forget the everyday stress at work, and the heavy traffic on my way back home. But I could not sleep; a flashing image came to my head that lasted for a second or two before it disappeared.

Vadim, my grandson, threw himself on me and hugged me, his body fell into my breast and he embraced me again and again. But when he raised his head, there was something that glowed in both his two eyes. He stared at me with his two eyes covered with white spots. As I cuddled and cradled him in my arms, it was hard to stop crying. I wanted to grasp him again and would cover him with hugs and kisses, but he was not there.

Again, I was so angry with myself when seeing the vision that brought me anguish. I sat on my bed and sobbed. I had that extreme feeling of unease. It is so unfair for a baby to experience the difficulty of sight. Was that vision another message from God?

I prayed hard. I begged the Highest, that if those images were true, please would He help us to overcome the pain, and let Vadim be healed. My meditation was interrupted by my anger. I was angry that my child and grandchildren had to suffer the consequences of my husband's congenital illness. Vadim was only two years old. It was too cruel and too early to let him experience hardship in life. I still remember when Lysiane had her cataracts at the age of three. I ran to Lionel in his bedroom still awake, listening to old music from a cassette. I informed him of what I saw in that vision, but he did not say a word. He remained silent and contemplated. Then he told me to forget it and go back to bed. But I remained awake the whole night. I was tormented, unable to decide whether or not to call my daughter that evening to inform her about Vadim's eyes, but what for? I didn't want her to feel the anguish like I had.

Lionel and I visited them in their apartment that weekend, and as usual, Vadim was full of energy playing with his toys. Sometimes he showed us how to re-construct the broken cars and lorries. He was full of wisdom. I was not able to tell Lysiane about my visions. I never told her that I have this capacity of viewing visions, as I don't want her to be scared of me. But perhaps she knows it?

Two weeks passed swiftly. White spot that had started shading Vadim's eyes. Now I was thinking that Lysiane's eye operation had been successful, and same with Typhaine. I thanked God that Vadim's eye intervention was also a success.

Why that congenital disease exists! I spent a lot of time in meditation trying to find hope and rewards for the sufferings we have endured, and to spare my grandchildren from misfortune. And I asked pardon from God, to forgive me for being weak, although my faith in Him remained strong.

Sasha

Sasha came to our world safe and sound. She was a cute little darling with big brown eyes and brown hair that was almost blond. Lysiane's delivery was smooth as Sasha came easily by herself. The nurse and the midwife were stupefied seeing her come out so effortlessly. My fourth grandchild, now seven years old at the time of my writing this memoir. Time passes so quickly. She was born in July 2014 in Pavillons sous Bois, France. I find it impressive to see this young child who has already begun to learn how to read and has already memorized many poems. She has the drawing skills that she got from her parents, and she also loves to dance, which she may have gotten from me and her elder sister Sabrine. Sasha has a beautiful voice like her sister Typhaine. Like her brother and sisters, she attended kindergarten from the age of 3.

You would never be bored with Sasha. Unlike me, she has very strong conversation skills, and she is not shy. "You know Lola," she says to me [they call me *Lola*, meaning grandmother], "I won't be in the baby class anymore; I am big enough now, I'll be attending the primary class this coming September." She was full of enthusiasm while showing me her drawings. I would miss her and all the grandchildren terribly if I spent my retirement away from them in a country far away, like the Philippines. For me, they are safer to stay in France.

While writing this memoir, my spirit was wandering, tracing the times of past years and present. Lots of unforgettable adventures happened before, during and after my teenage years. Now I meditate not only for my own life but mostly for the future of my four grandchildren who drastically changed my life. My husband and I love them very much. How I long to be possibly to be with them for the rest of my life.

I can never forget my past: my spiritual life in Cabadbaran where I have the privelege of been visited by the Holy Spirit that had changed my life; the interrupted schooling at the age of nine where I became responsible for my two younger sisters; the near-death and out-of-body experience at the age of 10 that had allow me to have a glimpse to Heaven; my difficulties in elementary school where I was not welcomed; my teenage misery having to work to provide for my parents instead of focusing on high school; my college experiences as a working student; and my love affairs where I was courted by someone, while I was in love with someone else. Then it continued during my college days where I became brave and hard-hearted as I was concentrating on my studies and constantly trying to helping my parents and siblings improve their lives, rather than being pre-occupied with my own affairs.

What had I done during my adolescence years? I had some different travel experiences like the scariest landing in Bangkok, before my arrival in France; then several car accidents; and now I was a grandmother cherishing my grandchildren. Will I still be there when they obtain their university diplomas, and their first jobs? Will I still be there to witness their weddings if they choose to get married? It was so difficult for me to establish the connection between my feelings and my inner self, and to choose who I would live my life with. I sometimes am persuaded that it was life that chose for me who to live with. Was I really intended to be the wife of my husband Lionel? And him for me? Now I am long married, blessed with one daughter who made me a grandmother. Time is going by so fast. I should stay in harmony with my body and spirit, must channel my energies and with God's help, everything will go well.

I became mature before my adolescence period. I was looking back over my childhood, when I became an adult, longing to be young, also when I became a mother, trying to recall my errors. And now more questions arose. Could I be a good grandmother to these children?

It was hard for me to not to see my parents in Philippines for nine consecutive years: from August 1993 to May 2002. And I missed the opportunity to attend their Golden Wedding Anniversary in August 25, 2001. I am the eldest of eight children, and I know very well that my father would have liked me to have been present during that memorable celebration. I was also not present for their 65th Wedding Anniversary in August 2016. I am terribly sorry; living abroad had mean that all the pain of remorse and regret continuously dig into my aching heart.

Lysiane, our only daughter, has given us four grandchildren. Lionel had two brothers: unfortunately, neither of them had children. Lysiane give this gift to her father, by choosing Tchermnykh as the surname of her four children. My husband and I love them very much, so much that we would give our life for them.

Could I be able to face the most difficult trials and to gain victory throught Jesus? Could I still see heaven and live eternal life with God?

Clairvoyance and Visions 1982–2020

In France, I also experienced dreams and visions about myself and people not in the Philippines. Here are some of the more interesting or alarming things I witnessed, or times when I experienced some kind of clairvoyance.

Searching for a job is challenging. Some people may have wrangled a job through a friend; others find something through families. In the early 1982s, I was searching for a job in France, away from my family in a country far from my homeland. This brought me many difficulties, particularly during interviews. French was a requirement much of the time. As I was not a native speaker, I had many battles to overcome.

The pain and humiliation of finding a job remain palpable even today. But this experience taught me patience, even though I cried a lot. I went to school to learn French, but they said I also had to work on my accent. I was discriminated against during the selection of job applicants. There were many times when they implied or said indirectly that it was clear I was not born in France; the said my diplomas were not valid in France, or they questioned my professional experience in the Philippines, saying that I did not have the required skills for the positions.

I drove my car when searching for a job, which was my constant struggle. I learned sufficient evidence that some employers preferred hiring job applicants they already knew, or one who came recommended. They also often preferred people who drove their own car to go to work, to prevent employees being absent due to a transportation strike or lack of transportation infrastructure, especially as some places were inaccessible for buses and trains.

At the age of nine years, Lysiane took her lunch in the school canteen and could walk home alone if I wasn't early enough to fetch her from school. One time I came, but she rejected me in front of her friends; she said she could manage to go home alone this time; our apartment was only few yards from her school, to be fair.

I was ready to accept work in an office, even for a simple office employee position. I had one missed opportunity when I had to miss an interview for a job at the Embassy of the Philippines in Paris. I concentrated on my baby's eye appointments in 1986-1987. In the agency of employment, they said to start to work in France, this time, training in office management is necessary especially that I had no experience dealing with computers in an office setting in my previous jobs in the Philippines. There was no computer yet at that time.

I grasped the internship opportunities, with chances to train in the procedures used in office activities, including speech, written or image processing and communication, using electronics, IT, telecommunications, and administrative organization. Then I gained my first employment in the French National Railway Company for two years; it was a part-time job (half-days) that enabled me to spend my spare time with Lysiane. That year was followed by a full-time job, but only for temporary employment, then other temporary jobs. I signed up temporary mission contract in a temp agency called Kelly Services in Paris. The agency would send applicants to the companies who needed our services; I carried out several missions for different companies in France for a period of time. I was well-paid but I had to adjust each time I had a new mission that brought me to a new local site. One of my missions was to replace an employee who resigned recently, as a bilingual secretary in the office of the International Railway Union [*UIC-Union International de Chemins de Fer*] in Paris. When that mission was finished, I went to another school of training dealing with international trade to improve my knowledge about the current market. These positions together helped me acquire different experiences across a range of businesses and commerce. I also worked as a bilingual assistant for a wholesaler store in the department of litigation investigating fraud. We had to deal with fraudulent bank cards and unsupported cheques, and I dealt with many foreign customers. It was a pity that despite opportunities I might have had in the Philippines, I never learned how to speak Chinese fluently. It would have been very useful in the commercial sector.

A memory: I never stopped moving and learning. If I was not at a job, I was in an internship or studying. In October 1995 I went to the United Kingdom for three months to practice my knowledge of translation between French and English, while studying international business. I was able to leave home because Ghislaine, Lionel's elder sister retired earlier than expected due to the closure of the company where she worked. She was living near us in Stains, and so she could watch Lysiane when Lionel was late from work. Lysiane's school was between her apartment and ours. I called Lionel almost every day from Bournemouth, so there were very high telephone bills each month.

There was a transportation strike for the trains, metro, and busses on the day before the departure to Bournemouth. My colleagues and I ran to catch the only bus that brought us to our school in Paris. I stumbled on the first step, with my right ankle swelling up almost immediately. The pain lasted several days. Despite the sprain, with my ankle wrapped with a stretchable bandage, I went with my classmates to England without hesitation. I wouldn't have wanted to miss the training, and we received payment from the government for it.

One day in Bournemouth, our whole class visited the offices of *The Bournemouth Daily Echo* where I spoke with the manager. He offered me a job with an attractive salary, and a furnished apartment. I was greatly honoured to have been chosen from among my classmates. However, I would not have wanted to leave my family in France, as Lysiane was still in primary school, and Lionel was working at the university. What would be the use of having a high- ranking position if you had to leave your home and family behind? If I had been single at that time, it would have been a great opportunity to take that job. Our professor was very disappointed, more so than me, and he said there was no other student he could think of to recommend. The editorial house gave me a gift, a sample of their printing design, that I saved as a souvenir. He said their editorial house would always be open to me in case I ever changed my mind.

The majority of my classmates were smokers. It was freezing cold outside, so they smoked inside the classroom during breaks. The smoke made me cough and gave me breathing problems and nose bleeds, so I was happy when our classes finally finished.

However, I never regretted taking those months in England. I was declared an "outstanding student."

When I came back to France, I was called for another job interview. I was soon hired as a bilingual secretary, the assistant to the department head, before I was employed permanently as a manager in another department of the same company.

Meanwhile, I had a recurring dream which showed the place where I found my first job, and *then showed me an image of a logo* that kept on flashing in my head. I only understood later, when I saw the building in real life, after I got the job. The same logo was used by that semi-public business that employed me as a casual secretary for one year. Later I became a manager there and stayed until retirement. Interestingly, after I have signed the contract of employment, I never had the dream with the logo again.

My diploma in Bachelor of Science in Commerce – majoring in Business Management – had to be validated by the University Paris VIII before I was able to officially enroll, even though I had passed the entrance examinations in both French and English. My aspiration was to become an interpreter, as I wanted to teach English in France once I retired from my job. But destiny gave me a different path. My university studies were interrupted to take care of the baby twins, while Lysiane continued going to university for her degree.

A memory: I wanted to go to school to learn French immediately when I arrived in the country, but there were always hindrances. First of all, I arrived France at the end of October and got pregnant two months later. Often I felt nauseous or faint. When I felt better, Lionel did not want me going to school because he thought it was too dangerous to attend classes for adults in the evening, as the area (Clos St Lazare) had a lot of crime and violence. There was a free training school, but you needed to request a place from the Communist government. In the end, but Lionel did not allow me to make the official request.

I met other Filipinos who lived in Paris. They said several Filipinos had earned college and university diplomas in the Philippines, but they had not been validated, so they worked as house maids, hotel maids, street cleaners, janitors, and other positions due to the problem of language. Some doctors worked as private nurses in the residence of rich or famous people in Monaco, where they had the perks of housing, free meals, and a return ticket each year for Philippines. And as soon as they had earned enough money, they went to school for validation of their certificates and diplomas. But those who came to France with their children had a harder time; most of them worked as labourers, but had the consolation of being able to send their children to school. Many let their children finish their studies first, then went back to the Philippines to retire.

I had made sacrifices for my four-year course in Commerce in the Philippines, yet in France I had to obtain equivalents of my diplomas by undergoing new exams to the French university. I had to look after the education of my young daughter first, and so I waited until she was big enough to go alone to her school.

In the National Employment Agency, I met several people who were not naturalized French, some who had just arrived in France a few weeks previously, but they had already received a lot of financial assistance from the French government. Some were living in hotels for free, including coverage for medicines, and they went to school to learn the French language and took exams for free. Yet, they were not refugees. Whereas I had received nothing. The *Agence National Pour l'Emploi* said that despite the fact that I was unemployed, I was not a priority. They cannot grant me the training for free because they said I was naturalized as French, had a husband and a child, and lived in an apartment. I was shocked by their answer! Then I regretted the timing of being a naturalized French citizen. I understood right away why there were lot of foreigners coming to France in the 1980s, and lot of jobless, homeless French people. I could not see the logic in the government system of distributing funds or assistance. I could not even figure out what support existed. I was dependent on my husband, and he did not tell me how to get financial aid in France.

I finally returned to university in 2001-2002. I obtained the equivalent of my diplomas, acquired a good job, helped to pay for building our new house with extra comforts, and drove my own car. I was successful on many fronts. However, even though I had finally achieved career success, I experienced a lot of injustice. I wrote and spoke fluent English better than many people, and that aroused jealousy between colleagues. Once again, I saw that jealousy can be the cause of many misfortunes. It's regrettable how people's jealousy can have damaging effects. Some people could not accept that I was the most suitable person for a position, with the best professional qualifications and experience. They considered me like their worst enemy. A jealous co-worker who considered me a threat was very difficult to deal with, and caused trust issues, making a healthy working relationship impossible. I was despised. One promotion that was meant for me was given to somebody else. However, I was still promoted in the end: my job was reclassified to a higher level with a salary increase corresponding to my promotion.

I persevered in my career, despite difficulties, and obstacles of all kinds that I had to overcome. With goodwill and energy, I managed to find a stable job with responsibilities in a field where I could apply my personal experience and professional skills, and feel fulfilled until retirement. All those interminable efforts and endurance were rewarded. All this belongs to the past now. I have an ample monthly pension from the social security system in France. I'm living at the side of my husband with compassionate love, my daughter and my grandchildren are just near me. Those are my fabulous graces and blessings from the Highest. God is good.

The upside-down bridge dream

I started having visions of a bridge at the beginning of December 1999. One evening after work, I was driving on the highway but abruptly I saw a flash of a green bridge upside down, under the sky. I said to myself that I was just so tired that it led me to have some kind of hallucination. I continued driving until I reached the end of the highway, where I was able to park my car for a moment, and I contemplated. I should have stopped driving that day, but I was still far from home.

Once I'd arrived home, I described the vision to Lionel, but he did not seem interested and ignored what I said. I thought maybe he did not believe me, so I did not insist. Two days after that vision, I had a dream:

The ceiling and the walls were turning around me. At times there were pictures or ads or information with pictures of nurses and doctors, and also other people in consultation, midwives, images about health welfare. I came to understand that I was on a bed rolling around the long wide corridor. I was dizzy looking at the walls that kept turning around me. There were people in white uniforms talking to me, asking me questions, calling my name repeatedly: "Madame Tchermnykh, can you hear me?" I did not answer them. Instead I kept checking whether my husband was present, and then I awoke.

At once, I told Lionel about my dream and he answered: "Maybe it's because you're not yet used to your new job. As you are dealing with different laboratories selling their different medicines and products, there are lots of ads and discussions mentioning different medicinal products." What he said reassured me.

While driving to work that morning, the dream was still so vivid it refused to leave my mind. I persuaded myself that Lionel was right. The dream was the result of reading all the documents we received each day from the laboratories. There were so many applications for marketing authorisation for their medicines that we typed each day.

Then one week later, I dreamed again, a continuation of the previous one:

> *The rolling bed passed through a corridor full of closed doors. At the end of that long corridor, there was a door open to a bedroom showing me two empty beds. Between the beds there was an agitated old woman, but I wondered if she was sitting down because I only saw her face and the top half part of her body. She was calling out for someone to help her. I wondered why she was moving her head so much. I heard the voice of a man informing me: "This is your room, Madame," and then I awoke.*

A few days passed, and I managed to forget the dream. Christmas celebrations were very near, and I was fully concentrating on reviewing my list for Christmas: running to stores, making the decisions, and keeping track of our list for Lysiane's gifts and for every member of the coming family reunion. I was wondering how it would be this year, the first without Lionel's mother, Huguette, who had passed away on January 12 the previous year. It had been one day before Lionel's birthday and two months before I started working in my current job in March.

By 1994, I felt that I deserved a brand-new car, why not? One that would be more comfortable to drive, with comfortable seats with lumbar support, and so on. I was thinking about how to improve my daily life, but I also realized just how materialistic I could be sometimes.

We found a two-year-old car, a red Ford Sierra, five seater, comfortable which had run only 22,000 kilometres. It still seemed new because the former owner worked with Air France and was driving the company car to work, while his wife - a policewoman drives her own car,

This car helped us in looking for a house to buy in the country. Sometimes Lionel's brother-in-law, and Lionel's two elder sisters, came with us as they were also looking for a house in a more peaceful and secure area. But they abandoned their search, while Lionel and

I continued. There were many inconveniences in that time of trying to buy a house, so that we were often exhausted and frustrated. I was humiliated when the builders told us that our budget was not enough to buy a house. Another time, we had signed and paid the construction contract fee with an initial payment of 15,000 francs; however that company went bankrupt and we couldn't get our money back.

We had almost forgotten our failures which gave us about a year of humiliation. Then one day, we received an encouraging proposition from another real estate agency and builder of individual houses, who convinced us to have an initial appointment with them. They said we could discuss building a new house in the future, and we might also recover the amount we had paid to the other company. Two agents came to our home, a project-manager, and an accountant, who studied our financial information.

In one week's time, we had an appointment with an architect. We signed the contract for construction after having seen their proposed allotment, with beautiful panoramic views to the back. It was a place where we could see both the sunrise and sunset. We talked about the size and the shape of each room and corridors inside the house. We obtained bank loans to be paid off in 20 years. The construction in Beaumont-sur-Oise, a suburb situated to the north of Paris, started in May 1999 and finished in December.

Here's the story: Lionel and I had chosen this suburb because the cost of living in Paris was too high, and this house would see us through retirement. We made some concessions and sacrifices to save money: I had to stop my horseback-riding, which was quite expensive. Lionel reduced his habit of going to restaurants every weekend. We held back on the shopping, and walked more, in order to spend less on petrol. We concentrated our spending to the food we needed, and on our daughter's schooling. We were fully focused on our project, but it did not prove to be easy.

We had some disagreements with the architect and the project-manager for the construction. In fact, I sensed it during our first meeting. I had detected dishonesty, that had led me to feel a spontaneous rage of anger, I became out of control. I was almost sure he cheated many people. Knowing I had sensed their plan, I told them that if they were not honest, their office would be closed.

It was customary to shake hands when you meet people, especially during the business meeting, but there, I was struck by the strength of my conflicted feelings towards the man in front of me. He was smiling, but he gave me so much stress and violent feelings of anger. I was horrified. I was afraid of what would be my next reaction, and it was unbearable, because I sensed some immense trick he would try to play on Lionel and me. I controlled myself because at that very moment, what I sensed had not happened yet. I tried to overcome my negative feelings and to convince myself I was just being sensitive and paranoid. Meanwhile, my husband noticed my nervousness, but I could not tell him yet the reasons why I refused to sit down in with of the manager of the construction. I tried to regain rationality in that challenging situation, even though I felt breathless.

We had several meetings with them about our house construction despite my sense of their dishonesty. We were told to sign the plan, which was different than what we had agreed. Right away, I said firmly, "I am sorry, I can't sign that, and you know very well why." I dashed out of their office and Lionel followed me to the car where we had discussed animatedly all the way home. I informed the bank and requested them to not pay the constructor for the unfinished services, and to take a penalty because of the irregularities of the construction methods. For example, the proposals for the style of the front of the house, the wall between the kitchen and the garage, as well as the staircase were different than what we agreed. One week passed, and we did not hear from them. Later, they made some compromises and we finally agreed.

Luckily, with our vigilance, the plans for our house were finished despite several upsets. Two years later, their construction company was dissolved not because of me, but because another other clients claimed mismanagement and demanded a refund.

Lysiane's cards

One afternoon at the beginning of December 1999, Lysiane was 17 years old and sitting on the carpet of our bedroom in our apartment, playing with her Tarot cards. I did not know when or how she learned it. She said: "Oh la la, Mama, you will have a car accident. But no need to worry, you will have fears, but no physical injury. You will have some difficulties, but you could adjust to the situation, then everything can be alright, and you will have a new car." She said as if it was just normal, talking to me like an elder. I was stupefied.

I did not really pay attention to what she said; she was just playing. I asked her to stop reading the cards. She did not answer.

I still remember that she read the Tarot for my sister-in-law Claudie. Lysiane said:

"Tata Claudie, you will receive an inheritance from your very close family." Despite Claudie's eagerness, I interrupted Lysiane, because I had guessed what she was going to say. I sensed that something would happen to Claudie's husband, and I didn't want Claudie to know ahead of time. I already sensed that Pierre would die soon, but at that very moment he was still actively working. We could never have guessed that he was going to die early. I was even afraid that he would not be able to reap the benefits of his retirement days, because he was only 59 years old. Just two months later, he died, and their insurance endorsed a considerable sum to Claudie and to their children: Hugues and Tatiana. They bought a nice house in Vendee, western province of France.

I hoped that Lysiane would not think of playing her cards anymore. Then one day I was worried, because she had not returned home on time. I wondered where she was. The meal that I prepared for her had gone cold. I heard the small voices of young girls of her age, giggling and talking in front of our entrance door. I sneak a peek through the peephole of our door, and I saw her surrounded by three classmates, doing the card reading. I was so mad that I tore her cards into small pieces in front of her friends, and warned her not to do it again.

I did not see her playing nor reading the cards for some weeks, but when I was cleaning her bedroom, I found new handmade cards that she had made by herself. She had replaced all the cards by drawing the same colours and the same images on some card paper. Again, I tore them into small pieces before she arrived from her college. As soon as she came home, had noticed what had happened to her cards, but she did say anything. However, she forbade me from entering in her bedroom again.

The car accident

The new house was finished after seven months of construction. It has large windows in each room. We got the keys in December 1999. But we still had to paint the walls and the interior before moving in. The painter and a family friend called us fully excited, early on the morning of 25th December, and informed us that he had convinced someone to work with him starting that day to paint the interior of our house. Knowing it was very difficult to find someone to help him, I thought it was an opportunity to finish the painting, and I didn't want to refuse the motivated painter the work, even though it was Christmas.

Despite our lack of sleep due to the Christmas Eve celebration, I drove to Beaumont-sur-Oise, 35 kilometres away from where we were living. There were only a few cars on the highway.

It had been raining the whole week, which made the area quite muddy. To reach the house without tumbling into the sticky mud, we lifted some large flat stones, and some old broken asphalt that was extracted from the road to cover the twelve meters mud from the sidewalk to the house. We lined them up like a little footbridge and walked on them to not lose our shoes in the mud. The area in front needed to be cemented, and there would be a fence and gate. Our newly-built house stood in front of us, but we realized that much work was still to be done, like the construction of the path leading to the garage, a fence around the house, terraces in front and behind the house, the front garden, and the backyard.

We worked hard that day, and at around 1:35 p.m., we were very hungry. We decided to go back to our apartment to take our lunch and rest. I drove the car, Lionel was in the passenger seat, sleeping and snoring. His head was covered by a woollen hat. I knew he wouldn't want to be separated from his hat, even inside the car. He was surely much more tired than me. Then my eyes started getting heavy, and I could hardly concentrate on the driving. I had probably closed my eyes for a second when I suddenly realized that my car was rolling at a high speed towards a green bridge which joined Pierrefitte and the City of Stains. I should have made a turn following the road, but it was too late, I missed the bend. Instead, I was driving right towards the bridge with my right foot stepping on the accelerator   instead of stepping on the clutch pedal and the brake.

My red car hit the high cemented pavement, and immediately flipped over, with the four wheels facing upward, still spinning. The witnesses said there were no vehicles directly in front or behind our car, which was lucky. There was a woman in a car at some distance behind, who called the police. She said she had seen the accident, but was not able to understand how it was exactly happened because when she reached us, our car was already upside down. An Indian restaurant near the bridge also called the police, so the firemen, the ambulance and the police all came at the same time to save us. They said it was lucky that our car did not caught fire, while we were still inside.

We were in unusual position inside the car: our heads were on the floor (the roof) while our feet were up high. Fortunately, Lionel had well-fastened his seat belt around his chest and waist, while I had loosened mine, which had caused me to be ejected from my seat, while the car was rolling over repeatedly. When it had finally stopped, but upside-down, Lionel's head touched the car's roof.

"I walked out from the car by myself," he told me later. "I crawled between the car-door opening that was half-blocked by the pavement. The firemen could not open the door, so the police had helped me by breaking it open wider."

I was just above Lionel. The firemen straightened the car to open the door wider, which helped them to pull me out from the car. Then they laid me flat down on a stretcher but on the ground momentarily. They needed time to prepare inside the ambulance, and while they were checking out on how they could help me, I opened my eyes. And there, I saw what I had dreamed before the accident: the sky and the green bridge. Now I understood why the bridge in my dream was turned upside down, seen in reverse under the sky.

Diagnosis

I was in shock and had a cranial trauma. I heard them saying many things I did not understand. Lionel was with me in the ambulance, and said that while we travelled to the hospital, I was only half conscious. The police checked my papers in my bag and asked him to confirm that I was indeed Mrs. Tchermnykh, the Municipal Councillor of the City of Stains, as it was written in the card. The ambulance drove at its highest speed with the siren blaring on the way to Hôpital de la Fontaine. They said I was seriously wounded and had the risk of internal haemorrhaging.

I was conscious but was felt hungry when we reached the emergency entrance of the hospital, where I was surrounded by a medical team. At the time, I saw different images around the wall and ceiling of the room, ones that I had seen in my dream, but this time it was all real as I was not dreaming anymore. In the X-ray room, I was perhaps half-conscious or half-asleep, as I suddenly found myself alone and naked on the hospital bed; that made me furiously mad, and uncomfortable. When the doctors reappeared, I grabbed anything to cover myself, but they were very alert to prevented me from moving, as they were worried I was maybe seriously injured. I told them I was so hungry, but they did not give me anything to eat, as I needed to undergo blood tests and X-rays first.

"I know myself very well," I said. "If you don't give me something to eat, I will surely collapse." I begged them. Maybe I had convinced them, but it was too late;

everything became dark, and I fainted.

I woke up with a cervical collar and an IV in my arm and I felt better. I found myself wearing hospital's clothes, and as soon as they have finished all my medical examinations, they had me lie down again on the rolling bed. Suddenly, I saw again the rest of the images that I had seen in my dreams. The bed rolled through the corridor and turned a corner, and they said, "Here you are Madame." I was astonished to see all the same as in my dream the bedroom with door, opening showing me two empty beds. Between the beds, there was the agitated old woman that I had dreamed of before the accident.

Then I understood why I saw only the top part of her body. She was sitting on a chair between her bed and mine, but her hands were tied on her armchair.

"Why is she tied?" I asked the hospital attendants.

"It is because she wanted to escape from the hospital, and it is dangerous for her to go out, because she doesn't remember her room. She cannot go home alone because she never remembers where she lives" they answered.

Before the evening, Lysiane and Lionel visited me with Hugues, Lysiane's cousin. I was happy to see them. I noticed the sourness of my daughter's face upon looking to me with a cervical collar around my neck, as if she wanted to tell me that what she had seen in her cards was right. She remained silent while our eyes met. I wanted to hug her, but I was afraid for my neck and she was hesitant to touch me.

The meals they served in the hospital at quarter to seven in the evening were not I wanted, and despite my hunger before the accident, I lost my appetite. I noticed that the woman on the other bed had eaten her dinner, and I was quite reassured to see that her hands were not tied anymore, and she was free. She was smiling at me. For sure she liked me as her roommate.

I was not feeling well the whole evening. I had this foreboding feeling: I sensed danger would come to happen, and I did not really know what, but worry invaded my spirit. Unable to sleep, not even a single second, I got up and I walked around inside the hospital. I felt tense, and I removed the neck brace around my neck.

As I closed the windows, I sensed the strong storm would come to blow very soon, so I wanted to leave the hospital. I went to the nurses' station and asked them to let me go.

"Mesdames," I said. "a storm is imminently approaching us here, so fast." They ignored me. I begged them again to let me go home, as I heard the noise of the wind in the trees. I sensed that several trees will soon fall across the road.

They did not believe me, so I became mad. I pointed my fingers to the head nurse and said: "Madame, listen please, you cannot go home either. There will be logs that fall across the road to prevent you." And immediately I felt the kind of stiffness that made it difficult for me to continue talking. I was afraid I would collapse again. There was no chair near me, so I sat down on the floor.

They said: "What did you say? What have you seen? What did you hear?" The nervousness in me had suddenly disappeared. The nurse put my cervical collar back around my neck, and they were all looking from to one another, as if telling themselves that I was a fool, or I maybe I had lost my senses due to the head injury. I thought of the woman with me in the bedroom, where she was forced to remain seated, with her hands tied to her armchair. I decided to keep silent.

Two men in white shirts came with the nurse and both stood in my sides. They gave me a tablet and a glass of water and instructed me to swallow it. They said it would help to calm me down and sleep. I pretended to have swallowed it. The way they looked at me freaked me out, and I was afraid they would restrain me like the woman in my room. I returned to my bed still fearful and shaken, but at the same time, I was about to burst with uncontrollable anger towards the nurses. I cried, finishing with terrible headache. I was thinking of Lysiane and Lionel, and I was getting so stressed thinking how could I call them, as the telephone in the hospital for patients to use was out of order. I asked the nurses to let me to call from their office, but they did not let me. Instead, they told me that it was not the time to call, and that I should relax and sleep. Feeling frustrated, humiliated, and tired, I swallowed the tablet that was almost melted, hidden under my tongue. I lay down on my bed and closed my eyes.

At dawn, the wind was blowing so hard that it sounded as if the glass in the window frames might shatter. And this time it was uncontestably real, as everyone felt the storm that had struck France. There was a cracking sound of great trees falling, and the sounds of the objects flying in the wind. I wanted to look out the window to see how it looked like outside, but it was too dangerous to have it opened, and that increased my nervousness. All my thoughts were for my family at home.

One of the nurses who I had seen last night, and argued with, came to see us in our room before breakfast was served. She stared at me, but no words came from her mouth. I knew that at that very moment she had realized that I was absolutely not crazy. Although I would have had liked to have told her that what I had sensed would soon happen, I preferred not to say anything. My thoughts were with my family and our newly-built house. But she noticed that I removed the cervical collar again, and she placed it quickly back around my neck, speechless despite my refusal as I did not need it at all. What I really needed at the time was to use their phone to call my husband and make sure he and the family were okay. I stared straight to her eyes, begging. I finally convinced her because she gave me her duty-phone from the inside pocket of her belt. I rang home, but nobody answered. It was either that they were still sleeping, or the telephone at home was cut-off due to the storm.

The nurse was impressed that the woman at sixties, my roommate, behaved well, sitting quietly and calmly on her bed. She went out from our room without tying the woman's arms on the armchair, and I was more than delighted. I continued thinking that my roommate would be pleased to have me in her room and although she did not talk to me, probably due to the language, she kept on smiling at me. She did not speak French. She did not seem like a crazy woman, but only that she suffered from dementia or Alzheimer's.

After breakfast, I roamed the hospital to see if a doctor was present to sign my request of discharge, so that I could legally leave the hospital. However, not a single doctor was present yet, as they were all blocked away from the place. No car had been able to make it along the road due to the fallen trees and branches blocking the roads, and many telephone and electricity lines were disconnected.

Here are some details I learned from a news report later: Around Christmas 1999 Central Europe was struck by two storms that caused severe damage in France, Germany, Switzerland, and Italy. Satellite images showed the first of the two storms, called Lothar, rapidly crossed France and Germany on 26 December. It started off as a frontal wave over the Western Atlantic just one day before, crossing the ocean at a speed of more than 120 km/h. After hitting France and the Paris area early in the morning, the storm's centre crossed into the Frankfurt area at 11-12 o'clock on Sunday morning.

Later after our lunch, a doctor said I could go back home the following morning, but I contradicted him right away. I insisted on telling him categorically that it was a waste of time to keep me in the hospital, as I was already feeling better and I was terribly worried for my family. I needed to absolutely go back home that day. I signed a paper, a discharge note that allowing me to be released and checked out legally from the hospital and asked him to give me the means of communication to contact my family.

Hugues came to fetch me from the hospital and brought me home. I was so happy and relieved to see Lionel and my daughter safe and sound. I immediately called Nicole, my colleague, and a friend, to find a way to fetch us from our apartment and asked her to bring us to the car pound to take back the stuff we had left inside the damaged car, and then go ahead to Beaumont sur Oise to see if our new house was not damaged by the storm. It took two long hours instead of a 30 minutes' drive for Nicole to reach to our apartment, because some roads were closed for safety but everything was going fine. Lionel, Lysiane and me went with Nicole to the car pound, we found the things we left in the red car. We proceeded to Beaumont sur Oise, about 35 kilometres away. Luckily, the new house had not suffered, and nothing was damaged. I was relieved. But I was so sorry for our neighbour's new house; the roof was damaged, with some tiles blown off.

Upon seeing the damage to the car, it was unbelievable that we survived from the accident. The picture of the wreckage stayed in my mind as I wondered how Lionel and I survived that horrible accident. I am haunted with this question in my head:

Shall I be afraid after dreaming of an empty bed? Does the empty bed signify my destiny?

Lionel later remembered the experience with a smile. "My mother, who passed away in January the year before, was probably watching over me and protecting me, because when I was getting out from the car, I still had my woolly hat and the hood of my winter jacket. My head was doubly- protected." In my view, it was possibly just the fact that the car turned upside down that made the hood press against his hat. My head, on the other hand, bumped the roof because I had loosened my seatbelt while driving, as I always detested the feeling of being too tightly squeezed, which triggered my claustrophobia.

But it was a miracle that, despite the serious damaged of the right side of the car (passenger seat) where Lionel was sitting, he was safe and sound. And God has my eternal gratitude again for saving both our lives.

Moving into the new house – 2000

All our furniture was brought by two grand lorries, except a few other heavy things that we brought in a utility van that we rented. It was my first experience driving that van which was much different from a car, but I am proud that I could do it. We also rented a car for 48 hours to bring us back home to Beaumont. When I had stayed in the hospital after the accident, our packing had been interrupted, and some pieces had to be hand-carried. And there were some delays in packing, but we moved into our new house as scheduled – on January 6, my birthday.

The movers were all very motivated, and the weather that day was great for a winter day. Beaumont sur Oise was bathed in sunshine, and with temperatures above zero centigrade, which is rare for that time of year. Those were my excellent birthday gifts, thank God. Thus, we became the new Beaumontoise. All those difficulties were nearly forgotten, like my bad feelings about the architect, the car accident, and the storm. We now owned a large space of more than 1000 m2 for our future garden or a parc for the coming grandchildren, and fruit trees for Lionel and me. Our one and only daughter was only 17, but I had always felt we would be surrounded with children and see them running in our house and playing in the garden. And all those flashes of visions came true, because two years after we settled in Beaumont, we had two lovely granddaughters, Sabrine and Typhaine, followed by Vadim, then Sasha.

But life was less comfortable without a car, especially when you bought heavy things like a pack of bottles of water from supermarket to hand-carry them back home is quite a difficult task. We could not fetch our grandchildren from the railway station, and struggled to get to work when there were strikes, and so on. Claudie had proposed to us to buy her husband's old car, and we agreed; but it gave us lot of trouble. One early morning I was not able to drive to work when the car wouldn't start. When I told Claudie about the car, she wanted to refund the money we paid, but I did not dare to accept it.

Pierre, Claudie's husband who passed away three years before we had moved to Beaumont, had paid for an expensive car repair, but he died before it was finished. Hugues recovered it from the repair place and parked the car for three years in their rented garage. But he had been cheated as nothing had been repaired.

Message from my late brother-in-law

The day before the accident and before Christmas, I heard a voice calling me while I drove my red car. Lionel was with me as a passenger, and also heard the voice calling out my name and there was nobody in the road, The voice was so clear but seemed from far, but I recognized Pierre's voice. I said: It's impossible, it could not be Pierre?

On that same day, his son Hugues, who had not driven yet his father's car tried to take the car out of their garage, but he had hit the car on both sides against the garage exit. He decided not to drive it anymore. That very evening, I dreamt of Pierre Pieztrikowski who passed away three years before. He sent me his message through my dream.

He was walking around his car, scratching his head, letting me understand that he needed to do something about his car. It had only stayed in his garage after his death, and yet renting the garage place was an additional expense for his family. He was probably asking me to help his wife and his children to save or to sell his car.

That is why I refused when Claudie offered me to refund the money, and I was happy that I did. Then Pierre could rest in peace. And I did not dream of him again.

I asked the Peugeot garage to repair the parts that Hugues had damaged, and if they could also check the engine and make any repairs before to drive to work. But they said the repairs would cost more than a new car and maybe I should just to leave it to them, and they would take care of the rest. Otherwise, my car would go to the junkyard, but I would still pay for the labour and services. But I couldn't afford to leave my car like that. I was no expert, but I knew it had potential. It ran on diesel and had a turbo engine which made it very powerful; I hoped to find an interested buyer or dealership.

Meanwhile, the Peugeot dealership made me a nice offer for a brand new car. They studied our finances, and with some sacrifices, I was able to buy my very first brand new car in a green-bottle colour in 2000; for me that was my compensation from my accident. It had five doors and five seats, paid for in monthly instalments basis with no deposit. Then I remember what Lysiane told me before the accident: *"Mama, don't worry you will have a brand new car."* But I did not dare to ask her if it had really been written in her cards, or that was her own intuition. I hoped not; she should not be like me or it would be so challenging for her.

Then I needed to find someone to buy Pierre's car, but I did not know yet how to sell a car, as I had never done it. Should I make an advertisement? But how? Should I stick a poster in the car window with my phone number? Or maybe contact the buyers of old cars? I really did not know what to do. Ten days passed, my new car was delivered, so then I had two cars: Pierre's car in our front yard, and the new one inside our garage.

But my trouble of how I could sell the car was suddenly solved miraculously. One Sunday afternoon, by chance, a man happened to be walking by and came to ask me if I would sell my old car as he wanted to have it for his son. I was surprised to see him. Lionel was out for a walk in the forest with Rayna, our dog, while I was cleaning our front yard. My husband was not at home and I needed to discuss it with him first. I proposed for him to come back two hours later so that we could speak first.

The man was insistent. "But Madam," he said, "you must sell your car because you have new car now and I need a car for my son." I did not like his way of pressing me, as if he was ordering me to sell the car immediately without waiting for Lionel to come back. So I asked him how much he would offer for the car, and he quickly answered 2,500 francs. I then tried asking him for 3,000 francs which was only half of the amount I paid to Claudie. He agreed without hesitation. I understood that he was really interested to buy it. I informed him that the car had troubles. But he did not say anything, instead, I showed him inside the car. He turned on the engine which sounded a little odd, but he looked at me with a smile. I wondered what had pleased him with my car?

"I know how to repair it Madame," he said with persistent smile. I realised that maybe he was a mechanic. The car's engine had not been starting, although I had tried. How come it worked now? If I had known that it was working, I would have had asked him for more than 3,000 francs. But it was too late for me to change my mind. I told him to come back with the papers in two hours' time, and he left. I thought that Lionel would be there by then. However, I was wondering how the man could procure papers for the legal sales and transfer of a car when the offices were normally closed on Sundays. The man surprised me and came back before Lionel did, showing me all the necessary papers for the car.

Still, I was quite bothered because Lionel was not home yet. The man had possibly noticed the car standing near our garage so that he had prepared all the necessary papers before he asked me to buy it. I really don't know. Anyway, we both signed, and he left with the car. I even forgot to give him the duplicate key, he was in such a hurry. I was still feeling amazed that I had sold the car without much efforts. After it was done, I realized that the garage where I bought my new car was surely interested, because they knew they could repair it and could sell it a higher price.

When Lionel came back home with Rayna, he was of course surprised not to find the car in our yard anymore, and we kept talking about the buyer. I did not really expect anything that it could be as simple as that when I had been so worried about how to sell the car. How come that the man knew that I wanted to sell the car? Who sent him? Was he working in a garage? Which garage?

The following Monday morning, I asked the Peugeot garage, and all our friends, if they had sent someone to buy my car, but not one of them had. They all told me that they did not even know that I was trying to sell my car. It may sound unusual, but in my mind, I think it was probably Pierre's spirit who sent the man to buy his car, in order to give his car a second life. So that was surely the reason why he called me while I was driving?

Another memory: one Saturday afternoon a few years before, Hugues was 18 years old, and he came to our apartment to ask me about his father's health. I did not dare to tell him the truth, that his father was critically ill and that his days were numbered. Outwardly, there were still no signs or visible symptoms of his cancer of the lungs. However, Pierre, despite the advice of the doctors, was unable to stop smoking, which was the principal cause of the cancer. At that time, he still looked healthy.

I informed Hugues that his father would probably have some pain in his legs and foot (I saw in a flash Pierre walking with a limp) that should be treated. Two days later, Hugues came to see me again and told me that his father was suffering pain in his legs because of the varicose veins, and a sore foot because a piece of metal had dropped into his foot while repairing something in his shop. Hugues added that, despite the treatment, his father was strangely very tired, which seemed very unusual. I knew he loved his father, but I also knew that he was not yet ready to accept that his father was dying. I felt the pain for him and for his elder sister,Tatiana, and their mother, Claudie.

The Tchermnykh family always held a family reunion each New Year's Eve, but that year (1997) the party was on the 3rd of January. Pierre was there, but he did not eat well since he received injections as treatment for his cancer. He was telling everyone that despite his chemotherapy treatment, he had kept his hair, and he giggled proudly, combing his hair with his fingers. I remember that every time I offered him food he did not refuse, and he ate all the foods in his plate. Everyone was very happy to see that he had such a good appetite. But I sensed it was the last day that we see him that way. He died three days later.

Are my dreams warnings?

I met with three car accidents that I dreamed of before they happened: in December 1999, March 2017, and February 2018. Each case was different.

The second was special, because I had dreamed about my father first, so it was like a warning. I had ignored that second dream, and I tried to be so careful in driving, But I had forgotten that even when we are driving carefully, the other drivers are not.

A white van hit my car from behind at speed. I saw myself immobile at the middle of the highway where I heard lot of noise. I heard lorries all around me and people dressed in in yellow vests calling me. I turned my head and I saw the white van stuck behind my car. There was a woman driver who suddenly turned on the engine with a roar and then the vehicle disappeared.

On 30 March 2017, in the midst of heavy traffic, a woman drove a white van while speaking on her phone (not hands-free). She was concentrating on the conversation, but she lost track of the driving so that she hit the back of my car, and caused some light damage. My head snapped back and forth, giving me whiplash. I was in shock for a moment, so I was not able to move for a while and my car's engine also stopped working. Despite the noise all around me, I heard some people giving me instruction from the left side, but far from my car; it was impossible for them to get closer because vehicles were running at full speed at rush hour, and I was between two lanes.

The people trying to help wore bright green and yellow jackets, giving me the signals to bring the car to the side to be safer. Through the rear mirror, I saw the white van behind me with a woman driver still talking on her phone; she was not able to escape because of the cars moving on both sides. I suddenly realised that it was unsafe to be inside my car in the middle of the three-lane highway. I was afraid and panicked, feeling pain in my head and neck. I made up my mind and pressed the warning button and called the police through the integrated phone of my car.

The police asked: "Is your car working? Please turn the key and drive your car to the side of the road. You must get off the highway."

I had forgotten to turn the key to start the engine. But I was afraid, the cars and lorries came so fast on both sides that it was hard for me to drive to the side. I asked the police to come to guide me. They answered that someone would come, but it would take time. And I suddenly saw the white van with woman driver rushed away, so I tried to follow her. She drove so fast that I lost her, luckily I memorised her plate number. I told the police that I lost her, and I gave her car plate's number. The police continued to talk to me. One of them asked me if I was wounded, and I told him about my neck. He advised me: "You should go directly to the hospital, right away."

The radiography indicated negative results. But I had pains from my head down to my neck and shoulder, surely because of the shock. I tried some medical treatments such as radiography and physiotherapy. Despite all the treatments, my pain lasted from March until May, and I couldn't work. Long-term, it was more the psychological harm that remained. Although I was a careful driver, others were careless and dangerous. My treatments were interrupted because I had to attend my father's funeral in May 2017.

Nine months later, I dreamed of another car accident in early February 2018; I was so worried that I had to take leave from the office. I did not drive for a whole week to try to avoid another accident. It had snowed abundantly, and it was so dangerous to drive anywhere, although I did not see any snow in my dream. When I returned to work on Monday the 12th of February, everything seemed alright as there was no more snow. But at the end of the week, on Friday the 16th, I had the accident that I had foreseen. I understand now that once I dream of danger, no matter what precautions I make, and despite my prayers to prevent it, it will come to pass.

I always asked myself: Why do I have predictive dreams? What is the purpose of dreaming about the coming danger when you cannot avoid it?

The night before the accident on the 16th of February, I dreamed of Lionel's deceased mother, and I woke up late that morning:

Mama Huguette was there standing in front of me, and close, but she was looking somewhere else. Then she turned her head towards me, and I saw in her expression that she was experiencing pain or had eaten something sour, and she left. She seemed to be trying to announce some kind of incident. I wanted to ask her what she meant, but she was gone. I suddenly saw my own car being hit by a big white lorry crossing the road at full speed. I wondered why the driver was there, when in fact my light was green. My car was thrown to the right side of the road, and I was lying there.

I immediately told Lionel about that dream, as it really worried me. He said: "White van again? What do all those white vans have against you?" At first, I did not find the words to answer him. Eventually I said, "usually when I dream of your mother, she is serene, but this time she was so different and not at ease."

I was swamped of work waiting for me at the office, so despite the dream, I drove my car that early morning. I was at the intersection of the city of Pierrefitte. At the stoplight, I started my car when my light went green. Suddenly a large white van came from the left, driving at full speed, and cut off my route. I braked, but the van hit my car and damaged the left front side of my car (my side) by knocking it into the right lane of the road. The key went off the dashboard and also all the things I placed in front of me. I was severely shaken. I felt a strong pain in my whole body the next day. I had wondered why the driver of the van went through a red light; he should have not been there at all. Luckily, I was not driving fast. But the bodywork of the car was badly damaged. The headlamps were broken, and the damage was more serious this time. Luckily, I was not physically wounded.

Again, I wondered: why do I have these dreams, when I can do nothing to prevent the accidents? Why does God did not hear my prayers? Although my life was not in danger this time, I suffered psychological effects once again. But God had always protected my life, and I have not been too seriously injured in the car accidents. With all my heart, I always honour Him, forever giving gratitude and sincere thanks for saving me.

On Saturday evening, 17th February, Ashley phoned me while I was still in bed. She said she felt like calling me but didn't know why. I told her it was late, and I was hungry, but I did not feel like getting up to eat. What was strange was that I was about to call her when she called. Anyway, I couldn't drive my car as it was still damaged. As our conversation went on, though I was afraid to frighten her, I informed her about the accident in my dream and once was again it was realised, and it troubled my mind.

When filling in the forms to report the accident, the driver of the white van wanted to put all the fault on me by making false statements. When in fact, it was he who was undeniably in the wrong and had caused all the damage. I defended myself by looking straight into his eyes and said: "If you are not punished by the power of the law for your faults today, you would be doubly and seriously punished by the Highest authority in the future." And he had probably realized that what I said was true, because he tore his paper in half.

But I was worried for the repairs of my car. It was badly damaged, and it cost a lot, while my insurance was still examining the details of the accident. Eventually, on the 8th of March, I received a letter from my insurance confirming that the accident was not my responsibility, and all the repair costs to the car including all my medical examinations would be paid by the insurance of the driver who caused the damage. That news helped me to have an excellent sleep that night.

In France, Premonitions Are Stronger

As soon as I settled down in France in 1981, I re-started seriously experiencing dream premonition concerning mainly my family members, relatives and close friends living in the Philippines. However, when I was in Philippines, I often dreamed about other people, but seldom about my family.

One day in 2018, I informed Mama through webcam that I saw her in my dream, and I asked her to be extra careful because I saw her fall on a floor that was shining with water. Her face looked pained, and I saw her holding her hand as if it was hurt. I did not want her to get worried about the dream, so I told her: "Mama, it was as if you were trying to catch fish on the floor in the living room." She laughed. But one week after, I dreamed of her again, and this time Mama fell to the floor again but not in the same way. I called her again the next morning to warn her not to do anything that might put her in danger, but that day Mama told to me that she fell down the day before. She said that she was wiping the floor with a wet rug and when she stood up, she lost her balance. She fell sideways, catching herself but hitting her hand on the wet floor. She said, "Don't worry Sarah your dream is now finished."

A few weeks later, we were all happy that her hand was getting better. But she lost her balance again. She said she tried to hold on to something to prevent her from falling, but she really hurt her hand that time and she needed to have an operation. I had dreamed about her hands twice and she had suffered injury twice in her hands. Mama became disabled in the use of her hands, so that it was very difficult for her to cook her own foods and she had trouble using her hands to eat. I was mad at myself, thinking that if I hadn't dreamed the accident, maybe nothing would have happened.

But how can I prevent myself from dreaming?

I had another dream, this one about a motorcycle accident with Dave, my nephew, where he was seriously injured. Years later, as I said in chapter 15, I dreamed about my brother Dan's ambush, where he and all his passengers were asked to strip down while the bandits searched for arms. If Dan had brought his revolver that day, he would have had been killed. But what was strange was that I felt the pain that Dan had suffered. I even went to the doctor to ask his assistance on how to ease my bruises and pains. And I also dreamed the explosion of the tanker that Dan was driving, although it was good that he was not inside the truck when it exploded. I was feeling suffocated when the water had showered down on the tanker by the automatic fire detector machine and the fire stopped.

What was worse is that I have no power to prevent my premonition dreams from happening, and I am sometimes unable to detect where it will happen, unless I can see faces of my family members or friends. For example, I sensed that a bomb would explode in Davao's International Airport, and I saw the face of my cousin Domingo Palma standing behind the car, but quite far from the explosion. I wondered why I dreamed of that explosion before it happened. He was the only son of Mama Modesta, the elder half-sister of my mother Dominga. Luckily, Domingo was not wounded.

I also saw in my dream the bombs that fell over Bancasi airport, and on 4th Infantry division and the firing between the Philippine Army and the rebels. I recognised the faces of some of those soldiers who were wounded from my time working in the ROTC office in Butuan. Some of the people I knew died.

Vivid dreams about catastrophic events are very troubling, like the famous typhoon Philippines Yolanda in November 2013 which I had sensed ahead of time, where six thousand people died. I was almost sure that it would happen in my country because that dream showed me several coconut trees uprooted and houses in Nipa Huts destroyed.

I was so horrified that I refused to tell anyone, although I also felt guilty of being unhelpful to humankind. I dreamed of several earthquakes, but I only found out the name of the places when I saw them on the television the following day.

I was asking myself about this kind of premonition: Was I having an auditory verbal hallucinations? I recall: Even before an accident happened, I had already heard in my spirit the sound of a car hitting my neighbour's gate. I looked through the window, and there was nothing. But few minutes later, a car smashed the gate of my neighbour.

One day I heard my daughter calling me: "Mama please open the door, I have my arms loaded." I opened the door and there was nobody. But few moments later, I heard my daughter calling me again as the previous time: "Mama open the door I have my arms loaded." And this time she was there with two bags in her arms. Astonished, I told her: when I opened you just a while ago, there was nobody. She answered: "Mama, I just arrived from shopping," Looking at her face, you could tell that she was annoyed of what I said.

Another times I heard the phone ringing with a colleague on the line. Strange. I picked up the phone but nobody. Few minutes later, the phone rang and this time my colleague was really there. She said: "Sarah, I dialled your number but my phone rang." I was confused about what she said.

Why do I hear sounds or voices before the scenario come?

Premonition about Sister Cecilia's mother

I dreamed of the death and burial of Sister Cecilia's mother, just three days before she died at the age of 103 years. We went to Cabadbaran in 1981 with Sister Cecilia, who warmly welcomed us and introduced us to her sister Elizabeth at home. Lionel, too, had the chance to meet their mother, who was 98 at the time. She died in 1986.

In the dream I saw vivid images of the burial of Sister Cecilia's mother. There were a lot of adults with children walking in a procession of two lines, holding lit candles and most of the children were holding flowers, roses in red, yellow, and white. I heard myself participating in the prayers as I sang with them. Sister Cecilia was at the head of the procession, just behind a coffin carried by four men.

I awoke full of serenity. This seemed to happen when I enter into a premonition dream, and participated in the prayers. But would a dream always be announcing a death if I participated in the prayers?

When Lionel, Lysiane and I visited my parents and family in Butuan in 1989, we also visited Sister Cecilia at Sacred Heart Convent. I told her about that dream and asked her why other people and children were holding flowers instead of lit candles during the burial.

At first, she asked me: "How did you know that?"

"It was in my dream," I answered.

"Candles are dangerous to the children because of the risk of hot wax in their hands. To prevent them from being burned, they were asked to carry the stalk of roses instead of lit candles," she explained, showing me her sweet smile as usual.

I still remember that, as a child, Nanay often brought me with her to the store of Sister Cecilia's parents in Cabadbaran to buy ropes and other material for the pigs and carabaos. I used to call her father, Yoyo Tiyoy, who would touch my head while mussing my hair, after I kissed his right hand. He was not a tall man, but he was robust with a bald, shiny head. I often had fun in emptying the transparent jar full of candies displayed on top of his desk, and they would let me fill my pockets with different sweets. He and Nanay often laughed and enjoyed the conversation, because Tiyoy was a joker, and his customers loved him.

Sister Cecilia is our cousin. Her mother was the youngest sister of my grandmother's mother whose family name was Beray. Sister Cecilia's father was the cousin of Esperanza Jamboy (my grandmother). Sister Cecilia, a nun, is my great-aunt and served as my teacher for English grammar and composition when I was a student at Urios High School.

I continued to experience more intuitions and premonitions, and some were small but eventful; others were quite surprising, even if they did not affect me personally but referenced situations with large crowds of people. I still felt emotionally involved, but more intrigued by these experiences.

In 1978, my professors in Butuan City Colleges, Mr. Colina, was a Professor of Mathematics. He and his wife, Mrs. Colina, Professor of Biology, introduced me to a pastor, their friend who also had a "spiritual gift." I asked him for advice. Even though I was not officially in their congregation, he helped me to understand my journey with God. He warned me not to go on a large body of water, and that I should avoid joining busy crowds. I was perplexed at the time, but both his predictions came true.

Premonition dreams often prevented me from sleeping. I kept on dreaming of Sister Cecilia and I thought maybe I was cursed. But she became my spiritual adviser, now retired and living in the Ampayon Convent, in a suburb of Butuan City. She advised me to accept my situation.

I still remember when she said: "Sarah, live with it without fear and accept it as a privilege as what you possess is a gift of of the Holy Spirit. And there is no reason to fear, these are signs of God's love for you." She was firm in her beliefs.

Her words kept repeating in my head. However, I couldn't help but continue to ask myself, why me? Then I remember when I was visited by the Holy Spirit at home in Mabini, Cabadbaran.

"You should write down your dreams that rattle you," she advised me. "This will help you move away from nervousness, and give you the serenity you need. Perhaps it might allow you to understand better, and you could turn to your dreams for spiritual guidance," she said, looking deeply to my eyes. As I was her previous student, she reminded me about my abilities and writing.

For years, I ignored her advice. Somehow, I did not feel like writing, or I didn't have confidence in my own capacity. Since that time, I tried to convince myself to write this memoir, although it was hard to decide what to include, and where to start. I told her all about my pain, failures, and successes. She kept insisting, telling me again to write.

It took the death of my father in 2017 to trigger in me the strong desire to express myself in writing at last. I am so eager to tell Sister Cecilia that she is right, and I finally found the inspiration.

I saw Sister Cecilia, with her inviting smile, in my dreams. I really hoped to see her the following year (2018) to tell her about the dreams. But I was not able to visit my family in Philippines that year.

In France, I had been dreaming of her often since December 2018:

> *I sometimes saw her walking along the seashore, smiling at me while slight waves came near us. This reminded me of our last promenade; other times she was standing in front of me in the church, as if reminding me I could find her in religious place.*

In November 2019, I asked my mother many times, despite her age of 85 years, to take my sister Imelda and go see Sister Cecilia at the Sacred Heart Convent in Butuan. Sadly, Mama learned that Sister Cecilia died in January 2019. She is buried in the cemetery inside their Convent compound of Ampayon.

I am now living with great remorse. I was not able to tell her that I am writing my memoir at last, as she advised. I really wanted her to know how she inspired me, before she was called to go home, to spend her eternal life with God. Today, remorse gnaws at me constantly.

Sister Cecilia told me once that the premonition dreams, visions, and intuitions which I confided to her, before she went to Manila, were full of efficacy. According to her, the events happened exactly as I pictured, during her Religious Mission, and when she went to Cebu City, in Cagayan, and so on. She was full of enthusiasm upon relating these experiences. I started to believe in myself, and trust in my intuitions, premonitions, and precognition.

"I hold onto my memories of Sister Cecilia," Lionel met her for the first time in the ship just after we were married in Manila, heading for Butuan. I had been kidnapped, but luckily escaped and then the police accompanied me to the boat that was waiting for me to leave. It was Sister Cecilia who was there and helped me with my anxieties and confusion. Her spiritual advice calmed my nervousness and augmented my faith in God.

"At the midst of darkness, there is light, God is present," she often said, reminding me of faithfulness to God.

Going back in 1981: From Butuan, Sister Cecilia brought us by bus to Tago, a town located in the central part of Surigao del Sur where she was assigned to work as a nun. She invited Lionel and I to spend the night in the convent. But the Mother Superior was quite reluctant to allow us to stay in one bed together, although we informed her that we were already married by a Judge in the Manila Court of Justice. However, she was still not satisfied despite seeing the wedding rings on our fingers, because she would have liked to know that we had a church wedding. She was hesitant to receive us in the convent until she learned that our church wedding was scheduled to be held in France. At that point, I was not able yet to show our photos of our civil wedding in the court, as they were not developed.

The following day, the Mother Superior brought us from Tago to the convent of Tandag. There we met the Bishop, who told us a lot of interesting stories which led us into a long conversation. Lionel loved Tandag, even if there were no comfortable accommodation or commodities, because he had enjoyed his conversation with the Bishop so much. He was so thankful to Sister Cecilia for inviting us to come with her to Tandag. In the afternoon, we took a long walk along the seashore. The sea was so beautiful and inviting in a turquoise-blue, blue like the healthy sky.

But Sister Cecilia warned us not to go near the sea water; she said the sharks come near the shore. She added: "It is the deepest sea in the world, where lots of shipwrecks happened. This part of the ocean is now called: the ships' cemetery."

Their old convent needed to be modernized, but they were waiting for a donor or a sponsor to help them fund their project of renovation. The road in Tago was not paved, and so it was so dusty everywhere. At the midst of our conversation, I told her: "Sister Cecilia, don't you know that one day, this convent will become new, and all the roads will be paved?" We looked at each other but I wondered why I had said that.

The next morning, Lionel and I left the convent at dawn for Butuan. Our preparations to leave was difficult, because there was no electricity that day and no water for us to wash. There was only one candle to light, and yet it was almost finished. We had to leave our room before the candle was fully consumed. We had some difficulties going down the stairs and paths because the candle was in the room, and we were trying to be quiet to not disturb anybody in the convent. We took a jeep that brought us to the bus terminal, and the sun was already rising and hot.

The departure of the bus was delayed for more than one hour. I looked around and we were happy to see Sister Cecilia there standing at the middle of the terminal with the same Sister who had accompanied her to meet us at our arrival in Tandag. They had surprised us. It was amazing to see them standing amidst the crowd of jeepneys, cars and tricycles, waving their hands while calling our names, as if a divine power had protected them, and they were not conscious of the danger, despite all the vehicles crossing around them; it was not very organised. People and mostly children with the Nigo on their heads selling fruits and drinks. They handed us two big sandwiches and cups of coffee that they made themselves. It was so nice of them. In fact we did not expect them to come to the bus terminal.

We ate our breakfast on the bus while waiting for the driver. We did not know what was the reason for the delay, but it allowed us to have a lovely conversation. That was one of our happiest moments with Sister Cecilia. In my mind, I thought that if the bus was intended to get delayed, it was so that Sister Cecilia and her companion could find us in the terminal. Thus we were able to take our breakfast together; God is good.

Back in France in 1983, we received a letter from Sister Cecilia. She said she would like to bring us to Cabadbaran during our next visit to my parents, so that Lionel could see her sister Elizabeth, her husband and the children in Cabadbaran; Lionel was delighted with the idea. But we returned to the Philippines in 1986, Lionel met Elizabeth, Sister Cecile, and their mother.

There was a fiesta celebration in the nearby town, and we were invited everywhere to taste foods; it was too much because it was hard to eat in every house. We also visited several places in the countryside, where we walked through the small but thick forest. There were some walks that took us to places where we had to traverse a river, and cross streams by walking across a trunk of a coconut tree knocked down as a high bridge over water covered with stones and rocks. One time it was getting dark because of the tree canopy and dense vegetation. Lionel had never traversed a single coconut trunk like that before but we successfully reached to the other side of the river safe and sound. Then we were welcomed by the inhabitants, who proudly offered us their home made foods again and again. We had to eat so much because it was hard to refuse their hospitality. We tasted all their foods, and the inevitable consequence occurred. We had insomnia at night, caused by indigestion and bathroom runs.

Since those memorable visits, we kept on corresponding by letters with Sister CecLaila until the time when we learned that the letters were delivered already opened before it reach to her, and our presents of money or gifts were taken. We had wanted to send her some presents to thank her for being so kind and helpful to both Lionel and me, but they were stolen. Maybe criminals can detect when something worthy is inside the envelope. I was ashamed and depressed by the negligence and dishonesty of those post office employees.

Only a few years later, during our visit in 1993, Sister Cecilia said, "Tago's convent was renovated and looks new, and the roads are now paved. Did you know that our Mother Superior was remembering you both? Before she died in 1992, she asked me about you. She said that if you came back to the Philippines, she would be happy to see you again in the convent." However, Lionel and I had never had the chance to go back there.

Dreams, Visions About Family in the Philippines and Australia

Sometime in 1987, my youngest brother Melchor never quit my mind. I wonder if that was the cause of my dream one day at dawn. The birds were already singing in front of my bedroom's window. For me it was too early to get up, so I remained in my bed and dreamed:

> *The noise of the crowd: people in the kitchen talking while cooking; people drinking; children running here and there; and among the people were Melchor and his wife. There were lot of movements and the sounds of noisy vehicles. I could distinguish the sound of the tricycles. One of them was the tricycle that Melchor was driving. I tried to see who the people were inside, but the tricycle suddenly turned upside down and fell down the slope of the roadside. I heard the crash, tilting and falling, "cling clang cling." They were the noise of calderos and casseroles falling,*

breaking, and rolling down the slopes... I saw Melchor far away from his empty tricycle. He sat on the ground leaning against something. Despite the darkness, I knew he was frightened but conscious, because I saw his eyes blinking.

I awoke, and phoned my parents to alleviate my worries. As usual, my father answered the phone. I asked him about Melchor: what was he doing and where he was.

Tatay said, "You had a dream again?"

I described to Tatay about my dream and I asked him to tell to Melchor not to drink alcohol that night when driving. He should be extra careful and avoid driving late at night. It was a pity I could not say what day he should not drive.

Two days later, I called my parents again and I learned that Melchor was driving his tricycle with casseroles and calderos filled with food to bring back home, foods from their fiesta celebration. A big truck was behind Melchor's tricycle and he had to stay close to the edge of the road to prevent him and his tricycle from being hit by the truck. Unfortunately, the tricycle was off the asphalt, became unbalanced and flipped over. It went down the slopes of the roadside as Melchor was thrown from the driver's seat. He lost all the food from his tricycle, scattered along the road. But despite the fright and bruises, Melchor was luckily safe and sound.

Why is it I dream of my family while I am in France, whereas I dream about other people when I am with them in the Philippines?

Dream of Amelie

Most of my dreams that happened at dawn had a significant importance. I could never get bored when contemplating about Amelie's life. One time I had an amazing dream of Amelie in 1989:

Amelie was so pretty, wearing a sky-blue shining long sleeved dress. She seemed to be sleeping peacefully on her bed inside a transparent rectangular box, floating calmly on water. In spite of the tide, the wind and light waves amidst the ocean, she was untroubled. The water was a clear bluish turquoise, and her blue dress was reflected on the water.

I awoke full of admiration of how lovely she was inside that transparent comfortable box. Then I kept on searching about the significance of that dream. I was worried about her when I learned she was having troubles with her husband. She said that at the beginning, Len was kind and gentle, they even went to the Philippines together in 1988. But their happy marriage only lasted two years.

The more I think of that dream, the more I grew confused. I was not afraid while dreaming, but I felt terrified when I awoke because I did not know what it meant. I had kept on asking myself, was she breathing inside that transparent box? Was she only sleeping? I wondered if I should inform her about that dream, or should I just keep it to myself and wait? I didn't want her to be stressed about it.

A memory: in August 1989, Amelie came alone to the Philippines, leaving behind her husband in Australia. She trusted him, and said that Len was busy working. Lionel, me, and our seven-year-old daughter were also in the Philippines, and together we went to Davao with her and Imelda, to visit our sister Nelly and her family. We visited the beautiful tourist spots and a children's park where Lysiane and Heidi played together. Amelie and I enjoyed shopping together.

We stayed in the Peninsula Hotel where we enjoyed the meals served in the restaurant. Amelie, Lionel, Lysiane and I were around the dining table waiting for our dishes to be served when *I suddenly felt uneasy as if something was about to happen, but I did not know what.* I hurriedly left the table and unknowingly, I went straight to our bedroom. There I saw the sparks of a fire under the window, while the smoke spreading throughout the room. The air conditioner had caught fire. From the room I phoned the reception, and two hotel employees came with fire extinguishers. I scolded myself later when I realized that with all the things we had in the room, I had only taken the packages newly-bought from gift shops that day.

The hotel management apologised about the incident. It was not just an inconvenience; it could have been fatal. I was happy that my premonition had warned me. They transferred us to a better room, much nicer than the first one.

I asked them: "What if I had not come to our room? You should have smoke and fire detectors in every hotel room, then it would be more reassuring for your customers." Nobody answered me. They just looked at each other. I was hoping someone would write my suggestion in their logbook.

We returned to France while Amelie proceeded to Butuan to spend the remaining days of her holiday with our parents. Once back in Australia, Amelie phoned me crying. She said she had just arrived from the Philippines and was shocked with what she had discovered when she came home.

"Manay, Len had betrayed me, there are traces that a woman had been with him in our apartment. Len had an affair with another woman," she said, sobbing and devastated. That news was like a bomb that had exploded. That turmoil tore my heart into pieces. I could not understand anymore what she was telling me because she was crying so much. I could not find a way to ease her pain. I knew nothing would bind them together again.

 I waited several months until one morning, she called me back.

"Manay, I am free, I divorced Len." she announced with relief. She married to Len in March 20, 1987 and divorced him in 1990. Evidently it was an inevitable and wise decision, I told her.

Amelie stayed alone for more than a year in her apartment. She said it was horrible for her staying alone at home; she was scared if there was a noise, and her nights seemed like an eternity. I was so worried for her. It was good that she got a job that kept her busy during the day.

Then about a year later, a new story started in 1991. Amelie called to tell me excitedly that she met a nice guy, and they planned to get married. So, I started to think that maybe the absolute interpretation of my dream was that there would be great changes for Amelie, a new marriage, and a new life. I was so happy for Amelie. She was no longer alone in a foreign country, sleepless and crying and scared when she heard some noise in the middle of the night.

In September 1992, she married Stephen Kelly, a young, divorced man. Amelie became his second Filipina wife, and he, her second Australian husband.

"Manay I hope you could meet Stephen, someday," said Amelie proudly.

Lionel, Lysiane and I came to visit them in Australia in August 1993, for a short five-day stay before we proceeded to the Philippines. We got to know Stephen and his elder brother Albert, as well as Amelie's charming in-laws.

During the first day of the trip we slept almost the whole day. It was so difficult with the jet lag; Australia is 10 hours ahead of France.

The second day, Ashley came from her visit in Sydney with new friends. She cooked us a fabulous meal, and then we visited places along the seashore. The third day it was Stephen and Albert's mother who came to cook the meals; the fourth day we went to the park with Albert's children. Lysiane really enjoyed playing with the other children. I found it interesting that they conversed in two different ways: Lysiane spoke French and Emily spoke English with strong Australian accent but somehow they understood each other. It was funny to hear them. On the fifth day we had to leave for the airport to catch our flight to the Philippines.

One thing that amazed me was when I saw a photo taken from Amelie and Stephen's wedding day, Amelie was wearing a dress of the same colour that I saw in my dream: the "blue dress." I was again stupefied.

Amelie got an office job in 1990. I remember she said she was stressed because her boss was always checking up on her, observing her through a glass dividing wall. I imagined that each office was like a square fish tank and the employees looked like fish turning around inside, being observed by their boss. This could cause any employee to experience tremendous stress and worry while performing their job. Thus, Amelie said she often suffered backache and that she couldn't handle working long hours anymore. She decided to quit her job. Having good experience in administration, she applied to a hotel and she was hired as a supervisor in maintenance at a Novotel hotel. I was so proud of her. She said all the employees under her command were tall and fat especially the men, and she was much smaller than them. She sometimes felt uneasy giving them instructions because of their size, but she remained brave and courageous despite all. She continued giving direction without hesitation and held to account those who didn't do their job in accordance with their instructions and the hotel regulations.

Then I had had another dream: *Amelie holding a baby. I felt good while dreaming.* On the other hand, sometimes my dreams would play a kind of naughty trick on me, so I was quite perplexed. I wondered if she could get pregnant, knowing that she had sadly miscarried two babies. The loss of her second baby made her take the drastic decision to stop working altogether, to be free from stress. Maybe then she would have a baby soon, as they really wanted to have at least one child. I prayed for her, that her wish would be fulfilled.

A few weeks after that dream, I received good news! I was so excited to read Amelie's letter joyfully informing me that she was pregnant. I was overwhelmed to read her description of how wonderful it was to feel her baby in her womb. I laughed and cried while looking on to her photos. I don't know anymore how many times I looked at the photos, with her showing me her growing belly. Her dream came true. God is so good.

A healthy, cute Karen Kelly was born in November 1994. The new parents were so happy and excited upon holding their newly born baby. Tears fell as I looked to their photos repeatedly.

After she'd grown, Karen graduated nursing, and is now actively working as a nurse, in one of the most reputable hospitals in Australia.

Visions of Ashley

During our five-day stay in Australia in August 1993, Ashley was there for the first time, with a tourist visa for three months from April, but she had been granted an extension of another three months visa by the Philippine Embassy in Australia. I was so happy to see her together with her twin. She was about 31 years old, and during our conversation I shared her my vision of her:

You will be obliged to return to the Philippines before the expiration of your visa as tourist. But you should consider coming back to Australia later, and this time you will live and stay, as you will meet someone, and you get married with him, but I don't know the date.

After six months, Ashley's visa ended, so she returned to the Philippines in October. However she came back to Australia, again as a tourist in June 1996, to take care of little Karen, who was two years old at the time.

Ashley's visa was due to run out in December, but she did not return to the Philippines because she met Ronaldo, an Argentinian. They fell in love and got married in October 1996. Thus proving my premonition true. In France, I had a dream in September 1996:

Ashley was surrounded with friends helping her at a party. She wore a purple-red dress that fell slightly below her knees. The next night, I dreamed of her again just after their birthday in September. She was still surrounded by friends, and this time she wore a long white gown with more people around.

I tried to analyse the dreams. The way the people embraced her, the first was probably an engagement party, and the second was a wedding. When I dream twice in close succession about the same person, the dream in my experience always has significant meaning. The next day I sent her a letter, informing her about the dream.

Communication was difficult at that time. The news and feedback took so long because we had to send things through the post office. Sometimes letters were late to arrive or never reached the right destination. There were no cell phones, no Facebook, no emails, and the long-distance calls cost so much from France to Australia that we only made them on special occasions. Anyway, I seldom called my sisters in Australia, so I did not hear from Ashley for a long period of time. I was excited, but I started to feel some doubts every time I thought of her. Since I was so curious and at the same time not sure of the meaning of that beautiful dream, I prayed that Ashley would receive my letter and that I would receive hers very soon.

She wrote me back eventually. I learned she was madly in love and now married to Ronaldo. She said she had worn a purple-red dress for her engagement party and had their civil wedding ceremony in front of a judge in October 1996 wearing a long white gown. They had two witnesses, a Spanish-speaking couple (from Argentina) named George and Mariluz. She wore the dresses I saw in my dream. She said that they held another party celebrating their marriage where all their friends were invited on November 10, 1996, and again she wore a long white dress.

I was so happy that the premonitory dream I had for my dear younger sister were positively what happened in real life. Two years later, Ashley gave birth to Andrew in August 1998.

Sometimes positive intuitions are strong, but I needed to keep them to myself, as some sensorial perceptions are hard to explain. I could never tell someone that the coming events would absolutely be happened, as I never depended solely on my intuition, but included my prayers and real-life observations.

One day, Ashley told me that the owner of the house where they were living wanted to sell it, but Ashley couldn't afford to buy it. They needed to look for another house to live quickly, because the owner had already found a buyer. I was worried about their situation, and wondered how I could help them. One week passed, I felt like calling Ashley. I think it was through a webcam I told her:

Don't waste time, you must ask the owner if he has another house for rent, because while I was thinking about a house, I had a feeling of joy. There is another house for rent with two fruit trees in the yard which might be intended for you if you can contact him urgently. However, it is smaller than the house where you are presently living.

In that the same week, Ashley informed me that they found a smaller house with two apricot trees in the yard from the same owner. The owner also promised them that a terrace or a veranda would be constructed so that all the things they had from the previous house could be kept and arranged nicely. I was pleased that my intuition was precisely right again. I was very happy that my feelings and enthusiasm were correct, and that Ashley and her husband were able to quickly seize the good opportunity in good time.

Ronaldo had severe backaches where he was working, so he resigned and was looking for another job. Ashley asked me, "Manay, do you think there is hope for Ronaldo to find a new one?"

A few weeks after, still through webcam, I informed Ashley about my feeling or intuition that Ronaldo would be working in a public institution where he would be dealing with a lot of children.

Ronaldo applied to a job with Sunshine SDS - Special Development School and got the job. He started work in 2012 as a teacher's assistant for disabled kids, aged from 6–18 years old (it is a primary and secondary school combined). He has used his computer skills to help the teachers with their computers' problem as well as working with the children. Ronaldo worked in that public school until he retired in 2017.

Segundino's trajic death

When I was living in France, I dreamed of Manoy Gunding a few days before he died in 2000. I had never dreamed of him while I was still in Philippines. I phoned Tatay at once to tell him of my vivid dream of his tragic death:

Segundino was facing the sea, sitting on the log lying in the sand of the seashore. Suddenly I heard the sound of breaking noises several times: bang bang bang bang! It was a strong, deafening noise, so much that I covered my ears not to feel the painful hazing sound of the flying bullets which pierced when they reached Segundino's body. Then there was a huge plume of dark grey smoke that covered his body. He fell down to the sand, lifeless, and the smoke faded away into a grey fog. The next image was a form of a large wide box, open and approximately 1 1/2 meters wide, by 2 1/2 meters long, and one meter deep. There was something inside, also covered with smoke. Then at last I saw his face in front of me, getting closer to mine. It was as if he wanted to touch me, he wanted me to reach him, but I could not see his hands. I extended my hands to touch him, but he was moving far away until he faded, and the smoke faded away too, gradually. But then he came back, and I saw him so distinct with his body surrounded by smoke again. His clothes were covered with small holes. Then the smoke faded away and he disappeared. I waited to see him again, but only silence remained.

Shocked with the idea of a tragic death of Segundino that felt vividly real, I remained immobile on my bed. I sensed Manoy Gunding needed my help for his soul, he needed prayers to ask for mercy, to ask God to pardon his errors and sins. So I prayed for him. Were my prayers enough for his forgiveness? Only God knows.

I phoned Tatay and asked him if he had seen Manoy Gunding recently, because I felt he needed our help. "No Sarah," Tatay said. "I have not heard from him recently, but he visited us several weeks ago and he seemed alright."

"Tatay, can I call you back next week to find out if you have heard from him?"

"Of course! You can always call me. I hope I will have some information about him for you by then."

He should have been told not to go to the seashore. It was so dangerous to go to the sea, but I don't know which shore, I admitted.

I phoned Tatay again six days later, he said Manoy died and this is how he described me the details of Manoy Gunding's death:

He had a date with a friend near the seashore, but the woman did not come. There was another woman who came but did not approach him. Instead, she stood at a certain distance and called out to him, but Segundino did not recognize her voice. When he turned his head to see who she was, several bullets of an automatic weapon were fired at him with no chance to escape. He fell to the ground wounded, and died with several bullets lodged in his chest and other parts of his body. According to the testimony from witnesses, there was a cloud of smoke that had spread from the bullets that remained in his body while other bullets passed through him.

He had been almost six feet tall, handsome, and charming. Lots of women, married and single, were attracted to him since his early years and even past when he was already married. We don't know the reasons behind his murder, but most of us in the family think that he was a victim of a woman's revenge.

Explosion of a tanker

It never quit my mind: I saw my brother Dan sitting in front of the steering wheel of his cittern [a tanker truck or a fuel tank full of gasoline]. There was something written around the body of the tanker, but the image went so fast, I could not read it. Dan bent his head down, but I did not know if he went out from the truck. Then I heard buzzing sound and saw sparks of light at the rear, followed by the loud sound of an explosion and there was fire. There was a moment of pause, then I saw flashes of water which were like the water from fireman's hose, but it was so high and was dropping onto the truck. There was no more smoke, but this time, I did not see Dan in his seat in front of the steering wheel. I wondered where he had gone. The water continued which looked like a waterfall. I was awakened because of water that dropped into my face.

I hopped up from my bed and called Tatay right away. I sensed my dream shows urgency. I said to myself, Dan should not drive but I don't know what day. Tatay already guessed I had dreamt again and he asked me: "About what dream this time?" "Tay, I answered. I dreamed about the tanker and Dan was in front of the steering wheel, there was an explosion, then there was waterfall; do you know where I could reach Dan?

"He was driving his tanker until late yesterday, Monday evening, and he came to see us before he went home. He said he would drive again on Tuesday," said Tatay a little worried.

I called Tatay again on Wednesday and he said: "Dan came this morning and informed me about the tank's explosion happened yesterday – Tuesday afternoon." He said he was not in the truck when it exploded, but he did not say why. He had probably gone out from the truck: it was either that he saw the sparks of the fire, or maybe he'd gone out to buy cigarettes. In any case, he was not inside the tank truck during the explosion. There was a detector which detected the heat, smoke, flame, and gas fire inside the parking area where the tank truck was parked. The detector signaled to an automatic system that poured water down when it sensed fire. **Now Dan was technically unemployed,"** Tatay explained. Tatay knew very well how it worked there because the company where Dan was working was not far from my parents' house.

Dan was ambushed

Years later, another dream - 2014

> *Dan was driving his van full of passengers, probably Japanese or Chinese people who were not fluent in any of the national languages of the Philippines. They may have been doctors or medics because there were medical equipment and bags full of medicines. Two armed men came and ordered Dan to leave the vehicle. Those men were carrying bullets arranged like a belt around their waists; they also were armed with knives and rifles. One of the men struck Dan with his gun. Dan stepped out from the car with his hands up. He was hit in his face and fell to the ground, moaning; I also moaned with him because I felt the pain when he was kicked many times by a man in dark uniform hiding bullets and weapons underneath. They stripped Dan naked and the other passengers too.*

I awoke wondering where I was and felt relieved that it was only a nightmare. That dream was so strange because when Dan was hit, I was also hit, and I felt the pain. I was hit in my ribs. I prayed they would stop hitting me. I was awakened by Lionel and for a moment

I feared he would also harm me. It took me a minute to realize that I was having a nightmare. Lionel said that I had been moaning with my arms covering my face and that he did not understand what I was saying. I got up from my bed painfully. It felt like my ribs were broken and I could hardly breathe, while my head was weirdly aching. My face was full of bruises as if I had been being struck by something hard.

Lionel took me to see our doctor. Doctor Lim asked Lionel: "What have you done to your wife?"

"She was fighting with someone in her sleep. When I woke her, she tried to punch me and kicked me furiously," Lionel answered smilingly.

I knew the doctor was just joking, but he was also wondering or curious what had really been happened to me. I was surprised when he said: "I knew someone like you in Vietnam." I was delighted, knowing that I was not alone. But I had to keep on asking myself: How could it be possible to feel the same pain of what my brother felt? How I wish I could talk to Dan to satisfy my concerns. Unfortunately, we did not find time to talk to each other about this incident.

One year later, Ashley and I were talking about our upcoming travel to Philippines in September 2015 and happened to mention Dan. She confirmed to me that indeed Dan drove his van with three or more passengers and had been ambushed in Tandag, Surigao. One passenger was a doctor, with a bag full of medicines and drugs for the treatment of children and adults in acute and emergency situations.

The first thing that the bandits demanded from Dan was his revolver, and luckily he had left it at home; otherwise, he would have been killed. Dan and all his passengers were ordered to completely get undressed, put all their money and jewelleries on the seats, and then told to go out of the van with their hands up over their heads. The men then continued searching for something in the van.

Dan was able to bring all his passengers to a safe place, even though it was not their destination. He came home with his bruises all over his face, on his body, and with broken ribs, so he went to the hospital.

Holidays in Hongkong and Australia

Amelie and Karen visit Europe

Since she was a small child, despite danger, Amelie always tried to ignore her fears, so as not to be deterred from experiencing new adventures such as travelling to other countries alone, for example Singapore, Thailand and others.

Excitedly Amelie announced me in the phone that she would be having a tour of Europe with her 10 year-old daughter Karen, including a visit to us in France. Then I had no news until I received her postcard, dated 4 September 2005, telling me that they were already in Rome. They had attended the Holy Mass in St. Peter's Square held by Pope Benedictus XIX, and they would take a guided tour of the Vatican and the Sistine Chapel. They had walked all day long, visiting several places and saw many things. However, she said she still preferred Australia; for her it was the best country and she felt very lucky to live there.

Their tour of Europe consisted of: Austria, Azerbaijan, Belgium, Finland, Greece,

Germany, Italy, Czechoslovakia, Switzerland, England, and they arrived in France on the 10th of September. Karen was able to meet her small cousins: Sabrine and Typhaine were three years old at the time. Lionel and I brought them to Lourdes. The next day we visited the Chateau de Versailles, then the Eiffel Tower, Disneyland, and other places in Paris.

We chatted, exchanging ideas about holidays, families, the situation in the Philippines, and others. We had funny conversations as well as disagreements that revealed our likes and dislikes. What mattered was not so much the words, but simply the pleasure that we had together. I love her and my niece, Karen and I was greatly happy with their visit. We had not seen each other in person for 12 years.

Lionel retired from his job in October 2010, then we travelled to Australia in December and stayed there until 6 January 2011. It was like our second honeymoon. It was the first time that Lionel and I had travelled without Lysiane, who was busy taking care of her 8-year-old granddaughters. She was also working. All my thoughts were with them.

From Paris Charles de Gaulle airport, we had a stopover in Hong Kong before we would reach Melbourne. We were exasperated waiting for our delayed flight, but we were excited to hear the boarding announcement. Our hopes were dashed when the customs agents stopped us while we were in the queue for boarding. We apparently looked suspicious in the eyes of the Chinese customs officer. It was humiliating. Lionel and I were told to follow them, and they requested us to open our hand luggage. On the first hand, I was confident, knowing that we had been checked many times at other airports with no problems. Lionel had stayed longer with the French customs team during our departure from CDG because every time he passed by the metal detector, it rang. All was removed from Lionel like his belt, keyholder, hat, purse, and shoes, still the machine sounded. The same thing happened upon our arrival in HongKong, but everything was alright because they allowed him to go ahead

We really wondered why the customs authorities were so determined to find something suspect from our hand luggage. In fact, we had not left the departure area. They sprinted to my hand luggage. "Open your bag, Ma'am and take out your belongings then place them on the table," said the policewoman. They took my U-shaped head neck cushion and turned it upside down repeatedly while all our co-passengers were already on the plane, waiting for us.

I would have preferred to leave the neck cushion behind and go, but they retained us longer. "You can shred it if you want sir, or keep it, but please let us go now," I said. "We are already late, and the aircraft might go without us."

But they did not answer; they continued examining it and we had to wait. Then one hour passed and I was fed up. I made a sign to Lionel and we started to walk towards the plane, but the policewoman held my arm.

"You can go ahead Madame, and you can leave your husband with us," she said.

"That's impossible," I said. "I travelled with my husband. I won't go without him, and the luggage is mine."

Her policeman colleague whispered something to her ear then he said, "You can go." That was all, they did not even arrange my belongings into my bag. Once home in France, we realized that it was maybe because of the staples and wires inside Lionel's chest that stayed in after his heart surgery that were detected by the machine.

We visited Amelie and Ashley in Melbourne. We were so happy meeting Ashley's son Andrew and Ashley's husband, Ronaldo for the first time. They were waiting for us at the Tullamarine airport with Amelie. Ronaldo drove us directly to Amelie's home in Victoria. Ashley, Ronaldo and Andrew stayed in Amelie and Stephen's residence. I was impressed by the size of their house which was normally occupied by only three: Amelie, Karen, and Stephen. For me, it was like a palace. It was a pity that I did not know yet how to do ballroom dancing at that time. Their parquetted floorings was so inviting, would have been perfect for a dance floor.

We spent a nice holiday full of laughter thanks to Ashley who was then reconciled with Amelie. I can still remember the letter from Ashley saying that she did not invite Amelie and Stephen to her wedding in October 1996, 14 years previously. But that was forgotten now. Ashley was an expert in telling funny stories. It made our stay with Amelie and Stephen's residence so agreeable. The laughter was so irresistibly contagious that it made our days full of good humour. I love people who make me laugh. It allows me to forget the high expenses, and the lousy, hypocritical and self-centred people who try to put us down to feel superior; laughter allows us to forget any family troubles and exasperation because of certain jealousies, suspicions or misunderstandings. It helps us to forget frustrations in life. For me, laughter is the best remedy to many of life's mental and physical ills.

One evening, Amelie's husband was already in bed, Karen too, and Lionel in our room. Amelie, Ashley and I continued chatting in the living room. Ashley had a talent of making us laugh so much that I almost lost control. I gave them a demonstration of how to maintain a flat belly. No need to advising her about her diet, because we had eaten a lot of cake that Ashley and Amelie baked, and we still had the intention to eat more, especially the cassava cake that I loved the most. I gained two kilos while staying with them, as I couldn't resist all the cakes they baked. Ashley was already complaining about her increasing weight, so we tried some sports in the middle of the night to try to get rid of the belly fat. Ashley kept making me laugh as she had trouble following the instructions and we went to bed at 2 a.m. In the morning, Karen was telling us how noisy we had been, disturbing her sleep. Stephen said he heard us giggling until morning.

We celebrated Christmas Eve with them, and before the arrival of their friends, Amelie distributed some Christmas gifts were so happy receiving our share. She distributed to all of us paper crowns that we each wore while eating our Christmas dinner. It was full of fun and the foods were delicious; Amelie cooked very well.

On New Year's Eve, the family went altogether with some friends to the top of the hills where lot of fireworks and firecrackers were lit. It was so beautiful to observe the villages located down the hills lit up with fireworks flying into the sky in different beautiful colours. We stayed on top of the hill until the midnight's wishes and hugs for a happy New Year 2011. Our New Year's Eve was so colourful, with the temperature of 40° C. I thought it was good that Amelie used her air conditioner at home to make everyone more comfortable, but Lionel hated it. He always moved away from the cold air, didn't like the noise either.

I can always recall one time when Lionel tampered with the air conditioning in our hotel room in Manila. The machine completely stopped working and it was too hot. He was selfish, as he was happy with the result, while I was furious with him because the air conditioning was no longer working at all, and I could not tell the hotel because it was our fault. So, I left the fridge open the whole night. I thought it could make the room cool, but it remained hot. I stayed awake the whole night, while he was snoring loudly. Evidently, Lionel and I are not compatible when talking about the weather. He loves a hot climate in the summer, while I prefer the fresh season of spring.

That vacation was very memorable because we were with Amelie and Ashley, and we felt like well-off tourists, spending money without worries. I did not feel that we were wasting money because we were all so happy. We enjoyed eating meals in nice restaurants, roaming around Melbourne, visiting different tourist spots and out-of-the-way places: Balarat Village, the zoo, and the homes of Amelie's friends; we even went bowling with Amelie, Ashley, Karen, and her friend while the men stayed home.

The next day, Stephen drove us to Sydney, almost a ten-hour trip. Maybe we would have taken a little less time in the car, but we had two GPS devices that disagreed with each other: one said to turn right, and the other indicated the opposite. We finally reached Sydney after Amelie and Stephen decided to follow just one GPS.

We had such lovely experiences every day. We crossed the bay by boat from our hotel to the other side of the sea. There was bright sunshine that morning, although we felt the wind blowing around us, so we had a lovely visit to the Opera House located in Sydney Harbour. We admired its white sail-shaped roof, of which Australians are so proud, like the French with the Eiffel Tower, and the Americans with their Statue of Liberty. I was fascinated by the creativity and talent of the architects who had created the innovative design.

The following days we also visited the well-known Sydney Aquarium, located in the ocean, which showed us many kinds of aquatic life. The different species of sharks fascinated me with their fearsome looks: Blacktip Reef, Grey Reef, Wobbegong, Whitetip Reef, Grey Nurse and Port Jackson Sharks and others. It was amazing to see those giant sea creatures swimming alongside the smaller fish, sea turtles and stingrays, with tails like a sharp saw which could surely fight back against the sharks.

The sea animals were turning around us, over our heads and under our feet, as if we stood inside the aquarium too. The only difference was that we were protected by glass, and we were dry. Lionel and I felt as if we were inside a ball of water, standing in the middle like a living plant. We observed those aquatic creatures roaming all around us from all sides. I filmed them with a camera that I bought in a Melbourne store to have souvenirs of the experience. But I kept on thinking: what would happen if the glass walls and floors should break?

At the beginning, I was not comfortable with the idea of roaming around the aquarium, walking on transparent ground. It was eerie. I was even wondering if the transparent floor could crack. I was also afraid that those sharks might break down the walls and could eat us whole. But there were lot of children and babies carried by their parents, so I finally had decided to trust the quality of the environment and have faith in my destiny. The sharks were enormous, measuring about seven meters long; they could have easily swallowed half a dozen of people at once.

Once we left the aquarium, the weather had drastically changed. There was the strong cold wind and rain was whipped up, as if a tropical storm was going to flood parts of Sydney. The climate in Australia can suddenly change, and we need to improvise with thick coats or raincoats.

After visiting those lovely places in Sydney, it was raining cats and dogs and quickly the road was flooded, so we went back to Melbourne by train. We spent our remaining days at Ashley and Ronaldo's place. We really appreciated Ronaldo's warm welcome. Ronaldo is my brother-in-law and most of all, a friend. My sisters gave me a surprise advance birthday party. Amelie and Karen were there, as well as Ashley's Filipina friends, a day ahead of the normal celebration, as Lionel and I were going back to France the following day.

However, before the party was held, I had a long conversation with Ashley. And while listening to my younger sister, a future vision occupied my mind. One of my prescient visions occurred: *seeing her cooking and dancing in a wider place.* I was trying to manage my emotions so as not to interrupt her. She said her husband is a kind guy, and that they were not rich but were happy together because they love each other. One thing made me more than delighted looking to my sister: she was so alive moving faster than I had ever seen her in the Philippines.

I encouraged her to look for a job for herself. I sensed it was the right time. I worked to convince her that it would be better to have a salary of her own, and to gain a comfortable retirement package later, so she could manage life without being totally dependent financially. I said: "I am sure that your husband will be happy for you. Also, there is freedom. When you have a job, you can go to the Philippines when you want to. You know, we can never obtain something if we don't make certain efforts to look for it. If you continue to search for a job, then you will find one, as you will deserve to have it. Believe me, we can only reap the fruit from the seeds that we sow. I am sure of what I am telling you, because I made strong efforts in searching for a job in France, which was so difficult for me because of the French language." I told her it took many months of studying French before I was accepted working as manager, where I had to speak both French and English on the phone. I had to also write in both languages, for my work with national and international laboratories.

She explained that she wanted to find a job, but every time she got one, it never lasted, or she did not like it after all. In fact, she had some interviews lined up, but she was stressed that she might not be accepted.

I said: "Just go to your interviews, so that you can gain experience in how to interview, how the working world works. Even if you don't like the job, it can allow you to acquire some experience and that you can add it to your curriculum vitae."

She wanted to visit our family in Philippines. I told her that it could be possible if she got a job. I encouraged her to think about being a cook. "I like all the foods you make, and I love all the cakes you bake, and I appreciate the happiness in your face when you are cooking and baking. You could be a cook or a chef. I am sure you would be successful. Maybe you could join a school to learn something which could be added to your cooking skills. Never lose hope if you fail once or twice, just keep going. I know you might lack trust and confidence, and that is quite normal, but don't worry so much about that. The time will come for you to accept an offer of a job. Keep going and you'll be successful because at this very moment while I am talking to you, I really feel you will reach your goal of a job you desire."

I can still remember the small game I made for her and Amelie when they were still babies. Ashley choosed the picture of a mother cooking with the music and dancing.

"I will try", she said.

"Ashley," I said. "It is not a matter of trying but doing it. Follow my advice, and even though you will be in your 50s, continue your search and surely you'll find a job."

A few weeks later, in January 2011, Ashley spoke to me through webcam. She said she had enrolled in a one-month course, to obtain the Certificate 3 in Childcare. And that was the beginning of her new promising career.

In July 2011, she got the work-placement qualification in Childcare, 120 requirement hours done successfully. On her last day of the placement she heard about a vacancy in the kitchen, and that they had been looking for a cook for a very long time. I encouraged her to apply for it.

"Manay," she said, "I didn't think anybody would believe me applying for that job, as I still did not have enough experience, but in the end, I got it," she announced excitedly. God knows she deserved it. The director of the company called the centre and asked them to hire Ashley, as they appreciated her so much and were afraid that another centre would snatch her up.

A few months later, Ashley told me that she was upset and did not know if she could still manage to continue working. I told her to be patient and forget the stress, without knowing she was on the way to success.

Later, Ashley said "I can't believe I survived all the stress and pain, including backaches. I worked hard and showed a good performance and obtained an excellent recommendation from my manager. I now have a permanent job!" In August, in an office party, her boss confirmed that she had the job she wanted. I was so happy for her. At the time of writing, Ashley remained working as a cook where she was much appreciate by her boss and coleagues.

Imelda, our youngest sister, was still living in Philippines with my parents at that time. She went to Australia on a tourist visa. Stephen, Amelie's husband, signed a request for her to visit Australia with the hope that she could possibly meet someone she liked and get married. My three sisters were together in Australia (Ashley, Imelda, and Amelie), and how I was so eager to join them. In any case, I was so happy for them, I don't know how many times I kept looking at their photos.

Ashley was full of emotion when her boss told her that she could have 20 working days for a holiday. After her work that day, she went directly to the flight centre and obtained a booking for the Philippines; still, she found it hard to believe. She called and told Ronaldo, so excited that she could go back to the Philippines for the first time in 10 years. She had not been there since she went with her son Andrew, for the Golden Wedding Anniversary of our parents in August 2001.

In 2012, she went to the Philippines, this time all by herself. She was so proud to tell me: "This time it is completely different. I'll will be spending my own salary. I will spend a vacation granted from my job for the first time." She was overwhelmed. Until this year 2021, she's still working for the same company. She got all that she was longing for. She goes back to the Philippines nearly every year since then.

In October 2018, Ashley asked me my feelings as to whether her son Andrew would find a job. I answered her with my feeling and I said: "There would be job offers and Andrew will be employed with the second offer, not the first one." A month later, Ashley informed me that Andrew got the job which was the second offer and was Andrew's second option.

Lionel and His Unforgettable Adventures 1969–2019

My loving husband Lionel deserves a chapter all his own. He has had so many adventures, before he met me, and then us together. His passports are decorated with stamps from all the countries he has visited. In addition to the Philippines, he went to Malaysia, Pakistan, Singapore, Sri Lanka, and Thailand before we met. He has also been in places across Europe, such as Ireland, the United Kingdom, Sweden, Germany, Italy, Turkey, as well as to Australia and the United States. He was a die-hard traveler, despite problems with his eyesight, which did not prevent him from taking the many trips abroad.

He loves reading poetry, is deeply passionate in world history and politics, and walks or hikes for exercise. He says hiking in the natural environment is a kind of meditation, giving him a better understanding of things, and promotes a balance of the physical, mental, and nervous systems.

My beloved husband is now fed-up of hearing me tell him about my premonitions and visions, begging him to help me remember them. I often woke him in the middle of the night to report on these vivid and undesirable dreams, as shared in the chapters below. Lionel said he will surely not be able to remember all my dreams that I confided in him; his brain has become saturated, although his memory is still good. No one lasts forever, of course, so he too has advised me to share all my spiritual experiences, premonition dreams and visions through writing a memoir, before passing to the "other side."

Lionel was born during the Second World War in January 1944 in Stains, France. He was one of ten children to a Russian father and a French mother, he was baptized at home urgently by the priest because of the war. He wishes he could write the memoir of his father's long and hard experiences.

Lionide Aleksandrovitch Tchermnykh was born in August 1892 in Viatka, Russia. Lionide was already a Captain in the Czar's Army at the beginning of the civil war in Russia, and was wounded. When the Czar and his family were assassinated by the Bolsheviks (Communists), the Czar Army became the White Army. Lionide fought with the White Army but was wounded for a second time. He was an officer of the 2nd Kornilov Shock Regiment as Staff captain in Gallipoli. He had participated in the first Kuban campaign in 1918, and was rewarded with special St. George Medal for having fought and been wounded twice.

He came to France as a refugee, and died in May 1970 in Paris, when Lionel was 26. I said to Lionel, by coincidence, my father Tatay Eco also died on the same date in May, albeit many years later. Lionel's elder sister, Sylviane, brought Lionel with her at the age of 6 on a very long walk in the Paris area and beyond, some 14 kms (there and back). Since then, he has always loved long walks, especially when the weather is hot. He couldn't stay in one place without practicing his favourite hobby – walking miles and miles, even if it upset his hosts or went against tradition. At the time we met, Lionel had already visited different areas in Butuan for his walking holidays and adventures. Some of my friends had seen him walking in Agusan Pequeño, a place far from New Asia and Obrero, about 10 kilometres from his hotel. He said he has the blood of a military officer, like his father; he would always defend himself and never back down against any danger.

A few weeks before Lionel came to Farmacia Rosita where we first met, he had already been in Surigao where he encountered the Governor. There, he asked for permission to penetrate into the jungle with the Army's protection. The Governor rejected the request, saying that Lionel could be mistaken for a rebel himself. When Lionel later informed me of his desires, I thought he was totally crazy, and absolutely unaware of the dangers. For example, the rebels were imitating the military uniform of the Philippine Army, so it was difficult to distinguish them from true soldiers.

I was impressed when Lionel came asking my Commander to provide him with an escort to bring him to a dangerous area where he could meet the rebels. He said he wanted to meet the men, not to sympathize with them but just to learn something about them. But I told him that his request was impossible. Lionel went ahead and met both my Commander and the Assistant Commander, but he never shared with me what they talked about. He did say that he had asked Major Referente to let him go with his men to patrol in the jungle or to the critical area where rebels were hiding. But I put a stop to this plan, despite the presence of the Philippine Army who were assigned to protect the area. I felt responsible for Lionel and would never be able to forgive myself if the worst were to happen.

To make Lionel forget his desire to meet the rebels, the Assistant Commander Captain Rara visited us at my parent's house to discuss it. Then he invited us to his residence where we were warmly welcomed by him and his wife

Lionel at risk in Northern Ireland – 1970

Recently, Lionel told me about some of his experiences, and said: "Whenever I was in danger, my angel was constantly vigilant and protected me."

In 1970, Lionel was working at the private company in Stains, one that made soap, shampoo, and detergents for washing clothes, and also wax. Lionel was stubborn and even a bit self-absorbed, as he never heeded to the advice of his parents or his friends either. He insisted on his adventures. Once he made decision, no one could hold him back. He decided to go to Belfast in Northern Ireland in 1970 and stayed one month despite the civil war. This was for a holiday and also to practice his English. There he encountered a young student named Colette, who became his fiancée later. Their relationship lasted four years.

For bed and breakfast, Lionel stayed in the house of a professor who was teaching mathematics and French. He met other French students, who were also there to practice their English. He also had friends who were on the Republican side, living in Ireland.

One day, Lionel took a long walk, and then he stepped into a pub and waited for his Irish friends. But they were late. Musicians and singers usually came to this pub singing folk songs. While waiting for his friends, he enjoyed listening to their songs and he wanted to record them on his tape recorder.

Suddenly, two men appeared and asked him "Are you bugging us? Are you spying on us?" They probably thought that Lionel was secretly recording someone's conversations. They were speaking in their colloquial phrases, so Lionel did not entirely understand, and he answered: "Yes." Immediately, these two men, in civilian attire, arrested Lionel, informing him that they belonged to the provisional IRA, (Irish Republican Army) and that he had no choice but to follow them to their car.

He was brought to an unknown place. There, he was questioned like a spy for the whole day. They asked: "Do you know someone living here? Who are they and where are they living? Can you tell us their names and their addresses? Tell me their job, what are they doing?" And so on.

Lionel answered several questions while they were checking the cassette to see if anything sensitive was registered. But the tape recorder was empty, as Lionel had no time to register any songs, because the two men had surprised him.

The tone of their voice became aggressive and they said: "If you can't prove to us that you are not a spy, we will shoot you." And they repeatedly told him not to look at them, instead, he had to turn his head while they pointed their revolver at his head. He was so shocked!

This time, he understood they were determined to kill him. Lionel was so rattled, he was unable to recall the names of his friends. It was only at that very moment when he realised that in a second to come, his life on earth would be terminated, that he remembered. He was able to prove his innocence because he had friends on both sides of the conflict.

At around 6 pm, after about seven hours, they released him. "Now you have nothing to fear from us, and you can enjoy yourself around here," they said to Lionel with a smile.

Lionel was so relieved that he did not know how to thank his guardian angel. "For the first time I was so happy, roaming around Ireland feeling free," he said with great relief.

The people were divided into two camps: there were the Unionists, who wanted to remain within the United Kingdom and were in favour of English rule; on the other side were the Irish Republicans who wanted the end of British rule in Northern Ireland and reunification with Ireland. But the conflict and his experience with the fighters did not scare Lionel away. In 1972 and 1973, he spent his holidays in Dublin and visited the

Republic of Ireland, where he was serene and happy.

Kidnapping in disguise, a victim of his own generosity – 1979

At the end of August 1979, Lionel stayed in Manila while waiting for his flight for France. We had met in Butuan, but were just friends at that point. He checked-into a lodging house called New Lodge, (founded by Imelda Marcos, the wife of the late dictator, President Ferdinand E. Marcos). The room measured only 2.5 meters wide and 4 meters long, with room for just a single bed, a toilet, a shower corner, and a sink. He did not want to stay in a 5-star hotel, as he would only be using it to sleep for three nights; he loved to meet people through walking during the day.

He journeyed around Manila Bay as a tourist, while observing the people and talking to them. He encountered a young man, and they talked about life and everything. The man followed Lionel to his lodgings that he had already paid for. The man noticed Lionel's lodgings were too small, so he invited Lionel to stay with him in his apartment. Naively, Lionel agreed to stay with them for the full three days.

There at the man's home were his wife, a baby, the wife's sister, a brother, and a cousin called Tony. They were six in the family including the man, but Lionel had forgotten to ask his name.

The first day, Lionel noticed there was nothing to eat. He went with the man to the supermarket to buy some food; the husband bought many things for the whole family, while Lionel acted as a financier. After their lunch, Lionel wanted to take a walk and to visit some places, but he was prevented from going out, they told him many reasons not to go, so Lionel obeyed, but hesitantly.

On the second day, again he was not allowed to leave the apartment because they always finding reasons not to go out. This time Lionel realized that he had become their prisoner. He was wondering if they would let him take his flight for France. He was very worried, and his enthusiasm for visiting places disappeared. Instead, he tried to figure out how to inform the police about his situation, but there was no telephone in the apartment. The police did come, to ask what a stranger doing in the apartment. Lionel was about to ask for help from the police, but the man threatened him and said to tell the policeman he was a friend.

Early in the morning, a man from the lending business came to take all their things in their apartment and said that those possessions were not enough to pay all their debts. Lionel then understood that he was there to pay their debts, and he realized that his life might be in danger. He said he was always thinking on how to contact me, as one of his only friends in the country. But he was in Manila, Luzon, while I was in Butuan City, Mindanao.

Lionel contemplated and asked himself later: "Was I really in danger? In fact, I didn't feel like I was, like was in Northern Ireland or Pakistan, especially since the lady's husband naively confessed to me that they were on police surveillance. I didn't even ask why. Maybe because I started to experience intense fatigue at the end of my stay. I actually felt that they were behaving strangely, but nothing more. Although I did not understand why the wife was going out to work at night, and the others were jobless and quarrelled often."

Despite the noise from this family, he was able to sleep in the room. When he woke up in the morning, he was surprised to learn that the husband had been fighting with a cousin in the kitchen. A knife was involved and Tony was seriously cut and brought urgently to the hospital. The husband was in prison and the cousin in the hospital. The wife begged him to pay the bail to free her husband, and the hospital fee for her cousin. He paid it all. So the husband was released from jail; and Tony was discharged from the hospital with a big bandage around his arm.

Lionel said, "How could I refuse? I went to the airport feeling free and with empty pockets; but I am in peace with my conscience."

"It was when I arrived in France and I opened my suitcase that I discovered that I had been robbed of a lot of things, and some were important to me. So I wondered if they would have had let me go, if there had not been the quarrel with a knife. It was a blessing in disguise! I was safe and sound in the end. So maybe I was supposed to come back and see you again, Sarah," he said, smiling and mocking me a little.

He continued: "If I had known, I would have had not paid for the New Lodge in advance. I should have booked a five-star hotel. I would surely have paid less than what I had spent for the man's strange family, and I would have had visited several places in Manila too," he said with regret. He has learned not to be so trustful to strangers now. He said it was a threatening and dismal experience, but he stores it in his mind as part of his collection of different adventures and stories from the Philippines.

Saved by our loyal dog – 2016

What would you do if you were lost where it was foggy and dark? And if you didn't know anymore where you were in the thick forest, or which forest at all? It would be scary to hear the sounds of animals around you, like deer, fox, and boar, and to be the mercy of your dog, the only one who could sense the way in the dark amidst of dense forest.

In 2016, Lionel went to the forest with Rayna, our 7-year-old dog. Rayna is a Dobermann Pinscher, and serves us as our guard dog, known for her offensive abilities, her proud, determined appearance, and strong character. She is Lionel's loyal and courageous companion, who would surely always fight against animals if necessary.

They had started a long walk on a hot summer afternoon, as usual. Lionel was following a narrow foot path along the forest and noticed it was not their usual way home. He did not realize the sun had set a long time ago, and he did not find the signboards to follow. Rayna had drunk the three litters of water; the bottle was empty, and she was still thirsty. There was no more car noise, as they were far from the road. They obviously were very lost. Lionel asked Rayna to find the way back home, and Lionel followed her hoping to hear the sound of cars. He opened his ears to follow the noise, thinking that it could help him to be close to the road and the way home, without knowing that they were walking towards a sloping and perilous path ahead.

Rayna usually would stop walking stay in front of him, to protect him from the animals; for example, one time she protected Lionel when a family of deer was crossing their path. But this time, it was different. Rayna stayed behind him, walking at a slow pace. Lionel insisted on walking in the dark, pulling Rayna along while she whimpered. She refused to keep walking by gripping the ground with her claws, pulling the leash backwards.

Lionel didn't hear the noise and the cars' vibration anymore, so he asked Rayna again to continue walking, but Rayna whimpered, and disobeyed him. Instead, she lay down on the ground and looked at her master, her eyes lit brightly staring her master seemed to be begging her friend not to go ahead.

Lionel wondered why Rayna refused to go further. He thought she had seen an animal. He was convinced of danger and fear took over his mind. But he could not see anything unusual in the dark. He went ahead to see what was wrong, while Rayna stayed sitting on the ground, though she remained alert observing her master by staring at him; every time Lionel moved, Rayna barked. Lionel held the leash extended to the maximum length, and went ahead to see what was there. He discovered it was the end of a small narrow way. There was then a dangerous descending cliff, stony, rocky, with sand and gravel along the side of a rough slope. There was no security fence, and Rayna had sensed it before him. She knew that it was a steep and dangerous slope, and she was scared they might fall if they kept going.

If they had rushed together down that small path along the dangerous Sonia slope, they would have surely fallen down together. But Lionel no longer knew how to go back, the path ahead was the only way he could think of for returning home.

Lionel tried not to let Rayna be separated from him. The dog had a light-up collar and reflective leash, improving the visibility in the dark forest but walking a dog with a black coat created extra challenges. Rayna was used to walking far distances, even more than him, but it would be extremely difficult to find her at night. They must have instinctively been careful not to be separated from the other. However, Lionel, seemed not totally aware of the danger around him. He held the leash in his right hand, while his left hand was grasping on the branches of trees and bushes for balance. The loyal Rayna showed the way for Lionel, guiding her master to find strong branches so as not to fall. Sometimes, Lionel's footing was unsure, and he became more dependent on the branches and bushes as they descended the steep path, until they finally reached the flat ground. Both of them were relieved. Rayna was so overwhelmed that she pulled hard on her leash, running home faster than ever.

"Holala! I can't believe it, but we finally got home. What an ordeal," he said. "Luckily, all is well that ends well," he exclaimed, relieved.

But I was mad at him at the time because he was only thinking of himself. I found him arrogant and self-absorbed at times. He never thought of the worries of his family. What he always thought about was walking day or night, rain or shine, for him it didn't matter. I even tried to get him to wear bright-coloured clothes for his safety, but he categorically refused.

I was waiting nervously, so worried, because there was no light in the forest and Lionel was unreachable, his telephone had no network or low battery. I also didn't know which forest they were in as there were several nearby: La Carnelle, l'Isle Adam, Montmorency, Coye la Forêt, etc. We love the fresh air and oxygen in the forest, but these forests are connected to each other. Without paying attention to the signs, it was very easy to get lost.

I had also once been lost in the forest. On my way driving home after work one day, I decided to buy something for the fridge. And after I left the store, I decided to take a short-cut, but I got confused. There were roadworks, so I took a small road that I thought would join the freeway in the direction I wanted, but it was the opposite way. Night fell and I had been driving for more than an hour through endless winding narrow roads, in the middle of a thick forest. I saw some animal footprints that scared me. A few meters ahead, I saw the three beautiful full-grown deer and their fawn. Then a couple of boars crossed the road in front and behind my car. I was freaking out in my mind, while remaining still in the car, in order not to scare them, or else they could have damaged my car and harmed me. The boars were beautiful with their brown-orange-vanilla coloured coats. They were strong creatures that stood taller than my car. They crossed the road, seemingly calm as long as they were not disturbed. My fear for myself grew when I noticed that my petrol tank was indicating close to empty, yet I still did not know how long it would take to get out of the forest before the petrol was completely gone. I reached the gas station and filled the car's reservoir, but had consumed a lot after because I was really lost. I had no GPS in my car to find my way home.

At the time, Lionel reported my disappearance to the police. My colleagues informed him that I left the office at 5 p.m., while I didn't reach home until nearly midnight because of the heavy traffic and being lost. It was all due to a mistaken short cut.

Another time, in Manila 1981, we were newlywed. Lionel and I both remembered when we walked around the city the long way, taking the whole day because again a supposed short-cut was actually a wrong turn. First, we walked along from Rizal Park to Manila Bay, then to Intramuros and Fort Santiago. We visited the National Museum, and returned late to our hotel smelling the delicious dishes. But that was a wonderful experience, because we had realized that we could roam around Manila, visiting several tourist and non-tourist spots, by walking, rather than taking a car or a taxi and spending time in heavy traffic.

The Metro – 2018

In 2018, Lionel was on a walk alone in Paris, roaming with pleasure around the *Jardin de*

Plante until late in the afternoon. He needed to take the metro to go back home; it was already rush-hour and the metro was crowded with many impatient travellers. He walked along the wall-side of the corridor, to prevent himself from being pushed by the crowd.

To reach the subway platform, he thought of using the shortest way – a kind of short-cut. He however lost concentration: he was going the wrong direction. He was surprised facing a long staircase. He wanted to step back, but it was too late. He missed the first step and fell backwards!

He later told me, "I missed the first step, and for a fraction of a second, I thought, that if I would miss more steps and start to fall, I would crack my skull on the concrete floor below. I did not want that to happen, and it was like I was hovering over the stairs, while I shifted quickly into a sideways position, falling down with difficulties. I don't know exactly how, but I skidded down to the bottom while still remaining upright. I still can't believe I made it. Maybe my mother was there, watching over me. She had protected me well, as always. I was overwhelmed with relief, inhaling a deep breath, and sighing a big sigh of gratitude. I thank God for saving me."

Friendly Spirits

The spirit of the glass ceremony – 1977

It was not a simple game but a dangerous one, to confront a ghost that you had invited during a ceremony. It was an interesting and scary experience, but also an exciting one because of the mystery of the demonstration of the spirit. Even though I don't regret having this experience, but I prefer not to attend that kind of ceremony again. I would not recommend it to anyone to experience this phenomenon, as it could be dangerous, especially for a naïve beginner.

One day in 1977, I was invited to stay a night at my cousin Ramon's house in Cabadbaran. In the evening, Ramon conducted a ceremony called the "Spirit of the glass." I did not know in advance how it was going to work.

Although this was more than 40 years ago, I still remember some details. There were two young women, their neighbours, who came to participate, and that increased my curiosity. We were four around the table. Ramon set a square table at the middle of the sala. He placed a square wooden board on it that covered the whole table and some information was written in the wood. There were letters and numbers from 0 to 9 in a circle, and another field saying things like good, bad, yes, no, hello, bye, happy, sad, marriage, death, and so on. Each one of us sat on a side of the square table.

Ramon closed all the windows and doors of the house and he lit four candles. He was holding a glass and he made a prayer in a language that I didn't know. Then he placed a drinking glass upside-down at the middle of the table. He instructed us to call the spirit of someone who had recently died. I started to get upset because to call the spirit of the dead scared me. We all placed one finger onto the glass without pushing it; we were just supposed to follow the glass, concentrating on a personal question, without revealing it to other participants.

Among the four of us, the spirit I was calling was someone who had died only a few days before; her name was Mrs. M. We called out her name while our fingers remained on the glass. Ramon called to her and invited her to join us. He asked her to confirm if she was there, and the glass moved to the position that indicated "yes." When she was asked to confirm her name, the glass pointed to all the letters of her name in order. I started to feel faint, because it was the name of the spirit I was calling. I was so anxious, but at the same time, very curious to know what would happen next.

We had to ask only one question at a time, one after the other, and soon it was my turn. I was a bit freaked out; my dead friend was there and I felt her presence. I wonder what my face looked like, as I was pretending to feel okay about this and not to disturb other's concentration. But I was trembling inside. We were allowed to ask only one question, so I have asked her: *who will I marry?* The glass started to move. I wondered if it was because of our nervousness where all our pulses joined together, but the glass pointed to the first letter of the family name of the person I would meet in 1979 in Farmacia Rosita of Butuan: T. I could not believe it, and I started to feel numb all over. How could she know someone I didn't even know? For me it was impossible to understand. Then I waited for the next letter and it pointed to the second, the third and then all the letters were completed. Other people were having a hard time to spell it, but she knew it very well. I still could not believe it. I removed my index from the glass because I had my answer, even though I didn't know the name yet. Others removed their fingers at the same time as me because they said they did not understand the letters or the name which had only one or two vowels: E and Y. They all believed that the spirit had been playing with us. While we were all complaining, the temperature dropped. We felt a strong sense of cold.

The glass continued to move slowly by itself, when in fact, all our fingers were far away from it; at the same time one candle blew out, then the second, the third and the last candle. All the candles were put out by themselves. We all felt the cold air shifting, swirling around us. Everyone was freaking out. A thrill of cold air surrounded my body, as if an air-conditioner started to blow our hair upwards with freezing air turning around us. Ramon was still praying while I followed the others who ran up the stairs to the bedroom. But I was frozen to the stairs. I could not move anymore, shocked by this manifestation of the supernatural. It was surely her: Mrs. M. I was afraid, thinking that she had followed me. I had only able to move when Ramon came near and reassured me that the spirit had gone. I wondered what prayer he said that made her flee?

"Ramon, do you think she was angry with me because I disturbed her?" I asked, but he did not say anything. I guessed that he was not afraid at all, or maybe he was a good actor. He finally said he had conducted several ceremonies, but that was the first time that a spirit had manifested in that way. Usually, the spirit called had a difficult time to arrive, while this time the spirit came so fast.

"That's because she knew me," I said. "She was our neighbour, you know."

I went back home to Butuan the next day, early Sunday morning. In the evening, everyone participated in the Novena prayer for Mrs. M., the spirit I had called the night before. In life, she had always been arguing with her family about cleaning the toilet bowl. She was always angry when someone left the toilet in a mess, and I agreed with her. I know all that because I was working during school vacation as salesgirl in the family's sari-sari store in New Asia. Mrs. M. was a schoolteacher in Butuan. After she caught her husband with another woman for the second time, she had committed suicide by swallowing the product used for cleaning the toilet bowl. It was so sad,

 I went to her house that evening to participate the prayer for her soul. I went into the kitchen first, looking for Mama, but she was not there. Instead, I found my godmother, Gloria, washing the dishes together with some of our neighbours. She was Mrs. M's sister-in-law. I unintentionally overheard their conversation about the reason of Mrs. M's suicide. And I suddenly heard the strange noise: a tickling "cling cling-clang, cling-clang-cling." The stainless ladles which hung against the wall of the kitchen just above the sink were clashing and banging to each other. I approached them, and the noise became stronger, as if I was being invited to look at them.

"Listen everyone, do you hear that?" I asked the others, but nobody had heard it. So I told them to look at the wall and there, they were all surprised seeing the different ladles swinging to the right then to left.

The ladles continued moving violently, as if they were dancing and at the same time, their movement became stronger that I was afraid they would be thrown off the wall. I observed them, curious, while the others had already gone to the sala where the prayers were being held. My mother appeared suddenly at my side; pulling my hand, she brought me to the lounge to participate in the prayers. I had been looking for my mother as soon as I entered that house, but I could not find her. She was the one to find me. I would have had liked to speak to Mrs. M. first, to ask for her forgiveness for summoning her to the ceremony the night before. She was probably angry with me for disturbing her. I turned my head towards the kitchen. The noise had stopped, as the ladles on the wall had stopped swinging. So, my fears disappeared, and lot of people participated in the prayers.

At home, I wanted to tell my mother that Mrs. M. wanted me to be scared, because we had invited her to be present during the spirit of the glass ceremony. But I was reluctant because of the consequences that might follow. I knew very well that Mama was always scared when we spoke about ghosts. I finally told her several weeks later, and she was mad at me. I explained to her that my curiosity had caused me to participate, because I had not believed what the others had been telling me. At least, now I knew.

Sonia's spirit confirms her presence – 1987

Fred, Sonia's son, Sylviane, Lionel and I were sitting around the rectangular kitchen table at our flat on the 13th floor while I was reading the Tarot cards that Sonia had chosen. Francing from Farmacia Rosita had taught me how to read the Tarot cards, so I brought them from Philippines to France for my personal use. I was reading them just for fun, as I never took it seriously. But Lionel told his sisters about it and they often came to our place and asked me to read their cards. This was the last time I handled those cards; I threw them away after cutting them into small pieces, because I realized that they showed a fuzzy negative trick that day.

I noticed in Sonia's facial expression that she was asking questions to the cards, and taking it seriously. She put her two hands on top of the cards, and I suddenly felt like fainting. Cold air touched my shoulders, and I saw the shadows of people around the table. But these were not our own shadows which gave me goosebumps. I stopped the session and told them that I did not understand what the cards had showed. I knew they were all frustrated, but that session was attended by the spirits, and Sonia's cards showed her approaching death.

I called Tatay Eco in the Philippines and told him all about that incident. He advised me to stop reading cards and to go to church regularly. I was intrigued to what Tatay had told me, but I fully understood what he meant.

We spent two weeks holiday at Sonia's place that year, and she invited us to come again the following year if we didn't go to the Philippines. I had really no intention to go to her place, because I knew she was dying but I didn't want to say no. Once we were there, she announced to us that she had cancer, and we did not dare to refuse her invitation for the next year.

Back home, one morning we visited Lionel's mother and brought her some selected dishes that I cooked for my birthday celebration. The phone rang, and I knew that Sonia passed away because I smelt her perfume, Nina Ricci. I was very near the phone, but I did not lift the receiver. Instead, I asked Mama Huguette to answer, because I sensed it was Fred on the line to inform us that her mother died, and I was right. But I was angry at myself again, as Sonia died on my birthday, 6 January. It had ruined my birthday celebration, though it was not her fault, of course.

The following year, even though she had passed away, we went for a short holiday in Pontarlier, in the northeast of France, in answer to her earlier invitation and to fulfil our promise to her. We stayed in her house for five days. Her son Fred, who was living in the village not so far, was there and welcomed us. On the first evening, Fred said I could choose any bedding for our bed from their dressing room. Once I entered that room, I suddenly felt a shiver, very unusual as it was a hot summer. Although I did not have the power to see her, I sensed that I was being observed and I felt her presence. I immediately told her that if she was there with us, she could give me a sign. Almost immediately, a handbag fell down just in front of me, but I was not scared. Maybe it was her own way to say hello. Now that I was sure she was with us, I greeted her with

"Bonjour Sonia." Although I did not hear any answer, I was sure she was still with me.

At night, I had to go to the comfort room, and again I felt her presence on her chair near the window close to the lavatory door. I did not have the choice but to talk to her, so I said: "We wanted to keep our promise to come to your home, and I was hoping that you would be pleased to see us. But if you are not happy with our presence, kindly give me a sign and we can go back home." I stayed awhile and I waited. Then I felt the cold wind that swirled around me. The fresh air went upwards and gradually vanished. I sensed she had left. Then I heard Lionel calling me, wondering why I was staying so long in the bathroom.

The following morning, Lionel and Lysiane went for a walk along the small streets of Pontarlier. I knew how they both loved walking, while I preferred to stay at home to clean Sonia's house first, before sharing the summer lodge with Fred and Serge, who had just arrived from Sarcelles. We were scheduled to visit the city of Doubs, about 10 kms away. We also planned to go to a summer riding lodge far from Sonia's house, before going back home to Stains. Fred had offered us to bring us there with his car. Meanwhile, I was searching for their vacuum cleaner. I was about to pick it up when I felt something strange, as if someone was standing near the vacuum cleaner. I felt like I was being observed again and I knew it was Sonia. But I was not afraid because I know she had loved me as her sister-in-law. So I started talking to her normally. She probably wanted to talk to me too, but unfortunately I did not have the power to hear her voice. We both felt the lack.

I continued talking to her. "Sonia," I said, "I love staying at your house, but it is never the same now that you have passed away. However, you should know that even though you are not anymore in this world, I am hoping that you are happy where you are." Then I continued cleaning the house with her vacuum cleaner. She probably did not like the noise of the machine, and so she left. That was the last time I felt her presence.

Before leaving, Sonia's children, living from different cities, came to stay for holidays, and the house was full. They said they did not feel any presence of their mother and grandmother except, Sandine, her sister.

Sandine said she heard the voice of Sonia. "She is a bad woman," the voice said.

Sandine told us that Sonia was informing her that Fred's companion was not the right woman for him, and not a good mother to his daughter, Cindy.

Years later, Fred found someone else. He married Madeline, a librarian, and took

Cindy with him. After that, Sonia did not manifest anymore. She must have liked Madeline better as a step-mother for her granddaughter. This is my own interpretation.

Françoise says goodbye – 1996

Francoise, our neighbour, stopped by one day in January. She was intrigued by my Christmas tree still glowing bright. She thought it was unusual, seeing the Christmas tree still lit up, even after New Year's Eve. I answered that it was my birthday, and the Three Kings celebration.

"Oh really? So, we've got the same birthday, what about celebrating it together?" She asked, smiling. She was our neighbour who lived two stories above our apartment.

"That idea is fantastic," I said. "Please come down in one hour. I will bake our birthday cakes and we shall eat them together." I was excited.

I baked three different kinds of cakes: chiffon cake, banana cake and apple cake. Françoise amazed me because aside from eating some parts of two of the cakes, she also devoured the whole apple cake by herself. I wondered if she had just wanted me to be pleased. I informed her that I had some problems making the apple cake, but she said she loved it very much. I was so embarrassed because the apple cake's appearance was less attractive than the other two; the apple juice had overflowed from the baking pan and burnt inside the oven, deforming the shape of the cake.

"It doesn't matter, it did not affect the taste of the cake," she said, giggling. At first, I had doubt whether she just didn't dare to disappoint me, but then I sensed she was sincere. I explained to her that I had to take it out from the oven and remove all the burnt cake pieces which had stuck around the baking pan. Only then could I place it again inside the oven to let the apple cake finish cooking. However, when I took it from the oven it deflated to such an extent that it went flat. Anyway, we both enjoyed our simple birthday celebration together. That was the last time I saw her alive.

At 7:00 a.m. the next day, Françoise came to say hello and goodbye just after her last breath. I understood she had a happy passing. She stood at the bottom of my bed and said goodbye just when our alarm clock rang. She was so pretty, and I smelt the scent of her perfume. She let me know that she was freed from all the pains she had endured.

Without thinking, I was about to hug her as we always did. I first put my feet into my slippers, but when I raised up my head to reach her, she was gone. And that was the way I understood that it was her spirit who came to me, to show me that she was feeling free and happy. She died in a happy state.

Lionel had gone to work, and I was preparing to go to the market. I had planned to go upstairs first to see Françoise first, but Murielle knocked at our door crying. She was informing me about the death of her elder sister. I told her that I was about to go upstairs when she rang. She stared at me frowning. I understood her reaction. "How did you know it before me? "she asked me angrily, but not surprised.

Here's the story: One afternoon, a few months before Françoise's death, Murielle came to ask me to read her cards. I said that I didn't read cards anymore. She insisted while showing me her own cards. She wanted to know whether she could have another baby. I answered her that it would be quite difficult, but I did not know why. I did not dare to tell her frankly that what I had understood while reading the card was about a young woman who was very sick. She stared at me and asked if I had seen something. She said she could tell that I did not know how to tell a lie, so I told her what the card showed.

Murielle lived one story above us, while Françoise was on the 3rd floor; we were all on the same building. Three weeks passed, and Murielle came back happily informing me that she was expecting a baby. I told her frankly that the card said she was not pregnant anymore, though I did not know why I said this. She came out from the comfort room crying and mad at me. She said she was slightly bleeding. She had miscarried her baby. She did not come to see me again until that day, the day her elder sister passed away.

I explained to her that Françoise's spirit came into my bedroom smiling, and seemed alive.

I was sitting on my bed still thinking about Françoise' visit and I did not hear my doorbell when Murielle rang. So she knocked at the door. I said to Murielle that Françoise was with me in my bedroom, she visited me just after her last breath. I went up with Murielle. There the doctor confirmed that she died at 7:00 in the morning, exactly the time when she appeared in my room. I was honoured and flattered by her visit. For me it was a real privilege that a spirit comes to see me before to joind the afterlife.

I remember the day when I sensed she was dying, though nobody would ever have guessed that she was sick because she was active, young, and beautiful. And she was only about 40 years old. I did not realize that I uttered to her that she would die very soon in small voice.

Lionel was at my side and started shaking my arm. "Why did you say that? I hope she did not hear it," he said angrily.

I was upset with my reaction. I did not want to tell anybody. So, when I sensed that she was dying, I should have just kept it to myself. But I do not know why I uttered the words to her. Maybe it was because I sensed it so intensely that it was hard to keep quiet. Again, as usual I was furious with myself.

The next Saturday morning, I accompanied Lionel to the laboratory for his blood test to monitor his heart-problems. On the way home we met Françoise, who announced to us that the result of her analysis showed that she had breast cancer. This time I did not say anything more, but I felt so uncomfortable in front of her, knowing that she would die so young. How could I dare to tell her? Knowing that the person would die made me feel sick and I remained awake the whole night.

Oftentimes, an ambulance came to bring her to the hospital and back home, even at the middle of the night. From time to time, I went upstairs to visit her, to say hello and to encourage her although I knew very well that she would be leaving soon. I felt so guilty with my hypocrisy. Then, at last, she confided to me.

"My room is well-equipped with costly medical equipment, but I can't anymore feel the comfort. My real comfort is no longer at home, but elsewhere," she said morosely. I understood what she meant. At that very moment she had already accepted her eminent death, and I knew that she was ready to pass to the other side.

She knew that her husband was having an affair with a divorced woman living next door, but knowing she was doomed to die, she was indifferent. She agreed to ignore their affair, because her husband had fallen into a profound depression due to her cancer that had strongly affected him and their three children.

From our terrace, I used to bring fragrant roses and carnations to her tomb, when we were still living in Stains. I can't forget when she said that she could not help herself from going to her open window, usually in the morning. She liked to observe the flowers, roses and carnations, admiring their beauty, and to breathe in the scents of the fragrant flowers growing on our large terrace. She said that she envied me, with all those blossoms blooming proudly which invited her to stay at her bedroom's window. I did not know that she was observing me every time I took care of my plants. I was happy that she'd loved the flowers I had planted in my terrace, like we did.

Huguette in her coffin – January 1998

I had never met a family laughing around their mother inside her coffin. Huguette Dufour, born in Paris-7éme arrondissement, was married to a Polish man, Stephen Andre Prozko, and they had two daughters: Sonia and Sandine. However, Stephen died very young, and later Huguette married Lionel's father, Lionide Tchermnykh. They had eight children, five girls and three boys: Lydia, Sylviane, Regine Serge, Claudie, Ghislaine, Lionel and Fabien, who were all born in Stains.

Huguette was the most extra ordinary mother in-law that I could have ever known. I immediately felt at ease during our first meeting. I was very lucky to have her as my mother in-law. I had felt the affection I needed from a second mother while living in France.

One day, Huguette told her daughters in front of me. "Whatever will happen to me, and if ever Lionel harms Sarah, I will do the best and necessary for her, as what I would do for my own daughter. You should take care of her as your sister," she said. I know she was sincere. When she was dying, I prayed that she wouldn't pass away on my birthday. She died at 89 years old on the 12th January 1998, between my birthday and Lionel's.

She was hardly ever unwell since I arrived in France in October 1981. Then one day, I heard she had eaten some oysters, that had given her a stomach ache and since then, she was not feeling well. She had diarrhoea and the doctor had prescribed medicines for that, but there was a complication as she stopped going to the toilet anymore. The effect was being reversed, so the doctor gave her another, but the result was making her worse. Her body did not accept all the medicines that the doctor prescribed for her. One week later, her health was deteriorating, she shook her head when I wanted to kiss her. She was not herself, no longer the healthy smiling mother-in-law that I had known. She had suffered so much, and that day I sensed she was dying.

The following morning, I called Ghislaine, who had been staying with Huguette, and taking care of her. I also asked Claudie and Lydia, who were just leaving next her house, about their mother.

"Mama is getting better," Ghislaine said. "She has already taken her shower and put on her favourite dress. She arranged her papers in her handbag, and she has agreed to go to the hospital. She is ready. We will bring her in few minutes, but we are waiting the ambulance."

For Lionel and me, it was excellent news, especially that everyone in the family wanted to bring her to stay in the hospital to be well-cared for, monitored and treated with appropriate medication, but she had always refused. She really did not want to be in the hospital. She said she preferred to stay at home to feel better, rather than to feel more sick while staying in the hospital.

After we had taken our lunch, and while our daughter was still in the school, we called Ghislaine back, as Lionel wanted to hear his mother, to be reassured, to check that she had gone to the hospital. I had a premonition of the coming sad event. I noticed that Lionel felt the same, as we both not able to finish our lunch correctly. Worry was in the air.

Ghislaine answered the phone: "Mama is resting on her bed," was what she said.

I felt more worried, because Lionel's mother never took her nap on her bed. She had always preferred to stay on her favourite armchair in the lounge after watching a film, so for me it was not a good sign. At more or less 4 p.m. that afternoon, I phoned again, and Ghislaine told us that it was finished; their mother had died on her bed serenely.

Huguette's wish had been fulfilled, she died in her house surrounded by her daughters: Ghislaine, Lydia and Claudie. The doctor was there too, and the ambulance, but Huguette had already passed away. Lionel did not move from where he was standing when he heard the news. I was worried, as he had a heart problem that was not yet treated because nobody in the family knew that he had had a congenital condition since he was born.

Meanwhile, it was so strange, but I did not feel like crying. Then I remembered all the jokes we had shared together. But I also remembered all her dreams that she had confided in me. We were so close to each other, she even defended me when Lionel was angry with me. One thing I remember most was when she told me that she kept on dreaming of her late family members almost every night. She said they were all waiting for her. She was probably joking, but the truth was revealed as she would surely have been welcomed by her relatives who departed before her.

The embalming was done in her house immediately after Doctor Lim confirmed her death,. She was already in a coffin when we arrived. Everyone was there including the children except Fabien, who was living in Japan with his wife, Noriko.

I always found Huguette to be so naturally pretty. She did not have many wrinkles at the age of 89 years old. She never put on makeup. She looked so peaceful, full of serenity in her open coffin. I kissed her forehead before I joined the circle, all of us surrounding her in the middle of the lounge. Everyone was laughing, except Lionel who felt strange seeing his mother this way. And although I did not hear the whole story, I started laughing with them, as it was so contagious. Regine, who continued telling her funny experience was out of breath and coughing. Everyone's face became red, not because of sadness, nor of colds, but because the stories were undeniably funny. The atmosphere in the house was full of gaiety; we didn't feel like crying, but on the contrary, we all felt like laughing as if being tickled. And the laughter had no end, because everyone was telling all their funny stories of their life, one after the other. I had never heard a mourning family who could not stop laughing, in front of their deceased mother in an opened coffin. It was incredible. I felt that the laughter was the will of Mama Huguette. Once again, her wishes were realised.

A few weeks before her death, I came alone to see her while Lionel was at work and Lysiane was in school. I found Tatiana, Claudie's daughter, also Camille and Leah, Lydia's daughters, in the kitchen crying as if they had lost someone. I asked them why were they crying, and why they were not in School. Marquis, Mama Huguette's loyal dog, a German Shepherd was lying immobile on the ground in the garden. They said he had eaten plants in the garden that had been treated with slug-killer and he had been poisoned. And there, I understood now why they were crying. Everyone loved Marquis; he was a loving companion, and a loyal guard. The children in the family had played with him in the garden, taking walks, and they even brought him to the lake where he had loved to dive. Marquis had been a gentle dog, a friend and a member of the family, and Lionel had loved Marquis very much too.

Lionel told us that evening after work, while walking along the sidewalk in Pierrefitte, a dog that looked just like Marquis stayed beside him and walked with him. Lionel had tried to drive the dog away, but it insisted on staying at his side. It was as if they knew each other. They walked until they reached the bus station, but still the dog refused to go away until the bus stopped in front of Lionel. Again, he tried to drive the dog away, and he was afraid that the dog would attempt to follow him onto the bus. He said: The dog looked exactly like Marquis, but it was impossible that Marquis could have been there." And when Lionel arrived home, he learned that Marquis died in middle of the day. He was stunned. I sometimes believe that a dog like Marquis has a loving communicative spirit. It was as if the dog was a divine messenger and spirit guides to Lionel. Did Marquis's spirit want to inform Lionel that he was leaving and wanted to say goodbye? Was Marquis a dog totem ?

"Dogs offer people "an ordinary, extraordinary grace," writes Jean Houston, author of the book *Mystical Dogs*. "Look in their eyes and you find *beautitude."* [a state of utmost bliss] and I agree.

I remember one of the last times I saw Mama Huguette on her favourite armchair, she was watching the television as usual, a film. After we have kissed each other hello, I sat near her without saying anything and she switched off the TV. Then she said: "Sarah, when it is my turn, please remember that I never would wish for everyone to cry. When life is finished, it means it's finished. There is no choice but to let me go." Then she started telling me about her dreams: "My parents, my sister Odette and my brother Andre were around the table smiling at me, as if they were all waiting for me. The other night, there was my first husband Stephen Andre with our daughter Sonia. And last night, it was Lionel's father, together with people around him, people whom I have not met yet, but in my dream, they were there smiling at me too, so inviting and friendly. I dream almost every night now, and I see all those people who are gone. Maybe I can meet them when it will be my turn, probably soon. So, there is no need to cry for me because there, where I should go, I will never be alone," she said, laughing. We laughed together, again and again. Yet I did not know why I was laughing. Then she added, "*Tout ira bien,*" [all will be well].

At her burial, everyone in the family was present, even Fabien came from Japan, and the neighbours too. For me it was logical that Huguette did not know the people around the table who seated with her late second husband, Lionide, Lionel's father. Those were his Russian family, whom Huguette and her children had never met.

Bekka's spirit visits us – June 2012

It was at the beginning of summer in 2012, a sunny Saturday morning. At 7:00 a.m. in Beaumont sur Oise, Lionel and I were still in bed discussing my job and our plans of traveling together to Turkey that year, the possibility of also visiting my parents in the Philippines at the end of that year.

A lot of birds were singing outside, many of them on the terrace, waiting for Lionel to come with breadcrumbs. But our conversation was interrupted when we heard a strange noise downstairs. It was like a pair of scissors that a barber would use to cut a man's hair; for a moment we did not move. We remained in bed until we heard the door of our lounge. It was as if the wind blew inside the house, and our internal double doors banged together, like clapping in the air. I was thinking that we had forgotten to close some windows downstairs.

Then there was another noise, like a person was searching for something inside the drawers, mixing up our spoons, forks and knives. At the beginning of the noise, I heard something like a hissing, then the clinging sound of a chain moving on the floor; Lionel also thought of the garden materials. But those things were all in the garage or the cabin at the end of our property, about 200 meters from the house. The doors continued banging that way, as if our young grandchildren were playing with them.

Lionel was not able to move from our bed. The noise got stronger, so I hopped out from our bed naked as a fish, while Lionel was calling to me, reminding me that I had no clothes on. I darted through the stairs, no time to get dressed. I had to check whether all the doors and windows were closed, as well as the drawers in the kitchen. I confirmed that all windows were closed, and our kitchen utensils were still arranged.

I thought of Bekka's spirit. He was the husband of Lionel's elder sister, Lydia. Bekka died in June 2012 at the age of 76.

As soon as I reach downstairs, the noise stopped. I remained still, as I felt cold air moving around me, lightly lifting up my hair. I sensed that I was being observed and I felt ashamed because I was not covered. The fresh air continued turning around me, and I was almost sure that Bekka was there. His funeral was scheduled for at 3:00 p.m. that day, June 11.

I spoke to him. "Don't worry Bekka," I said, "we will attend to your burial this afternoon, and I will pray for you, then you may rest in peace." The whirling fresh air continued to caress me for a while, but I was not afraid. Then he left, and the temperature returned to normal.

Lionel appeared at my side already dressed. He examined again all the windows and doors to find there were well-closed. "Do you think it was Bekka?" he asked. "Were you afraid?"

"Yes, it was Bekka who came and caressed me slightly, but I was not afraid," I said. "He needs help. We should pray for his soul. And we must absolutely attend his burial this afternoon or he will be disappointed."

Earlier that year, Bekka had been present during the family reunion as usual, which was held at my mother in-law's house in the middle of January, instead of the New Year 2012. I knew he was suffering from cancer of the stomach, and I had not seen him for almost a year. He looked pale and much thinner than the last time I saw him. But he was always smiling during the celebration. I was thinking that perhaps he was hiding his pain.

That night he had wanted me to stay at his side during the photographs; I was a bit embarrassed in front of Lydia and their three daughters, because he had put his arm around my waist and brought me tightly against him, and he bent his head towards mine. I tried to pull away, but he was stronger than me. When I looked at his face our eyes met, I felt goosebumps. Although he was active and alive that day, I saw him dead. That was the last time I saw him alive.

Lydia's spirit comes to kiss her brother

Can you smile when you're in pain? Not me. You can read it on my face; I can't pretend to not be in pain. In 2014, a surgical intervention was scheduled, for severe back pain, but at the last moment, I didn't go to the hospital. I paused, knowing that the surgical procedures were not 100 percent successful. Some risks are considerable, and I was concerned about the potential complications caused by anaesthesia. I had developed chronic lower back pain, the "lumbago." Yoga and other sports practices were not enough to soothe the pains of rheumatism and arthritis of the fingers. As I got older, the acute pain in my back woke me up at night. So, I had to take time off from work to undergo physiotherapy sessions, rather than taking medication. I endured many exercise sessions to develop certain muscles around my spine, and it worked. Episodes of painful spasms decreased. I'd even become more flexible, which allows me to have more fun when dancing.

Then I heard about the spa treatments where many people were satisfied with the results. I booked for both the spa and the hotel in Dax, in the south of France, about 400 miles away. We travelled by TGV which took us about 4 hours to reach Dax on August 17, 2014. I could never forget this date, as it was the date of our civil wedding at the Manila Court of Justice in 1981.

However, three days before we left for Dax, my sister-in-law, Lydia, died of breast cancer about two years after her husband Bekka, died. On the Saturday night, at a quarter to midnight, Lydia's spirit came to visit us at our home in Beaumont-sur-Oise, on August 16, 2014.

We were unable to attend her funeral on Monday 18th because we were leaving early on the morning of the 17th and we could not cancel our scheduled departure, the hotel, train tickets, and the spa cure which was already well-planned and everything was already paid which were not refundable, not even by our insurance, and we had devoted a lot of time and effort to get it just right.

Still, I felt a little guilty about leaving, with Lionel unable to say goodbye to his sister. So we decided to visit Lydia's body in the funeral home, to show our pain of losing her. We appealed to Lydia's daughters to allow us to see their mother in private before leaving for Dax, even if it was complicated as we couldn't just visit her on a whim. Lydia was inside a refrigerated coffin. She had to be removed from her freezing chamber and temporarily transferred to another reception room, and placed on the bed without radically changing the temperature. This way, we were allowed to see her, touch her, and offer our last farewell.

Lydia was radiant on her bed. I kissed her on the forehead to say "hello and goodbye" while explaining to her the reasons why we could not attend her burial. But I was absolutely shocked at how icy Lydia was! She was so much colder than my mother-in-law, Huguette, who was embalmed at home.

Lionel stayed further away from Lydia's bed. He did not dare to approach her. He was so sad, and I was worried about him because of his heart problem. He did not have the courage to express his emotions, he just stood motionless and alone, a little away from us. I asked Lydia to understand that her brother would go with me, even if there was no cure planned for him. Despite my best efforts, I failed to convince him to have spa treatments with me.

The feeling of cold remained on my lips until we got home. I touched my lips while I was driving because I felt like they were swollen. It reminded me of the local anaesthesia during my dental care. I don't regret my decision to come to see her and kiss her. I was satisfied and felt relieved. I had a great time with her when she was alive. We had shared funny stories, and she was so good and loving to me. She deserved my last greetings and respect.

A few weeks before Lydia's death, she no longer accepted any visits in her home nor in the hospital, because she had not felt comfortable facing visitors. She didn't want to show herself diminished by her illness. But this time in the funeral home, Lionel and I had the privilege of approaching close to her body, even for a short time, while talking to her mentally. Her three daughters Irene, Camille and Leah did her funeral makeup to make her cheeks appear less pale and make her lips red. They were caressing and hugging her so many times. Lydia seemed only to be sleeping peacefully, despite all the pain she had endured from cancer. I was almost sure that she would be so happy watching her three daughters around her that day: touching her arms, caressing her, and kissing her cheeks over and over again. Meanwhile, Lionel had not uttered a word.

The day before we left for the spa, our luggage and accessories were all ready for the train journey early the next morning. We tried to go to bed as early as we could, but I didn't know why, there was always something to place in or take out of our luggage. We had to check again and again, before we finally went to bed late.

I tried to fall asleep, but I couldn't stop tossing and turning until I ended up sweating, so I pushed my blanket away. But later, I was cold. I took back the blanket, but still there was no way to sleep. I didn't feel comfortable at all nor able to explain how I felt. I sensed something was going to happen that night. But of course, I didn't know what. I couldn't do anything but wait. I had already felt that kind of feeling before, when I felt the eminent arrival of a violent storm of December 25, 1999, the morning after my first car accident with my husband.

Lionel had already fallen asleep in his room. But despite the silence I did not hear him snoring. I thought it was a something unusual. I doubted he would stay awake like me. And suddenly, I heard a strange noise from the bathroom, at exactly 11:45 p.m.

At first, I thought it was just a bird on top of our window calling with an extremely high pitch sound, then it sounded like a nail clipper. But then it changed; the noise sounded like a pair of scissors cutting hair and then the sound sped up, becoming faster and faster, so fast. It became louder, sounding as if someone was hitting our radiator and tumble dryer with a big coin, determined to attract our attention. I was angry with Lionel. I wonder why he was making all those different noises.

We both shouted at each other and were angry almost at the same time. I yelled nervously at him from my room next to his, and asked him to stop the noise or I would go crazy. But he yelled at me because he thought I was cutting my hair and nails in the middle of the night. The noise kept going so loud. Then I heard him coming out of his room leaving his door open. He went into the bathroom and the noise stopped. What was he doing?

There was a long silence. I waited and waited. My heart started to beat faster. In that time waiting for him, I began to get frightened. I wanted to leave my room to see what happened, and see if Lionel was okay. But I felt like I was nailed to my bed because I couldn't move. Silence persisted. I was more intrigued. I wondered why Lionel hadn't said anything.

Finally, he went back to his room and closed the door behind him. In fact, he usually left his door open, like I did. But this time, he closed it. I wanted to ask him about the curious noises we had heard, but it was perhaps no longer necessary because I understood that it was a phenomenon, a paranormal activity that had prevented me from moving, as if I was tied to my bed with my own blanket. But I was burning with curiosity, so I called out to him anyways."

The only answer he said was: "Shhhh... you should sleep now. I will explain it to you tomorrow," like he was whispering to a young child. It intrigued me even more that I ended up being mad. At the same time, I was afraid that Lydia's spirit would return. I felt my body stiffening. It reminded me of the "spirit with the glass" session at my cousin's house in the Philippines, many years earlier.

I glanced at the door of my room which remained wide open. I always leave it open during a hot summer. I thought if Lydia really wanted to see me, she could have gone straight into my room. This time I was able to move to close the door, but I had no more courage to get up. The emotions had exhausted me. However, I started to panic. I turned on the light and glanced at my clock on the nightstand. It had already passed 1 a.m., then 3 a.m. and I could not manage to sleep, not anymore. The dawn was almost there. I was already thinking, wondering what Lionel had observed about the activity in our bathroom at midnight. I was sure he had seen or sensed something paranormal. I wished I could have seen it. Unfortunately, I was not allowed. I understood why: Lydia didn't want me to see her, and I had to respect that. I tried to convince myself that I had not forgotten anything; I kissed her during our visit to the funeral home to say goodbye, but Lionel hadn't. So, I presumed she was there to say goodbye but only to her brother, not to me.

We had both spent a sleepless night, but we stayed in bed. We were tired when we finally arose, while our minds were still wandering. I tried to forget the phenomenon and look forward to the spa, while making sure that we did not miss our train. We took quick drinks for breakfast: chocolate with milk for me and coffee for Lionel at 4 a.m. While I was driving our car to the station, I asked him again, but he told me he would tell me better on the train. We left the car in the car park, and took the train to the Gare du Nord in Paris, as there was no direct train to Austerlitz from Persan-Beaumont. We took a taxi from there to Austerlitz International Station – our official departure area – and from there we finally left at 5:15 a.m. as scheduled for the city of Dax.

Yet, Lionel still hadn't said anything on the train. He may have been trying to understand the visitor or the surprising event in the bathroom. It probably troubled his mind, but I didn't know how to comfort him. I thought how shocked he must be. I had insisted on asking him again what had really happened, but he categorically refused to say anything. I realized that he was not ready yet. So, I preferred to keep my mouth shut.

Suddenly he looked at me. "I'll tell you about everything as soon as we get to the hotel," he said firmly.

"Why at the hotel? Come on, why don't you tell me here on the train?" I was really insisted, my curiosity pushed so much that I made him angry. I could assume that what he was going to tell me was surely one of those events that had strongly stunned him, the most shocking he had ever known in his life.

As soon as we reached to our hotel, I had to go out and make my way among the festive crowd to get to my medical appointment on time. My doctor was already waiting for me to determine which thermal cure would best suit me.

While waiting for our first dinner at the hotel restaurant, I was again so eager to know whether or not it was a phenomenal activity he had experienced in our bathroom. He finally decided to tell me about his mystical, paranormal experience. You can't imagine how excited I was to hear what he said:

When I got into the bathroom, I was surprised to hear a slight slip like a light thing gliding against the wall, like a breath of fresh air coming from nowhere. I felt observed but loved. I stood still, a little confused. Then I felt a breath of fresh air passed around me, caressing my cheek ... The fresh air surrounded me for a few seconds, then it vanished. I was not scared. But I felt a kind of languor, an inexpressible feeling, as one sometimes feels on a summer night under the rays of the moon. It's a strange experience that I hold onto, and will remain etched in my memory. Now I know that it was not just a simple event, but supernatural one. It took me a while to understand that Lydia's spirit visited us that night, and she kissed me.

I was thrilled to listen Lionel who spoke with intense emotion, and he breathed with long, deep sighing breaths. I remembered that Lydia would always kiss us traditionally when we visited her at home or when we met somewhere. While we were in the funeral home, Lionel was extremely tense, so he was not able to kiss his elder sister. He couldn't even approach Lydia's bed. It seems to me that Lydia did not dare to leave our world without kissing her brother first, before leaving for the other side. I hope Lionel felt honoured. For me, it was so nice of Lydia, to kiss her dear brother before she could join the world of the afterlife.

If I had not had spa treatment, do you think Lydia's spirit would have come to kiss her brother?

My Godmother crossing over – 2018

In France, I dreamed of my baptismal godmother, Gloria Montilla, who had worked as a nurse in Butuan Hospital, married to Reynaldo Calo. In the dream:

> *She was so vivid in front of me and so gentle, smiling as usual. She did not talk, but she was telling me in my head that she was happy. I can still see her radiant smile, and she gradually vanished.*

I awoke with the image of her smiling face in my mind. I realized she came in my dream to tell me she was crossing over in a happy state. I called Mama right away to tell her about Gloria, but it was impossible to reach her that day.

One week passed, Mama said on the phone, "Gloria died during the evening two days ago." My parents and Gloria were close friends.

I was grateful I'd had the chance: I visited her at her home in January 2013. Gloria was like a mother to me. When I was a child she brought me to the hospital where she worked when I had health problems like diarrhoea, flu, and infected tonsils. She took care of me when I was a baby, and she helped my mother a lot. I would have liked to have seen her in person and bid goodbye before she had left to the other side. However, I felt gratified and honoured that she came into my dream smiling so much, telling me she was free. She had suffered a lot due to being diabetic, and constantly having to inject herself with insulin to live longer. One day, I will probably meet her again, on the other side.

As a teenager, after working with the couple who were both professors, I worked for my godmother. As always, I studied during evening classes in Urios, but I was taking care of Gloria's two small daughters, during the day. It was not an easy job to take care of the two children at the same time. I used to let Wena take a nap in the afternoon, but she was always pretending; one time she escaped from home and started playing in the neighbourhood while I was taking care of her newborn baby sister. Gloria was working in the hospital and Reynaldo, a policeman, had no fixed time to return home. It was either late at night or early in the morning. When at home, the parents were often needing to sleep during the day, due to working such long night shifts. Mama Moding, my aunt, washed their laundry and brought it back ironed. In the evening, she stayed on at my godmother's place to watch the children, so I could attend my evening classes.

During the day, I would review my lessons while washing the dishes. I pasted my lessons in front of the faucet and continued reviewing, even when I was cleaning the house. I reviewed my physics, algebra and geometry lessons and problem-solving. I used whatever paper I could find, like the back of their calendar, to compute variables into equations and to work out the solution to some complex numbers. My efforts were repaid because I graduated valedictorian from my high school. However, I was not working for them anymore when Gloria gave birth to her baby boy.

Serge – 2018

We kept on calling Serge, Lionel's elder brother, but he did not answer the phone. We thought he was at home, but no one had heard from him since before Christmas 2018.

At that time, I told Lionel to insist on speaking to his brother because I sensed he needed help.

"He called me the other day, I'll call him tomorrow," Lionel said, ignoring my pleas. But he did not call him.

I kept asking him to call his brother, until he got irritated. When he finally called, there was no answer. Lionel thought he had probably gone with a friend for a holiday. Lionel and his elder sisters tried to call him again to wish him a happy New Year, but still he did not answer. His family and his friends wondered what was wrong.

On that New Year's Day January 2019 we informed the police about our worries. They came and broke the window of his apartment and discovered Serge's corpse decomposing, sitting on the couch. It was terribly sad. We learned that he died alone before Christmas. It reminds me of my maternal grandmother who died alone at home, despite having many children and grandchildren.

Serge was an interesting man. He had fought in the war in Algeria as a volunteer paratrooper for 27 months. He lived with his wife Chantal for 20 years. Unfortunately, they did not have any children. He earned a good living working as a manager in the sales and marketing division of a wholesaler distributor. Their company was distributing office materials like stationary paper, pens, scotch, and others to the retailers such as libraries and big offices in France. However, the company where he worked was dissolved, and he then lost his job. One year later, his wife died. Serge became depressed and got sick in turn. He had an operation for cancer of the throat, probably due to smoking cigarettes and drinking alcohol.

Special Experiences

Municipal Councilor

There was chaos and stagnation in the municipality of Stains, located in the northern suburbs of Paris, 16 kms from Paris Charles de Gaulle airport. The population was growing increasingly dense, becoming the hiding place for criminals, burglars, drug dealers, violence, and teenage delinquents. It was like a toxic virus had invaded the city, and kept spreading. Stores and trades run by the French inhabitants or the "Stanois" were obliged to close one after the other. The city of Stains, for many, became unliveable. They had to escape and settle in the provinces where they could find peace and dignity. Lionel and all of his brothers and sisters were born in Stains, but had lost their hope of bringing back the elegance of their birthplace, which had once been a beautiful and peaceful city.

One day, my husband and I were contacted to be on an apolitical list entitled "Renewal of Stains" for the 1995 municipal elections. Although we were touched by their consideration, we didn't want to get involved in an election. Not only that I do lack knowledge of politics, but I also hate it. But to do them a favour, we were persuaded to put our names on the list of people running for Municipal Councillors on the condition that we would not be at the top of the list. Though we were passionate about some issues such as crime, drugs, and delinquency, we didn't agree on how they handled crime in the city. We did not want or expect to be elected. But by the evening, surprise! We were told that we had been elected to the list of the opposition to the outgoing Communist municipality with very little difference of votes between the parties.

We had no choice at that point. Honestly, I trembled. Anxiety invaded my spirit, as the challenges and responsibilities commenced. That municipal election's result made Lionel and me members of the Municipal Councillors in Stains for five long years.

For the outgoing councillors, who had been re-elected regularly since the end of 1945, our election had the effect of a tsunami over our opponents. It was unprecedented. The elected representatives of the Communist majority could not bear to have a real opposition. This triggered some very aggressive hostility towards us that lasted throughout the mandate.

From that moment on, we became the focus of hatred from young and adult offenders who were Communists. We endured threats and violence almost every day throughout the mandate. It was a scary time. It was difficult coming home after work. We were greeted by glass bottles which were thrown at us along our way. Rotten fruits were crushed on our front door, and syringes strewn around the building lobby. They destroyed lamps, burglarized our garage, and invaded our terrace, breaking everything. One night an offender kicked our entrance door and taunted us by launching objects at our large glass windows, while we were inside our apartment. Our life became a real nightmare. It was fortunate that we got away without being physically harmed.

This experience remains a painful and unpleasant memory. We confronted several hurdles; we were prevented from doing our job and duty properly as City Councillors. As a result, many people who had voted for us and had encouraged us to make political and social changes in Stains were disappointed. What scared me was that everyone we know and loved would be affected. Nevertheless, we completed our mandate against all odds.

We had to recognize that we were abandoned by the first and second Municipal Councillors (members of our team), who did not take their tasks seriously. We were left alone to face a hostile and aggressive environment. They were not always present during the sessions. Fortunately, we were blessed with the chance to build our new house in a more peaceful place far from Stains. Once the construction of our house was over, we left Stains in 2020, and we stayed out of politics for good.

The challenge of being a juror – 1996

I had no knowledge on how trials worked in France before my experience as a juror. I know that I am so sensitive and emotional, and I was afraid that this would give me some trouble in making my decision. I didn't want to have a guilty conscience, or to live with remorse. But I had to face this when I was selected as a criminal assistant juror in the Tribunal of Grand Instance of Bobigny for 15 consecutive days.

At the beginning, I was quite anxious about how to deal with it, as I thought it was preferable for me to be recused so as to not get involved. However, it proved to be a challenging and memorable moment in my life. The experience was disturbing and surreal, but then I realized that despite the difficult circumstances during the trial and to give judgement to the accused, it was in the end worthwhile. It was a fascinating experience, and I would love to be selected again. I would willingly go back to my experience as a juror at the Assize Court without hesitation.

Before it started, I was surprised to receive the first simple letter from my municipality in June 1996. I wondered what I'd done wrong, or was it a privilege to receive it? I decided to open it in front of my husband. The letter was informing me that my name had been drawn by lot from the electoral list by our Municipal Mayor to serve as juror in the Tribunal de Grand Instance de Bobigny. I presumed that it was not necessary to have any legal knowledge in order to perform the role of a juror. Then they proceeded to jury selection. They had to check if I had not been previously convicted of a crime or of an offence or serious penalty. My name, date of birth, home address were taken down and I needed to answer by sending back the questionnaire to the court. I was reticent to reply because I wasn't sure, having no judiciary experience. However, it was clearly stipulated that refusal can be accepted only with a valid medical reason. I was in good health, so I sent it.

Two of my sisters-in-law, also residing in Stains, told me that they had received the same first letter from their municipality but that was all; there was no second letter. Whereas I received my second letter at the middle of July. It was another simple letter informing me that after fulfilling all the conditions required to be on the jury, I was definitely selected, and I would receive a convocation as confirmation. I had started to get upset and prayed that the convocation would not reach me. I did not want it but what could I do? A week passed, I did not receive anything, so I thought my prayers had been answered.

I was about to forget my worries about serving on the jury, but then in August I received the letter of convocation, designating me as a juror for the session of the Assizes Court of Bobigny from 1st October to 15th October 1996. There was also a copy of the citation from the Prefecture of the Seine-Saint-Denis, telling me to introduce myself to the Court of Assizes of Bobigny, Palais of Justice at 9:30 a.m. on that day.

Copies of the different cases were attached to the convocation, and I was astonished to read about the various sessions with their corresponding dates, designation, nature of cases and even the full names of the presiding Judge, lawyers and Advocate General, the names of the civil parties and defendants, as well as the names of witnesses. I was overwhelmed to know that the Court of Assizes only dealt with criminal cases, which has gave me goosebumps, even before I was called to perform my duty as juror.

I continued to ask myself whether I could cope in my role as a juror. But it was too late. We were given a kind of pamphlet with practical details, and also the oath of the juror. I read them attentively many times to help me understand how it would work. It was mentioned that as a juror, we are called to bring our contribution to help improve the work of the justice system, which gave me the courage to do my duty.

I was determined to appear on time to the Palais of Justice on the 1st August 1996 in the city of Bobigny. As it was my first experience, I could not sleep the night before. Would it be safe to drive my car there or would I get stuck in a traffic jam? Should I allow two hours to get there, or maybe more? So many questions arose in my head. Finally I was in the courthouse on time, well-armed with my summons and citation. We were almost 50 jurists who appeared at 9:30 a.m.

After checking for those who asked for a medical exemption, we were invited to enter a large room and instructed to sit on the bleachers, which occupied most of the room. Just like a classroom, names were called alphabetically by the clerk of the Court and, lucky for me I had time to observe those who were called first. I started feeling acid circulating in my stomach. I felt feverish and faint. I had a cold sweat on my forehead while waiting for my name to be called. I hated that feeling, and I did not know anymore whether I wanted to remain there or not. I knew I was not there to watch a film in the cinema, it would not be a passive act. I jolted when my name was called, about to faint again. Our names were written on a paper individually, and once we were called, they were placed in an urn. After everyone had been called, they started the draw.

If your name was drawn, you would come down from the bleachers and walk in front of the two parties: the prosecutor and the defence lawyer, and they would choose to recuse you or not. If you heard "recused" then you were not chosen to be on the jury of the first trial. My name was drawn, so it was my turn to walk around to a kind of platform. I was terribly stressed. I felt so tense that I could hardly walk normally between the lawyers, although I had prepared myself to hear that I would be recused. However, both parties said nothing. Astonished, I continued walking and I returned to the bleachers. I was one of the selected jurors for the first day of trial, but still I did not feel relief. My cold sweat continued.

On that first day, we received training from the judging board, and the explanation of how the Court functioned.. There was also information about the list of jurors in each session and the numbers of alternate jurors to form a special list. A Judge, the President of the Assize Court, gave us some insight as to how to deal with our emotions before, during and after the trial. We learned where the courtroom was, and where we would perform our duty as juror. I was inspired knowing that to serve as a juror was an important civic duty. We would be participating in the judgement of crimes within the Assizes Court and be a kind of judge in our own right.

We were also oriented to the place where to take our lunch, a place to relax, and I was quite reassured that we always kept together as jurors, without mixing with non-jurors or others present in the Court. One of my fears was that a member of the criminal's family might recognize me later, outside of Court. But in the end, they could not recognize us, because the jurors were placed on the balcony at an elevated level in the courtroom, away from public. We took our lunch in our reserved canteen; we parked our cars in a secured underground parking and there was secured exit that nobody could follow us through. The one stipulation was that we could not talk about the different cases and trial sessions among us, except during the deliberation; We could not chat about it with others, not even to our family or friends at home. There were no cell phones yet at that time. If they had been in general use, they probably would have been prohibited.

There was a beautiful garden just in front of the court canteen inside the jury compound, with benches around the trees where we stayed during our short break. In addition, the jurors received compensation for our time, with a daily session allowance which including meals, a transportation allowance, a residence allowance, etc.

Those who were recused could go home and needed to come back the next day. We were 35 jurors to form the session list and finally, 25 were selected as jurors. We were instructed to sit at the right side of the stands, and 10 alternative jurors formed a different list to the left side. There were more instructions, information, and reminders about our behaviour, how to control emotions, what to expect and what to do during trial. Then we proceeded to the Assize Court for the first day.

The civil hearing began at 2:00 p.m. I became one of the jury of selected citizens seated alongside the professional magistrates and the Judge. The trial began. Most of the time, the trial was animated with contestations and yelling from both sides. The room was evacuated often, or the trial was adjourned.

I was confronted with criminals who had committed terrible crimes. I was sometimes affected and had conflicted emotions. Could I sentence a father of four children, because he killed the man who raped and killed his wife? Could I sentence a mother who killed her husband because he raped and killed their young daughter? I tried to apply my own life experiences to make good judgements of the facts as presented, and not to be influenced by the accused's personality.

Each juror needed to keep their emotions in check, and this was sometimes hard to deal with. Bloody images, such as photos showing mutilation, were exhibited to us to enable us to judge the level of the atrocity of the crime. One time I felt so awful upon looking them and I was about to faint. But I forgot my own emotions when I suddenly saw an armchair swiveling behind me where nobody was sitting anymore. My co-juror had actually fainted. We found him on the floor under the chair. The jury withdrew while awaiting a doctor, and took advantage of having a break with enjoying a pause, cigarettes, lunch, etc. The trial was postponed to 2 p.m. The process started over with an alternate juror seated in his place.

Sometimes it was very boring. Once, a young juror who seated to my left, was already half asleep, and tried moving her armchair slightly back and forth from time to time. I was disturbed by her restlessness. I knew the Judge had noticed her sleepiness, but he did not say anything. I wondered if he was just being understanding and humane. I felt even more sleepy than she seemed, and I had hardly rested. It would be embarrassing if I had fallen asleep by accident. The magistrates were just at my right side; it would be too easy for them to detect me.

Our jury consisted of half men, half women; half white, half black; ages from teenagers through to the elderly, with different professions. We tried to hold our emotions in check during the trial, so as not to delay or to have to restart the deliberations. I had to ask myself once we walked to the jury room to deliberate, "can I cope?"

In the jury room, we all sat down, finally relieved it was time to decide. During the deliberation, each verdict needed to be unanimous, which was not easy. There were times where we had to restart our deliberations due to divided opinions, where we had to re-examine our notes, remarks of conviction and so on. There was a coffee maker that fed most of my co-jurors often, while I only took a small bottle of water; I can't dare to drink coffee, otherwise it really enhances my nervousness. Believe me, it was not a holiday. It was sometimes hard to reach a verdict. We took turns speaking, and the Judge was there at the last minute to answer our questions and assist us in making the final verdict. Conviction was sometimes complicated. We had to agree as to whether it was a first or second degree murder. Sometimes the deliberations were adjourned then restarted, and we returned home very late in the evening. Sometimes we had long hours of deliberation, which required an overnight stay and then we returned home the following morning.

Each life sentence was always unbearable to the accused and their family. After the pronunciation of the verdict, the room would be immediately evacuated. The convict's family would scream, cry, and shout their frustrations, anger, hatred, horrible cries of revenge; the atmosphere became heinous. I understood their strong distress, but there was nothing we could do differently. We could hear them very loudly, as if they were using a microphone. Fortunately, we were secured on an elevated level, so they couldn't reach us nor to focus their eyes on us.

My horse riding adventures – 1991-1998

One day in 1991, we had our walk in the parc of La Courneuve. I was fascinated to have discovered that one of the leisure and cultural sports activities there was a horse riding in the UCPA Equitation. [*Union des centres de plein air*] or union of outdoor centres. My desire to ride a horse grew. I still remember my childhood experience riding on the back of the young carabao, even though I had no knowledge as to how to steer an animal, so I ended up by being thrown from carabao's back, landing with a crack on the dry and hard ground. By coincidence, Lionel's nieces Camille and Leah also loved horse riding, but had no experience in dealing with horses either. Together we signed up. I promised to myself to learn how to ride a horse properly. This time I took regular riding lessons twice a week. For eight consecutive years I had a riding lesson and a galloping/ jumping lesson every week. At that time, I went there on my all-terrain bike, so I could directly enter the Equestrian Centre located in the middle of the park. Cars were not allowed inside the park; they had to be left near the entrance.

We rode different horses each session. We had to clean the horse before and after each session: clean or wash. I learned how to mount a horse, how to saddle, and how to install the 'tack.' I was always checking that the safety stirrups were well-adjusted for the length of my legs, in order to be completely comfortable for both me and the horse when we rode. However, I had a hard time putting on the bits and bridles. I was afraid to put the bit in a horse's mouth at the start. I was thinking, "what if he bites me?" It was so impressive to see all the large teeth. I also worried when I had to clean the horses hooves. I was afraid he'd kick me.

But later I learned to talk to my horse before the ride. I found it so moving, so affectionate when our eyes would meet and there would be this profound look. Horses started to recognize my voice and they liked to hear their names. It was the beginning of our friendship and complicity. I learned the methods and successfully passed the examination on the basic dressage, before proceeding to the higher levels.

It was funny when I rode a horse named Nenive for the first time. She was trained to work the aerobatic in such a way that she also made a kind of performance while I was on her back. I knew that she was doing what she wanted, because I did not know how to command her. She was trained and disciplined to work in a circus, and she retained those habits that gave her a funny attitude. It was my first day for a ride, and by chance, she came across with me and made everyone laugh. She trotted like a soldier marching in the parade, and she bowed her head so many times that that I felt so tired trying not to fall.

In eight years' time I rode 46 different horses. Among all them, for me, Surprise was the best. Now, they're all gone, and younger ones have replaced them. Like all other cavaliers, I had my riding gear, including a helmet and a driving whip.

Every time I went home, my nine-year-old daughter would ask me, "What was your horse's name this time, Mom?" Lionel would help me to remove my boots before I jumped into the bathtub. I walked like a duck after my first riding lesson, with muscle aches and pains from my first attempt to gallop. Sometimes I slipped from my horse's back while galloping or jumping. But those were some of the most beautiful and unforgettable experiences I ever had.

During weekends, Lionel, Lysiane and I went to visit the horses in their stables. We love to give carrots to my favourite horses. At the very beginning, I had preferred Crin Blanc, because he had helped me achieve my very first successful gallop without being thrown off.

One time we found three of my favourites in a row. There were Crin Blanc, Nenive (both white in colour) and Faraman (also white but with black spots). Lysiane gave a carrot to Crin Blanc and immediately, Faraman put his head under Nenive's body to take it from Crin Blanc's mouth, and Nenive did the same. It was funny to watch their behaviour. As soon as you asked them to stop moving, they behaved like wise obedient children. I had to bring more carrots to avoid quarrelling and jealousy amongst the horses. Sometimes they would try to snoop from my bag. We loved to go near the horses' boxes. One time, Verde, who was injured during a competition, was not in good mood. He pretended to bite Lionel because he had not yet received his carrot. General also pushed Lionel's shoulder so impatiently, waiting for his turn to receive his carrot, and so on. I loved getting to know their different personalities.

One afternoon, I was forced to rodeo despite myself. The horse was so distraught that she no longer obeyed me, jumping around, bolting and eventually jumping over the heads of people before coming to a stop. I almost caused a fatal accident to me and to the others. The horse I was riding was only between 2 and 3 years old. So active, so alert but afraid of lightning & thunder, and other things too.

On this day, I had brought with me a satchel, as always, to hold the materials needed to clean and prepare my horse. It held things like the body brush, mane comb, curry comb, hoof pick and a perforator for leather to add a hole on the strap leather to adjust the length of the stirrups. Our jumping session that days was wonderful, and when it was over I was feeling very satisfied. I was gratified with Surprise's excellent performance.

When it was time to bring back our horses to the stable, I took the satchel from the ground, and I placed it in front of me and against the pommel on Surprise's back. When Surprise started to trot, the things inside my satchel hit against each other and made noises that frightened her. She immediately became nervous and uncontrollable. She kicked in the air then stood on both her hind legs. I was off-balance, not ready for the rodeo, and I thought I was going to fall. I did not expect her to gallop with colossal strength and absolute intensity. I could not feel my feet on the stirrup anymore, and I thought she might throw me off. Luckily, I still had the reins.

I dropped my satchel to the ground, hoping that would calm the animal, but Surprise continued galloping, wildly. She jumped over the fence of the quarry and jumped over the head of my fellow horse-riders outside the track. She refused to enter the stable. This was despite all the efforts of the five monitors (Stephen Andre, Jean Yves, Cyril, Florence, and Mr. Lequin) and all the other riders present in the centre who had gathered to form a chain to block the way, but it did not stop Surprise.

I heard people yelling. The reins were slipping from my hands; I clung to her mane and concentrated on not being thrown off. I lost hope of stopping her. I trembled while looking to the people in front of us, afraid that harming them would be all my fault.

Guided by the monitors, more people from the centre stood in front of my horse, and Surprise finally stopped. I was in the state of shock. It all felt surreal. I did not dare to look at the people behind me who were kneeling on the ground. They tried to shield themselves from Surprise's hooves. I was afraid that someone might have been wounded. It was one of the worst fears in my life! Luckily, nobody was hurt. I was not reproached by the monitors about the incident.

However, one rider was so angry with me after my horse had jumped over his head while he was crouching down. I apologised at the time, but he followed me in the stable and pointed his fingers towards me while uttering angry words. I did not hear what he said. I was so afraid that my surroundings seemed silent.

Before our next session started, I told him again that I was so sorry of what had happened, but it was not enough. He was so mad, unable to forgive me. I started to be afraid of him, but I had dared to ask him: "What would you do if you were me, riding an uncontrollable horse?"

He did not answer.

"My horse and I did not hit you," I continued. "I beg you to pardon me for being unable to control my horse. I did not expect to frighten my horse."

Still he did not say anything.

I was consoled that he was not hurt physically, but I was so sorry that he was psychologically affected. In the end, my horse had not stepped on anybody. I was just so stupid, in that I put my bag on the back of my horse. I was hoping to become a good cavaliere someday. But I can't go back to the past to erase my errors.

I learned later that Surprise was sick. I saw her outside the stable separated from other horses. She died a few days later. Although I was affected by her death, I was so thankful and happy that I had rode on her back and we had spent many fabulous riding sessions together. She was such a magnificent horse. She was so active, and she obeyed easily without being asked twice. I am fairly short, and Surprise was tall, so I needed a mounting block in order to climb upon her back. Otherwise I needed another cavalier to assist me while I hopped unto her back. She had an extraordinarily beautiful reddish, shiny dark brown coat with a thick black mane. You could immediately distinguish her, even from far away. It is a pity that a disease killed her while she was still so young. I felt a pang, missing her every time I entered the equitation centre in the park.

Most of the time, I instinctively knew when something was amiss on my horse. A horse's nostrils relax when they are happy. We all knew the usual signs, and read the signs expressed by the eyes, ears, tail, it gives you feedback. Though horses sometimes have deadpan manner, I could hear my horse laughing with contentment, for example when we played Horse Ball. This was a really fun game for the horses and the riders both, where we took turns throwing a ball through a ring. The sport was a cross between polo and basketball. We were on the backs of our very vigorous and fast horses, well-trained to participate in the games and making points in a good mood. It was the great way to break the routine. How I loved those enjoyable sessions. I still miss them.

Of course, the horses were sometimes bored; they love playing as children do. They were sometimes seething with impatience to be brought outside the stable. Jumping was my favourite session. I also loved our sessions of hillside climbing, which were sometimes thrilling and intriguing. We crossed through woods and bushes. We also had internal competitions. We always had to be aware of contact, the pulse, and tension of our horses. The centre gave us sessions in performing, lessons in jockey riding, riding bareback (without a saddle), as well as Amazonian riding.

I was surprised to see my photo taken from far by someone after our riding session, though I did not know her. Although the photo look blurred, it is my great souvenir with Crin Blanc. Unfortunately, it was taken from the end of the evening just when our session was finished. At that time taking pictures was prohibited as the flash could frighten the horses, especially when it was getting dark. I had no cell phone and no video camera at that time to provide me with other photo souvenirs. All these unforgettable rich adventures remained fresh in my heart and spirit.

After the second year, I successfully passed my higher-level exams, and I was ready to participate in some competitions of show jumping. Leah and Camille stopped riding after one year, while I continued until the 6th Gallop Level. Unfortunately, I had to stop attending sessions because of the lack of funding. I paid 1,200 francs for one class at the beginning for every trimester. Later I paid the 2,400 francs each trimester, because I took two sessions a week. I had to make some concessions. It was hard for me to decide because I really loved horse riding. But I had to choose between paying for expensive riding lessons for my pleasure and sport, or to save money for the construction of our future house. Meanwhile, I understood that to realize a dream, certain sacrifices are demanded, and it is difficult for me to fulfil all my dreams at once, and at the same time.

Before I quit, nothing got in the way of my riding: not rain, strong winds or snowfalls.

I faithfully went to La Courneuve on my all-terrain bike for eight consecutive years. During my last two weeks of horse riding, I still could not believe that I had to stop the sessions. One day after the session, I waited for everyone to bring back the horses to the stable. I went in the opposite direction. For me, it was the first time to really enjoy galloping away from the stable, away from the other riders. I galloped as far as I could without Cyril, my coach, noticing at first. It was fantastic.

Alas, Cyril ended up finding out me and he scolded me like a child. He said: "You may not feel like you have to stop, but your horse needs to rest." He was furious. "And as your monitor, I am responsible for the horse and for you. It is good that no one was hurt."

On two other occasions I went over some jumping obstacles, then I joined other riders who were performing the *Le Cross* competition, jumping over tree trunks in the park. In fact, I was not supposed to join in because I was not in their category. But I was a bit stubborn, and I wanted to prove to myself that I was capable of riding a horse under different circumstances to a higher level. That was my last day of horse riding.

Once we had moved to our new house in Beaumont-sur-Oise, I tried not to think about my missing the horseback riding, but sometimes my mind wandered. I thought of making a stable for a horse in my garden. I still loved horseback-riding. The feeling of riding a horse, whether a small trot or a full-out gallop, is an overwhelming feeling of freedom. Then I thought that it would only be possible if I could buy a wide space of land to raise and ride my horse at any time. Unfortunately, I realized my garden, and the land we owned, would not be enough for a horse. A horse would need a stable and equipment, as well as comfortable bedding, food supplies like hay, and fresh water. A horse would need lots of exercise, veterinary care, feeding equipment, a barn, pasture, and maintenance. I wondered how I would cope with the expenses and time while working full-time. But I couldn't forget my excitement when watching an international jumping competition on the television. How I had loved the beautiful horses, performing their roles of champion with such excellence. Afraid to experience another delusion, I tried to forget that desire.

My feelings towards my husband – 2012

Lionel and I received the holy sacrament of matrimony during the Church wedding ceremony on December 14, 1981 where we both made our vows before God. We spoke the words of commitment to be together, to cherish each other as husband and wife, for better and for worse, for sickness and health, and so on. And because of the holy Sacrament and those vows, I remained married and respected the sacredness of our marriage.

As a wife, I wanted to take stock of the gift of marriage. When you've been together for years, it's obvious that your husband knows your likes and dislikes and vice versa. But I discovered some characters and manners that I did not expect. I never imagined that I would get bored or fed up with married life one day. We both became unknown to each other, so irritable and impatient. We argued so much, for small trifles, for a "yes" or for a "no." He raised his voice, something I couldn't abide, and I lashed out of anger. I thought of breaking up, moving out and filing for a divorce. Dealing with such animosity was difficult. My life seemed like a hell.

I had that kind of midlife crisis where I felt so tired and fed up with my life with him. I had even thought it was my depression that had ruined my marriage. Something inside of me felt as if I would be cutting off my right hand, but I was feeling numbed about the marriage. I had had more than enough of my job and the people around me; I was fed up with my daughter and my grandchildren, fed up with my colleagues. I had a strong feeling of impending doom. I lost trust in everyone. I was thinking my friends were not really friends. I did not know anymore what to think. I lost courage and felt sick. I did not feel like eating, and I was not sleeping well either. I abandoned my desire to attend dance classes. Worse, I did not even feel like praying. I was hopeless and helpless. Though it was nearly unbearable, I remained married, maintained my job, and kept driving three to four hours a day (morning and evening) to work. I had no choice, as I did not know where to go or who to talk to. I felt so alone. The doctor prescribed me lot of tablets to take, but they had too many side effects, and I did not feel healed.

One day Lionel gave me an ultimatum: "If you don't help yourself," he said, "I will bring you to the psychiatric hospital and I will leave you there without rendering you a single visit." He was firm. His statement awakened me from the nightmare. I never would want to stay in the hospital. Instead, Lionel brought me again to the doctor, who told me that he could not perform a miracle, that only I could help myself now. He said if I slept well and ate nutritious foods, my appetite would come back, and then everything would be alright.

At home, I had thrown away all the medicines, and I filed for some leave from work. I stayed at home for three straight weeks, while Lionel went out almost every day. He would go for long walks, to a restaurant with friends, take a guided hike, or stay at Lysiane's place to be with our grandchildren on Wednesdays or when they were not in school. I stayed alone in my dark room crying. I was even mad at Lionel when he opened my room's windows. I did not want him to come near me. It was so hard, as if I was getting crazier without the tablets.

Lionel and I travelled to Turkey in October 2012, where we experienced somewhat bad and good memories (see below). However, I did not take a single anti-depression tablet until we returned to France. For me it was the beginning of veritable deliverance and success.

In December of the same year 2012, I travelled to the Philippines all alone for the first time, searching for comfort and advice. But as soon as I arrived in Butuan, I learned about the difficult situation of my sister Nolwen due to her mahjong gambling. It woke up my mental health condition and augmented my problems with depression. My healing process was abruptly interrupted. I realized how the power of depression could kill you. I asked God to drive away the evil that had been continuously tormenting me.

I stayed with my parents until January 2013, and I confessed to them about my marriage and my conflicting feelings towards my husband. Just speaking about it to someone made me feel a bit relieved. I was really surprised with my parents' full understanding. I was especially surprised of the way my father reacted. He had the beginnings of dementia, but he was very lucid that day.

My travel from France had been smooth and comfortable. And by luck, I stretched my back on an empty row of seats until we landed at our first stop over in Guangzhou, China. Joan and James fetched me from Ninoy International Airport in Manila, the second stop over before Butuan, and they brought me to a hotel. It was the first time I had travelled alone without Lionel, where everything was pleasant. I had the sensation of being somewhere, my mind was empty and relaxed. I was not feeling lonely on the plane; my mind floated. I felt no fear nor worries, I was free.

When I returned home to France, something had shifted; it was like a miracle. Upon looking to the old folders in the big drawers, searching for some space to arrange our old photos, I found Lionel's letters to me from 38 years ago. I thought I had lost them during our move from the apartment in Stains 18 years before. I felt I was being invited to read them. I read them full of intense emotion. His letters had a tremendous effect on me. It replenished my love for him. It made my love even stronger.

It would have been so cruel to him and so painful for me if I committed the greatest error of my life. The idea to leave him was so self-centred and inhumane. I would never have been able to forgive myself, and would have had guilt throughout the rest of my life. His love for me is eternal. His letters touched the most profound depths of my soul. I felt guilty for even considering it, although I am still at his side. I still love him. How lucky am I to have someone who always loves me, despite my difficult character and swaying moods?

God had touched my heart! I had come to believe that God is never absent, even when evil is palpable. And great love manifests from the deepest parts of my heart, and gives me the power to overcome trials and hurdles in life. With Lionel at my side, no matter how serious the problems are, and how strong the storm is, I will be able to stand again. As a pure and powerful energy, based on love, God has a fantastic and magical effect on my life.

Sometimes things can be complicated when I let my bad emotions dominate. I sometimes lose control and make hasty decisions. It also can affect my ability to communicate. I am sure that Lionel had suffered with my faults, like my lack of organization and bad temper. But he never complains, as he loves me.

My pledge of love had faded. I remember when one day, I told him straight that I did not feel the same feelings of what I had for him before. "I am not in love with you anymore," I said.

I was surprised with his answer, full of immense sincerity and understanding. He said " Don't worry, love. It is probably because we are getting old, then everything changes." I did not even dare to have asked him about his love for me, because I always knew that no matter what, he loves me and always will. Now I rediscovered my lost love. I am really feeling God's eternal love.

Exhilarating hot air balloon ride – October 2012

For the first time ever, in October 2012 we participated in some organized travel, a tour package to Turkey from Antalya to Cappadocia. Organized travel is quite interesting, except that it was very tiring as we had to change hotels several times during the trip. In addition, you had to get up early in the morning in order not to miss breakfast, or you could be left behind. If your bus left without you, then you would be lost and in trouble! It was like that with no time to recover because we had to move every morning for eight consecutive days.

Our flight landed in Antalya and we stayed one night in the hotel. The first morning, we travelled along the seaside in a special bus. Our tourist guide was sharing all the details to every place, while visiting several cities like Ankara, the capital of Turkey, Bodrum, Izmir, the côte turquoise, etcetera. The bus ride ended in appadocia, where we took a hot air balloon flight – the "Montgolfier."

I wonder if it was because I was still under the influence of such depression that I was not afraid to board the hot air balloon, I've forgotten my vertigo. Lionel said he is naturally an adventurer so he was not afraid. We're all gathered at dawn in the restaurant and took a light breakfast. The Montgolfier organizer said to have a flight in favourable weather conditions, we must be in flight before the sunrise and before heavy wind comes. We witnessed how the hot air balloon was inflated. The burners were on, heating the balloon. We're about 20 people standing inside the gondola conducted by the young hot air balloon pilot without any security measures (no belts) except some safety instructions. It's fun seeing the spectacle of all the other balloons flying over the mountains. Sometimes we were much higher, lower or on the same level with the other balloons which gave us an amazing and breath-taking sensations, being inside the large square basket attached to, and hanging from the balloon. While we're in the atmosphere, the landscape was even more fascinating seeing the remnants of the past and the rich nature! It was so impressive to see the different forms of Rocky Mountains and the remnants of a dormant volcano crater.

We flew over mountains, slaloming between the chimneys, seeing the other hot air balloons nearby in the atmosphere and over the magical landscape. It felt like our Montgolfier was moving slightly, and turning along the air waves was so impressive.

I know that earth rotates which makes the sun's light shift. Our hot air balloon arise facing the magnificent sunrise. It was my so wonderful and unique experience watching the animation of the sunrise which flashes its colourful rays: pink, red and orange into the sky. As we were at altitude, I was fascinated watching on how the sun rose to the horizon and continued ascending into the atmosphere. When the sun reached facing the moon, the moon disappeared. It was as if the sun had swallowed the moon. I was like a young child admiring the wonder to that breathtakingly beautiful process of rising sun.

The balloon rose into the air about 3,000 feet, and we remained in the Montgolfier for an hour. The wind led our Montgolfier turning a little faster in the atmosphere that we all stopped commenting, then silence reigned. We settled to the ground more than a mile and a half from where we took off.

Despite all the difficulty of having to move every day, it was wonderful that we were able to visit several sites of antiquity: These were ancient sites and Greco-Roman ruins such as a Grand Theatre, the ancient Greek city in the process of restoration dedicated to the Dées (Aphrodisia), the huge marble colonnade of the city of Aphrodite, the numerous sarcophagi, the white marble enclosure surrounding the city, and the Roman arenas at an altitude of 700 meters where gladiators used to fight. All these were being restored. We walked a lot, moving with the crowd, and luckily my shoes: Basket Sneaker, fitted me comfortably. We even visited underground cities dating back to the early Christians.

The Turks were kind and helpful, but some of them dared to flirt with me in front of my husband. Lionel said he saw this, but he didn't say anything until after we reached home in France. He said it didn't matter because I was depressed, and he knew I did not mind. I did not know he was hurt because he did not say anything. He only revealed this when I was writing this memoir. He said he was about to hit somebody one day on the trip. I realized how I was unaware of my surroundings. I was really in a bad mental state. I felt like I was on another planet.

We visited the famous landscape and breath-taking fairy chimneys, the underground towns, and the churches carved out of rock in Cappadocia. In the evening, our guide brought us downtown and we were welcomed in an authentic Turkish restaurant and met by whirling dervishes dancers. They said it was the night for their religious ceremony where the whirling ceremony was performed. It was fun to watch them turning for hours, remaining in the same place. I didn't know anymore how long they kept on turning. I felt dizzy watching them spin like a top, except that they never fell.

There were women dancers too, wearing bright red, orange, and yellow, dancing the so-called fire dance. The men were separated from the women dancers, and the men turned faster and longer than the women. Our guide reminded us not to cheer them because it was a religious ritual. I am well-disciplined so I obeyed. But the rest of the audience applauded at the end of the ceremony even though they were told not to. When the whirling dervishes stopped dancing, they invited us to dance with them. They took our hands and we danced in a chain of people. We were told not to break the chain. Many people were there, so the chain seemed to go on forever. We went around the lobby, outside the hall, but the chain was so long that we went through many different rooms inside the enormous building. At times we were in rooms outside with no roof and it was freezing. But eventually we came back inside the restaurant's dancing hall, profusely sweating.

Before we were brought to our hotel to rest, our guide brought us to different stores in Avanos,_and we were carried by the crowd inside the Turkish store selling floor carpets. I ordered a carpet which cost 4,000 euros and be delivered in France. They asked me for a down payment of half the price. But I told them I would send the check. I was confident my credit card was used up. I did not know yet at that time that they succeeded taking the down payment of 2,000 euros through my credit card. We were also taken to jewellers and I bought a set with a ring, earrings and a pendant. We went to another store selling leather products. The leather coats and jackets were so expensive, but they were so beautiful that I was tempted. We didn't know that they were tricking us, and asking very high prices. We only learned it later when we were in another hotel. The salesmen were always surrounding us, crowding us. One particular salesman kept on whispering to me. "Madame, you can never find this outside our store, our products are genuine, you can't find them even in France." He was sort of hypnotizing me, while I was unaware that I was using up the money that was intended to buy a new car.

The following day we were in our luxurious hotel to relax at last for another eight days. There were lot of stores. We discovered the same products, the same quality of leather coats and jackets but much cheaper. We realized we had been cheated. But it was impossible to return to the tricky stores which was so far from our hotel; we would have needed to hire another bus to go up there.

I joined some sport activites everyday: like *Tai-chi* (an ancient Chinese discipline of meditative movements), and zumba dance before breakfast. We also had a lovely swim in the turquoise sea water wearing plastic sandals because of sharp stones. In the evenings, we participated in the quizzes. Lionel had fun finding correct answers. I had a Turkish massages in the hammam, my first experience. This is a scrub and then a rinse, and the place was set up in such a way that I was always carried by the water every time the hammam boy poured the rinse over me. The small boy would then run as fast as he could to reach the other side and catch me so I wouldn't fall, as I was covered with suds of soap that made the tub more slippery. There were also foot treatments with tiny piranhas placed inside an open aquarium; I even dared to put my feet inside, and they loved to eat the dead skin off. As I said, as if I was floating, my mind was full and empty at the same time while Lionel was having an exceptionally long walk around the hotel, exploring a wide beautiful landscape. There were lot of tourists, many were French. I was likewise proud to have been one of the hot air balloon passengers. In the end, our stay in Turkey was for me an exhilarating and memorable experience.

Ballroom dancing 2013-2021

"Mama, you are dressed like a beggar," said my 31 year-old daughter, as if she was ashamed to show me to her friends.

My colleagues and friends recommended that I needed to take better care of myself. They said, "Sarah, wake up! Watch how you dress, go out to the beauty salon, sign up for dance school, attend yoga sessions, go to the movies, swim, travel, shops and attend parties."

I could not find the right words to answer them, but I thought they should mind their own business. However, later I realized they were right. I was trying to forget my dark days. I had trouble finding the time or energy to take care of myself. I asked God to send me His Holy Spirit to guide me..

After Turkey in October, I went alone to Butuan in December 2012. We were in our parent's yard fully lit with natural lights and by the glittering quivering colorful garlands hanging in our balcony. There also was the light of firecrackers exploding in the sky. While we were watching the fireworks I suddenly felt like dancing. The neighbours were launching fireworks and playing music. Tatay, at age 81, came in front of me and we danced together until he gave-up, exhausted. Our audience were Mama, Nelly, Heidi and Imelda, while the neighbours were watching us too, envious. The midnight sounds exploded with our wishes for "A Happy and Prosperous New Year 2013." It was my first New Year celebration with my parents since I had left for France in 1981. I still have the image of my father dancing, a nice memory that gave me a new perspective: that I should try to learn ballroom dancing.

In France, I decided to find it. I said to myself that maybe it wasn't too late to re-start learning how to dance, and in February 2013 I was officially enrolled in the *École Tango Noir*, a dancing school. My heart was full of joy. In fact, I yearned to become a member of a school three years before, but I was discouraged when the professor asked me to bring my own partner, and I had nobody.

The course focused on the standard and Latin sport dances, It had started in September so I was extremely late, but that did not matter because with a little perseverance and my passionate love of dancing, I caught up with the missed choreography. I had loved dancing since I was a young child. I remembered being in the discotheque with colleagues and friends where you could throw your arms, kick the ground, turn yourself around, raise hands and jerk your body on the dance floor; but that had nothing to do with the ballroom dancing choreography.

I heard my mind murmuring, saying "why not enjoy dancing on the polished boards of the dancing hall, Sarah?" I told myself it was time to transform my habit of old fashion dancing, jazz, and disco with the modern choreography. I followed several courses, and I am proud to say that I learned the art of dancing. I was very attentive to our professor's technical instructions. I can still hear Gilbert, our coach, who assisted the professor in teaching us the right posture for performing the choreographies. In a loud voice, he would say, "Sarah, don't look at your partner, look to the left, heads-up, keep in contact with your partner not to lose him. Lift your elbows." He would always have to remind us to look to the left, keep the head tilted high, and not look down at our feet. "Be tall and graceful," he would say. "You need to stay flexible, bend your knees, and take bigger steps."

I would return home satisfied with what I had accomplished in each class. While dancing, I still had in mind the years of my horse-riding days, another discipline that I'd worked hard at. Whereas now, I was dancing. For me, dancing is an excellent sport to practice and it builds fitness although sometimes it is physically challenging. Little by little I made progress. I became more self-confident and was encouraged to continue. I had never had so much fun in my life, and now a new chapter of my life was beginning, with wonderful social connections of the wider dance family. I discovered new kinds of emotions and feelings. There also grew wonderful friendships between co-dancers. We all we danced for the pleasure of embracing life as it comes, while being carried along by our passion for dancing. Our amazing professor, who managed both strict and friendly, was the key to us becoming the most successful ballroom dancers we could possibly be, remaining elegant and highly respected in our society.

On the other hand, dancing is a healing process. When I dance passionately, I forget my own personality, transforming myself to a new person carried by indescribable new emotions. I forget my dark days and feel revitalized when I hit the dance floor. I started to feel happier inside and I discovered who I was. Dancing has allowed me to discover a new family of friends in the Tango Noir school.

I learned to laugh. I am even sometimes scared, seeing myself smiling and a bit stunned to hear myself exploding with laughter, because I never used to laugh so much. The benefits I acquired from ballroom dancing was what changed me mentally and physically. I was surprised to find myself feeling happy at my job, even when I was swamped with work. I was now smiling on the phone and even when dealing with dossiers and unprocessed files. My colleagues had to notice my good mood. I also sometimes tapped the floor under my desk, thinking about the choreography, while typing the keyboard of my computer.

It is a wonderful moment for every dancer in all levels during the dinner, or tea dance party, where everyone is welcomed to the dance floor to try out routines, wearing smart clothing. We were not graded while dancing, so we danced comfortably for our fitness and for our pleasure to dance. It felt so alive and sophisticated. I feel better when I dance and proud of myself of being able to dance the following: cha-cha, rock, salsa, rumba, jive, tango standard, slow waltz, Viennese waltz, quick step, a little bit of samba, Argentinian tango, and tango waltz. We had the opportunity to meet other dancers from other schools during these parties, where we could see dancers of all ages flocking together to move their toes on the famous parquetted dance floor. It is also the time for us as pupils to determine what levels we belonged in, and trying out the different choreography we had learned in each session.

One weekend, I was invited to a party organized by the association. It was a pity to see that many people remained sitting at their table, seeming to be annoyed. The music played by the orchestre was so exciting. I invited some men sitting around the table next to ours to dance the slow waltz with me, one at a time; they said they had not danced for a very long time. So I was guiding them, and we cheerfully enjoyed dancing. They danced with their wives afterwards, and the dance floor became crowded. Giselle, Tatiana, Florence and Nicole, my friends and co-dancers from Tango Noir, were surprised I did that, and me too. My timidness had disappeared!

I likewise discovered for myself how I could dance with quality, elegance, allure, and good posture. It is not a competition against other dancers, but just a chance to be proud to show how much we had learned and to show my gratitude to our excellent professor Marie-Jo, whose popularity soared. Thanks to her, I humbly achieved my goal.

Mama Dominga

Mama possessed the gift of healing. Was it a spiritual gift? She told me she had discovered that she had special abilities when she was only seven years old, just when World War II was declared in the Philippines in 1941. The Japanese occupation entered Cabadbaran the following year.

Her adolescence was full of healing activities, which became a ritual for her and with her eight children. It was very hectic from her 30s to her 80s. She healed sprains, twisted ankles and wrists, light, and closed fractures, blows, bruises, burns, contusions, intestinal troubles, stomach aches and other disorders by a simple touch or a simple massage. Many people benefited.

Did she have the spiritual gift from birth?

Dominga was born in Cabadbaran in March and was baptised on 23rd March 1934. Her father disappeared during WWII, under the five years of Japanese occupation in the Philippines.

Nanay was on her own to bring up Dominga and her younger sister Benita. Dominga was not a doctor. She never went to college. However, since her early childhood she proved very effective at healing people, which I consider miraculous.

Like my late grand aunts Yaya Tatang, Yaya Idad, and Nanay Pantay, Mama had the ability to heal people with herbs. She knew the names of all the medicinal herbs we used, and she even showed them to me when we still lived with her in Cabadbaran. Those plants are hard to find nowadays.

One day Dominga, Benita and Esperanza (Nanay) were eating a meal when a mother knocked at the door. She came with her feverish child. He had spent a sleepless night suffering from a sore throat after swallowing some fishbone that got stuck in his throat. She begged Esperanza to help the young boy.

Nanay asked Dominga to touch the throat of the child. She was hesitant but at same time intrigued by her own powers, so Dominga obeyed her mother. There was no way of testing her abilities ahead of time, so she had doubts whether she really had a gift of healing. She touched the swelling throat of the young boy. It became red. Without knowing how or why, she had an effect. The little boy returned back home with his mother, happy and healed.

Since then, her curiosity over her powers grew. That revelation was spread throughout the barrio of Mabini, Cabadbaran and beyond; people came from far villages and barrios when they heard about her healing. At the beginning Dominga was doing it against her will, as she was not sure of what she was doing.

"What if it doesn't work?" she asked repeatedly. She was quite afraid for the reaction of the people if it went wrong, especially the adults. She was not yet in the habit of using her hidden gifts. She was not even fully convinced that she actually possessed a gift.

Several years passed. Dominga continued consciously healing people. By the age of 13, she was serious about her work. Simply by touching or massaging lightly the problematic part, and silently asking God to be with her in healing the patient, they would leave happy and satisfied.

People sought her out. They followed her wherever she lived, coming to see her from different cities until some doctors in Butuan city complained. They said that she was intruding on the medical profession. It was true that Dominga was only a simple Filipino girl who had not studied medicines nor had any qualifications. Dominga's ability to heal people, especially children, became well-known throughout Cabadbaran and Butuan City. Then we heard some rumours that there was a complaint filed against her. Former patients, children and adults reassured her not to worry, because she had many witnesses in her favour. People argued about the coming hearing. I heard them saying:

"We the defendants will form an association between us, ready to fight and defend Dominga."

Meanwhile, Dominga was waiting to receive a subpoena so that somehow she could explain in the court, in vain. "I only had one simple statement, I never harmed anybody, and I never asked people to come; but when they came, it was to seek my help, so I helped and healed them. I'm very happy about it, but I never demanded anything in return." Said Dominga to me many years later.

She never received any subpoena asking her to appear in the Court of Justice after all. Shecontinued healing, mostly children. People asked her to assist a mother to deliver a baby, as she had successfully done many times in the past. Years passed, even some doctors and their families became Dominga's patients and were healed; they had witnessed Dominga's gift and her efficacy. So this time, unlike before, the doctors asked for Dominga through intermediary services like the City health clinic, who without hesitation would have granted her a license. But Mama refused, because she did not want for people to have to pay for her services.

She said: I am just the instrument; the gift was not from me, but from God."

On the other hand, Mama refused to do the job as a midwife working in the prenatal health centre asit was too great a responsibility, and the people would still continue to come to the home even at the middle of the night. Mama lost her privacy since she started healing people. My father was so patient, but even if he had wanted to object, he had no choice but to allow his wife to be approached by people who needed her at all hours. When her patients were unable to walk, Dominga didn't hesitate to make a trip to reach them. People came at any time; sometimes she forgot to eat or to take time to rest.

She continued healing people while we were in New Asia. I thought she might have a peaceful life once they moved to a new place, but I was wrong. People followed her to her new residence in Sintos subdivision. More and more people, mostly mothers, brought their children to Dominga and they returned home healed. Mama was always happy of her accomplishments, but she became so tired and restless.

In France, I dreamed of her twice. One day she slipped on the wet floor she had just cleaned and had to have surgery on her right hand. A few days later she fell again, and her left hand needed an operation. Little by little, with the advice of the doctors, she started refusing to accept adult patients, but still concentrated on healing children. Later, again with the advice of her doctor, she stopped healing people for good in 2018 for health reasons, at the age of 84. It was the time to think of taking care of herself instead. My nephew, James, put a sign board attached to the gate informing the public that Dominga had stopped healing.

At a recent visit to see family in Sintos, James, my nephew came with his wife Joan and their baby daughter and said: "Tita Sarah, how I wish that Lola Dominga will have a very long, lasting life. She heals people, especially children. She is a mother of perpetual help." James shared his opinion in a manner of a joke, but the truth was revealed. It had awakened my sensibility that led me think of preserving my mother's experiences of healing people into my memoirs here. I retired from work in 2019 and have been thinking about working on her autobiography.

Dominga is healed from arthritis – a miracle?

When she was 57, for several months Dominga suffered from terrible arthritis. It got so bad that she became dependent on Tatay to get out of bed for several weeks. Tatay said despite the massages he gave to his wife many times a day, she remained unable to take a single step. She had no appetite, and was so weak that the arthritis effectively confined her to bed.

In May 2002, although it was not planned, I visited them in Sintos because Tatay was very ill. While I was taking care of Tatay, Mama told me about the days when she was seriously sick in 1991.

"It is nice of you Sarah to come to visit your father," she said, "but you never came, not even Amelie, nobody visited me when I was in bed for several weeks unable to stand." She was full of bitterness and melancholy. I felt my neck both stretching and constricting, as if I had swallowed a bone stuck across inside my throat. I had a painful pinch on my heart upon listening to Mama, expressing her feeling of being abandoned and ignored. I was really sorry to hear about it. I had never known that Mama had held onto that feeling of animosity and bitterness inside her heart for so many long years. I felt her pain. It was excruciating. She even seemed to ignore my explanation. My poor Mother, she had really been hurt.

This remind me of this proverb: "The past is well spent: if you stir it, do you find anything but bitterness?" – Jean Simard (Quebec writer, teacher and translator, author of novels and essays).

At that time, I was taking care of Lionel, who had heart troubles and had been in hospital many times. Lysiane was only eight years old, and still needed me badly, as I had to bring her to school and bring her back home. France is just so far from the Philippines. In Australia, Amelie was in the process of divorcing her first husband; she also had to find a job to make a living, and stand on her own two feet. At times I wondered whether Mama understood me when I said that I never forgot her, despite our distance. I hoped to ease some of her sadness and pain, as I knew she needed to feel that she is loved. Of course, we love her same as we loved Tatay, she must not forget that. I was hoping that she would feel better now that she had expressed her bitterness. Then she told me the story of how she was finally able to get up and walk again after several weeks of being confined to her bed.

The Holy Virgin Mary visits Dominga

When I phoned Mama in 2017, she was surrounded by my three younger sisters: Nelly from Davao City, Nolwen in Butuan City, and Imelda from Dumaguete City. They had come to celebrate with her All-Saints Day, All Souls Day, and to commemorate our father's death who passed away only five months before. Dominga was full of joy, her melancholy gone. She remembered the moment as if it had only taken place yesterday. This is how she told her story:

One afternoon at three o'clock, I saw a bright white light in front of me. I was not dreaming; I was fully awake. The Lady was embodied with brilliant white light, so much that I could hardly see her face at first. She was dressed all in white standing in front of me and against my bed. The light glowed from her body and I finally realized that she was the Virgin Mary. She wore a white dress with a light blue cape around her shoulders that reached down to her feet.

The image of the Holy Virgin Mary is always fresh in my mind and I can never forget it. Mother Mary spoke to me so that I could finally get up and walk. Francisco had left the bedroom to prepare my meals that he used to give me in bed, so I was alone when the Holy Virgin Mary appeared. When your father came back to feed me by giving me spoonfuls, the Holy Virgin Mary had left.

Needless to say, your father was overwhelmed seeing his wife already out of bed and on her own feet, healed. I miraculously recovered all my mobility when in fact, I had been unable to get out from bed for several weeks.

At first, I did not tell him of what happened during his short absence as I did not realise yet the impact of the event. I wanted to be sure I was not dreaming. Naively, I did not realize how lucky I was to have the privilege of being healed by our Holy Virgin Mary. The only thing I was sure was that I managed to get up from my bed and walk by myself without the help of your father. I was really surprised that what I had seen was true; the mother Virgin Mary had really visited me and healed me while I was confined on bed. I owed my endless gratitude to the Holy Virgin Mary.

My mother was full of laughter and faith as she told us this story.

A scary creature pops out from nowhere, was it a devil?

A few days after the appearance of the Holy Virgin Mary, Mama has acquired a certain force and energy that she had never felt before. Her spiritual experiences augmented her faith in God. She said the Virgin Mary asked for many prayers to save the earth; all parishes, even the remotest barrios needed to honour the Virgin by letting her visit every household together with the image of "Our Lady of Perpetual Help." Thus, Dominga wanted to fulfill that mission. She told me the story:

Before dawn, at three o'clock in the morning I left the house and walked alone along the small road with the aim to reach the house where the banner of the *Birhen Sa Barangay* (Image of the Holy Virgin) was held for one night. We needed to bring it along to transfer it to another household while we prayed the Holy Rosary along our way.

After the appearance of the Virgin Mary in my bedroom, I was not afraid of the dark, but suddenly a strange creature dropped in front of me. I tried to ignore it and said, "no matter what and who you are, I am not scared of you." I was wondering where it came from and how it fell out of nowhere, as there was not a single tree above my head and no forest either around us. It had dropped heavily with a strong groaning sound like a heavy black lion, but it howls like a dog. It seemed to have randomly popped up, and it tried to block my way to the church. Was it a devil ?

Despite the dark, I quickly contemplated, and I was able to differentiate that it was just like a huge black dog with two big green eyes flashing at me. But it was an unusual size, and it triggered my curiosity. It was probably a devil who wanted to block my path, trying to prevent me from accomplishing my mission that day.

Meanwhile, all the dogs from the neighbours were barking, and they came near. The creature put itself in a position of attack, standing in front of me trying to scare me by opening its jaws showing me his long sharp teeth. The dogs formed a circle and blocked the devil, thus protecting me against the attack from that huge black animal. All the dogs were incredibly intelligent; they grouped themselves altogether and attacked that huge, weird animal. It disappeared in the same manner as it appeared – suddenly.

All the dogs then stopped barking. I asked them to follow me and they obeyed. I really appreciated how they had protected me by forming a circle around me. And they followed me until we reached the road where a friend of mine was waiting for me to join the others to go to the house with the Birhen Sa Barangay. Then the dogs went away, leaving me quite reassured. But it is strange, I sometimes wonder if that animal will ever appear again.

When I phoned Mama Dominga after these stories, sometimes she says she was alright, and other times she had pains and worries. One time she complained that she pities her dresses, which only remain inside the dresser. She wanted to wear them to go to the church to attend the Holy Mass. There were other times when I called, and she informed me that her helper was not there for some reason. I noticed in her voice that she was afraid to be left alone at home. I understand how she felt, as she was with Tatay for 66 years.

How my parents met – was it love at first sight?

They celebrated their 50th golden wedding anniversary in August 2001, and their 65th (diamond) wedding anniversary in 2016. Those were the rare accomplishments of their long-lasting and passionate love. They were both in love at first sight. I was not able to attend their two wedding anniversary celebrations, unfortunately, but family members sent me videos which I treasure and hold precious.

Francisco was sometimes a joker. He made me laugh when telling me his story of young love. He had his awesome way of telling the story in deep Visayan dialect, with actions. I can just imagine how pure was their love. He told it this way:

When I met Dominga for the very first time, my heart was beating so strongly and irregularly that I was choking. It was not merely a crush, but I was falling in-love, terribly. I was terrified with my tremendous feelings urging me to go near her and kiss her immediately, but having a face-to-face conversation was impossible. I was somehow able to whisper secretly into her ear that she was so beautiful, and I knew she heard me. That was a relief. Her elder sister Modesta was there, which was frustrating. Dominga was reluctant to look at me. She turned her head away when I looked at her. But when she suddenly looked at me, our eyes met. There, I knew she felt the same. Her eyes sparkled, and her cheeks changed into rosy hue, but she had to pretend nothing changed. She hid anxiously her twinkling eyes while searching for an occasion to look at me. But when she turned her head again, she makes her eyes big pointing to warn me not to approach her. The next day I was determined to kiss her, but she jerks away and stopped me.

"Stay away from me or you can never see me," Dominga warns me but I know she did not mean it. "Dominga was so shy, which made our communications uncomfortable, because she was afraid of her elder sister. Modesta was so strict and vigilant. I understood she did not want Dominga to have an affair with me." Said Tatay Eco.

The intensity of Tatay's revelations made him cough and then laugh. I was also laughing so hard. It was a wonderful day together with him. Mama later told me the rest of the story:

"One day, Modesta, asked me to take care of her baby boy, and I accepted. It was a good opportunity for me to come to Butuan. And I did not know when I would return to Mabini."

Modesta was married to Anatalio Palma, who came from Tubigon Bohol, the same town as Francisco. They both worked in the New Asia Sawmill, but Anatalio had a higher position than my father. He lived in their house as boarder, and that's how my parents met. I have fun on this: My mother's name is Dominga and Modesta's boy was named Domingo. Mama took care of the baby Domingo and as he grew, he had thought that Dominga, my mother, was his mother, as they were always left at home together while Modesta and Anatalio were enjoying good times with friends or going out to the cinema.

My mother was bored taking care of Domingo, and she was about to return to Cabadbaran when she met Francisco, and they both fell in love at first sight. Mama recalled:

> One evening, Francisco was not able to enter the house by the entrance door because he was delayed by his barkadas. All the doors were locked by Modesta, who was so strict regarding rules and regulation to be respected.

> I heard a timid whistling under my window, and I did not dare to leave Francisco outdoors for the whole night, so I allowed him to enter the house by passing through my bedroom window. I really did not believe that he could enter this way, but he did it successfully. Yet he could not go out from my room, because he was afraid that Modesta might see him, so he climbed up to the wall then jumped into his room which was just next to mine. However, I felt a new sensation of freedom.

Dominga got pregnant at 18 years old, while Francisco was only 21. He was not ready to marry her. He still needed to find the financial means to hold a marriage celebration. He eloped with her to Babag, assisted by the Montilla family. Dominga's family was furious and looked everywhere for them. Dominga developed a terrible nervousness and was so stressed all day long, knowing that her elder sister would be very angry with her. Modesta had been responsible for my mother and their whole family from Cabadbaran were blaming her. A civil wedding was held and later, Francisco and Dominga got married in the church with Zoila Montilla, (the mother of my godmother), as their witness or godmother.

I presume that, in the womb, I was particularly affected with the stress and anxiety during my mother's pregnancy. She had an increased risk of miscarriage, but I was delivered normally. However, I had an exceptionally low birth-weight. Perhaps this is also one of the factors why I have emotional problems today, because of my mother was feeling anxious during her pregnancy. I feel that I have a specific genetic vulnerability that makes me so nervous and sensitive. Mama once told me proudly: "Oh you were so tiny but strong; you had started to walk at nine months. You were one of the smallest in the class, but not the weakest." I was flattered.

At the time of writing, Dominga is now 87 years old, and she needs people to take care of her. She has fragile heart. Nowadays, she has a helper with her at home to do the household chores, and especially to stay with her at night. She said she needs someone to wake her up and soothe her when she has nightmares.

Mama and my birthday

Mama Dominga made a promise to herself and to God. She had always done the nine days novena prayers each year before my birthday, in the chapel of my birthplace, Capella de Senor San Vicente. This was because she said I was born such a small baby and she was thankful that I survived. Although I continue to have some problems with freezing up and stopping breathing when I'm upset, as I did when very young, I think her prayers did have an effect.

In recent years I asked her to stop the novena, as it was already difficult for her to go to the chapel without someone to accompany her. She stopped the novena after my birthday in January 2017, we would just have to pray directly to God together and I would be alright.

She said: "Sarah if ever you feel sick like when you were a baby, you must pray the nine days novena asking help from Señor Saint Vicente and the Holy Spirit."

There was no more novena prayer for my 66th birthday in January 2018. It was not to compromise our faith and devotion. I still pray to God and trust Him. I know that whatever He does for me will be the best thing that could happen in my life. I submit myself entirely to Him, and I have faith that everything will be done according to His will.

Mama informs me about Tatay's health

I was unable to travel very often to the Philippines, so I tried to call my parents frequently.

Mama informed me over the telephone in May 2002 that Tatay was sick, and she was so worried about him. I had to go to the Philippines in May, before I would be needed back in France for Lysiane's delivery scheduled in September. If I hadn't gone I would have felt immense guilt for not seeing my father.

Luckily, I obtained a flight for three days travel with two stopovers in Bangkok and Manila. All my thoughts were for Tatay. I prayed that he would get well soon. Lysiane was five months pregnant of her twins, and she found it hard to understand why I had to leave for Butuan. I did not have enough time to tell her my reasons, as I was afraid that if I left it any later I would have the dilemma of choosing between her, the babies and my father.

Once at my parent's home, I rushed to see Tatay, who was still in bed. He had hardly opened his eyes and was unable to stand up by himself. Mama said that he had been like that for the previous three weeks. In order to understand what Tatay was suffering, I asked Mama to show me all his medicines. Tatay had four types of medicines in four different colours. I read that two medicines were for the same pathology, for heart failure, so I believed that Tatay was a victim of overdose. He was taking two capsules in each medicine, then other tablets for his headache and another for his stomachache. I am not a doctor, but when I had read the notice of those medicines, all what Tatay had suffered seemed to be the side effects of the beta-blocker. He had overdosed on the medicines incorrectly prescribed by his doctor, and that had provoked side effects such as headache, nausea, blurred vision, diarrhoea, and a slow heartbeat.

I assisted Tatay to get out of his bed, to have a walk around inside the house to help his blood to circulate. But he told me that he was dizzy and had a headache, so much so that he could hardly open his eyes. He felt cold in his fingers and toes, so he felt the need to stay in bed all day long and covered despite the hot weather.

It was a risk, but I stopped giving medicines to Tatay and observed him. We brought him to another doctor, and then to laboratory for the blood and urine tests. Then the new result of his blood tests and the doctor's diagnosis showed that Tatay's heart had been slowed due to the beta blockers, making it difficult for him to do his daily normal activities. So I was right: the medicine was too much. He also was choosing not to take trips away from home anymore, because of his problems due to the side effects of the medicines he took.

Mama needed some rest, so I took care of Tatay personally, helping to ensure that he didn't miss his medicine or not to take them more than once. I only gave him one capsule for his heart and stopped giving him the medicine for the headache and for his stomach. I slept on the same bed with him to observe him the whole night until he got better, because Mama said that he was complaining of feeling cold. I controlled his medication and observed the eventual reaction.

The following morning I was so touched looking Tatay getting up with a smile, he said he had passed a good night's sleep, and he was hungry. That was a good sign! That day, he took all three meals. It was wonderful to see him walking normally, no more headaches and no more nausea. He wasn't feeling cold anymore and was feeling good. We were all relieved. Two days passed, and Tatay was roaming around inside and outside the house, inspecting what was wrong like checking the electrical installation, changing the electric bulbs, watering the plants. He was returning to his daily activities.

What if I had not come to Butuan to see my father?

Before I left Butuan for France, weTatay and I had an interesting conversation. He said he still remembered my daughter Lysiane running after the chickens and the goats when we visited them when she was young. Now he was imagining her as a mother of twin babies, my grandchildren. "How I wish I could see Lysiane and her babies one day," he said with a smile.

I asked Mama Dominga recently if she would like to come with me to France then she can see her other great-grandchildren, but she answered: "That would be nice, but at this time of my age, I am happy to remain in Butuan, in this house, where your father had stayed with me. Your language is different in France, and I would surely miss my friends here." I tried in vain to convince her, but I fully understand her.

Reflections on My Family History and Ancestry

Mama was recalling stories about my two great-great aunts, our ancestors that I lived during 1957-1959. I remember playing with them when I was a child of five and six. I only learned recently from Dominga that they died at the age of 135 years old. To my mind, this is great news and an unexpected revelation that some people in my family could live so long. If ever there was a good journalist at that time, my two great-aunts would have been headline news. I am proud to have lived a part of my life with them.

"Why did you not tell me that they were my great-aunts?" I asked over the phone.

"Oh Sarah," she said, "you were still so small, but now that you ask me, I confirm to you that they were your old great-great aunties. They were Esperanza's aunts" Then she added with a question: "Sarah, do you think I can reach 100 years old?" We both burst into laughter.

"Of course," I said. "But only if you wish!" We laughed together again like old friends. I had not often heard my mother laughing that way with me very often, not even on the phone. She had changed a lot, that she could more easily joke with me now that I was a grandmother myself. I told her to enjoy life and not to think about the sadder things. This was surely what my father would have wished for her, that Mama should enjoy living on earth before she joins him on the other side.

Once again, Mama failed to tell me some of the most important information that a child should know, especially as it concerned to our own ancestors and family, even ones we never met. I now understood why they looked alike, wearing the same Spanish style clothes as Nanay did, because they were born during the Spanish colonial rule of the Philippines. I also understood why I had been feeling so close to them and they were so tender to me. I remember feeling guilty towards the other children, because I received a very nice treatment from those ladies. But if those children had known that Yaya was my great-great aunt, they would have surely not been jealous and cruel to me. Now I feel reassured that when I pass away, aside from Tatay Eco, these women will all be there to welcome me to the other side.

Yaya Idad, Natividad was married three times, and had thirteen children, but they all died before she did. She played games with me on our yard and sometimes on a smooth surface like the asphalted street, as there was only one bus that passed twice a day. She enjoyed jumping and every time she jumped, one slipper was left behind her, and I put it back under her feet. Every time I did that, she kissed my forehead lightly, and she would touch my head and smile. I still feel her love and affection even now.

Yaya Idad was so fun. She was always smiling. She almost closed her eyes when she looked at me and she giggled like a baby. She spoke like a young girl, sometimes like a very small child. Part of her head had white hair, and other sections were like baby hair. Her teeth were so fine, and some were still growing like babies as well. She was dynamic and active, but unluckily her back was curving. Despite that, she played games very well. She jumped so high when she won. She loved it so much that she would sing a Spanish melody in high pitch with sharp voice. She also danced the *kuratsa*, a Spanish-Philippine folk dance, in front of the children. They sometimes mocked her, but I always defended her not knowing that she was my great-great aunt, my ancestor. The family name 'Jamboy' were Spanish names like Esperanza Jamboy, my grandmother.

Then one day, she said she was too tired to play. "Oohh, Bebe now I must go home, I maybe rest now as I have already played enough," she said, kissing my head. But before she left, I remember her turning to look at me and she hugged and kissed my forehead again, stronger than usual. She gave me a big smile and told me not to pay attention to the children's remarks, and she added, "they are just kidding." And she was sending me her flying kisses; it was a very long bid goodbye, waving her hands like a small girl. She made a quick dance of the kuratsa, and then she left.

When I saw her figure in the distance, I sensed that it was her last day. That image of her, in her Spanish attire and her smile, imprinted on my brain. As if she had transmitted her knowledge across my mind, I understood she had also had a love of dancing. No wonder why I loved dancing too.

The children who were with me were so naughty. They were always mocking, and I would defend her. I told them that there was no need to be impolite and disrespectful to Yaya because anyway, she would die very soon. I did not want to tell them, but I sensed that Yaya Idad would die that evening. I would have loved that the children to have said a proper goodbye to her.

Nanay said: "She was 135 years old, it was the time for her to rest."

The following day the children learned that Yaya Idad died, and accused me of being the cause of her death. They threw stones at me. They accused me of being a witch because they believed that I intentionally let her die. If only Mama had told me that she was my great-great aunt, perhaps the children would have not been so cruel to me.

From that time on, Nanay told me not to go out anymore to play with those cruel children. She instructed our black dog Guro, not to let the children enter our yard. He stayed in front of the gate made of bamboo covered with sampaguita, a sweet-smelling flowering vine. Guro was always loyal to his post and he barked whenever the children came too close. One day, I saw Nanay talking to the children near our gate. I wondered what she had said to them, but the children did not bother me anymore.

Yaya Tatang, the other aunt who also died at the age of 135, was the one who healed Dan's broken arm. She was more firm and strict than her elder sister. When she talked, everyone had to listen to her. She possessed the same ability to heal people with herbs, plants, and trees as my grandmother. However, we were already away in Butuan when Yaya Tatang died. She had been married twice with seven children, all who also died before her. Now I understand why they looked alike (Nanay, Yaya Tatang and Yaya Idad); they possessed the same ability to heal people by natural products. And I had the privilege of having that experience of being with them. I will always keep in my memory all that I have learned from them.

Now at the age of 69 years old, everything is becoming clear, and all these things are coming back to my memory as sharp as when I was a child. I am really surprised to know that while writing, I discovered more memories that were just hidden in the lexicon of my mind. It astonished me that I remember those events that happened while I was only a baby.

Mama Dominga, still having an excellent memory at the age of 87, is a major source of information for my memoir. Although I have some memories of my own, I still needed to confirm the exact dates of events that happened during my childhood. I updated the events by glancing to my diary, talking on the phone with her while recording our conversation, and asking my siblings and friends. While talking to Mama, both of us discovered that we find some past events so funny, and Mama was going through them joyfully. In fact, some were not really funny at the time, whereas this time, those horrible things which happened especially during the Second World War could easily be recalled. I was astonished listening to Mama giving detailed information about each event.

Before this time, when I asked her details about my childhood, she used to answer that she was too tired or couldn't remember. While now, she is very interested recalling so many things when asked. She has a dynamic functioning brain. It's fantastic! Before, perhaps, she never knew how to express by herself, but I felt that she had many things to tell us, more than she wanted to reveal. I wonder: Was Mama also being guided by Tatay after his death?

Esperanza Jamboy (Nanay)

When we were living with her, Nanay told us stories about when she was a child, and her connection to where we were living. Cabadbaran, Agusan del Norte was Nanay and my Mama's birthplace. It has a suburb called Mabini, the place where I spent the happiest moments of my childhood.

Esperanza Beray Jamboy was the full name of my grandmother, whom I called Nanay or Nanay Pantay. She was born in 1896 and died in March 1962 in Mabini. I would never forget that day, because there was flood in Butuan where we were living, near my father's work.

Nanay's first marriage was in 1914 to Brigido Yubit, whose parents were the tenants of the Jamboy family. They were blessed with nine children: Francisca, Natividad, Baldomera, Raymundo, Edmundo, Mariano, Felipa, Vicente, Supriano, and Modesta (my mother would come later, in Nanay's second marriage). All her children were born in Cabadbaran.

Nanay always wore a particular Spanish-style dress, even when she worked on the farm. Clothing played such an important part in society. I enjoyed watching her with her beautiful Spanish attire, especially when she danced the *kuratsa*: the Philippine folk dance of courtship. She also had special dress for church.

Her first husband always worked hard and was a loyal tenant of the Jamboy family, but he was fed-up managing the hectares of land that was entrusted to him. For a change, he went to Davao together with his eldest son Raymundo and his three daughters: Francisca, Natividad and

Baldomera. They all found jobs in Davao. Meanwhile, Brigido, who had suffered from lung infections, only worked for few more years. He died in 1930. Raymundo, their son, served his country as a sergeant in the Philippine Army and was wounded and killed during World War II, leaving a small pension to Nanay.

Felipa, Nanay's middle daughter, stayed in Cabadbaran, and was married to Gregorio Gamayon from Pandanon, who also owned and cultivated his own parcel of land in addition to the land that Felipa owned as a share from the Jamboy family, Esperanza's father. They had ten children: Narcisa, Feliciano, Juan, Natividad, Teodoro, Carlito, Pedro, Yokyok, Gregorio Jr and Saturnino. At the time of writing (2017), they are sadly all gone.

The four younger brothers (Pedro, Yokyok, Gregorio Jr and Saturnino) were my favourite cousins, and likewise my favourite playmates. Every day they passed in front of our house when going to school. Their's was the Agusan Trade School, formerly called the Northern Mindanao College of Arts, Science and Technology. I admired their courage of going to that school everyday under the heat of the sun, at a considerable distance – 10 kilometres from Pandanon; yet I never heard them complain. When the weather was bad or when they were not in their school, they used to stay in Nanay's house and work. Pedro scrubbed the floor throughout the house with the coconut husk until it was so shiny that even the flies slid along the floor. Pedro took care of me and treated me like his younger sister.

The Philippines was always among the world's top coconut producers. Nanay had large coconut plantations for commercial purposes in her own fields. I enjoyed watching my cousins and uncles working to provide coconuts to market. First, they had to do make the *copra,* a dried sections of the meat of the coconut which was an awfully long and labourious process. Then it needed to be dried safely in order to prevent the growth of any harmful mould. This meant that they needed to be left out under the sun for at least four or five days in a row. I still remember now a moment when Pedro put his hands around my waist and lifted me so high and spun me until I felt dizzy, when they were all so happy after all the copra was sold; it was always big family effort.

Sometimes the cousins brought me to the field where there were plenty of root crops to reap: sweet potatoes, cassava, pao, *ubi, gabi* and others, but I usually had to go back home, my skin covered with allergy rash. Those root-crops were simple to cook as you simply boiled them in water until they were cooked. Cassava root is somewhat similar to the potato, in that, like the potato, it is starchy, inedible when raw, and bland in flavour when cooked. Cassava flour is made to bake a cassava cake. It was always my favourite cake, and Mama was so talented in baking it, with the taste of it remained on our tongues for a long time.

Nanay told us stories of how she was 36 years old when she was remarried in 1932 to a handsome guy named Simeon Ramacula. They were blessed with two daughters: Dominga, my mother, and her younger sister Benita. Nanay also delivered twin babies stillborn during the second world war. Dominga and Benita did not remember anymore how their father looked, as they were only eight and five years old, respectively, when Simeon left, maybe not knowing that Nanay was pregnant. Once the war was over, Simeon disappeared. Everyone in the family thought perhaps he died during the war.

However, in the late 1992, 50 years later, the news spread that Simeon Ramacula was still alive, with another two children, and had worked in the National Power Corporation in Iligan, the country's largest provider and generator of electricity. He was born in 1895 and died in Marawi in 1992 at the age of 97. My younger siblings and I were his great grandchildren, but he passed away without meeting us.

How Nanay survived World War II

Imperial Japan invaded the Philippines on 8th December 1941. They occupied Cabadbaran between 1942 and 1945, when they occupied the whole of the Commonwealth of the Philippines.

Another story Nanay told us was this:

"When we heard that Japanese were coming to occupy Cabadbaran, men were digging big holes secretly under the ground to let their family hide. The hole was not comfortable and we were cohabiting with snakes. Luckily, snakes afraid of bombs kept themselves in spiral and did no harm to us. When the Japanese reached Cabadbaran, they were keeping all the civilian men into the prison, and if they did not obey, the Japanese soldiers never hesitated to shoot them. They were everywhere. They were appallingly ferocious and brutal, killing the men and leaving the dead and crippled bodies in the streets." Nanay sighed.

Mama Dominga recalled later:

"Nanay was pregnant of the twin babies who were stillborn. I was eight years old and my younger sister, Benita, was five. In our small house, we pulled the curtains closed in the room during the labour, but the Japanese soldiers suspected us of hiding someone as a spy. They rushed into the room and found the poor two babies, and a group of women who helped Nany give birth. The soldiers were frustrated as there was no male in the group. An officer took his sword and stabbed the babies. The babies were already dead, yet he dared to kill the babies again with his sword. The Japanese soldiers were so inhuman, and their cruelty was deplorable. They were likewise cruel to the animals. The soldiers became crazy after drinking too much tuba-wine. They played with their guns and shot all the animals that passed in front of them, pigs, chicken, goats, cows, carabao and cows. When the Japanese left the premises, only then we could go out from our hiding place and take care of the dead animals. The Japanese soldiers were happy when they came to Mabini, as they never went hungry because they could find everything to eat in Nanay's property. But they could not eat all the animals they killed; it was too much for them, although they were sometimes more than 20 Japanese soldiers in patrols." Mama said with nostalgies.

Modesta, Dominga's sister, hid separately in a secret hiding place with several beautiful Spanish porcelain plates that Nanay inherited from her great-grandparents. She helped Nanay by cooking food, washing clothes, and bringing some materials to the hiding place, while Benita was always holding Nanay's skirt. When they heard lots of planes turning around the sky over Mabini and sometimes just above their heads, they ran to their respective holes. And they felt so sad for those who were trapped by the warrior planes dropping bombs. Many dead bodies scattered along the roads and fields.

Yoyo Supri, Mama's half elder brother was the father of Manoy Gunding. Yoyo Supri's wife left him for a younger man, and he struggled to take care of baby Segundino. So Nanay brought him home and raised him with the help of Dominga who was eight at that time and helped to take care of him. Mama said she was like a mother to Manoy Gunding, who was only five months old at the time.

Mama explained a particularly worrying episode:

"One day, when we were about to eat our lunch, I did not find baby Segundino to feed him. I realized that he was not with us; he was left alone at home. I had to forget my fears of the falling bombs, and even though I spotted many dead bodies scattered along the roads and in the fields, I ran back to our home. I found the baby alone, crawling across the floor. He was not crying, but was calling out for his mother. I felt such pain in my heart and wondered what would had happen to me if the baby was not there anymore. I loved him so much. When I felt such fear I often felt the need to go to the toilet, but the house was quite far from our hiding place, so I went in nature instead. I hid baby Segundino in the midst of the thick bamboo grooves, warning him not to make a single noise and that he must not leave the place, and he obeyed. Unconscious of the danger, he would play, waving his feet in the stream. Luckily, he was not killed by the bombs. He was kept safe by his loving guardian angel. Before the combined American and Filipino troops, including recognized guerrillas, started to fight back against the Japanese, two Japanese soldiers discovered our hiding place against the bombs and came often to inspect whether any Filipino soldiers were hiding with us. We spent sleepless nights, afraid what would happen next. The next day, the American and Filipino troops attacked the Japanese troops on the roads between Butuan and Cabadbaran in March 1945. Our underground shelter trembled; the war was so near us, we had to cover our ears with our hands or a cloth to protect our hearing from the deafening sounds of the explosion of bombs dropping non-stop all around, and also the battle in the streets. We continued praying that the war would soon stop. We weren't harmed physically, but the psychological effects remained. Several houses in our neighbourhood were destroyed, the coconut plantations were damaged and animals such as carabaos and cows died. The tanks that covered the roads in Mabini were destroyed, as Mabini is located between Butuan and the town of Cabadbaran where the Japanese made their camp.

The Japanese surrendered. While we were in our hiding place, some people from the aboriginal communities came from the mountains to loot empty houses in the towns and barrio of Mabini. They took with them all the things they wanted like clothes, blankets, food, and useful items from the kitchen. One evening, we'd noticed that no Japanese were in the surrounding area. We were all so tired and feeling ill, longing to wash ourselves, put on clean clothes, and have a nice meal. So, we decided to go out from our underground hiding place and return home, to rest and sleep, hoping that no warrior planes would drop bombs and no Japanese soldiers would come to frighten us. Nanay's house was quite big and comfortable, but when we reached home, we were all shocked: Nanay's house had disappeared, burned to ashes. We had nothing to put on, no more place to rest and nothing to eat. We're all devastated.

When it was confirmed that the Japanese lost the fight and had left Cabadbaran, our men came back to their respective families. We built a little refuge, a small cabana made in bamboos, tied with two different kinds of fibres: the *abaca*, (strongest natural plant fibre) and the *rattan*, (the climbing palms with tough stems used for wickerwork). My elder brothers, Supriano, Vicente and their friends made our refuge strong and comfortable," Mama explained with nostalgic."

Later, the people in Mabini rebuilt Nanay's house. It was a strong wooden house with whole tree beams, tall walls, and flooring in all robust woods. This was the house that I knew and where I spent a good part of my childhood. Esperanza organized the people in Mabini in how they could restart farming, coconut plantations, repair the irrigation system.

The war had lasted for almost five years, and Manoy Gunding had grown up believing that Dominga, my mother, was also his mother.

Benita was married to Bonifacio Peleño from Bohol, and lived together in Bohol. Dominga brought Segundino to Butuan where she got married to Francisco Serohijos, my father. Manoy Gunding stayed with them as I was born. At the age of 11, he took care of me and had watched me grow. He also took care of my younger siblings Dan, Nelly and Nolwen when they came along.-

As I described above, I was five years when my mother decided to go back to Mabini, and we lived together with Nanay. However, Tatay only stayed with us on the weekends, as he was working in Butuan, 29 kilometres away. But Manoy Gunding was there. I remember him carrying me on his shoulders while walking back and forth to the upper part of Mabini near the village of Pandanon. Together with my whole family, we went to watch a theatre show, managed by my godmother whom I called Maninay Brenda, and also our cousin, who lived nearby. Maninay used to dictate the text of the scenes that the artists would utter, complete with action behind a large curtain separating the front and the backstage. The presentation ended so late at night, I can still recall. I fell asleep on Manoy's shoulders and he carried me along all the way home.

Unpaid taxes

Nanay died at the young age of 67, due to a cholera epidemic. Then there was trouble with the inheritance. I could never forget that when Nanay died, nobody was with her. Her daughters of her first marriage who were still alive only came after her death to claim their share of the fortunes, even though they had not been at all interested in working as farmers.

Mama said that there was the unequal treatment between her and her elder half-sister. Modesta, who acted with a sense of superiority, intimidated her. Modesta took all of Nanay's belongings and brought them to her own home in Butuan. But most of those things were quickly destroyed by the earthquakes and typhoons. I said to Mama: "It's a pity had you not brought home some of Nanay's beautiful Spanish dresses. I had loved them all."

Esperanza Jamboy's family had owned several hectares of rich land, and they were the landlord of the Yubit family, the tenant. This truth was confirmed by Francisca, eldest daughter of Nanay, who came to Butuan in 1962, just after the burial of their mother. All the five sons of Nanay had already passed away. I did not get to meet those three uncles: Raymundo, Edmundo, and Mariano, because they died before I was born. I only knew Aunt Filipa, Yoyo Supri and Yoyo Vicente. I had also seen my Great-Aunt, Purification, I called here Inse Puri, (Nanay's elder sister). In remembering their names and stories, I have kept all their memories alive.

The children of Nanay unluckily learned that there was a high level of unpaid taxes, going back many years due to inefficient management. Now even if all the land was sold, the sale would not have covered the unpaid taxes, including penalties. And they still had to pay inheritance tax. The land included several plantations: coconut, coffee, cacao, sugar cane, pineapple, banana, root crops, and so on. All those properties came back to the younger generation of my grandmther's family, the Beray-Jamboy family. They paid all the unpaid taxes. It is really sad to know that members of the family only came to claim their shares; they did not offer to take care of their mother when she was still living.

Dominga, Dan and his wife

I saw in photos how so elegant Mama Dominga was with her pink coloured dress that she wore during the wedding of Melchor's daughter Anne-Melord married in December 2018 to Lester Ronald. It's a pity that I was not present, not even Ashley and Amelie. We were in Philippines in 2017 for Tatay's burial and I was not ready financially to go back that year for the wedding. Then the covid-19 pandemic beginning 2019 to now 2021 prevented us to travel. But Dan had deceived me again because he lives in Butuan and he did not attend the wedding.

His wife Betsy was always in conflict with Melchor's daughters. And that conflict had slashed through the structure of our family social world.

In January 2019, Mama was seriously ill. My brother Dan and his wife Betsy brought Mama to the hospital in Davao. There was no vacant bed in all the hospitals in Butuan at that time due to the epidemic of dengue fever, and Mama was diagnosed positive. Mama quickly recovered on the same day, and she was back home in the evening.

"Francisco's spirit visited me in big smile," Mama said. But she did not specify if she had seen Francisco in her dream, or in a vision while awake. For me, my father was so happy that Dan finally showed his generosity. It was the return of the black sheep.

I can never forget Mama said to me, laughing: "I will probably live longer Sarah, because Francisco was smiling so much when facing me. Maybe he will still have to wait for me a bit longer." Even though she forgot to tell me how she saw Francisco smiling, I was so happy hearing that my mother felt better.

I spoke to my mother on a video call the day before her 85th birthday. She was happy expecting her birthday. It is not too late to put our words into action, showing her our affection and how we love her by concentrating our time for her, and finding ways to help her. Talking to her on the phone that day allowed her to express herself and ease her worries and pain of losing her husband. I just reminded her that her husband had wanted her to be happy.

This reminded me of my vivid dream I had just before hopping out of bed one morning, where all Tatay's words were significant, brief and precise. I was confused as to whether it was a dream or real because of how vivid it was. My encounter with him was so intense that I could almost touch him.

My departed father appeared to me, sitting on his favourite corner of our living room, on the chair at the left side of the window facing the small road. His eyes blinked as if he was trying to understand something. I asked him where Mama was, and he answered: "Your mother is still preparing. Tell her I am waiting for her and she can come with me when she is ready." He faced the road as he used to do when he was still alive. I was so near to him, I wanted to hug him, but I awoke.

That dream remained in my mind. I sobbed. I had not been able to hug him before he left. I understood that Tatay was sending me a message for his dear wife, and although he had a spiritual happy crossing, maybe he could not be completely happy without his wife. But at the same time, I know that he wanted Mama to carry on a happy life on earth, even during his absence, until she is ready to join him. They had been together for 66 years. Now, he is just waiting patiently, because Dominga is not yet ready to join him on the other side.

I strongly sensed that Tatay was reminding me, being the eldest child in the family of eight. He was sending me his message to take care of my 85-year-old mother. This is my personal interpretation and spiritual growth. And despite that I know he is watching over both Mama and me, I miss him. Yet, life on earth is not everlasting. Now I am in a dilemma as to whether I will stay with my mother in the Philippines to serve her and to let her feel that I love her. But to do that I would need to abandon my husband, who also needs me in France. He needs weekly medical check-ups due to his heart condition, and he is getting old like everyone else. I need to be with him to listen, to know each result of his medical consultations.

Dominga's love for Dave and his family

Mama Dominga did not only take care in her second grandson Dave, but also Dave's daughters Kylie and Hansel since their birth.

A memory: In 1978, I was wondering why Mama was crying. I followed her into the kitchen and there, she was carrying a 12 month-baby, Dave, in her arms begging him to eat the sweet soft rice that she had prepared for him. Dave is the second son of Dan and Betsy. He was sick, had a fever and a diarrhoea, while his parents were playing mahjong and not looking after him. My mother became a parent for the second time round for her first two grandsons, Carter who was born in 1975 and Dave in 1978, because Dan and Betsy were not taking responsibility for their two sons. They were maybe reassured that Mama was there to take care of them.

I took off to find where they were gambling. I found Dan and Betsy, playing the game with total concentration, despite the fact that their sick child needed medicine and care. I was so angry with them, I was about to turn the mahjong and table upside down, but I tried to remain calm and not get too upset, to show my respect to the people around them. I reminded them of their responsibility to take care of their sick child, instead of playing mahjong day and night. The child refused to eat and was getting weaker, that he needed to be brought to hospital.

As Dave grew older, his grandmother (Mama Dominga), always gave him what he asked for. Mama placed him as the highest priority, and the other nephews and nieces who came later became jealous. I heard Mama say to him: "If your parents can't take care of you, I will do it." Mama made a promise, and I was sure that she would use all her power to fulfil it.

Mama not only took care of her grandson, Dave, but she also – decades later – assumed responsibility for Dave's family. Dave went off to live with another woman in Davao. He left his wife Beatrice, alone to raise their two young daughters: Kylie was born in June 2001 and Hansel in June 2002.

Dominga became a second mother to Kylie and Hansel. She made many sacrifices to make sure that the children had enough food and things necessary for their growth to allow them to grow in good condition while Dan, and his wife Betsy, the grandparents to the babies, ducked their responsibilities. They did not support them physically or financially.

I can still remember when I visited my parents in May 2002, when Tatay was sick. Dave's wife was renting a house in the town of Buenavista. Before I returned to France, Mama asked me to go with her to visit Beatrice and the baby Kylie, who was only 11-months old. I had witnessed how Mama missed the child. She hugs the baby in her arms, eyes full of tears. She was terribly missing her, while Beatrice was expecting her second baby Hansel, born the following month. Mama went there to give her financial support and foods. Mama had a wonderful blessing of being a grandmother, she has all the quality that we need for a grandmother. I understand what Mama felt during those time. As a grandmother myself, I admit that our emotions towards our grandchildren is undiscribably special than what we had for our own children. For me, nobody can do for little children what grandparents do. A grandmother's love is forever.

Memorable Moments with Tatay

Tatay was a handy-man, a carpenter, an electrician, a security guard and a labourer. He was 21 years old when he got married. He never had the chance to go to university, but he had an excellent memory. He could compute everything without using any calculator or machine, didn't even need a pencil and paper. He was good in geometry and mathematics. I was always impressed with how smart he was. I am sure that if he had gone to university, he would have had been a brilliant student and could have achieved success in whatever course he might have chosen. Although he was not perfect, he was above all, a loving father.

In August 1984, Lionel and I spent our summer vacation in Butuan with our 23-month-old daughter. My parents' house was an old one but was built in hardwood that Tatay had restored, renovated, and later enlarged to accommodate his big family. The house became strong, safe, and appeared like new. I was immensely proud of him and still I am. But the typhoon that struck the Philippines in 1984 destroyed my parents' house as described in Chapter 12.

Tatay was an excellent neighbour. He built by himself a wooden bridge which all the neighbours used to reach the road when there was flood. It was a temporary bridge which became permanent because the place needed it; there was so much mud when it rained. There was no neighbour who helped him, and I felt bad for Tatay, when I watched him continue to work despite the rain. In any case, he was happy doing it, and liked to be a good neighbour to everyone. He worked without counting his time or efforts, working silently and with strong conviction. That what was important for him: to accomplish a masterpiece which would be useful to everybody, and make everyone happy.

When I visited my parents in 2013, Tatay at the age of 82 was still so active in performing the tasks that had always been his responsibility at home. One time I was awakened in the middle of the night due to the noise of Tatay's inspection tour – he roamed around the house to see if all the electric bulbs were working. I caught him standing on the chair because he wanted to remove the light bulb in the ceiling of the balcony. He said the light was flickering, and it would be dangerous if it burst. He even went outside the house to check if all the lights were working. Before he returned to his bed, he opened the door of my bedroom, but it was not to check whether I was in my bed. I understood later that it was just to check if the lights outside my bedroom were working well enough, looking through my windows. I know why he was doing it. It was because he used to check everything in and around the sawmill when he was working there as the company guard. He did it at home when everyone was asleep. Only when everything was all checked, could he go to bed.

When we were still small, we would sleep under the mosquito net, which was an effective way to repel mosquitos. Tatay would always check that everyone was safe inside our mosquito net. Well, it was not only to check whether or not we were inside the net, but also to burn any mosquitos that had entered. I saw him catching mosquitos in the candle fire. He was so clever in how he did it in such a way that nobody was ever harmed or burnt (except the mosquitos). It was so unpleasant, the itchy hives were so hard to ignore that they woke us and made us scratch. For most people, mosquito bites are harmless, but for me the bites would result in large red bumps, creating itching lesions on my skin.

As a father, Tatay was sometimes tough but fair. He was a hard worker and not self-centred. "Wherever you are," he would say, "either in the city or somewhere, you must be home before midnight so that we can celebrate the New Year's Eve altogether. Our family will always be complete and united no matter what," he reminded us. I always knew that my parents loved to see all their children come home to their unconditional love.

Spending New Year's Eve at home with your family can be a fantastic opportunity to bond, have fun together, and for the children to have fun with food, drinks, games, and activities. But it wasn't always a joyful celebration at times when food was scarce. But despite poor times, my parents were always striving to find special foods to be served on that occasion as we gathered the whole family around the table.

One New Year's Eve when I was a teenager, I was not at home. I was always aware that being the eldest, I must not deceive my parents by not breaking their rules. It was essential that children respected the disciplinary measures. In order to encourage my siblings to respect the rules too and follow the discipline code, my responsibility was to demonstrate obedience first. For me it was not about strict rules, but just rules that must be respected.

On my way home, there was a kind of rain of bright sparks from all the firecrackers flying. Fireworks exploded everywhere, which created some competition between firecracker operators. They were competing to produce a lot of noise and the biggest bangs. There were fuses wrapped in a heavy paper casing to contain the explosive compound. I was afraid of the bright sparks that could have dropped unto my head, so I opened my umbrella to be protected while running home, my way crowded with people, especially children, all excited to watch the fireworks. They seemed to enjoy facing the danger while waiting for another deafening explosion. I still had three kilometers to go, and I sprinted to reach home before midnight, but I was interrupted by firecrackers were dropping all around me. I was afraid that some debris would explode on me, so I was running home, trying to protect my eyes.

My Aunt Modesta enjoyed putting some bundles of firecrackers in a *taro* [an empty kerosine can] to reach her goal of creating as much noise as possible and to be much louder than the others. Some children planted firecrackers in empty cans of Coca-Cola or Pepsi, throwing them into the sky to explode. There was no coordination or organization at all, so everywhere was a mess, but everyone was happy despite danger.

I arrived home at 20 minutes before midnight, with my umbrella full of small burnt holes. The whole family was waiting for me, except Dan who was detained by a friend somewhere nearby. The table was already set and filled with different foods that my mother had prepared. What I liked best was the *sotanghon* [bean-thread noodles] with sliced chicken, sweet and sour papaya salad, and *biko* [rice cake] for dessert. Mama shared some biko with our neighbours, and she came back home with some suman from them, which added even more beauty to our dining table. Then Dan arrived and the family was complete. It was symbolic, in that 12-seat table and benches made of *yakal* and *lawaan* hard wood were pieces that Tatay had heartily constructed by himself.

The pencil

When I was studying in Bading Elementary School (1963-1965) I reviewed my lessons with a kerosene lamp when there was no electricity. The mosquitos came at night, so I continued memorizing my lessons inside the mosquito net by candlelight then I was sure I could continue reviewing my lessons without being bitten, then I would pass serenely the examination the following day.

The examination day came. In the classroom, my teacher had distributed the tests when I noticed that my pencil was not in my bag. I panicked and felt very angry with myself. How careless I was! We had been all instructed to use a pencil to solve the problems in mathematics, and I was about to ask my teacher if she could lend me hers, when someone knocked on the classroom door. Tatay was there, drenched with sweat, raising his hand with my pencil. I was delighted, and my stress disappeared. Tatay was sweating so much that his T-shirt was stuck onto his skin. he blinked his eyes dimmed by his salty sweat dripping from his forehead, his thick eyebrows not enough to prevent it stinging his eyes. He had sprinted from home to reach to our classroom just before the examination had started, knowing how important it was to me. Considering that the house was quite far from our school, it was quite a feat.

I felt my heart bursting with gratitude while feeling my father's unending love. I hid my face not to show my tears to my classmates. I learned from Mama that when I left our house that morning, Tatay was already at work but he had forgotten something, so he went back home and found my pencil on the table. Then he sprinted to school. He knew it was my examination day. I could never forget how Tatay loved us. And I have this endless love for him, and I promised myself not to deceive him or let him down. Once again, my efforts were rewarded when I got the highest grade in the class. Some of my classmates were unkind and teased me. For them, it was unbearable to accept that I was the first in the class. I was extremely exhausted and fed up of dealing with their aggression. They pushed me to the limit to such an extent that I almost burst in anger.

While writing this memoir, I again thought of how Tatay loves me to pass the exam and how that pencil was important. What about if Tatay had not forgotten something at home, he would have had not found my pencil on the table.

My special chair

Tatay was like professional carpenter. He built me a chair for school, made of yakal hardwood, and donated it to the school when it was newly opened. It was more beautiful and comfortable than the other chairs. I was again so proud of my father. Some of my classmates were unfortunately envious. I knew that Tatay had made it with love.

One morning, I was shocked not to find my chair anymore and I did not dare to sit on a chair that was not mine. So, I remained standing, humiliated, watching my classmates sitting on their chairs. My teacher was asking my classmates, but nobody answered. However, when I returned to the class after our sport activities, I found my chair back to its place. I did not say anything to not to embarrass the person who hid it, even though I think I know who did.

I felt unwelcome in that class and they looked at me with disdain when I got the highest grade in the examinations. I had sensed it from the very beginning. The other bright children in the class were afraid there would be a fight between us because I showed them I was not afraid. They were not happy to hear that I came from a private Catholic institution. Some of my classmates were angry that I spoke fluent English to our teachers, and they skipped over me during recreation period. In any case, I preferred to remain alone in a corner, so as not to provoke their rage. My humiliation lasted three years, from Grade 4 to Grade 6, when I graduated as salutatorian instead of valedictorian although I had got the highest grades. I observed how the cruelty of jealousy can ruin relationships, and change behaviour for the worse.

Purok President

Dominga had been incredibly lucky with Francisco. Aside from being a good father, a carpenter, an efficient guard, an electrician, a mathematician, and the best handy man I have ever known, he was also loved by many people living in New Asia district. He was nominated as the Chairman of sport activities in *Purok* 1, our local district or zone. The following year, he was elected Purok President, where he used the role to promote better relationships between the younger generation and adults. He conducted and arranged informal and formal meetings which were opportunities to discuss different problems of the youth in and around New Asia District. As a Chairman of sport activities, he was able to find a common ground and goals that every member in the committee was comfortable working towards.

I once heard my father delivering a speech, much applauded and acclaimed by the audience. He had strong skills in press relations, and was an excellent team leader for organizing events such as benefit dances and sports activities. When he was involved, all the participants were energized and became more interested in participating in the programme of youth and sports, encouraged by his leadership. With his initiative as Chairman, youth activities progressed and participation increased. In addition, the committee collected money for the improvement of our chapel, the Señor Saint Vicente, from kind-hearted volunteers. Francisco successfully encouraged the youth and adults to concentrate on their love of playing sports, rather than criminal activities which created public and social troubles, common problems in other Puroks and Barangays.

Benefit dances were held almost every week to raise money for their projects, inviting people especially the ladies to join. Sometimes our Purok was lucky to have some ships that landed overnight and spending two to three days in the port, and then many of the crew would participate in the dance and contribute to the success of the fundraising. Unfortunately I missed most of those, as I was working during the day and had evening classes, returning home tired. But I could still hear the fun they were having with loud music and announcements. I sometimes went to observe the dance and the dancers after my classes. On popular nights, there could be a crowd of people, out onto the road, watching the dancers, making problems for vehicles passing by.

Among Tatay's children, Ashley, who loves dancing, had been searching for the opportunity to express her talent and creativity in dancing. As her sports practice, she danced to her favourite song, "Funky Town." She was much appreciated by her partners and became one of the favourite dancers. Amelie was not fond of dancing but sometimes went anyways to watch her twin sister having fun. Amelie and Imelda's volleyball team invested much energy in practicing for their games. Their constant practice gave them stronger muscles and endurance. They won the volleyball tournament. Melchor's team also won the basketball title. Our Purok became the champion in volleyball and basketball amongst the four different Puroks in New Asia. Our family, under Francisco's leadership, can say that we successfully contributed to the achievement of the Purok-1 projects in our Barangay.

On the eve of Fiesta, games were held during the day, and the winners were announced. Trophies were given to the final winners of the games. In the evening, the winning candidate, the "Queen of our Purok" was crowned, and then the dance was free for everyone to join. Everybody could dance with their chosen partners. Lot of people from other Barangays and Puroks came to join the Fiesta celebration, while the games and volunteer performances continued. Different stands were set up on the side, selling of snacks and beverages.

A memory: When I was 13 years old, I was full of curiosity when I heard for the first time the loud music amplified with a microphone, and an announcer inviting ladies to come to participate in the benefit dance. I loved to dance, but my sisters were still very young. I followed the sound and there, I found a dance floor surrounded with coloured electric lights hanging from wires above. Children and teenagers were dancing to the pop and disco music of 1965 in their own way; there was no choreography. so I just observed them.

Then the announcer instructed the children to give way to the lady dancers, who were dressed up especially for the dance. The children filled up the benches while the men stood on the other side of the dance floor. Little by little, small groups of people collected around the place and the cha-cha music played. Only three pairs of dancers started to dance. The second piece was another cha-cha, but the music was in Spanish. The third song was a rock-n-roll song by Elvis. How I loved it! I started to move my feet and hips, and a young guy, maybe the same age as me, invited me to dance with him. We went to the middle of the dance floor, and I immediately enjoyed dancing. I was about to go out from that place when another Elvis song started. Another man invited me to dance with him. He was much older than me, and I did not feel comfortable dancing a slow dance with him.

When the music stopped, Mama Dominga suddenly appeared behind me. She pinched my side, just below my armpit. I was about to yell with the pain. She brought me home. She was surely shocked to see her young daughter dancing freely with an unknown man at the middle of the dance floor. For her, it was too early for me to dance with a partner during the benefit dance. I understand she was not used to it at that time.

I did not have the chance to embrace the fun and joy of dancing with my full creativity like other adolescents of my age, unfortunately. Mama was so strict or maybe she didn't know. I missed the opportunity to express myself through the art of dance, which for me has always been very mentally and physically positive. Psychologically, dancing was for me one way to get rid of stress and problems, and forget all of life's shortcomings that you feel so keenly as an adolescent. However, at that time, my mother had surely not thought of it that way. I was even wondering if she was conscious of the damage that it caused to me emotionally, to be denied dancing.

The following year, my parents allowed me to participate in the benefit dance and I become famous in our Purok. I received lot of compliments. When Mama heard our neighbours admiring me for my talent in dancing, she told her friends that she was proud of me. I almost couldn't believe that Mama had said it. I was stupefied. I even heard her talking to other mothers who were also present that evening. "Oh yes she dances very well and she's my daughter," she said proudly. Unfortunately, my father was not the Purok President yet at that time.

The small house

My parents seldom bought toys for us, but Tatay always made things. When the twins were young, they enjoyed playing with whatever we had, despite our poverty when Tatay lost his job after the explosion of the sawmill.

There were some pieces of strong wood left unburnt after the explosion of the sawmill, which were not needed by the company. Tatay used them to build a small beautiful wooden house. It was about four square-meters in size, and about 1.60 meters high. Tatay installed electric lights and a traditional stove that we called *abohan*. Amelie and Ashley played inside that small house together with friends of their age, Tita and Daday Escobido, and they even slept over in that house for the night. They cooked sweet potatoes in a big kettle, and sometimes put ripe sarabia bananas for their snacks, watched by Nolwen and Nelly. I happened to eat their cooked ripe sarabia and sweet potatoes [*kamote*]. I am sure that my siblings can still remember how Tatay Eco had been a loving father, to build that little house for them.

Tatay saved me

One day, Mama made a delicious cuisine, and the recipe was the famous *Gisadong Isda*, a dried fish cooked in a small amount of coconut milk, mixed with some vegetable leaves and spices. All of us enjoyed the lunch. But just few seconds after I finished my meal, I couldn't breathe. I was about to fall when I stood in front of the mirror seeing my whole body covered with rashes, red spots, swollen red lips and red eyelids. It was my first time experiencing a reaction like this, and I did not understand what was wrong with me. Nobody knew I was allergic to that fish. I got sick and suffered all the symptoms including hives, nausea, headaches, and my breathing became short and terribly fast, the early signs of anaphylaxis. It was so exhausting to try to catch my breath. I could not do anything else but follow my breathing and wait to see what would happen next. That life-threatening allergic reaction appeared quickly. I could hardly move, unable to talk, unable to answer them when they asked me what was wrong. I was burning with fever, my eyes were red while my head seemed ready to explode. When I looked up, the ceiling was turning.

But Tatay quickly understood what was happening. He ran to grate a coconut, pressed it for milk and forced me to drink it abundantly. He placed one finger into my throat until I vomited. After a while I felt better, and my breathing gradually slowed down. Tatay had saved my life, although I suffered of diarrhoea after taking the coconut milk.

Another memory: Tatay coming home from work still sweating, but always smiling, looking to my youngest sister. Baby Imelda was crawling across the floor, then hurriedly stood up, gripping her hands to the security fence while waving her body to welcome Tatay home. But she ran away as soon as Tatay came closer, because she was afraid that Tatay would kiss her with his unshaved chin that hurt her skin. It was good that Tatay had installed the security-barrier, otherwise, baby Imelda would have escaped through the open door, but instead she hid under the bed. Tatay pretended not to find her as if they were playing hide and seek.

These simple memories are always important to hold onto, as it reminds me of Tatay's fatherly love.

Tatay saved Feliciano

Feliciano, whom we called Manoy Dodo, was Mama's nephew. One day in 1962 he walked in the flood barefoot. He had stepped onto a piece of wood underwater with a nail sticking out. The nail pierced his foot and caused a deep and painful wound on bottom of his foot. Luckily, Tatay was passing by. He said he saw Manoy floating on the river water unconscious. Tatay was smaller than Manoy Dodo, but he carried him on his back to reach home, walking against the current of the flood water that was above his waist while the rain continued. The flood was rising again.

After cleaning Manoy's foot with *aqua oxygenada,* Tatay lit his cigarette lighter. He boiled coconut oil on a spoon and poured it into the wound. Manoy trembled and groaned so loudly that I was about to run away. He had never had his anti-tetanus vaccination. Despite the first aid, his foot grew swollen and infected. There was pus leaking from the wound and red streaks all around it.

Manoy had a fever that had lasted three days, and Tatay stayed with him for two nights. As a child of nine, I observed how everyone was worried, but Manoy was not brought to the hospital. A friend of Tatay, who was not a doctor, but a natural healer came to examine Manoy everyday. He gave him some tablets to take and some medicinal solution to disinfect the wound. Evidently, the healer was reliable. Manoy got up one morning without fever and the swelling on his foot had diminished.

"Lucky that he was not diabetic," the healer said. Manoy Dodo recovered from his wounds, but he continued coughing.

A memory: I was alone on board of a raft that Tatay and Manoy Dodo had constructed out of branches of the trees that they had caught floating in the flood water one year. I was going to buy milk for Amelie and Ashley. The stores were flooded, and the merchants used their boats to sell their goods. But I was still small, and did not have enough knowledge as how to steer the raft. I had only a piece of rough stick that used to move it. I placed the cans of milk I had bought at the centre of the raft, together with other goods. Suddenly there was a huge log that came from the river that banged my raft, and one can of milk fell into the water. I jumped into the water to look for it while my small raft went farther, carried by the river water current. Luckily, Manoy Dodo passed by there and found my raft and he helped me to ride back, but I did not find the can of milk. I went home afraid of my mother's punishment. I feared that I had not been so clever in performing my mission that day, although I arrived home safely after all.

Manoy Dodo remained unmarried. He had also worked in the New Asia sawmill where my father was working. For many years, he lived with us during working days in our house near the Agusan River. He returned to Pandanon after the explosion at the sawmill.

When he visited us one day later, I sensed he was dying. As usual, he was so tender and smiling at me before he left, but of course I did not tell him what I knew: that he would die very soon. I informed Mama the next day that I was having intuition that Manoy Dodo would die, soon. But Mama got angry with me. She still did not accept that though not always, I can sense when someone is going to die.

Tatay Passing Away in 2017

Through a series of prophetic dreams, I was informed of Tatay's imminent passing away telling me about the event before he was called. The dreams also showed that Tatay was in a blissful state as he was illuminated by the divine beauty of Heavenly light. Tatay was with God.

My first dream occurred on April 19th. Different images were milling around in my head that were difficult to understand. I was able to return back to sleep, but then I was awakened by a voice whispering my ears, saying; "three-four." The numbers repeated in my head even when I was sitting up in bed. That whisper was stored in my mind, and only went away when I obtained my plane tickets for an evening flight to the Philippines, scheduled for the 3rd of May.

At first, I was wondering about those two numbers. I said to Lionel that maybe I should play the lottery, and those would be the winning numbers. But how could I win, with only two numbers? Then on the 24th of April, I dreamed again, and clearer this time.

I was in a big spacious house full of prestigious furniture, maybe made of narra wood. I said to myself it was a waste to have an immense house with a wide lounge, but nobody was around. I wondered who owned the house, and I awoke.

I returned to sleep almost immediately, which was rare. I saw beautiful places, small houses along the road, and suddenly Tatay was falling down. He was weak. He sat down, then he tried to stand up and fell down again to his seat, and then to his bed. He sat on the chair and fell again.

This dream repeated in my mind, so many times. For me it was a warning. I thought that Tatay needed someone to take care of him, so that he would not fall down like that.

I called Ashley, who at that time was in the Philippines with her husband. They attended the wedding of my niece Heidi, held in Davao in April. Amelie was the godmother, and her daughter Karen was one of the bridesmaids. After the wedding, I asked Ashley if she could please stay 10 days more in Butuan to take care of Tatay. I told her that I saw him in my dream, and he was tired, weak, and kept falling down.

Ashley answered: "Manay, you are being so negative," she said. "I can't stay more days. I must go back to work as planned. I have to return to Australia next Tuesday." She was not overly concerned.

"What about Amelie?" I insisted.

She replied, "Amelie and Karen will fly to Palawan where Stephen is waiting for them and continue their vacation and will have a tour in the Visayas region." Her words were like a gong ringing my ears. Despite her lack of concern, I prayed that somehow, there would be someone to help Tatay when needed.

I had no choice but to call Mama too and inform her about my dreams concerning Tatay. She got upset and refused to believe me. She was, of course, worried because this reminded her of the previous time when I dreamed of her falling to the floor, and she had, in real life, soon fallen and sprained her hand. Again, I had wondered why I have to know these things beforehand in my dreams, and yet I am powerless to stop the events most of the time.

"Sarah, I need someone to help me," she said, full of anguish. "I am not strong enough to carry or lift your father if he falls. I know, he is getting weak."

"Mama," I said, "I'll pray and trust in God, that when that time comes, there will be someone who could do the task. Don't worry, you will not be alone."

"Someone with strong arms," Mama added.

So, I made her a promise that there will be someone around her when the time came. Three nights later, I dreamed again.

There was unusual noise. The room was full of people who I did not recognize. I looked around, and saw my mother in the midst of them, but she did not see me. I did not know where those people came from, or why were they there. Some of them recognized me and vice-versa but they never spoke. I walked along the dark corridor. Reflections from small lights enabled me to recognize Johanna (my niece-in-law) singing with her guitar, sitting on a wooden sofa. In front of her was her daughter, Hansel, smiling while some young boys of her age were laughing. Then I returned to the group of people sitting on a bench in the wide balcony, a place with roofing but under an opened area. Mama was there, but where was Tatay? Dan was talking to someone where cars were parked in line. Dan's wife, Betsy, was standing at a bit of a distance. Former neighbours from New Asia were there at the other side of the balcony. I was surprised to see the deceased Victor Montilla was also there, or maybe it was his son. One of the twin brothers, Roy, was present too, I recognized him well. I had the impression that it was the same house of my previous dream.

I awoke confused. I wondered why I dreamed of Johanna and Hansel surrounded with boys at her age in that place? Why did I dream of Dan and Betsy and all those previous neighbours from New Asia? Two nights later, I dreamed it again. I was so tired with the dreams and broken sleep that I had trouble concentrating at work. I felt so sleepy that I put my head down on my office desk.

I was so tired the next morning, I remained sitting on my bed, but I needed to get ready and have my breakfast before going to work.

I was surprised hearing a gentle voice calling me: "Sarah."

I immediately answered, "Yes, Tatay?" Then I realized I was alone in my bedroom. Why was he calling me? Stunned, I went into Lionel's room.

"Wake up Lionel, did you hear that? Tatay called me," I said.

"What do you mean? Of course, I did not hear Tatay calling you. It is probably your imagination, or you are still dreaming," Lionel said.

"I know Tatay's voice very well," I replied. "He called me with a gentle voice. You should have heard him calling me," I insisted.

Another dream, on 30th April:

People were talking to one another, then a prayer was held. A lot of people were present. I participated in some parts of the prayer. Then I heard myself praying with the people in the same room. I awoke with the prayers in my ears.

I ask myself why there was praying in that house and why was I there? I was almost sure that something would happen to Tatay, so I started to think about buying plane tickets.

At work, everyone noticed how tired I was. Instead of doing my work, I was typing up my dreams on my computer, and I was surprised it was saved automatically. I told my colleagues that I just needed some rest and a good sleep. When I asked my boss to allow me to have two weeks rest in May, he did not refuse.

"You have not recovered yet from your accident?" he asked.

I did not dare to inform him that I kept on dreaming almost every night. On the 1st of May I dream again:

The sun had gone down., I entered a wide-open gate. I walked along a dark long pathway, and wondered why there was no light. I needed to go further to reach a light at the right side. Two young girls in white robes were playing, and one woman was with them. The children were happily speaking in loud voices. They were excited and shouting with joy. They seemed close to each other, maybe family members? But they were too far away for me to recognize them. Along my way near the entrance of that particular house, there were different vehicles parked along both sides. I saw a small lorry, a pick-up truck, motorcycles and cars in different colours: white, black, grey, and green. There were our former neighbours from New Asia, where we lived 25 years ago. Sitting on the benches were Lourdes Tolo, her daughter Lila, her son Eric, and Roy Montilla. But where was his twin brother, Rey Montilla? Esmeraldo Montilla was there too, looking like an exact copy of his father who died many years ago. I awoke wondering if the house I saw in my previous dreams was the same house.

My last dream before Tatay passed away:

I was walking while murmuring, feeling upset, walking along an endless dark hallway, I tried to find a way out.

"Where is the light?" I asked out loud, hoping that someone might hear me. I

continued, lamenting that the owner of that house needed to place more lights around the wide corridor. I noticed some lights further in front of me. "Where are the people living here?" I asked but nobody answered.

I continued walking, so impatient to reach the area where the lights were on. It seemed so near, and yet so far and hard to reach. I finally ended up at the end of the corridor, or at least I thought it was the end. But I needed to move to the right side to fully reach the illuminated area. Taking a slight turn to the left, I was stunned!

White lights were shining bright. It was so inviting in front of me. I was greatly amazed! White lights splashed around from above, illuminating the place. The lights had an extreme beauty that could not be expressed in words, and it healed my fears of darkness from walking in the hallway a moment ago. What was most surprising was that my father and mother were standing in front of me, seemed separated by a transparent wall because I could not reach them. I asked them. "What's wrong with you? Why are you both standing, separated by a wall? Why are you not in the same place? What happened?"

Mama was wearing a white blouse and dark skirt, looking down. She was so sad and sobbing. She crossed her hands against her stomach. It seemed like she could not hear me. She did not look at me either. She was not aware of my presence and she did not seem to be aware of Tatay. She was just in front of me, but when I tried to touch her she was far.

I was thrilled and envious seeing Tatay bathed with strong rays of brilliant white light from above that reached to his feet. The light was concentrated only on him, as he stood to Mama's right, beyond a transparent wall. I wanted to hold Mama, to ease her pain, but it was impossible to reach her though she was just there in front of me.

Slowly, Tatay started walking away and the light becomes round had never left him. As if Tatay was standing on a ring of light that has an infinite length up to the sky. When Tatay made one step the white light did the same, the light never wants Tatay to be out. It was so beautiful to see him there. He was good looking, younger, and bathed in beautiful light, walking slowly away from Mama. Light encircled his body, as if Tatay and the light were becoming one. He turned his head towards me, and our *eyes met. He gave me a quick glance while talking to me in my head. He stared at me, then smiled while giving me a sign with his eyes in Mama's direction, and I followed where he was looking. He looked at Mama, so I looked at her too.*

When I turned my head to look at him again, Tatay was gone and the lights too, they left together at the same time. Then I awoke.

This is my ultime interpretation: For me this dream was sacred, a gift from the Holy Spirit. I understood that Tatay would have a smooth crossing over, awaited with heavenly lights of divine beauty. He looked younger, strong, healthy and I could never forget his smile, all these remain in my spirit. Tatay was happy because he was called by God and this time Tatay has his eternal life with God. He went forward and then disappeared, both the mysterious light and Tatay gone together. He left me his words in my mind. I heard the complete sounds of his thoughts. Then only darkness was left. The restful, beautiful, and soothing light was gone. But before it was completely dark, I saw Mama's clothing, her white blouse and very dark skirt.

I know what I was seeing was a not an ordinary premonition dream, because it required quick action. My first thought was to find a flight for Butuan, pack my luggage and race to get out there. I felt so worried for a while, but then it dissipated. I really feel that Tatay was telling me about an event. I felt my stomach turning upside down while my heart was beating a million miles a minute, because I was not ready for him to leave. I started to panic again, but it was as if someone was telling me that everything would be alright, and then I felt serene. The images remained in my head. They were so clear and said: When Tatay left, the lights above and around him were also gone. They were gone together at the same time. This time I understood. My father was bidding me goodbye. He was happy and healthy, and God was there already waiting for him. Tatay was in a blissful state.

I hopped out of bed and darted to the phone. It was 5:00 a.m. in Paris. I absolutely needed to speak to my father. I sprinted to my husband's room while the phone started ringing. "Lionel," I said, "wake up!" You must know this dream! It was such an unusual dream and I need to know today what is happening with my parents. Why were they standing on the same path but separated by a transparent wall? Why was Mama was not aware of the presence of Tatay, just next to her? Although I had an ultime conviction about the interpretation of my dream, I wantedd to hear my husband's view.

"Lionel, can you tell me what the meaning is?"

"I don't know Sarah," he said. "It is probably because you always think of your parents," he said, trying to calm me down.

"No, I feel something unusual is happening with Tatay. This time is different from my previous dreams. I must find a flight for Butuan now."

"Do you think you can withdraw money to buy your tickets and some cash for pocket money? The bank is still closed. You cannot stay in the Philippines with nothing in your pockets." Lionel was in panic too, but same time he had understood that no one could stop me.

The flights that day were full, no vacant seats on any plane. An offer appeared in one corner of my screen which announced a last-minute deal. I became quite nervous, afraid to miss the offer as it was said "26 minutes, six passengers," then at eight minutes left, there were only two places left. I had to pay immediately, typing the numbers of my credit card in, and hoping I didn't make any mistakes.

Finally, I had the return tickets, on a flight the next day – Wednesday, 3rd May 2017. I had enough time to cancel all my meetings and medical appointments, as I had had a car accident only a few days earlier. But at that very moment, I felt that Tatay might be leaving while I was travelling. I kept in my mind his beautiful image which remained with my spirit: Smiling, happy, and full of bliss. I was sure he would have a happy crossing over.

On May 3rd, 7:15 a.m. Paris time, I needed to speak to Tatay immediately before doing anything. I was able to get through to Imelda, my youngest sister.

"Hello Imee, can you pass Tatay please?"

"Wait a minute Many. He is still taking a nap, but I will see if he can be awakened."

"Is he okay?"

"He is awake now, Manay, but he said he is so tired and has a headache. He tried to stand but sat back down immediately. Then he fell down abruptly to his bed. It is unusual for him, maybe he needs some potassium, and he should eat a banana."

"Please let me see Tatay, Imee. Please place your cell phone standing behind a glass of water or something so that I can see him clearly?"

"Alright Manay, you can talk to Tatay now."

"Hello Tatay, are you alright?"

He groaned a little. "It's you Sarah? So you are coming?"

" Yes, I'll be there on Friday, the 5th."

"Is it?" he said with a voice half-satisfied. I knew he wanted me to come right away. He had surely forgotten the distance between France and the Philippines. He had a hard time swallowing the banana. He had dark shadows under his eyes. He did not seem like he was feeling well at all. Then he gave me a quick smile and said he would go back to bed, without saying goodbye. That was the last time I saw his face, through video-call.

There was great panic at home. Mama, Nelly, Imelda and my niece Kylie were there. Imee's phone was still on, but nobody was looking to me, and I heard them saying that Tatay needed to be brought to hospital. I stayed on the phone, but nobody answered me anymore. They were all gone to the hospital. Being the eldest of the family I should have told them more about my dreams in the light of Tatay's hospitalization, but their phones were already off.

My confirmed flight schedule was to depart from Paris on Wednesday 3rd May and to arrive in Butuan on Friday 5th May 2017. I rushed to ask Ashley to make a room reservation for me in the same hotel where she and Ronaldo were staying, and to ask the hotel to fetch me from Bangcasi Airport on Friday at 6:30 a.m.

On my first stopover in Abu Dhabi International Airport, I heard the message that that my father had passed away. Francisco Pizarra Serohijos, born on October 10, 1931 in Tubigon, Bohol, died in Butuan on May 4, 2017. He was the son of Jose Serohijos and Enrica Pizarras, both born in 1895.

The Philippines is six hours ahead from Paris. Tatay died on Wednesday *3rd May*, five minutes past 6:00 p.m. Paris time. It was then five minutes past midnight, Thursday *4th May* Philippine time. Now, I knew at last about the meaning of the numbers; the *"three and four"* not only in my dreams but a whisper that was repeated in my ears.

The clothing at the burial was the same as in my dream

On Monday 8th May 2017, it was bizarre to see all the people who were in my dream were all present at the burial. My whole family: the adults, children, men, and women were all wearing white shirts and white blouses. I was especially astonished seeing Mama, wearing exactly the same clothing as what I saw in my dream, when she was standing alongside Tatay seemed separated by a transparent wall. In fact, I did not know that we would be told to wear white blouses or white T-shirts during the church and burial ceremony, as it was organized by my youngest sister, Imelda. I was blown away to see our clothing at the burial was the same as in my dream.

For a while, I stood alone, bewildered by the landscape around me and wondering whether I was at the burial or if I was still in my dream. I had even told Lionel about that beautiful green landscape, and that there was something on the ground and with a mountain that we could see from far away. Lionel was for me a kind of a computer database to record all the information about my dreams. When that data base started to feel overloaded he told me to write down my dreams and premonitions.

It was only when I was on board the airplane on my way back to France when I realized that we all wore the same clothes as in my dream. The landscape of wide green fields with flat gravestone (modern style) and the sky in my dreams were also the same as I saw during the burial. In fact, when I awoke from the dream, I had discounted those images of graves because I thought that the cemetery of Butuan did not look like that. But when I looked at the pictures that I received later from my family after the funeral, I recognised those images from my dreams before the sad event. I still wonder how it could be possible to enter into the wide green field that I saw in my dream.

During the burial, my heart was bursting with the overwhelming emotions of sorrow, suffering the waves of pain and bewilderment, and I didn't know how I could cope. Mama was there at my side. I was thinking how could she handle so much pain at her age, so I tried to be strong for her. I thought that I needed to help her overcome her sorrows while grieving, and not to feel the unbearable feeling of emptiness and numbness. I needed to be there to help her cope with the loss of her husband after 66 years together. And now, although it would be hard, she had to be strong to build a life for herself.

Although I know death is inevitable, I am a one of those who tend to live as though we and those we love are never going to die. We are shocked and distraught when we are met by the impending death of others, and now, Tatay was gone. We have to live with this unending pain of losing him. But I still have his memories, the happy, funny and loving memories of the time he shared with us. He had those qualities of a loving father. I miss him so much. I look at his photographs, and then I feel refreshed by those wonderful memories.

And now, I am writing his memories, and this may help me to forget the pain in my heart and keep his memory alive. In fact, I cried so much with emotion that was deeply ingrained in my heart, but I cried for me and not for Tatay, because I know he is in a blissful state. God called him to go home. Tatay is now happy in his true eternal life.

Divine guidance

A memory: On Saturday 6th May, I was in Butuan. Although I had really needed rest that afternoon after three days travel from France, it was impossible to close my eyes in the comfortable Grand Palace Hotel. I sensed I was not alone in my room, and my father's image accompanied me even when I closed my eyes. He was there, and I could almost hear his voice. He was happy to see me. I put on my clothes and was determined to see him, even though I did not know yet how to find where the funeral home was. I went out from my room and I started to explore. I had faith in divine guidance, and I let myself be guided.

In front of the hotel entrance, a tricycle without any passenger was there. I went inside it while staring at the driver.

"Where are we going Ma'am?" he asked. It took me a while to answer him, because I forgot the name of the funeral home, and I did not know the name of the road although I went there for a short visit with Ashley as soon as we arrived from the Bangcasi airport early that morning.

"Please bring me to Raniel," I finally answered him.

"Yes Ma'am but which one? There are three Raniel Funeral homes in Butuan. I know one near the highway, one near the commercial centre and I think there is also one around here," he said.

"Alright, please bring me to the nearest one then," I said, and he drove. It was so easy. The young driver dropped me in front of a wide-open gate. He realized that I was not sure of the way, so he was reluctant to leave me.

"Are you sure Ma'am, is this the one? Otherwise I can bring you to the next if you want. It is dangerous to stay alone outside, especially during the evening," he said repeatedly. It was nice of him to be concerned for my safety. He even waited for a while before he left.

I stayed standing still for a moment, not out of confusion but out of shock at what I saw. I recognised the place as the same as in my dream. I had not noticed it in the morning maybe, because I did not come alone and there was bright sunlight. Now that it was dark everywhere, it was just like my dream!

I continued being surprised. Once I was inside the compound of Raniel's, I saw a small shade used for the guards at the right side of the pathway, and the three girls were there: Rose-Anne, Laureene and Baba, the only difference was that although they were my nieces dressed as in my dream. The difference is I had not known who they were in my dream because of the distance. Then further ahead stood a house and again, I had already seen it. When and where was that? Oh my God it was all in my dreams! They were exactly the same places as I saw in my dream. It was incredible to be physically entering into the place I dreamed of for several nights. I felt strange, as if what was happening to me was only the result of a magician's trick. I realized I had penetrated into these places before my beloved father passed away, in my dreams. And this time, I was not dreaming anymore.

I knew I was supposed to be resting. My family had instructed me to stay in my hotel-room and to phone them as soon as I was ready to go to the funeral home. But I had forgotten all my tiredness when I felt the presence of Tatay, feeling that he was eager to bring me to see his friends.

As soon as I heard my brother Melchor's voice, I was conscious that I was not dreaming anymore. "Who is with you, Manay? Why did you come alone when we were going to fetch you from the hotel with Randy's car?" He was surprised to see me alone. But how could I explain him that I was experiencing the divine guidance? At that moment I realized that everything around me was real, and no longer a dream. But I was wondering, why was the tricycle driver waiting at the front door of the hotel? Was it a part of Tatay's spirit guidance? I did not request a tricycle, but it seemed that he was waiting just for me because he did not refuse when I got into the vehicle. The hotel security guard told me that it was prohibited for the tricycle to stand by in front of the hotel, unless the driver was there to drop off a passenger who was staying there. But why was there the tricycle seemed waiting for me. In any case, I was so happy that I arrived at the funeral home safely. Everyone was worried for my security, as there had been a lot of kidnapping and violence in Butuan.

I sensed the presence that allowed me to go alone. I knew it was Tatay's spirit who guided me to see his friends, and I was roaming around the funeral home with him at my side, showing me all our previous old neighbours and his close friends from New Asia. Otherwise, I would have had not dared to reach that dark side of the funeral home all by myself. I then understood why he brought me there. His friends, young and old men, were there, drinking bottles of beer behind the funeral home.

At first, I did not find Tatay while thinking of that particular house in my dream, because I found a lot of people praying in the chapel. Some were standing, and others were sitting on benches. In my dream I was not able to go forward as I woke up before. Perhaps Tatay did not want me to see his coffin and be worried. However, just to help me understand that he was leaving, and that he did not want me to be too upset, that is why he showed me he was surrounded by brilliant white light full of peace. This told me that that there was no need to worry. He was free from pain, had no more doubts or sorrows, and that he was called by our Almighty Father. I had again asked myself several times whether my dreams were the messages from God. And now I have the answer.

A memory: When I told Ashley about my dream several days before, she said to me: "Manay, you have so negative thoughts." So I hesitated to inform her about Tatay's eminent passing. But that day, I was ready to tell her everything to help her be prepared. Unluckily she did not answer the phone. Later, she told me that she had been feeling uneasy, and worried for some reason that morning. She said she went out from the hotel and walked towards our parent's home, but her phone was unable to connect to the network.

So I was not able to tell Ashley that Tatay lost his strength that day. I understood why Ashley was feeling anguished; it was because everyone was in panic at home. Ashley said:

"Kenny fetched Ronaldo from the hotel by car and brought him to my parents' home. Ronaldo carried Tatay into Kenny's car and they brought him to the hospital."

I was thankful that Ronaldo was there, so what I promised to Mama was fulfilled; when the time came, there was someone there strong enough to carry Tatay and take care of him. Every member of my family was present in the hospital except me, I regret. Though it can't forget my remorse, I take long breaths and try to remember that I did try to get on the earliest flight I could. The breaths don't really help, however.

Have you ever heard someone calling you just near and found out you're all alone?

I can still remember when Tatay called to me in a gentle voice: "Sarah". It was early in the morning just before I took my breakfast and a day before his crossing. I recognized his unique voice. I wanted to buy the plane tickets that day to be able to see and hug him once more. And now, it was too late. I am unable to reach him or ever speak to him again. I am not at peace that I was unable to reach Butuan before his death. I regret it so much. I could not grant his wish to see me, or to see all his children together around him before he died. I hope he can forgive me for that, as every time I spoke to him on the phone before, he had always asked me when I might be in Butuan.

"Come on Sarah, when are you arriving?" He always asked me gently, as if he was a child, begging.

Meanwhile, I was thinking that they should not have bothered Tatay with all those hospital devices and interventions, as he had already made me understand that he was happy to go. I waited to see if someone would ask me or inform me about Tatay's situation inside the hospital ICU (Intensive Care Unit). When James asked me my views about whether the hospital tube inserted in my father's mouth should be removed or not, I immediately answered to remove it immediately. The nurse would have seen that when the pipe was removed, if he was still breathing, it meant that those devices were not necessary at all.

They would have been better prepared if I had been able to tell them all this when I called Ashley, that this was his time to depart. But I didn't dare to tell my family the story from my dreams, that I had seen Tatay walking away bathed in light. I was afraid of their reaction, afraid that my family might misinterpret my telling to be some kind of cruel move against Tatay. In my view, Tatay should have been relaxed on his bed with a feeling of dignity, instead of being imprisoned by all those noisy medical devices preventing him from hearing the sound of our voices. The interventions prevented him from talking and sending messages to bid goodbye to his dear wife and his whole family. Now I understand why Mama keep on telling me in the dream, that Tatay was telling her something but she did not understand, as his voice disappeared although he kept on talking. But I have the strong conviction that Tatay was telling Mama that he loved her very much, was sorry to have to leave her, and that he would be waiting for her.

In fact, I dreamed of Tatay again a few weeks after his burial. He was telling me that Dominga was not prepared yet to join him. He added that he had all the time to wait.

I would have had gone to the Philippines earlier, before Tatay's death, but I was worried for my career. It was quite difficult to ask for time off at the same time as asking the administration to prolong my contract of employment, during a time of restructure at the office. I was stressed having been put in a dilemma between having early retirement and going to the Philippines; or I could retire later, prolonging my employment contract, meaning working longer and having a better retirement pension. I was working in a government and healthcare firm that was understaffed. There was a downsizing initiative, that had significant negative effects on my role. The changes meant that employees had to be creative and have better performance reviews at work. But my desire to prolong my professional career clashed with my eagerness to see my father earlier.

Now, I have this endless remorse that gnaws at me. I was not present for the celebrations of my parents' 50th or 65th wedding anniversaries, and I was also not there before his death. I am really sorry for that, Tatay, please forgive me. My only consolation is that I saw him in my dream in good health, younger and strong, and he threw me a big, serene smile of prolonged farewell.

I know he is happy, because he was surrounded by heavenly light, a brilliant, gentle white. I couldn't exactly express the way I felt when I was near to that light, which was somehow close to my face and at the same time far away and intangible. That light was so comforting and relaxing, which made me feel strong emotions and feelings that I had never felt before. I felt so sad when the light disappeared together with Tatay, who went away smiling at me. Mama still stood behind the transparent wall, not seeing her husband going away with his incredible white light. It was as if Tatay and the divine light were one, because when he moved, the light moved with him as if it was protecting him. I found myself in the dark, and I awoke to that early morning, the third of May 2017, full of questions. At the same time I was happy to have seen that wondrous light from above that illuminated and encircled Tatay's whole being. Even though it was just a dream, it seemed so real. It was one of my most revealing dream that would remain engraved in my mind and and in my heart.

Was he guiding me to write this memoir?

The immense pain of losing my father has gradually dissipated, being replaced by happy memories. Intuitive behavior and subconscious perception are sometimes fearful, but the death of my father has awakened my inner spiritual ability. Today, I am acquiring a new personality and developing a strong feeling that, after all, death is the beginning of new life. I feel more confident in God's love. Tatay's death was a very special event that changed my life. It was a turning point, as it led me to fundamentally understand my past. It's hard to believe that when I started writing this memoir, I suddenly remembered past experiences which had been buried in my memory such a long time ago. I am really astonished to discover the brain's potential to think methodically and retrieve these memories. I can now distinguish between me and my environments, thus allowing me to better understand them. It was as if Tatay had triggered my mature brain to grow new neurons that remain unlocked and flexible. This pathway has enhanced me to uncover some mysteries. It is like a new kind of perception, mixed with beliefs and conviction in faith.

In fact, Sister Cecilia's advised me a long time ago to write, but despite the efforts I had made seeking of inner guidance and inspiration, I had never been truly inspired, not until I dreamed the easy crossing of my father. It was the dream that continued, because even after he passed away, I was living in that vision and premonition, in real life when I visited the funeral home.

I don't know how long I will remain this way, but I have developed a feeling of more enthusiasm now for writing. Tatay awakened my mind and spirit. He revealed to me who I am. He gave me inspiration with unusual motivation, and he made me understand my potential to express through writing what had been recorded and buried in my soul and in my subconsciousness for so many years. So then, I am convinced of the benefit of sharing my spiritual experiences to the whole world.

When he was still in our world, I confided to him all my dreams that worried me, and I learned later that all those dreams came true. Sometimes I felt afraid to sleep, afraid of what would be the next premonition dream. Then I prayed to God, and He allowed me to feel the serenity of being protected. I am missing Tatay and asking God to help me heal, and He has probably answered me. Recently, He allowed me to encounter my father. He was so vivid in my dream, thus alleviating my sadness in missing him:

> There was a banquet and Tatay was there at the head table, sitting in a wheelchair. Other people left the dining table while he remained. He was looking ahead, and he blinked his eyes. I was standing just near his table in the dance hall, with other dancers and there were competitors behind me. I had to go out and I passed just behind him; but the closer I was getting to him, the more I could not reach him. He was looking attentively to a dancer wearing a Latin dance dress, who stood just beside me. While I was looking at him, he blinked his eyes again. I waited to see if he would look at me, but our eyes did not meet.

As soon as I awoke I sometimes thought that maybe Tatay was watching me dancing in the school or in a party? But why was it that Tatay was shown to me in a wheelchair? I learned later from James, my nephew, that he was pushing Tatay in a wheelchair during his last visit to the doctor for consultation. He said Tatay at 85 years old, was so happy riding on it and exclaimed his joy like a child.

In 2015 Tatay revealed several stories from his childhood, and he had talked rarely of the recent events. Tatay was speaking in English when I took a video. I happened to ask him about my dreams I had confided to him as a child. I was disappointed to hear that that he only remembered a few. Some of them he had completely forgotten. I was depressed that I could not confine my dreams to him anymore. But there were times when he could recall almost everything, I realized he was suffering from dementia. However, in 2016 when we asked him to say something about his birthday celebration, he had an excellent answer. Everyone was amazed of his answer, he was speaking English again during his birthday in October 2016.

"Today is my 85th birthday, it's unforgettable!" he said happily, and my family applauded, while my family was filming it all on video and sent it to me through Facebook messenger. I loved his answer. He had forgotten he had been forgetting some memories. But that day was so special. Everything was clear in his mind, probably because God allowed him to be happy on his last birthday on earth.

Now he is gone, but I feel that no matter what is happening, I feel safe and cared for. He became my spiritual guide. I sense his presence around me at times. Perhaps because I miss him, I feel that he guides my life in the right way. I sometimes feel his presence very strongly and that he is somehow communicating with me through my brain. This only lasts for a little while, but I know he is happy, and he will be there if I really need him. I ask a question and I receive answers in my dreams. I feel he is staying near, and that he is watching over me even while I write this.

Before he passed away, I dreamed of his death. A dream which appeared in many forms. Those dream showed me a particular place including the furniture, the surroundings, our previous neighbours, and other people whom I had never met before. I also saw the presence of my whole family. I am sure he was happy to have us there together.

On the 26th July 2017, I dreamed of him again. It was amazing that I felt safe and secure with his presence, I felt that he was there because he cares for me. I was feeling so comfortable because when I think of him, he has become my spirit of light and goodness. I even feel that he is around me at times when I am driving in my car.

When I think of him surrounded by that incredible white light, it also reminds me of the white dove, the Holy Spirit that visited me in my room at dawn, when I was only a very young child. I was visited by that magnificent, brilliant white dove that left me with strange feelings and questions, doubts, and hopes in my little head, but I was not yet five. I was still far too young to understand that it was the Holy Spirit. All these strong feelings seem similar to when I feel the presence of Tatay, and at the same time the presence of God Almighty, who is taking care of him. Now I believe and confirm that there is life after death, a life that never ends. It is the Eternal Life.

Tatay was not perfect, but he was a loving father. I think of him, and when I am feeling tired my strength is renewed. When I started writing, the first phrase I wrote was about of how I missed him, and in this context I know that I was being guided to an open portal of long past memories that I had kept with him. Now that he has passed away, those memories from my childhood are resurfacing. They invade my whole being, but still I feel guided by him.

My father's death triggered the need to trace and write down my memories. I often felt like I was running out of time to write, while also continuing to work in a professional capacity. However, lack of time is not a good excuse to put off writing our memoirs, because our memories across a lifetime do matter. Thus, by writing these words down, I am able to learn about myself, leave a legacy, and keep my father's memory alive.

The mysterious candle of an artist – June 2017

In the Philippines, there is a tradition of prayers for the dead: first it is done for nine days, then the prayers continue for 40 days. A memorial service is held on the 9th and on the 40th day after a family member's death. My family prayed for 40-day novena prayers for the eternal peace of my father's soul. However, I returned to France before the end of the novena.

I lit this candle (below) in my room for my late father. I watched the candle burning and was carried by my emotion, my breast tightened, I was terribly missing him. I wanted to blow the candle out before I went to bed, but the candle was only halfway burnt. I fell deeply asleep. When I awoke, the candle was already out but not yet fully consumed. I was overcome with unusual emotions when I saw it in the morning. I found it amazingly beautiful, full of mystery! A gift. But it is hard for me to explain this mystical experience.

Lionel said he did not come to my room to blow out the candle while I was asleep. "I did not enter in your room," he said. "And why would I blow out the candle when it was not done burning?"
We both admired the natural beauty of the candle in its formation. It seemed magnificently well-decorated. I could hardly explain it, so I will let you observe the photo, and you may describe it by yourself.

I was alone in my bedroom, so who blew out the candle?

How did the candle wax flow down without reaching the candlestick?

Who made the curves going up, and what made the knot wax formations like a handle?

Who made this amazing decoration in a candle which look like an artist's masterpiece?

I showed this candle photo below to my friends and colleagues at work, asking them whether they could give me some explanation. They examined it, and had different hypotheses, but no one had had the true answer. Anyway, I find the candle magnificent, with a kind of mystical and artistic beauty. For me it's a masterpiece of a great artist, but who? The answer can only be found in the depths of my heart. I remain so grateful that life has given me the chance and privilege to see and touch this candle, full of emanating love. I wonder how long it would remain visible, but no one can remove it from my heart. For me, it is a present from the good spirit who loves me deeply.

Shall I return home to the Philippines to stay?

Time moves by incredibly fast. I arrived in Paris Charles de Gaulle airport for the first time in October 1981, which seems only yesterday. I knew nothing about France, except that it is one of the most beautiful old countries in Europe and has become even more beautiful today. Paris is rich in history, full of monuments like the Arc de Triomphe, the Eiffel Tower and the Louvre, which is among the most beautiful and the largest museums in the world. Paris also houses the vast public library, le Bibliothèque de France, as well as the Pompidou Museum dedicated to modern art and contemporary painting, and the famous Notre Dame Cathedral and the Basilica of Sacré Coeur. Paris is also the city of lights, food, cheese, wine, fashion design, perfume, and so much more.

France has simply become my second motherland. In some ways I am feeling more French now than Filipino. It's not so long ago that my grandchildren leaned a lot on me, and on their mother naturally, whereas now it's obviously me who needs them more than they need me. I am quite confident that I can count on them. But I must count more on my own efforts to help myself, because it's evidently impossible to be always provided with assistance and be accompanied by other 100 percent of the time. I don't wish to be a burden to anyone. It is true that my grandmother was usually surrounded by her children and her grandchildren, yet in her last hour she died alone in her home. The neighbours found her stiff body on the floor. I continuously think of how we can avoid dying all alone. I try not to wallow in those sad feelings for too long and should run my life in accordance with the will of God.

Several questions get to the heart of the retirement dilemma. Things that worry me and lead to my indecision as to the choice to retire and stay in Philippines are as follows: the environmental risks such as the frequent flooding; the lack of health care, clear sanitation and equipment; ambulances are unrelialable; the costly medicines and hospitalization are not well-covered by the health insurance; the scarce distribution and unsafe water supply; a defunct drainage system in the subdivisions; too much air pollution which triggers allergies and diseases; galloping inflation, and the security issues like kidnapping. I hope that the new government would tackle some of these issues.

I was thrilled retiring in 2019 at 67 years old, so all those anguishes of back and forth trips in the middle of traffic jams to go to work is now over.

My daughter remains working as a Sanitary Social Worker. As a civil servant she had recently passed another exam and now waiting for her official higher rank appointment as

"Inspector." Thank God, my four grandchildren are in good health. Vadim, the only boy, and Sasha, the youngest girl, are still in grade school. Despite the Covid pandemic, Sabrine and Typhaine obtained their Baccalaureate. I am praying for their success in studies, acquire nice jobs and be blessed with excellent health and bright futures. For the meantime, the twins are now attending their first year of studies in two different universities: Sabrine is taking the literature and psychology courses to be a psychologist; while Typhaine is in law school.

Meanwhile, I am unhappy to be away from my mother and younger siblings. Often times, it's the small things that bring me the most joy; back home I can recall my memories from the past that remain in my heart and will cherish them forever. Likewise it is so nice to see people and spend time with old friends and relatives who are still in the Philippines. I cannot avoid the feeling of homesickness: Philippines is my motherland, my first home, and my first love.

Although life is not as easy in France as other places, health care in France for me, is arguably the best in the world. To ask a doctor to visit you at home in the Philippines is always a hassle. I feel more comfortable with the climate in France, which is mild and temperate, when compared to that of the Philippines. Now, unfortunately with age, and although I was born and grew with an overwhelmingly hot climate, high heat makes me very uncomfortable. I appreciate having four seasons a year. After living for 40 years in France, I have this inclination now, and will surely have a hard time to change it. I have been living in France longer than I lived in my home country. There are also times of great heat in France of course, but only in the summer.

I will sneak a peek to my bills on my computer, tapping on the keyboard finishing this memoir, and also trying out some fiction writing. I also have the household chores, garden work, and chances to gather together with my family and friends in our backyard, and maintain dancing as my favourite sport practice.

I will do my utmost to fulfil my responsibility of spending more time with my mother for a while, to let her remember the best side of me, and to let her know I love her. For the moment, the pandemic prevented me. I know that Mama is feeling the emptiness of losing her husband after 66 years of living together. I hope that I can help her avoid having sadness control her. She should have some leisure activities and friendship circles. It is so important for me to hear her voice with laughter.

Meanwhile, despite my great desire to return and stay in Philippines, and although the cost of living in Paris is very high, I realise that my life is here in France, at my husband's side. I need to be near to my daughter and my grandchildren, who are my motiving force. They allow me to feel confident, knowing they're all around me. For me, living far from them would be like a body without soul.

Nevertheless, hugs and kisses from them is enough. When Sabrine and Typhaine brought Lionel and me their unexpected little gifts: a 'Big Ben' on key ring that they brought from England and small gifts for Christmas, it was enough for us because we know that there was so much love behind those simple gestures. While our little Sasha, she runs in the garden and picks some little flowers for me, and that is her own way of showing her love. How I love them! I would have died for them.

My Other Childhood Adventures

At the end of our back yard stood the bamboo thick grove that grew in height along the stream of spring water and was home to a grand lizard, a monitor lizard. I started hearing its sound at 5 a.m.: "Tok-ko! Tok-ko!" The name comes from the sound of its hoarse cry as loud as the bark of a dog. Nanay said it was a kind of reptile I had never seen.

One morning I got up early to get a chance to see it while it was still singing its distinctive song, like a bell of a clock. However, it did not appear. This subject haunted me so that I became eager, persistently wanting to see that grand lizard. I was about to give up, when I heard that grand lizard singing again, but this time it was at seven in the morning. I walked to the banks of the stream until I got near to the bamboo grove where the sound came from, but it was not there. I stood motionless on the moist ground while looking around, careful to make no noise or sudden movements. Despite the thick bamboo stalks, the morning sun pierced between leaves swinging by the slight wind. I closed my eyes while the gentle sun rays caressed my cheeks.

When I opened my eyes, I spotted something on the ground just to my left; "A snake!" I feared. I instinctively stepped back on the slippery, moist bamboo leaves and lost my balance, falling down on my bum, out of breath.

I looked again at the shape next to me and was relieved to find it was only the molting of the snake. Luckily, the live snake had gone, only its old skin lay discarded and still in a spiral on the ground. It was inside a large hole that Nanay usually covered with banana leaves to keep the rain from coming in. She had prepared the spot to burn the coconut shells inside, to transform them into charcoal.

Suddenly, I heard the sound of a breeze or hissing that gave me pause, yet there was no wind? I felt as if someone was observing me. Then there was a drastic movement of the bamboo leaves. When I moved closer to the bamboo, hohlala! A giant reptile, gray-green and slight orange in color and about six feet long, was there in camouflage under the bamboo leaves, just above my head! I shivered and held my breath, staring at the freakishly large reptile. It stayed still with its claws gripping the bamboo stalk. I screamed silently inside and swallowed my fears, trying not to disturb the reptile. It looked like a crocodile with big, bulging eyes. I had to really focus to see it, as its color was almost identical to the bamboo leaves. I was sure it had been watching me since I arrived at the foot of the bamboo grove. It stared at me, blinking at me with its huge protruding green eyes before it jumped high up over the stream. The leaves swung back in place as it climbed to the bamboo on the other side of the bank of the stream. It could have come much closer, jumped on me and eaten me all up. Although I was initially terrified, I felt gratified for my patient nature. Now I knew what the grand lizard looks like, I believed Nanay when she said that a monitor could swallow several chickens at a time.

Bamboo grows amazingly fast, and produces multiples shoots. I have always been gratified with the smiling people buying the very young and tender bamboo shoots that Mama prepared. All were sold easily, especially when there were games: basketball for men, and volleyball for women on the other side of the game area. I earned some centavos that I shared with my brother to buy books, pencils, papers, or some candies or cakes. My brother Dan used to prefer rubber bands and marbles to play with, instead.

Punished by bees

One day, several ripe avocados fell to the ground. Nanay asked Dan and I to pick them up before I swept the dry leaves in the yard, to burned in the prepared hole. The ashes would later be used as a natural fertilizer. However, Dan would not stop his foolishness. He was stubborn. Instead of helping me, he was busy using his strength to throw small stones from the ground to the jackfruit tree, where the bees made their hive in one giant sweet juicy jackfruit.

Dan became shrewd and determined while doing foolish tricks. Despite our warnings, he made a slingshot, with a handle a Y-shaped branch from guava tree and elastic bands (that he cut from the old bicycle) to strike the hive.

Suddenly I heard him shout. "AyAyAy!" The bees took their furious revenge for having been disturbed and harmed while making their honey. He continued screaming while running towards the road. The angry bees chased him and stung him over and over again. I saw his eyelid, ear, neck, back, and his arms swelling red. At first, I made fun of him, but then, looking to his crumpled grimacing face, his eye almost swollen shut, streaming with tears, I pitied my poor brother. I felt sorry for him, but I remained firm.

"Now you are being punished by the bees, as you did not obey Nanay and me. I hope it will teach you a big lesson." I've been running errands all day, and was picking up the ripe avocados that covered the ground. But while I scolded him, he was already thinking about new tricks to do. I wondered if he was oblivious of the consequences to his actions. He had a fever the whole night that prevented any new plans the following day.

The private Catholic school – 1957-1961

My first years in school were spent in a private Catholic school, the Candelaria Institute, in Cabadbaran, Agusan del Norte, located in the valleys of Agusan Province. Our lessons were prepared by our teachers, who were nuns. They gave us a solid education with strict attention to spiritual matters. I attended the Holy Mass every Sunday and almost every day at the Cathedral Señora Candelaria next to our school. Through this, I enjoyed the proper spiritual practice, and I wanted to become a nun.

I was five years old when I attended the kindergarten class of Ma'am Toyay. Mama enrolled me as "Sarah R. Serohijos" instead of my full name, Baltazara (Sarah being a version of Zara, short for Baltazara). My teacher was a tall, charming woman in her 50s but was extremely strict in class. If you could not answer the question because you were busy talking with the other pupils, she wouldn't hesitate to force you to kneel at the corner of the classroom. She put heavy books on your hands and demanded you stretched your arms to the side. You would have to do this for 10 minutes, and if you dropped the book in that time, she would double the number of books in your hands. But I behaved well and she was kind to me. This made my classmates quite jealous because they thought that I was being treated as the favourite by our teacher.

I was one of the smallest girl in the class, and was happy to be seated in front, with nobody sitting in front of me. She had probably grown fed-up hearing from me, so she stopped calling on me even if I raised my hand to answer her questions. I often grew bored and yawned. I had a kind of daydream state that ended with me waking in quick jerks. I was silently seething when she would go over old lessons that bored me.

Before the end of June, Ma'am Toyay informed my parents that I would be transferred to the Grade 1 class. There it was more fun as there were more exciting activities. I participated with pleasure to all performances, such as reciting poems, making speeches, dance, and other presentations. Some words of a poem that I recited at that time was engraved in my little brain.

I had more fun doing my homework because we read relatable stories that provided us with useful life information. I was maybe too sensitive, at times, but this was my nature, I couldn't run away from my feelings. I even cried when I did a speech at school. It was just so hard to hold tears. But as my teachers said, my sensitivity was an advantage in expressing emotions. Because of that performance, I became famous in school in the field of theatre.

I easily cry when I am sad, but I also easily cry when I'm happy. I hate it because it often made me embarrassed in front of others, especially when I was not in a theatrical situation. I still don't know how to get rid of these moments of weakness and insecurity that enrage me. I cry, especially when I am prevented from fully expressing myself and it's unfair that people misunderstand me. In fact, I am just simply a human being who possesses feelings beyond what I can express.

During the Catechism classes that were always held in the church, we were told to memorize the Ten Commandments. I learned many things about our religion, but several questions raised up in my mind. Catechism was also taught in our classroom, but I was never satisfied. Most of my questions persisted and remained unanswered, especially about the Holy Spirit. I was in a hurry to meet someone who could help me understand what I witnessed.

I did not dare to ask my teacher directly, to avoid facing harsh words. I even regretted telling my classmates, who teased me unbearably until I got nervous. I cried. I never told them about anything more, hoping to retain a sense of respect, peace, and dignity.

When I was promoted to the Grade 1 class, I felt myself to be in my element. And despite my joy of finally being integrated into a higher class, I often had absent-minded episodes, as the image of the white dove with brilliant rays remained in my head. Often I startled when I heard my name and quickly answered "yes present" without waiting for the second call. Sister Maria, holding a long, fat round wooden stick about 150 centimeters long often woke me from daydreaming.

Why I did see the white dove while the others did not? Nanay, Mama, baby Nolwen, Nelly, and Dan were there, but they did not even hear the unusual sounds when the white dove appeared. Meanwhile, I always had this incredible feeling of joy and hope when thinking of the white dove.

One morning at recess, I was sitting on the bench when several grey birds came near me to eat the crumbs of my crackers that had fallen to the ground. Suddenly two white doves flapped their wings, flew over and swooped down over my head. One dove landed on my left shoulder just when the school bell rang. This white dove had stayed awhile with me and I waited for the dove to leave before returning to my classroom. It was not the same dove who visited me in my bedroom, but still it made me feel happy and content. For me, that recess-time was one of my best school moments, because a white dove had chosen to stay silently with me, even just for a short while.

Dragonfly warriors and my umbrella

One day, I discovered Dan's pocket full of sewing threads, but I could not fathom what for? His hobby was chasing insects like butterflies and grasshoppers, but his favourites were dragonflies. His hobby irritated me.

I couldn't look as he enjoyed tying each dragonfly with a piece of thread around its tail. I could imagine the sufferings of the insects and the cruelty of my brother. The dragonflies never had a choice but to fight against their opponent by trying to fly higher and out of reach. Dan took it as a game without realising that an insect could also suffer. I noticed the excitement of his face when he had succeeded in stemming the dragonfly's ability to soar.

Dan at age seven, dreamed of being a pilot of a fighter plane, to experience the adventure of flying low and dropping bombs into the heart of the enemies' area and shooting his adversaries. I did not know where his inspiration to become a pilot came from, when in fact we did not even have a television at home at that time.

One day, while walking back home, I was looking for a nice place to follow the call of nature (i.e.to pee). I placed my umbrella in the grasses to shield me from the view of others. I asked Dan to stay close and be vigilant so that the umbrella would not be blown by the wind, and he agreed. I was almost relieved. But I had a terrible urge to pee that I peed at the roadside just behind a tree. It was impossible for me to go further in the grass as there were plenty of bad herbs and shrubs that could scratch me. So, I placed the umbrella just behind the tree, not too far from the sidewalk. I started to take off my panty, and I was still peeing when a bus came up behind me at full speed. The bus blew my umbrella away. I screamed, asking Dan to help me grab the umbrella, but he ignored me. Instead of chasing my umbrella, he mocked me by showing the insects in his hands. I felt like I could not rely on him for anything, and, worse, I was convinced of his cruelty.

I wanted to run, but I fell down at once in the grasses because I have forgotten that my panty was still around my ankles. Dan ran away, leaving my umbrella behind. I caught him, but not my umbrella. I wanted to pinch his skin to punish him, but I had to run after my umbrella flying over the thick grasses and high bushes. It was to no avail. I lost it.

We were almost of the same age, as we were born in the same year, but he became my first enemy. He would punch me, and I kicked him to defend myself. We reached home one after the other. He always ignoring what I said. Yet my mother punished me, because she thought I'd left him behind, and I came back without my umbrella. I felt like Mama always preferred my brother over me. She often treated us differently, and though my love for her never waned, I felt betrayed when she didn't punished Dan the way she punished me, despite the full explanation of what had really happened. I admit feeling deprived of my mother's attention. I needed to be nurtured in the way she cared for my younger siblings, but unfortunately I did not get that affection.

A notebook of fighter planes

Dan and I used to walk on the paved road to school and back every day, with our lunches inside a netted shoulder bag. Nanay always wrapped our foods with smoked banana leaves to keep it well preserved and delicious. We usually took our lunch sitting on the bench of the park a few yards from our school, and we drank spring water from the fountain, which was shaped like a Christmas tree, beautifully decorated with large colourful shells around it.

One afternoon, Dan's teacher, Ma'am Toyay, knocked at our classroom door and Sister Maria told us to keep quiet as she opened the door. But they remained standing at the door and I was surprised when they called my name. I whispered, "what I have done wrong?" but no one said anything. Sister Maria asked me to follow Ma'am Toyay to her classroom, and while walking along the corridor she informed me that my brother was sick. I had to bring him back home. She handed me a hand towel and clean pair of trousers.

I found my brother silently sitting with his head bowed on his desk and his hands pressing his stomach. I asked him to stand up but he was reluctant to move, instead, he whispered: "If I stand from my seat, there will be a catastrophe." His grimacing expression showed me the evidence of his pain and it was urgent. I wondered what made him sick. We rushed to the riverside only a few meters behind our school. As it was high tide, the sea water had entered into the river. He ran into the deep to wash himself. I was happy to see him feeling relieved, and clean.

On our way home, Dan suddenly found lots of dragonflies and grasshoppers. I spotted boxes of matches on his hand while we walked home. I immediately thought of danger. I grabbed them from him, but I was surprised when the insects rushed out from inside. He was angry and punched me for freeing his insects. I kicked him to defend myself. I pitied those small insects, prisoners of his cruelty.

It became heavy for me to carry two school bags, one dropped to the ground, and it opened accidentally. With curiosity, I sneak a peek on his notebooks and I was surprised: There was not a single lesson written in that notebook, only drawings showing fighter planes firing their bullets against each other and dropping bombs against the armies on the ground. I was fascinated with his excellent drawings.

The paved road was melting due to the sun's heat, and our shoes sometimes got stuck to it. I asked him to stop playing with the dragonflies and to walk faster along the non-asphalted sidewalk, as it was covered with small stones and grasses. I held his hand to stay safe under my umbrella, protected from the sun and we still had another six kilometres to reach home.

A whip made of an elephant's tail

I admired my Nanay. She had a lovely Spanish-style dresses and even a Spanish-style robe which she wore when taking her after-lunch nap. She warned us children to also take a nap before playing outside. I enjoyed watching Nanay as she napped. Some hair that lay across her lips was jumping as she blews air by her lips and let it pass alternately through from the left side then from the right side of her lips that made a sound like a hissing musical instrument; for me it was funny and artistic way of snoring.

We were always so eager to play with the other children, playing the game called "The Black-Jack." It was an outdoor game, played by drawing a circle with chalk or a stick on the ground. To begin, each player was placed on the box "land." The first player needed to throw the pebble in box 1, and so on. We enjoyed jumping on each box. Dan enjoys playing with marbles or with rubber bands (*lastico-litic litic*) with our neighbours but all the doors would be fully locked. The balcony was open but had no stairs The only way to go down by the stairs was to traverse through the open *descanso*, a Spanish word meaning the landing.

We would need to jump from the balcony to the descanso before reaching the staircase. The narrow balcony was full colourful roses and bougainvillea flowers grew with sharp thorns so painful when they pricked our skin making jumping more difficult. Those times I failed to cross the void, and I abruptly dropped straight to the hard ground, I can't forget the immense pain and discomfort afterwards. The shock affected my breathing, and I had to make great and painful efforts to regain normal breaths and had stiffness and mainly in my bum and coccyx which lasted several days.

Dan climbed up to our bamboo-fence to escape, but his shorts got stuck between the beams and bamboo rods, which took him a lot of time to wriggle out of. He yelled for help and Nanay awoke. She showed us the *latigo*, a whip made of an elephant's tail. I knew it would be terribly painful. but I also knew that Nanay had never beaten us with her whip. When she raised up her arm holding it, Dan cried, closing his eyes tight and jumping before the whip hit the shining floor. Nanay was just pretending, but Dan and I were so frightened.

My little sister Nelly, clutching Mama's long wide skirt, while Nolwen was brought by Nanay to survey the rice fields in the farm. Mama asked me to stop whining and should nap before doing my chores of sweeping the dry leaves falling from fruit-trees around the house: Jackfruit, avocado, coffee, starfruit, guyabano, guava, banana, papaya, and pineapple which leaves look like a saw. I cleaned the yard every two or three days. Dan's job was to take care of the goats, moving them twice a day to the thick green grasses about 300 meters away from our house. Then he needed to fetch water to fill our jar with fresh spring water for drinking from the artesian well, which only few meters from our house. Nanay bought two small round metallic aluminium pails for Dan and me with a handle that could hold 10 litres of water each. My role was to water the plants and vegetables around our house, not allowing them to wither. We're all busy doing our chores all day long but full of joy.

Dan's broken arm and the strange ceremony

One Sunday afternoon, Mama and I were in our descanso playing the sungka (a popular game in the Philippines involving dropping small stones or cowrie shells into large holes on a long canoe-shaped board). Two friends chatted there with us, waiting for their turn to play when one suddenly said, "Look who is coming!"

Dan walking slowly moaning with pain. His lips trembled while supporting his left arm with his right hand. I had never seen him crying this way. Mama asked him what was wrong, but he couldn't answer. Instead, he showed his left arm, twisting down, broken, and swinging when he removed his right hand. We were all shocked. His arm hung down, with no strength, held only by the muscles and skin around.

Mama jumped down the stairs like a flying saucer and luckily caught my fainting brother before he fell. I stood behind them crying and embraced them with my small arms. Ernesto, the husband of our cousin Laling Beray, heard us screaming and came immediately. He took off his t-shirt and wrapped Dan's broken arm. He carried Dan to Yaya Tatang, Mama's great aunt. The younger sister of Mama's grandmother, Yaya knew all the remedies of natural healing with plants and trees. She and Nanay often gave advice to our neighbours and provided information about which leaves of the plants could be used for infusion and which trees to use for their bark, to drink after boiling.

Yaya Tatang was 107 years old at that time, and I was so skeptical of how she could heal my brother. I did not know yet she was healing people by using medicinal plants, because I was not living with her. Mama warned me to stay at home, and they all went without me. I lit a candle and prayed.

Nanay reached home with her basket full of vegetables. I informed her about Dan's broken arm. She sprinted to Yaya Tatang's house after she had instructed me to clean the string green beans that she had harvested. I cut some spices like garlic, onions, tomatoes, and red peppers, as I was told. I grated the opened coconut that was leftover from yesterday's lunch, using a Filipino traditional wooden coconut shredder, called the *kudkuran* in Tagalog or *kaguran* in Bisaya, used for scraping the tough coconut flesh. I squeezed it through the pure cotton-cloth to extract the white liquid, the coconut milk, then it was ready to be mixed with the vegetables. The freshly grated coconut made foods more delicious as it contained vitamins and minerals. But Nanay did not tell me to cook them, so I waited. However, the family did not return home that night. The big candle was consumed, and I felt sleepy. They all came back home while I slept; nobody took dinner, and Dan was not with them. He was held at Yaya Tatang's home and I was told that he would probably stay for several days. Mama lit another candle, and she was silent the whole next day, so worried for my brother.

Two days later, two men came to our house. I did not know who they were or why they came. But one man caught my attention. He never smiled. He was short possibly about 1.55 m and had a long beard. His head was wrapped with a thin red cloth, as a turban forming a simple knot at the end. He wore a plain white sleeveless T-shirt, and a dark gray Bermuda trouser. He firmly gave instructions to his companion to do different tasks, and I heard them talking about Dan's high fever and a ritual ceremony that they called it *Tigi* [a kind of faith healing or a pre-Hispanic ritual ceremony]. Nanay said it would drive away bad spirits.

Everyone sat on the wooden floor forming a circle. I sat between Nanay and Mama. Two of my uncles were also there, Yoyo Vicente, Yoyo Supri, and six of my cousins.

The man with turban was praying with his eyes tightly closed, using a bizarre language. He was turning his head from left to the right then up and down, as if he was drawing a circle in the air. He seated on the floor with crossed legs and feet in a lotus pose, like yoga, and raised his hands up and down. Suddenly, he jumped up so high that I was terribly frightened, I screamed. Then I raised my head and focused my eyes to follow his movements, as he almost reached the ceiling of our house. I was terribly shaken up and I cried. I wondered how he was able to have jumped so high and then drop onto the floor at exactly in the same place, the same position sitting on exactly the way he was before. All the while he uttered words that I had never heard before. After the ceremony, they all ate their dinner but I was already asleep on the mat on the floor. That ceremony had frightened me so much, it made me exhausted.

After more than a month-long stay at my great aunt's house, Dan came back home. He wore a smile as he showed me his healing arm, wrapped with large leaves protected by a thin, white cloth around. He had recovered fast in the end. He played alone with his favourite toy, the spinning top. I was happy watching him while he spun it rapidly on the floor. But as he played with it, the top left some marks on the floor that I had just scrubbed with a coconut husk for almost one hour, until it shone. Yet, in just a minute his spinning top had covered our shining floor with traces of dark spots. I had mixed feelings: I was delighted and relieved to see him using his healed broken arm to twist the stem of the top, using all his fingers. But I also resented his spinning top. Later, he played with our neighbours, it was challenging for him when they were three or four participants who joined a contest, trying to impact and destroy the other participant's top. The winner was the one who had his top with the least damage or had taken the impact without stopping spinning. Dan was not a good loser; he usually disputed his comrades when he lost.

My precious friend

The carabao as an animal fascinated me. It is a swampy domestic water buffalo native to the Philippines. They are slightly bigger than a cow and have larger horns, a strong, and hardworking animal, considered as the national animal of the country. So helpful for our farmer's daily activities, it symbolized the Filipino's hard work and perseverance, so it was a particularly important companion in the agricultural sector.

One beautiful sunny day with mild fresh air, and while I was looking after the fruit trees around Nanay's house, a man and his young son was on the back of the carabao. I was envious looking at them sitting serenely without giving any pressure to the animal. The carabao knew the way home walking silently. The rhythm of its steps and its graceful movements of its body produced in my head a dance music while watching them. They returned home after their difficult work. I wished that someday I could also ride on the carabao's back by myself and I would invite some singing birds to accompany us all day long.

The next day, I did not see them so I roamed around the fields. I noticed a mother and a baby carabao lying in a swampy puddle that was getting dry. Luckily, the sky was covered with dark thick clouds, the rain would soon fill it. Otherwise, I would go back home, take a pail, and fetch spring water for them from the artesian well so they would feel happier resting in well-moistened clay. The weather was so hot. I understand why they stay most of the time wallowing in swamps and mud. They are happy when there have plenty of water in their swamps, to protect against extreme heat, despite the flying insects that swarm.

While watching the baby carabao walking out from the swampy puddle, and as the mother was half asleep, I suddenly had the strong desire to ride on the baby carabao's back. She was not yet too tall for me. I walked closer to observe her and I was lucky that day. The mother remained in the puddle while the baby carabao continued walking and stopped in front of me. I stroked her side and she kneeled; I was stupefied! That was the beginning of our friendship. I wiped her back with thick large leaves that I took from the ground. Then I hopped unto her back, but I slid down to the ground. I climbed again on and rested first on my stomach as I tried to balance on her back, but I did not know how to place my body. I asked her to stand up by giving her a quick hit to her right side with my right foot, as I had seen others do. She stood up. I gave another kick to her left side with my left foot and she walked. Wow! It was so amazing! She understood what I wanted. She walked graciously with me on her back, and for the first time I was riding on my friend's back. That made my day a wonderful day. Riding on the back of my friend was for me a fantastic way of traveling. How I had wished the journey would never end!

But I was never fully satisfied. I was thinking it would have been more wonderful if I could make her gallop, but how to ask her? I had pretended to gallop on the wooden horse that Tatay had made for me. Although I did not want to jostle her, I slipped toward her neck and tried to hold her horns, despite the fact that they were not yet well-developed. Without knowing what to do, I tightened my knees and my calves against her ribs and stomach. She suddenly galloped at full speed, without giving me any time to think.

It was too fast for me and I was not prepared. I knew nothing of how to stop her, so I was upset. I panicked! I screamed but nobody heard me. I heard her mother mooing; she was surely looking for her daughter. Not knowing what to do, I let go of her horns and Bam! I was violently thrown away from her back. I found myself moaning on the hard and cracked ground due to lack of rain. The baby carabao went back to her mother's side, leaving me with bruises and a sore bum, but it did not matter in the end because my friend had allowed me to ride on her back.

That early morning, I went out to the fields to see my friends. They looked strong, healthy and adorable. I was happy observing them in their well-built shade and shelter. I laughed at myself, remembering how I was thrown off that time.

The farmers would keep their carabaos in a comfortable area under their *nipa* hut [Nipa is a mangrove palm, which could be used for roofing as well as the walls of a house]. Carabaos were cared for, like a member of the family and a friend. The carabao shared the quality of sensitiveness. They could not endure the heat of the full tropical sun when working the fields. They absolutely refused to work in the middle of the day if the sun is too hot, and I absolutely understand that; I also couldn't keep walking under the heat of the sun above 25 °C without protection, or else I fainted. A carabao would need an impromptu mud bath to be relieved from heat and fatigue, while I needed to stay under the shade of the trees or in an air-conditioned room. It was not a matter of comfort but survival.

A narrow escape

The plantation had plants of corn, rice, sugar cane, mangoes, long and green string beans and many other crops triggered fevers for me, and so they always left me alone at home, bored.

I wanted to climb a giant mango tree, or to a high mabolo tree, known as velvet apple that bears weird tropical fruit, but it triggered allergies because of the spikes on the twigs and leaves. The mabolo (or *kamagong* in Tagalog) is rare, which make the fruit expensive in the Philippines. It bears a majestic purple red skin coated with coppery hairs. Kamagong's heartwood is mostly used for highly priced carvings like organ ornament, statues for decorations, etc. One day I climbed that kind of tree, but I had to go home covered in swollen and itchy skin. Nanay treated me with the oil extracted from many different leaves of plants mixed with cooked coconut oil, that she prepared especially for me.

There was also a remarkably tall tree called *bauno*, which bore juicy rich fruit. Elders said it was full of vitamins, and it reminded me of the durian which has also white juicy flesh. I sheltered under the bauno tree to hide from the rain, but the drops flowing from that tree were enough to make my skin react, as if small round marbles had hidden under the top layer.

One day I went to fields that were far from our house for a change, so I could climb up to the high fruit trees. There, nobody could judge me by what I said or did not say, it was only me and the trees. I was been fed-up climbing to the fruit trees close to our house. I needed to see new horizons, where there was a guava tree to climb, a small tree with no thorns and smooth and flexible branches, well-suited to a small girl like me.

I still remember the last time I went there, and how unknowingly I faced mortal danger. I was sitting on the bough of the guava tree, rich with abundant fruit. Although I was protected from the sun by the wide leaves of the tree I climbed I could not ignore the afternoon heat of more than 40 degrees in the open field. From time to time, a swift breeze of fresh air took away any discomfort. I sang while climbing, feeling the freedom.

I was suddenly attracted to a fruit that was three times the size of a normal fruit. It was so different, shining with a beautiful yellow colour. But I had to climb up to the highest level of the tree to pick it. I was about to grasp it with my left hand while my right hand was carefully holding the trunk, but I discovered it was not a guava fruit! It was moving and stretching. At first I thought it was just the effect of the sun and the shadows of quivering leaves that had tricked my eyes and had prevented me to see it clearly. But it was unwinding, expanding, extending lengthwise, and something was growing in and out emitting a dreadful hissing sound.

Oh my God, it was the tongue of the snake! I fell. As I dropped, the branches swung violently, bouncing up and down. The snake was ejected from the guava tree and dropped just in front of me, on the ground full of twigs, small fallen branches, and thorny grasses. I would have liked to have sprinted away, but I was afraid to do a single step while the big snake was there, facing me with its mouth wide open. I was fixated by its sharp fangs, and its green eyes focussed on me wickedly. Its tongue was stretching towards me. I was petrified. I prayed for God to send me His angel to come and save me from a fatal bite. I was frozen with my feet stuck in the ground, having lost their strength to carry me. This was always my big problem: I could never move when I was dazed with terror. It was a huge snake with different colours: yellow, brown, and creams with yellow-green eyes. Somehow I snapped out of my fear and rushed away, jumping over the thick grasses and broken small branches while screaming as loudly as I could. I did not know where the snake was, thinking it could move faster than me, though it wouldn't be able to leap up, but it could have passed under the branches to go faster.

My sandals slipped off due to the wet grasses, leaving me to run barefoot. But despite the pain in the soles of my feet, I continued to run until I was exhausted and felt faint, unable to go further. I sat crying on the big trunk of a tree that lay on the ground, praying until I felt sleepy, saying: "My Lord Jesus Christ please come and save me."

I had thought I was dreaming of an Angel who came to save me, when I heard a voice. It said: "Wake up! Come with me, and I will bring you back home. Everyone was looking for you." He took me up in his arms. I opened my eyes when he put me in front of him on the back of his carabao. It was Manong, an elder from the village who my family and I trusted.

"Don't worry, I found the snake just when it was about to eat you," he said. " I saw its tongue stretching out to bite and grind you with his teeth, but I arrived just in time." I did not care whether Manong was joking or not, but I knew I had narrowly escaped from a fatal snake bite.

"Thank you Manong, you were my angel. But where is the snake now?" I asked him to be sure I was safe. He gave me a sign with his eyes; when I looked down, I saw the snake beheaded and tied with rattan lanyard. Manong dragged the snake with a string tied to the reigns on the left side of the carabao. "You and your carabao saved me," I exhailed with deep gratitude.

The carabao's march was relaxing. When I opened my eyes, all the members of my family were present and the neighbours too. They were again playing *sungka* with shells, in our descanso, but they were interrupted. They said that Manong's son had informed my family that they had found me in the middle of the field where I was prohibited to go.

I was so afraid, thinking of what would be my punishment. I continued praying, asking for the strength to cope with whatever punishment was meted out. The emotional shock from my confrontation with the snake triggered me a high fever for the whole night. Nanay was there with me, and she did not blame me. Instead, she made me an infusion of different leaves as usual that she picked from our yard and gave me a light massage from head to toe using the oil extracted from coconut and herba-buena leaves mixed together. It took me a week to fully recover from shock and fever.

Longing to climb a coconut tree

We were surrounded with coconut trees that constantly reminded me of Yoyo Supri. But he was not there anymore to show me how to climb them. It was a tricky business, and I did not have proficiency in climbing. But I was stubborn and intrigued as to how to reach the highest peak of the coconut tree.

One afternoon, I visited one of his coconut trees and I thought to try to see if I could do it without anyone's help. I started to go up by putting my bare hands around the tree, but I found my hands too short or the coconut trunk too thick to reach. I roamed around, searching for a smaller coconut tree, and when I found one that was leaning at an angle, I immediately remembered what Yoyo Supri told me that was been repeated in my head. "To be successful you must persevere in practicing how to climb the coconut tree," he'd said. I took off my sandals, but I felt pain on the soles of my feet when they rubbed the rough bark. I insisted placing my feet against the sides of the trunk, and I hopped onto the base of the tree, gripping it with my legs. I placed my feet into the holes that Yoyo Supri prepared to climb easier, and I started bringing my feet up one at a time. But I was not able to climb high, because the loops were far from each other. I used all my muscles and felt exhausted, much faster than what I had expected.

In the next few days, I tried to climb again and again, until I started to improve. I did not inform anybody, not even Nanay who had been my confidant. Then twice a week I climbed the same tree and made a lot of progress each time, as I felt less pain in my bare feet and hands, while my muscles seemed stronger. Oh la la! It was always a good sport practice. At the end of the day, when I lay down on the floor, I slept so well that Nanay was wondering what had happened to me, touching my forehead to check for fever.

One early afternoon, I was surrounded by other children, and shared to them of my desire to climb a coconut tree with bare hands. They challenged me to climb a very tall tree. I accepted. I said that after all I must use my knowledge and I climbed progressively, but not all the children were kind. One of them, a young man whom we used to call Iyoy, was about 10 years older than me. He had not grown tall but remained the size of a young boy. He climbed the coconut tree next to mine so fast, and the children were all teasing me. They challenged me to reach to the end of the tree and pick some young coconuts for them to eat.   I reached more than half the height of the trunk, and I looked down to the children becoming so small when I suddenly had vertigo. I started trembling, and I could not feel my hands anymore. I did not know anymore where to place my feet and I was incapable to find the holes. I felt dizzy, paralyzed, and I screamed for help. I closed my eyes, and I became deaf to everything. I did not understand anymore what they said. I prayed God to save me, while I was gripping around the tree as tightly so I would not fall. I was losing my strength, preparing to fall, but I was so young to die, so I was asking pardon from God for being so stupid and arrogant. "God, I entrust you my whole being." I had no choice but to wait, and I waited...

I felt so alone amidst the deafening silence in my head, thinking that all the children had abandoned me when I heard someone: "Bebe, don't be afraid, everything will be alright now." My heart sprang up, I recognized his voice.

He touched my feet, right then the left. It was the hands of Iyoy. I opened my eyes to see him, and he guided me down a ladder made of bamboo that he had placed against the coconut tree for me. As soon as we reached to the ground, I hugged him tightly to thank him for saving me. But I especially thanked God for sending me someone to help. My gratitude to Iyoy reinforced the idea that he was a kind-hearted young man. He became my angel and a great hero in my eyes. I had thought again of Yoyo Supri, perhaps he was there too, watching over me. On the ground, the people cheered, I thought they were gone.

Iyoy's mother was often drunk with the *bahal,* sour tuba. She told us the story of her pregnancy with Iyoy: "One day I felt vomiting and dizzy, so I lay down on my bed, but I felt an unusual pain in my stomach. I thought it was a bad gastro problem, so I went to the toilet. I felt something coming out and I took it with my hand, and I was surprise to see that it was a tiny baby's head!" Then she added, "I had eaten and drank all that was not good for the baby because I did not know I was pregnant." She was full of remorse.

The children mocked Iyoy due to his short height. He was always treated unequally, and he had a hard time joining in with the other children, who teased him unjustly. But after the time when he saved me, everyone became very nice and kind to him.

Holy Mass and the choir

On Sundays, I loved attending the Holy Mass. Going to church was part of our family's culture, a ritual I still follow today. Dan and I walked more than six kilometres to the church on empty stomachs. If we took breakfast, we wouldn't have been allowed to receive the *ostia* through Holy Communion from the priest. We didn't go straight home. Instead, we used to go to the grocery store to buy our favourite cake, called *liwayway.* The bakery's secrets were not divulged to their clients of how to make liwayway so delicious. I sometimes gave half to Dan, because he preferred to use his money to buy rubber bands and round marbles from a different store. I couldn't avoid my responsibility as an older sister, so I walked with him, even though the store was further away. It was always my duty to look after of him, and ensure that we arrived home together safely.

Sometimes I went to the church on Sunday by myself despite the distance, especially when it was my turn to be a choir leader during the holy mass. I belonged to a group of more than 20 girls and boys singing the chants from the church's balcony of the Señora Candelaria Cathedral. The pianist would give us the pitch of the song, then I sang the first line of the chant; the other children followed attentively to my signals and movements. I loved it.

Our uniform was a long white dress with short pop sleeves, with an integrated belt to tie around our waists for the girls. The boys wore white polo short-sleeved shirts and black trousers. Thanks to my teacher, by the age of nine I had proudly learned how to lead the songs. Sometimes it was stressful, but I never complained. All the other days of the week was tired out with running errands, or bored with the household chores. My energy was renewed at church, and it kept me going, when I was in choir. I loved to be in the church even if it was only to practice singing. We also got to sing every Friday afternoon, when our teachers instructed us to rehearse the songs, trying to improve them.

During the Holy Mass, we sang in the church's balcony in two groups. When the first group was taking the Holy Communion, the second group took over to continue singing the songs walking down by the stairways, forming in line just behind the nuns, who wore the white habit on Sundays. It was a great privilege for me to be in the choir, and I was honoured and proud that the teachers had selected me. They appreciated my enthusiasm as leader, and I worked hard not to disappoint them. I was sure that the parents were proud and pleased to hear us.

Nanay made me a satin white dress with two attached belts forming a ribbon at my back, but the ribbon could only be done once it was on. One early Sunday, I cried when nobody was available to tie my ribbon. I woke up Mama, but she was in a bad mood. When I went to find Nanay, she had already gone out. In the end that Sunday I was late. The following Sundays I hopped from bed much earlier than usual and stayed long in front of the mirror trying to tie my ribbon at my back without asking for help from anybody, and I did it with satisfaction. I walked back home from church happy. I grew my hair long, but that Sunday afternoon Mama was happy to cut my long hair to shoulder-length for the first time. I cried silently as I was already missing it, but she was right that when it was long it was quite hard to brush it quickly when I needed to rush to school.

My enthusiasm and good motivation in choir ended rapidly. The following year, Tatay did not allow me to be enrolled in school, because I needed to help Mama with the birth and care of my twin sisters: Ashley and Amelie. Although I continued going to the church, I was not with my classmates and co-singers in the church anymore. My pain was almost unbearable.

Segundino disappears

Around 1960, when I was eight, Manoy Gunding went missing. It was just for a couple of weeks at first, and then months, then a year passed, we did not hear about Manoy anymore. At first, my family thought he went to visit his mother's side of the family, but no one had heard anything. Everyone was worried and I was missing him so much. Others said he had probably been kidnapped and killed. The whole village was looking for him in vain. The *novena* prayer was held at home, praying for his soul. Many neighbours attended prayers over nine consecutive nights. But one afternoon he reappeared, alive!

We were about to take a nap with Nanay, when we heard a bus stopping just in front of our house. It has been long time that we had not heard the loud engine roaring like that. Guro, our dog, barked strongly. I went to the balcony and I saw someone coming down from the bus, but he was retained by the driver who continued talking with him. They seemed friendly. I was intrigued and sprinted down the stairs. Guro rushed to the opened wooden gate faster than me. I waited in front of the bus's door and waited.

Oh my, Manoy Gunding was so handsome, smiling, showing his two deep dimples in his cheeks. He took me in his arms, and I hugged him, and I don't know how many kisses I made to his cheeks. I was so full of joy. I loved the feeling of flying when he threw me high above his head. Everyone at home was surprised and so happy for his return. Nanay and Mama made a very nice dinner.

When Manoy was back from his visit to his mother's family circle, he told me about his time away, while lying with his stomach on the floor of our living room. He asked me to give him a massage by dancing on his back and I obeyed. I found it funny at the age of eight.

"You were absent for an such a long time, the people in our village believed you were kidnapped and killed." I said while kicking slightly his back.

"No, I was not kidnapped," he answered while he turned to lye on his back. "It had suddenly been decided, and I did not have time to inform Nanay and Manding [the name he calls my mother]. I went with a woman who invited me to go to Manila for a job. We were living in a small apartment. She introduced me to her friend who knew someone who had played a role in the movies from time to time. Then I was employed to play a certain role in the movie, like him. It was occasional work. At the beginning, it was quite interesting, and I discovered that the woman who had invited me was really in love with me, despite the fact that she was 10 years older. She took care of me. I shared with her all the money I earned, but later I was told that I needed to wait for the next film to be paid, but they did not know yet when that would be. I waited so long, until one day I played a simple role as a barman in a film and I liked it. Then I waited for another role in vain." He sighed. "I found a job as a barman in a nightclub and met plenty of women until it became dangerous, because the woman I was living with was incredibly jealous. She made it into a roaring scandal. She drove me away from her apartment without a single cent in my pocket. I did small jobs until I earned enough money to pay for the boat that brought me to Surigao, then I took a bus for Cabadbaran," Manoy explained and breathe deeply. As he spoke, I imagined his story like a film in the cinema. I wanted to ask him more about his life before he came back home, but he was already deeply asleep and snoring.

The missing fingers of my Uncle: Yoyo Vicente

Aside from being a farmer, Yoyo Vicente Yubit loved fishing with his only son, Fredo, my cousin. He also went – but more rarely– with his adopted son. Speridion was asthmatic, the son of Yoyo Vicente's first wife who died after his birth. At first, Yoyo Vicente went fishing for his own family's needs, but he also shared with us some small tuna fish from time to time. Later, he came home with many fish, so much that the boxes in his fishing boat were overflowing. Since then, he spent more time fishing, when he was not working in the farm. They were living in the higher part of Pandanon. They usually visited us riding their loyal hard-working carabaos.

Fishing became their source of income, in addition to the sales of their farm products. However, fishing as a livelihood was only seasonal, and it took a lot of time. Impatient, Yoyo Vicente found a radical solution to fill his boxes much faster and in less time than usual. But it was a tricky business because he used blast fishing.

Several months passed, and we did not hear of him fishing anymore. When he finally came to visit us at home, I noticed that his right hand was always in his pocket. One evening, many neighbours came to celebrate the end of harvest season in our yard. Initially, Yoyo Vicente used his two hands in tapping the table to make the music more vibrant, and invited me to dance on the table. But he did not show me his right hand. I stopped dancing, I bend towards him and asked him to show me his hand, but he refused.

A curious and naughty small girl like me, I put my hand inside his pocket while he was busy talking to the others. He was waving his left hand, holding a glass of *bahal*, a kind of sweet coconut red wine or tuba which was stocked within three days after the harvest, thus possessing a strong alcohol acidic taste.

My hand reached the bottom of his pocket, and I was stunned. His hand had only three fingers. He was surprised to feel my little hand inside his pocket and unknowingly, he raised-up his arm so quickly that I nearly fell from the table. I cried out. Because of me, everyone had noticed his right hand with only three fingers. He could do nothing to hide anymore after that, but he did not punish me.

An hour passed. He drank several glasses of tuba and became very talkative. He was telling his story about the loss of his two fingers. He said that one time when he started to throw dynamite to blast some fish, the launch did not go well. Unfortunately, it exploded too close to his hand. The surgical operation was successful, but he lost his thumb and his forefinger. After that incident, he never used dynamite to catch fish, not anymore.

Swallowing the fresh egg

One sunny day, my uncles Supriano and Vicente made a chicken coop in the backyard with netted bamboo fence. This was where female chickens (hens and chicks) slept at night. Nanay used to close the coop before she went to bed, to prevent predators from entering.

At the middle of the chicken coop, we placed the nest boxes where the hens could lay their eggs. These nesting boxes were made of wood and netted bamboo, which intrigued me. I thought they looked well-arranged. I noticed that the hens flew to reach a certain box, and then stayed. During the day, some hens were cackling but became silent once they had settled spontaneously into their respective boxes, and I was wondering what they were doing inside. When the hens cackled, I sensed they were happily announcing a victory. As they strutted around and cackled, I was even more intrigued. I understood later that hens cackled before laying eggs, probably because of their pains from labouring, and they cackled again after being settled because they were relieved. When all the nesting boxes were full, and all the hens cackled at the same time, it was really pretty noisy.

I was amazed to see that during the day, the hens and their chicks were free to circulate, as their bamboo and straw shelters were not closed. The chickens were free to go up and settle down and may have nevertheless chosen and marked their territory. Everyone had their own safe place to hatch their eggs.

As a child, I sometimes could be cruel and self-centred. One morning I woke up early to see what was inside the boxes. Silently I went into the chicken coop. I was sure that one box above my head was not occupied. I was too small to reach it. I piled up some wood and climbed up to see the eggs inside the box. I took one, caressing it while admiring its beauty. It looked the same form and colour as the eggs that Mama used to cook with, but the one I handled seemed perfect to me. Suddenly I thought of eating it, so I broke it against the edge of the wood and swallowed it raw. It was so delicious. I arranged the pile of wood not far from the nesting boxes in such a way that nobody would notice them. I was planning to eat another fresh egg.

The next morning, I did the same, but before my hand could reached the depth of the box, the mother hen pecked at my hand. I was surprised with a blow of its beak, ayyye! I groaned and fell to the ground holding my breath. The pile of wood tumbled down and scattered just below the nestling boxes. I cried quietly, but Nanay had heard the noise of the wood. My wound was bleeding. That's a good lesson for you Bebe. Now you know how stupid you are! I said to myself.

Nanay had noticed that the wood pieces below the boxes were all dispersed, but she did not say a xword. She told me to go upstairs and wash my hands. She was back with some leaves of the *herba-buena* plant. She rolled between her hands a clean leaf until it became damp. She pressed it and put some drops of it into my wound and warned me not to let dirt on my hand. And of course, I did not feel like taking my breakfast anymore, and yet I was not able to eat an egg. I drank a small cup of delicious coconut milk with pure grinded cacao.

Another day, there was a big snake inside the house, lying at the corner of the kitchen. "It had surely swallowed plenty of chicks that made the snake so fat," Mama said. Nanay stared at me and said: "It was not only the snake who ate the eggs and the chicks; I know someone else who loves eating the fresh eggs." I felt terribly guilty and ashamed. I admired Nanay how she directed the snake to go inside an empty kerosene can by her long broom made from coconut leaves and tightly closed the can. I did not know where she brought the snake in the end. She said that snake was not harmful to humans but could eat plenty of chicken. After this, Nolwen refused to let go of Nanay. She was gripping tightly Nanay's long skirt, even while Nelly felt comfortable leaving the house with Mama.

I enjoyed watching the chicken roaming in the backyard, led by the mother hen with her eight chicks forming a column like small soldiers waddling behind her. But I still had felt my guilt from having eaten one of them. I was even afraid that all the hens would cackle against me to mourn. It took me a long time to restart eating eggs, fresh or cooked.

I would have preferred to have been playing with the other children that afternoon, but Nanay needed my help.

"Bebe, catch it, catch it with your two hands," she ordered me.

"Yes Nanay, I am trying!" I said. But I was only pretending. In reality, I did not dare to catch one, especially when I already knew that it was the last day in the life of the young chicken. Nanay always had to catch it herself and put it in the closed small cage for the bird. I was so worried about the next step. She continued giving me instructions.

"Now you can fill the big *kawali* with water to boil," she said. The kawali is a round deep-frying pan, mostly used to fry whole chicken, or frying bananas or a *maruya*, and so on. I didn't want to hear Nanay.

"Bebe, you should learn how to prepare the chicken, even at the age of nine years."

I really did not know how to avoid it, and I cried while pouring the water into the kawali. The fire was growing high and bright under the pot, and my heart pounded so fast.

Nanay went downstairs to pick up some leaves to provide flavour and aromatic smells to the recipe. I was about to sneak away when she reappeared. She took the chicken from the cage and told me: "I will show you how to kill, pluck and clean a chicken after plucking." She took a sharp knife and cut the throat of the chicken. The blood fell into the bowl. She held the chicken's legs and placed it headfirst into the boiling water, and pushed it with a ladle made of coconut shell and bamboo handle until the whole body was completely submerged.

I was feeling the agony of the chicken while she continued telling me how to do it, but I closed my eyes and covered my ears that I only heard the pounding of my heart. My chest was about to burst while feeling the fear of that poor chicken in the boiling water. I hated Nanay that day. But the silence only lasted few seconds as I heard the chicken crying out. I opened my eyes to see that it had flown up and out of the boiling water! Even Nanay was surprised.

"How come that it is still alive even after that I have cut the throat and submerged it into the boiling water?" She asked herself.

"It was its last goodbye," I answered her. It freaked me out even more when it dropped onto our kitchen floor. I darted downstairs, crying, and escaped from the house. I prayed that Nanay would not try to catch me. I sprinted to the coconut fields and hid myself in the thick bushes and shrubs.

By lack of chance, Yoyo Supri was walking, just where I was hiding, and despite my reticence, he brought me back home. Nanay didn't say anything. I was so hungry, but I could only eat the cooked ripe sarabia banana of yesterday. It took me several months to again eat the meat of the chicken. Even now, I always avoid seeing how the live chicken is being prepared before cooking.

Weekends – trouble and nice moments

During weekends, a lot of people played team sports: there was basketball and volleyball for men and women, and many people came from other barrios to watch the teams play. Our uncles and cousins participated.

Vendors filled their tables with foods, and drinks such as *agre-dolce* [a sour lemon juice mixed with sugar], the *lamaw* or *butong*, [grated young green coconuts], and different fruits. One of those tables was ours. We also brought sliced bamboo shoots, cooked sarabia banana, some fried banana-maruya, sliced lanka or jackfruit, sliced and whole papayas.

Nelly and Nolwen were present too. Nelly took care the *nigo*, [winnowing basket] on her head full of washed fresh fruits like *balimbing* [star fruit] and *tundan* [a kind of banana]. She would actively roam around the playground, inviting people to buy her fruits, with Nolwen following her.

That day, the games were interrupted by a big fight: the players were punching and kicking their opponents. It all seemed out of control. Nolwen and Nelly were scared, seeing our uncles with their noses and mouths bleeding.
I stayed on my table, working hard to make sure that the drinks and fruits did not get spilled by the crowds in panic.

Nelly sprinted home to inform Nanay about the troubles, unaware that her fruits were falling out from her *nigo* on her head while she ran. She could hardly breathe, and Nolwen ran after her. As she tried to catch up, Nolwen also was picking up the fruits that fell. Her hands were too small to carry all the fruit, so that she pulled up her skirt and tied it in a knot to act like a small basket. Nolwen yelled at Nelly to stop running. They both arrived home with tears.

Nelly cried because of fears about our uncles' fighting; Nolwen cried because she was terribly angry to Nelly of leaving her behind. Nolwen slapped Nelly's face. Bang! Nelly's nigo fell upside down to the ground, empty of fruits. She had forgotten to report to Nanay about the troubles, and Nolwen forgot the fruits that she had kept in her dress that were now scattered on the ground. Nelly hit Nolwen back and they continued fighting and pulling each other's hair. Nolwen had a long curly light brown hair which became dark and tangled quickly.

Other times, on the weekend, Nanay often brought Nolwen with her when going out to bring home a gallon of fresh harvested sweet tuba. Meanwhile, Mama was out often, even though she was pregnant with twins, leaving me at home to do the household chores. Mama was often invited to attend meetings: they talked about interior and house decorations, dressmaking, cooking, and she was even hired to perform a demonstration to the other mothers about the usage of the tupperware, and some cooking utensils. I was proud of her.

One afternoon, we were waiting for Tatay to come home from Butuan. We sat on the staircase: Nelly, Nolwen, me, and Dan, and we sang our favourite songs. We were counting how many lovely songs we knew. Nolwen loved singing was often impatient for Nelly to finish her song. I was afraid they would start to fight. Nolwen stood up and sang loudly. She was our champion singer. Dan also sang a short song, that day, which was rare, but he quickly gave up and went away to catch dragonflies.

It was like a performance, and our audience were the cats in the stairways who rubbed up against our legs from time to time. We also had Guro, our big black dog, who sat near our wooden and bamboo gate facing us, as well as some birds eating the corn on the ground left behind by the chicken near our stairways. We suddenly dispersed when we heard the bus in front of our house. It was Tatay, with a brown paper bag in his hand and we rushed meeting him excitedly. Thus our weekend was full of joy. I love to remember those happy sweet moments together.

Dancing time after the harvest

At harvest time, people worked manually and cheerfully with sickles. They would wear hats and shirts or blouses with long sleeves to protect from the heat of the sun. They separated the grain of rice from the stems or straw by their feet; they use a *lusong* and *alho* [a kind of giant mortar and pestle] to separate the grain of the rice from the tares for local use. The lusong was either made of stone or wooden, and the alho was usually made from the wood of a long and straight branch or trunk of the guava tree.

They brought their dry threshed rice to the milling machine to get a clean white rice. While nowadays, the harvester machine combines several operations into one: cutting the crop, collecting the mature rice or corn from the field, feeding into threshing mechanism, threshing cleaning, and discharging rice in bulk directly into a bags. The combined milling machines remove the husk and the grain layers including threshing and drying. However, this machinery did not exist in my village in 1950-1961.

When the harvesting was over, Nolwen and Nelly, with other people of the village, picked up the corn still on the stalks that lay on the ground missed by the first harvester, working so fast. How I wanted to join them! And believe me, there was plenty to feed Nanay's chicken, who indisputably preferred the corn, although they were so independent, they could wander out and look for their own food. Sometimes, Nelly and Nolwen came home with bundles of beautiful corn that we cooked for our snacks. As long as we worked, we would never get hungry in Cabadbaran, as there were also fruits everywhere. Fishing was for food and amusement, and we were blessed with healthy soil, good crops, and vegetables that grew in Nanay's backyard.

The holy Mass was joyfully celebrated in the chapel of Mabini. People was extending their gratitude to God for a good season and excellent harvest that year. They used different musical instruments made of bamboo, like the flute and the organ. Gregorio, the husband of my Aunt Felipa, played the guitar and sometimes *a Bajo,* a kind of giant guitar with strings sounding lower than the usual guitar; others played ukuleles they made themselves, and Nanay sang Spanish songs. I remember one time she wore an ancient beautiful sky-blue coloured Spanish dress, and I was proud of her.

Once a year, sometimes twice, they came to our yard celebrating in a kind of fiesta the whole evening, where plenty of food was served and shared. After the meal, they would play their musical instruments again; someone put me on the table, and I danced with the music. Everyone was so happy. Some women, including Nanay, danced the *kuratsa.* Others tapped their hands to the table and their feet on the ground to prolong my dancing.

Epilogue

I sometimes thought that my encounter with the Holy Spirit in my early childhood and my dark experiences were there to remind me of God's call, as I constantly sought refuge with Him. I have learned to use the spiritual gifts that I have acquired from Him. I now understand what my mission is on earth. I had been lost, and He protected me countless times. My faith in Him continues to grow.

Feel free to the readers to believe or not to believe; I write on this page what I felt, saw, and experienced. I was not able to hug my father before his passing, I am full of remorse. I found myself typing on my keyboard my dreams of him and fell asleep in front of the screen. The next day I would write again, the computer was still on and I was surprised to discover what I have written. And for the first time I always feel like writing since then and I make it a priority.

I dreamed repeatedly of seeing a book near my face, the pages flapping by themselves, and allowing me to read. I wondered why I seemed to already know what was written in the pages. I sometimes awoke when the flapping of pages touched my face. As soon as I started writing, those dreams about books disappeared. And when I don't write, I have a feeling of guilt.

I acquired the power of knowledge in understanding the important lessons of my past and developed stronger determination to confront the challenges in life while writing this memoir. I also indulge in my lifelong passion of dance and my aspiration of writing novel.

Today, I lead a peaceful life with my loving husband in France. How I would especially love if I could choose the date and hour of my end so precisely, to avoid leaving that eventual burden of uncertainty to my daughter and my grandchildren. But I trust God to look after them. I entrust myself to Him and my whole being, and lead life according to His will.

CPSIA information can be obtained
at www.ICGtesting.com
Printed in the USA
LVHW010328111121
702980LV00004B/460

9 781006 531361